CENTRAL STATISTICAL OFFICE

CW00323311

Monthly Digest of Statistics

No 560
August 1992

Editor: PHIL LEWIN

14008

MORETON HALL.
REFERENCE LIBRARY

301
Statistics
510.

MORETON HALL

* 0 0 0 0 4 9 4 3 *

London: HMSO

© *Crown copyright 1992*
First published 1992

Proposals for reproduction of tables or contents should be addressed to Copyright Section, CSO Press and Publications Branch, Room D.115, Government Buildings, Cardiff Road, Newport, Gwent NP9 1XG.

ISBN 0 11 620540 7
ISSN 0308-6666

Introduction

This *Digest* has been prepared by the Central Statistical Office in collaboration with the Statistics Divisions of Government Departments.

The name of the department or organisation providing the statistics is shown under each table. Some of the statistics provided by departments are actually collected by other organisations such as nationalised boards and trade associations. The assistance provided by these organisations, too numerous to mention individually, is gratefully acknowledged.

The figures in the *Digest* are mainly totals for calendar months or monthly averages.

Provisional data

Some figures in *Monthly Digest* are provisional and may be subject to revision in later issues. This applies particularly to data for the most recent time periods.

Definitions

The 1992 *Supplement of Definitions and Explanatory Notes* was published in the January edition (No 553). This gives detailed definitions of all the terms and units used in the *Digest*. The following general definitions should be noted in using the *Digest*.

Area covered. Except where otherwise stated, all statistics relate to the United Kingdom of Great Britain and Northern Ireland.

Seasonality. Except where otherwise stated, all statistics are not adjusted to take account of seasonal factors.

Consumption and stocks. The terms 'consumption', 'disposals' and 'stocks' are defined in detail in the *Supplement* to the *Digest*. Figures of consumption and stocks are seasonal and should be used with caution. The stocks figures given may often relate to only part of the total stocks in the country.

External trade. Owing to differences in coverage and timing, figures of imports and exports are not always comparable with those for production, consumption and stocks.

Prices. Except where otherwise stated, all prices are shown on a current basis.

Money. There is no single correct definition of **money** and there are many liquid assets which are not included in any of the UK monetary aggregates but which nevertheless need to be taken into account on occasions when interpreting monetary conditions. Consequently, many definitions of money stock are widely used:

M0, the narrowest measure consists of notes and coin in circulation outside the Bank of England and bankers' operational deposits at the Bank.

M2 comprises notes and coin in circulation with the public *plus* sterling retail deposits held by the UK private sector with UK banks, with building societies and in the National Savings Bank ordinary account.

M4 comprises notes and coin in circulation with the public, together with all sterling deposits (including *certificates of deposit*) held with UK banks and building societies by the rest of the private sector.

Symbols and conventions used

Symbols. The following symbols are used throughout:
- .. not available
- - nil or less than half the final digit shown
- * average (or total) of five weeks
- † indicates that the data has been revised since the last edition: the period marked is the earliest in the table to have been revised.

Change of basis. A line drawn across a column between two consecutive figures indicates that the figures above and below the line have been compiled on different bases and are not strictly comparable. In each case a footnote explains the difference.

Rounding of figures. In tables where figures have been rounded to the nearest final digit, there may be a slight discrepancy between the sum of the constituent items and the total as shown.

Central Statistical Office
Great George Street
London SW1P 3AQ

20 August 1992

CSO Databank

Most tables in this publication contain data which is available on the Monthly Digest dataset, one of the datasets in the CSO Databank. The appropriate four digit identifier is included at the top of the column or start of the row of figures. This is to facilitate access to the data in computer-readable form and make available longer runs of data than appear in these tables.

The CSO Databank is a collection of mostly macro-economic time-series available on magnetic tape or disk. The tape format, unlabelled EBCDIC, is the same for all the datasets. The disks, either 3½" or 5¼" are written in ASCII text which can be loaded as spreadsheets and viewed using standard spreadsheet packages, such as LOTUS or SMART. Details of the service offered, and the schedule of charges, are available from the Databank Manager, CSO Information Systems Branch, Room 52A/4, Government Offices, Great George Street, London SW1P 3AQ (Tel: 071-270 6386, 6387 or 6381).

Contents

1 National income and expenditure

1.1 Gross national and domestic product[1]

	£ million									Index numbers (1985 = 100)					
	At current prices				At factor cost		At 1985 prices			Gross domestic product				Implied gross domestic product deflators[7]	
	At market prices									At current prices		At 1985 prices			
	Gross domestic product "Money GDP"[2]	Net property income from abroad	Gross national product[2]	less Factor cost adjustment[3]	Gross domestic product[4]	Gross national product[5]	Gross domestic product at market prices	less Factor cost adjustment[6]	Gross domestic product at factor cost	At market prices, "Money GDP"[2]	At factor cost	At market prices	At factor cost	At market prices[2]	At factor cost[8]
	CAOB	CGOA	GIBF	CTGV	CAOM	GIBD	CAOO	DJCU	CAOP	DJCL	CAON	FNAO	DJDD	DJDT	DJCM
1982	278 887	1 460	280 347	40 656	238 231	239 691	324 622	44 895	279 738	78.3	77.7	91.2	91.2	85.9	85.2
1983	304 314	2 831	307 145	43 231	261 083	263 914	336 503	46 355	290 148	85.5	85.1	94.5	94.6	90.4	90.0
1984	325 091	4 357	329 448	45 039	280 052	284 409	343 780	48 347	295 433	91.3	91.3	96.5	96.3	94.6	94.8
1985	356 083	2 646	358 729	49 367	306 716	309 362	356 083	49 367	306 716	100.0	100.0	100.0	100.0	100.0	100.0
1986	382 942	5 096	388 038	56 760	326 182	331 278	370 030	52 312	317 718	107.5	106.3	103.9	103.6	103.5	102.7
1987	421 198	4 078	425 276	62 901	358 297	362 375	387 718	55 539	332 179	118.3	116.8	108.9	108.3	108.6	107.9
1988	467 863	5 047	472 910	70 571	397 292	402 339	404 230	58 312	345 918	131.4	129.5	113.5	112.8	115.7	114.9
1989	512 221	4 088	516 309	75 233	436 988	441 076	413 394	59 974	353 420	143.8	142.5	116.1	115.2	123.9	123.6
1990	550 337	2 466	552 803	72 718	477 619	480 085	417 454	60 506	356 948	154.6	155.7	117.2	116.4	131.8	133.8
1991	575 607	898	576 505	79 960	495 647	496 545	408 288	60 013	348 275	161.6	161.6	114.7	113.5	141.0	142.3
Seasonally adjusted															
		AIMD		DIAA				DIAS							
1982 Q2	69 001	433	69 434	9 909	59 092	59 525	81 205	11 148	70 055	77.5	77.1	91.2	91.4	85.0	84.4
Q3	70 280	402	70 682	10 257	60 023	60 425	81 249	11 217	70 033	78.9	78.3	91.3	91.3	86.5	85.7
Q4	72 080	532	72 612	10 468	61 612	62 144	81 769	11 388	70 389	81.0	80.4	91.9	91.8	88.2	87.5
1983 Q1	74 267	797	75 064	10 590	63 677	64 474	83 199	11 501	71 698	83.4	83.0	93.5	93.5	89.3	88.8
Q2	74 801	374	75 175	10 847	63 954	64 328	83 754	11 514	72 240	84.0	83.4	94.1	94.2	89.3	88.5
Q3	76 629	1 002	77 631	10 778	65 851	66 853	84 330	11 559	72 771	86.1	85.9	94.7	94.9	90.9	90.5
Q4	78 617	658	79 275	11 016	67 601	68 259	85 220	11 781	73 439	88.3	88.2	95.7	95.8	92.3	92.1
1984 Q1	79 559	866†	80 437	11 018	68 541	69 419	85 884	11 881	74 003	89.4	89.4	96.5	96.5	92.6	92.6
Q2	80 576	877	81 455	11 322	69 254	70 133	85 654	12 217	73 437	90.5	90.3	96.2	95.8	94.1	94.3
Q3	81 479	949	82 431	11 450	70 029	70 981	85 676	12 064	73 612	91.5	91.3	96.2	96.0	95.1	95.1
Q4	83 477	1 653	85 125	11 249	72 228	73 876	86 566	12 185	74 381	93.8	94.2	97.2	97.0	96.4	97.1
1985 Q1	86 032	886	86 968	11 628	74 404	75 340	88 043	12 333	75 710	96.6	97.0	98.9	98.7	97.7	98.3
Q2	88 645	605	89 292	12 118	76 527	77 174	89 187	12 249	76 938	99.6	99.8	100.2	100.3	99.4	99.5
Q3	89 890	735	90 633	12 718	77 172	77 915	89 248	12 397	76 851	101.0	100.6	100.3	100.2	100.7	100.4
Q4	91 516	334	91 836	12 903	78 613	78 933	89 605	12 388	77 217	102.8	102.5	100.7	100.7	102.1	101.8
1986 Q1	92 940	1 045	94 011	13 501	79 439	80 510	90 884	12 887	77 997	104.4	103.6	102.1	101.7	102.3	101.8
Q2	94 756	1 180	95 976	14 098	80 658	81 878	92 090	12 937	79 153	106.4	105.2	103.4	103.2	102.9	101.9
Q3	96 396	1 377	97 801	14 377	82 019	83 424	92 962	13 131	79 831	108.3	107.0	104.1	104.1	103.7	102.7
Q4	98 850	1 372	100 250	14 784	84 066	85 466	94 094	13 357	80 737	111.0	109.6	105.7	105.3	105.1	104.1
1987 Q1	100 611	1 109	101 786	15 011	85 600	86 775	94 792	13 565	81 227	113.0	111.6	106.5	105.9	106.1	105.4
Q2	103 383	893	104 356	15 340	88 043	89 016	96 094	13 650	82 444	116.1	114.8	107.9	107.5	107.6	106.8
Q3	107 225	1 012	108 237	16 070	91 155	92 167	98 087	14 093	83 994	120.4	118.9	110.2	109.5	109.3	108.5
Q4	109 979	740	110 897	16 480	93 499	94 417	98 745	14 231	84 514	123.5	121.9	110.9	110.2	111.4	110.6
1988 Q1	111 735	932	112 694	16 705	95 030	95 989	99 600	14 244	85 356	125.5	123.9	111.9	111.3	112.2	111.3
Q2	114 919	1 192	116 267	17 567	97 352	98 700	100 499	14 448	86 051	129.1	127.0	112.9	112.2	114.4	113.1
Q3	119 039	1 252	120 440	17 953	101 086	102 487	101 617	14 633	86 984	133.7	131.8	114.1	113.4	117.1	116.2
Q4	122 170	1 047	123 509	18 346	103 824	105 163	102 514	14 987	87 527	137.2	135.4	115.2	114.1	119.2	118.6
1989 Q1	124 953	1 207	126 171	18 280	106 673	107 891	102 734	14 748	87 986	140.4	139.1	115.4	114.7	121.6	121.2
Q2	126 678	911	127 777	18 697	107 981	109 080	102 935	14 961	87 974	142.3	140.8	115.6	114.7	123.1	122.7
Q3	129 013	744	129 884	18 902	110 111	110 982	103 670	15 095	88 575	144.9	143.6	116.5	115.5	124.4	124.3
Q4	131 577	633	132 477	19 354	112 223	113 123	104 055	15 170	88 885	147.8	146.4	116.9	115.9	126.4	126.3
1990 Q1	135 029	-29	135 117	19 393	115 636	115 724	104 740	15 164	89 576	151.7	150.8	117.7	116.8	128.9	129.1
Q2	137 289	13	137 383	17 797	119 492	119 586	105 453	15 423	90 030	154.2	155.8	118.5	117.4	130.2	132.7
Q3	138 817	1 154	140 075	17 799	121 021	122 276	104 136	15 101	89 035	155.9	157.8	117.0	116.1	133.3	135.9
Q4	139 202	956	140 228	17 729	121 473	122 499	103 125	14 818	88 307	156.4	158.4	115.8	115.2	135.0	137.6
1991 Q1	139 806	-559	139 500	17 817	121 989	121 683	102 553	14 940	87 613	157.0	159.1	115.2	114.3	136.3	139.2
Q2	143 715	84	143 887	20 309	123 406	123 578	101 834	14 949	86 885	161.4	160.9	114.4	113.3	141.1	142.0
Q3	145 598	491	146 259	20 809	124 789	125 450	101 993	14 958	87 035	163.6	162.7	114.6	113.5	142.8	143.4
Q4	146 488	312	146 859	21 025	125 463	125 834	101 908	15 166	86 742	164.6	163.6	114.5	113.1	143.7	144.6
1992 Q1	147 058	452	147 510	20 360	126 698	127 150	101 054	14 730	86 324	165.2	165.2	113.5	112.6	145.5	146.8
Q2	..	..	..	..	..	..	..	..	..	..	..	..	112.5	..	..

1 Estimates are given to the nearest £ million and in the case of indices to one decimal place but cannot be regarded as accurate to this degree.

2 This series is affected by the abolition of the domestic rates and the introduction of the community charge. For details see notes in the UK National Accounts article in the July issue of *Economic Trends*.

3 *Equals* taxes on expenditure *less* subsidies.

4 The factor cost estimate of GDP is obtained from the market price estimate by subtracting the factor cost adjustment.

5 Gross national product *equals* Gross domestic product *plus* Net property income from abroad.

6 *Represents* Taxes on expenditure *less* Subsidies both valued at 1985 prices.

7 Based on the sum of expenditure components of GDP at current and constant prices.

8 Also known as the index of total home costs.

Source: Central Statistical Office

1.2 Gross domestic product: by category of expenditure[1]

£ million, current prices

At market prices

Final expenditure on goods and services

	Con-sumers' expend-iture[2]	General government final consumption Central govern-ment	Local author-ities	Total	Gross domestic fixed capital formation	Value of physical increase in stocks and work in progress[3]	Total domestic expend-iture[2]	Exports of goods and services	Total final expend-iture[2]	less Imports of goods and services	Statist-ical discrep-ancy (expend-iture)	Gross domestic product[2]	less Taxes on expend-iture	Subsidies	Gross domestic product at factor cost
	AIIK	ACHC	CSBA	AAXI	DFDC	DHBF	CTGQ	DJAD	DJAK	DJAG	GIXM	CAOB	AAXC	AAXJ	CAOM
1982	170 650	37 000	23 363	60 363	44 824	-1 188	274 649	72 694	347 343	67 762	-694	278 887	46 467	5 811	238 231
1983	187 028	40 654	25 133	65 787	48 615	1 465	302 895	80 056	382 951	77 529	-1 108	304 314	49 500	6 269	261 083
1984	199 425	43 142	26 618	69 760	54 967	1 296	325 448	91 852	417 300	92 669	460	325 091	52 576	7 537	280 052
1985	217 618	45 879	27 926	73 805	60 353	821	352 597	102 208	454 805	98 866	144	356 083	56 592	7 225	306 716
1986	241 275	48 801	30 580	79 381	64 514	716	385 886	98 319	484 205	101 070	-193	382 942	62 947	6 187	326 182
1987	264 880	52 040	33 309	85 349	74 077	1 388	425 694	107 031	532 725	111 868	341	421 198	69 074	6 173	358 297
1988	298 796	55 610	36 119	91 729	88 958	4 800	484 283	107 834	592 117	124 884	630	467 863	76 511	5 940	397 292
1989	327 386	60 527	38 502	99 029	101 842	3 155	531 412	122 791	654 203	142 704	722	512 221	80 925	5 692	436 988
1990	348 576	67 052	42 637	109 689	105 283	-275	563 273	134 107	697 380	147 758	715	550 337	78 917	6 199	477 619
1991	367 991	74 544	47 123	121 667	95 153	-4 705	580 106	135 819	715 925	140 571	253	575 607	85 717	5 757	495 647
Not seasonally adjusted															
1988 Q1	68 877	14 159	8 835	22 994	20 908	161	112 940	25 371	138 311	28 621			17 869	1 808	
Q2	71 825	13 498	8 902	22 400	21 035	557	115 817	26 764	142 581	30 839			18 226	1 353	
Q3	77 609	13 431	9 064	22 495	22 597	1 980	124 681	27 717	152 398	32 886			19 859	1 297	
Q4	80 485	14 522	9 318	23 840	24 418	2 102	130 845	27 982	158 827	32 538			20 557	1 482	
1989 Q1	76 005	15 114	9 352	24 466	25 576	1 580	127 627	28 042	155 669	33 160			19 137	1 625	
Q2	79 458	14 503	9 467	23 970	23 841	2 086	129 355	30 235	159 590	36 269			19 648	1 474	
Q3	84 480	15 238	9 668	24 906	25 306	1 352	136 044	30 968	167 012	37 432			20 949	1 342	
Q4	87 443	15 672	10 015	25 687	27 119	-1 863	138 386	33 546	171 932	35 843			21 191	1 251	
1990 Q1	82 349	16 397	10 129	26 526	28 108	132	137 115	32 231	169 346	36 984			20 516	1 507	
Q2	84 759	16 418	10 517	26 935	25 325	1 125	138 144	33 636	171 780	38 352			18 628	1 535	
Q3	89 515	16 739	10 828	27 567	25 791	43	142 916	32 969	175 885	37 005			19 921	1 378	
Q4	91 953	17 498	11 163	28 661	26 059	-1 575	145 098	35 271	180 369	35 417			19 852	1 779	
1991 Q1	85 830	17 866	11 303	29 169	24 999	-1 112	138 886	30 712	169 598	33 057			18 743	1 583	
Q2	89 388	18 664	11 730	30 394	22 573	-836	141 519	34 272	175 791	35 508			21 006	1 324	
Q3	94 887	18 795	11 883	30 678	23 655	-702	148 518	34 671	183 189	36 554			22 711	1 306	
Q4	97 886	19 219	12 207	31 426	23 926	-2 055	151 183	36 164	187 347	35 452			23 257	1 544	
1992 Q1	90 893	19 371	12 322	31 693	24 031	-477	146 140	32 978	179 118	35 224			21 376	1 844	
Seasonally adjusted															
	AIIX	ACHP	CSBK	AAXV	DECR	DGAQ	DIGS	DJAZ	DIAB	DJBC			AAXP	AAXW	
1988 Q1	71 787	13 570	8 821	22 391	20 373	222	114 773	25 985	140 758	29 157	134	111 735	18 328	1 623	95 030
Q2	73 419	13 895	8 860	22 755	22 196	-40	118 330	27 027	145 357	30 587	149	114 919	18 899	1 332	97 352
Q3	75 909	13 786	9 175	22 961	22 753	1 779	123 402	27 646	151 048	32 176	167	119 039	19 378	1 425	101 086
Q4	77 681	14 359	9 263	23 622	23 636	2 839	127 778	27 176	154 954	32 964	180	122 170	19 906	1 560	103 824
1989 Q1	79 283	14 586	9 365	23 951	24 763	2 068	130 065	29 174	159 239	34 464	178	124 953	19 738	1 458	106 673
Q2	81 140	14 919	9 447	24 366	25 324	912	131 742	30 102	161 844	35 347	181	126 678	20 138	1 441	107 981
Q3	82 399	15 513	9 741	25 254	25 502	1 213	134 368	31 045	165 413	36 585	185	129 013	20 421	1 519	110 111
Q4	84 564	15 509	9 949	25 458	26 253	-1 038	135 237	32 470	167 707	36 308	178	131 577	20 628	1 274	112 223
1990 Q1	85 772	16 045	10 153	26 198	27 128	287	139 385	33 431	172 816	37 984	197	135 029	20 890	1 497	115 636
Q2	86 630	16 682	10 514	27 196	26 945	446	141 217	33 852	175 069	37 970	190	137 289	19 341	1 544	119 492
Q3	87 610	17 002	10 886	27 888	26 026	-14	141 510	33 151	174 661	36 023	179	138 817	19 361	1 562	121 018
Q4	88 564	17 323	11 084	28 407	25 184	-994	141 161	33 673	174 834	35 781	149	139 202	19 325	1 596	121 473
1991 Q1	89 425	17 721	11 334	29 055	24 225	-1 062	141 643	32 456	174 099	34 382	89	139 806	19 291	1 474	121 989
Q2	91 385	18 729	11 737	30 466	23 950	-1 457	144 344	34 294	178 638	34 990	67	143 715	21 746	1 437	123 406
Q3	92 941	19 055	11 934	30 989	23 712	-1 316	146 326	34 630	180 956	35 409	51	145 598	22 238	1 429	124 789
Q4	94 240	19 039	12 118	31 157	23 266	-870	147 793	34 439	182 232	35 790	46	146 488	22 442	1 417	125 463
1992 Q1	94 657	19 226	12 355	31 581	23 299	-518	149 019	34 351	183 370	36 377	65	147 058	21 897	1 537	126 698

1 Estimates are given to the nearest £ million but cannot be regarded as accurate to this degree.

2 This series is affected by the abolition of the domestic rates and the introduction of the community charge. For details see notes in the UK National Accounts article in the July issue of *Economic Trends*.

3 Quarterly alignment adjustment included in this series. For details see notes in the UK National Accounts article in the July issue of *Economic Trends*.

4 GDP is estimated in seasonally adjusted form only. Therefore whilst both a seasonally adjusted and unadjusted version exist of the residual error, the attribution of statistical discrepancies to the expenditure based and income based estimates can only be made in seasonally adjusted form.

Source: Central Statistical Office

1.2 Gross domestic product: by category of expenditure[1]

continued

£ million, 1985 prices[2]

At market prices

		General government final consumption			Gross domestic fixed capital formation	Value of physical increase in stocks and work in progress[3]	Total domestic expend-iture	Exports of goods and services	Total final expend-iture	less Imports of goods and services	Statist-ical discrep-ancy (expend-iture)[4]	Gross domestic product	less Factor cost adjust-ment[5]	Gross domestic product at factor cost
	Con-sumers' expend-iture	Central govern-ment	Local author-ities	Total										
	CCBH	DJDK	DJDL	DJCZ	DFDM	DHBK	DIEL	DJCV	DJDA	DJCY	GIXS	CAOO	DJCU	CAOP
1982	197 980	44 421	27 228	71 672	50 915	-1 281	319 028	88 798	407 791	82 348	-815	324 622	44 895	279 738
1983	206 932	45 281	27 808	73 089	53 476	1 357	334 854	90 589	425 443	87 709	-1 231	336 503	46 355	290 148
1984	210 254	45 741	28 051	73 792	58 034	1 084	343 164	96 525	439 689	96 394	485	343 780	48 347	295 433
1985	217 618	45 879	27 926	73 805	60 353	821	352 597	102 208	454 805	98 866	144	356 083	49 367	306 716
1986	231 172	46 684	28 422	75 106	61 813	737	368 828	107 052	475 880	105 662	-188	370 030	52 312	317 718
1987	243 279	46 753	29 281	76 034	67 753	1 158	388 224	113 094	501 318	113 916	316	387 718	55 539	332 179
1988	261 330	46 942	29 544	76 486	76 648	4 031	418 495	113 150	531 645	127 964	549	404 230	58 312	345 918
1989	270 575	47 363	29 819	77 182	81 845	2 668	432 270	117 929	550 199	137 389	584	413 394	59 974	353 420
1990	272 828	48 609	30 956	79 565	79 904	-399	431 898	123 812	555 710	138 790	534	417 454	60 506	356 948
1991	267 988	49 913	31 842	81 755	71 853	-3 157	418 439	124 390	542 829	134 719	178	408 288	60 013	348 275

Not seasonally adjusted

	CCBH	DJDK	DJDL	DJCZ	DFDM	DHBK	DIEL	DJCV	DJDA	DJCY			DJCU	
1988 Q1	61 741	12 309	7 473	19 782	18 567	142	100 232	27 494	127 726	29 625			13 968	
Q2	62 750	11 419	7 394	18 813	18 256	453	100 272	28 529	128 801	31 670			13 656	
Q3	67 049	11 273	7 317	18 590	19 206	1 755	106 600	28 470	135 070	33 199			14 869	
Q4	69 790	11 941	7 360	19 301	20 619	1 681	111 391	28 657	140 048	33 470			15 819	
1989 Q1	64 261	12 139	7 452	19 591	21 149	1 281	106 282	28 114	134 396	33 465			14 248	
Q2	65 832	11 315	7 412	18 727	19 382	1 723	105 664	28 926	134 590	35 047			14 312	
Q3	69 026	11 822	7 434	19 256	20 054	1 301	109 637	29 327	138 964	35 218			15 445	
Q4	71 456	12 087	7 521	19 608	21 260	-1 637	110 687	31 562	142 249	33 659			15 969	
1990 Q1	65 552	12 456	7 588	20 044	21 614	-91	107 119	30 239	137 358	34 408			14 814	
Q2	66 790	11 942	7 725	19 667	19 228	851	106 536	31 147	137 683	35 432			14 700	
Q3	69 353	11 858	7 775	19 633	19 400	276	108 662	29 997	138 659	35 008			15 369	
Q4	71 133	12 353	7 868	20 221	19 662	-1 435	109 581	32 429	142 010	33 942			15 623	
1991 Q1	64 947	12 509	7 911	20 420	18 886	-829	103 424	28 816	132 240	32 233			14 473	
Q2	64 891	12 401	7 953	20 354	16 967	-461	101 751	31 227	132 978	33 936			14 276	
Q3	67 824	12 377	7 948	20 325	17 842	-140	105 851	31 165	137 016	34 508			15 286	
Q4	70 326	12 626	8 030	20 656	18 158	-1 727	107 413	33 182	140 595	34 042			15 978	
1992 Q1	63 834	12 623	8 072	20 695	18 481	-130	102 880	30 377	133 257	34 264			14 352	

Seasonally adjusted

	CAAB	DIAV	DIAW	DIAT	DECU	DGBA	DIAY	DJDG	DIAU	DJDJ			DIAS	
1988 Q1	64 223	11 714	7 418	19 132	18 111	129	101 595	27 936	129 531	30 052	121	99 600	14 244	85 356
Q2	64 544	11 820	7 373	19 193	19 235	11	102 983	28 874	131 857	31 490	132	100 499	14 448	86 051
Q3	65 931	11 605	7 394	18 999	19 288	1 442	105 660	28 568	134 228	32 755	144	101 617	14 633	86 984
Q4	66 632	11 803	7 359	19 162	20 014	2 449	108 257	27 772	136 029	33 667	152	102 514	14 987	87 527
1989 Q1	66 935	11 576	7 430	19 006	20 570	1 613	108 124	28 976	137 100	34 513	147	102 734	14 748	87 986
Q2	67 679	11 710	7 398	19 108	20 507	885	108 179	28 864	137 043	34 255	147	102 935	14 961	87 974
Q3	67 706	12 167	7 474	19 641	20 280	1 056	108 683	29 658	138 341	34 820	149	103 670	15 095	88 575
Q4	68 255	11 910	7 517	19 427	20 488	-886	107 284	30 431	137 715	33 801	141	104 055	15 170	88 885
1990 Q1	68 109	12 118	7 573	19 691	20 770	-31	108 539	31 106	139 645	35 057	152	104 740	15 164	89 576
Q2	68 692	12 135	7 704	19 839	20 407	328	109 266	31 384	140 650	35 340	143	105 453	15 423	90 030
Q3	68 257	12 205	7 816	20 021	19 609	93	107 980	30 456	138 436	34 431	131	104 136	15 101	89 035
Q4	67 770	12 151	7 863	20 014	19 118	-789	106 113	30 866	136 979	33 962	108	103 125	14 818	88 307
1991 Q1	67 507	12 486	7 896	20 382	18 286	-746	105 429	30 236	135 665	33 176	64	102 553	14 940	87 613
Q2	66 852	12 192	7 931	20 123	18 011	-827	104 159	31 265	135 424	33 637	47	101 834	14 949	86 885
Q3	66 830	12 524	7 989	20 513	17 926	-875	104 394	31 433	135 827	33 869	35	101 993	14 958	87 035
Q4	66 799	12 711	8 026	20 737	17 630	-709	104 457	31 456	135 913	34 037	32	101 908	15 166	86 742
1992 Q1	66 325	12 444	8 057	20 501	17 881	-23	104 684	31 339	136 023	35 013	44	101 054	14 730	86 324

1 Estimates are given to the nearest £ million but cannot be regarded as accurate to this degree.
2 For years up to and including 1982, totals differ from the sum of the components because of the method used to rebase on 1985 prices.
3 Quarterly alignment adjustment included in this series. For details see the UK National Accounts article in the July issue of *Economic Trends*.
4 GDP is estimated in seasonally adjusted form only. Therefore whilst seasonally and unadjusted versions exist of the residual error, the attribution of statistical discrepancies to the expenditure based and income based estimates can be made only in seasonally adjusted form.
5 *Represents* Taxes on expenditure *less* Subsidies, both valued at 1985 prices.

Source: Central Statistical Office

1.3 Gross domestic product at factor cost: by category of income[1]

£ million, current prices

| | Factor incomes | | | | | | less | | |
	Income from employment[2]	Gross trading profits of companies[3,4,5,6]	Gross trading surplus of public corporations[3,5]	Gross trading surplus of general government enterprises[3]	Other income[7]	Total domestic income[8]	Stock appreciation	Statistical discrepancy (income)[9]	Gross domestic product[9]
	DJAO	CIAC	ADRD	DJAQ	DJAP	DJAU	DJAT	GIXQ	CAOM
1982	158 838	31 176	9 502	216	42 266	241 998	4 276	509	238 231
1983	169 847	39 528	10 004	50	46 105	265 534	4 204	-247	261 083
1984	180 883	44 656	8 381	-117	50 227	284 030	4 513	535	280 052
1985	195 708	51 767	7 120	265	54 738	309 598	2 738	-144	306 716
1986	211 729	47 049	8 059	155	61 663	328 655	1 790	-683	326 182
1987	229 532	59 315	6 802	-75	68 462	364 036	4 725	-1 014	358 297
1988	255 357	63 950	7 354	-32	77 761	404 390	6 212	-886	397 292
1989	283 585	66 203	6 418	199	88 331	444 736	7 292	-456	436 988
1990	314 139	64 963	4 265	17	100 464	483 848	6 380	151	477 619
1991	330 928	60 950	3 050	121	103 542	498 591	3 277	333	495 647
Not seasonally adjusted									
1988 Q1	60 837	14 743	1 908	-16	18 485	95 957	1 312		
Q2	62 757	14 476	1 654	43	19 120	98 050	1 666		
Q3	64 683	16 152	1 576	12	19 794	102 217	1 475		
Q4	67 080	18 579	2 216	-71	20 362	108 166	1 759		
1989 Q1	67 760	17 172	1 995	110	21 110	108 147	1 970		
Q2	69 830	16 049	1 497	-53	21 800	109 123	2 039		
Q3	71 650	15 969	1 126	61	22 404	111 210	1 451		
Q4	74 345	17 013	1 800	81	23 017	116 256	1 832		
1990 Q1	75 388	15 846	1 202	32	24 254	116 722	1 718		
Q2	78 214	15 879	1 012	-11	25 108	120 202	1 650		
Q3	79 653	16 488	791	45	25 471	122 448	1 704		
Q4	80 884	16 750	1 260	-49	25 631	124 476	1 308		
1991 Q1	81 001	14 631	880	-4	25 629	122 137	911		
Q2	82 370	14 816	779	-4	25 812	123 773	1 232		
Q3	83 365	14 433	644	62	25 959	124 463	462		
Q4	84 192	17 070	747	67	26 142	128 218	672		
1992 Q1	84 747	15 171	491	26	26 516	126 951	1 010		
Seasonally adjusted									
	DIAC	CIAD	ADRO		DJBH	DIAD	DJCE		
1988 Q1	61 339	14 963	1 727	-16	18 469	96 482	1 215	-237	95 030
Q2	62 839	15 344	1 802	43	19 147	99 175	1 595	-228	97 352
Q3	64 666	16 492	1 931	12	19 788	102 889	1 588	-215	101 086
Q4	66 513	17 151	1 894	-71	20 357	105 844	1 814	-206	103 824
1989 Q1	68 266	17 471	1 764	110	21 114	108 725	1 882	-170	106 673
Q2	69 798	16 851	1 662	-53	21 812	110 070	1 950	-139	107 981
Q3	71 620	16 177	1 544	61	22 380	111 782	1 571	-100	110 111
Q4	73 901	15 704	1 448	81	23 025	114 159	1 889	-47	112 223
1990 Q1	75 896	16 122	942	32	24 279	117 271	1 631	-4	115 636
Q2	78 161	16 518	1 231	-11	25 097	120 996	1 537	33	119 492
Q3	79 593	16 554	1 165	45	25 444	122 801	1 831	48	121 018
Q4	80 489	15 769	927	-49	25 644	122 780	1 381	74	121 473
1991 Q1	81 521	14 637	909	-4	25 673	122 736	822	75	121 989
Q2	82 289	15 617	758	-4	25 772	124 432	1 113	87	123 406
Q3	83 275	15 314	717	62	25 924	125 292	589	86	124 789
Q4	83 843	15 382	666	67	26 173	126 131	753	85	125 463
1992 Q1	85 281	15 116	521	26	26 589	127 533	919	84	126 698

1 Estimates are given to the nearest £ million but cannot be regarded as accurate to this degree.
2 Wages and salaries, forces' pay and employers' contributions.
3 Before providing for depreciation and stock appreciation.
4 Including financial institutions.
5 Figures reflect privatisations.
6 Includes quarterly alignment adjustment. For details, see notes in the UK National Accounts article in the July issue of Economic Trends.
7 Income from rent and from self-employment, and the imputed charge for the consumption of non-trading capital.

8 The sum of the factor incomes before deducting stock appreciation.
9 GDP is estimated in seasonally adjusted form only. Therefore whilst seasonally adjusted and unadjusted versions exist of the residual error, the attribution of statistical discrepancies to the expenditure-based and income-based estimates can be made only in seasonally adjusted form.

Source: Central Statistical Office

1.4 Index numbers: gross domestic product; at constant factor cost

1985 = 100

	Output at constant factor cost			Service industries				Gross Domestic Product
	Agriculture, forestry and fishing	Total production industries[1]	Construction[2]	Distribution, hotels and catering; repairs	Transport and communication	Other services	Total services	Gross Domestic Product
1985 weights	19	344	59	134	70	374	578	1 000
	CKAP		DVJO	CKAQ	CKAR	CKAS	CKCE	DJDD
1984	104.7	94.8	99.6	96.2	96.1	97.5	97.0	96.3
1985	100.0	100.0	100.0	100.0	100.0	100.0	100.0	100.0
1986	97.1	102.4	104.5	104.6	104.3	103.6	103.9	103.6
1987	97.9	105.7	112.7	111.4	112.5	108.1	109.4	108.3
1988	97.4	109.5	122.9	117.9	118.5	111.8	114.0	112.8
1989	101.2	109.9	130.4	121.8	125.3	114.3	117.4	115.2
1990	108.2	109.3	131.8	122.9	128.1	116.8	119.6	116.4
1991	111.0	106.0	120.3	119.1	123.5	116.0	117.6	113.5
Seasonally adjusted								
1982 Q3	94	92.0	90.4	88	88	92	90.5	91.3
Q4	92	91.1	92.0	89	90	93	91.4	91.8
1983 Q1	87	93.1	94.0	90	89	94	92.5	93.5
Q2	85	94.0	92.8	91	91	94	92.9	94.2
Q3	86	95.2	96.4	92	92	95	93.8	94.9
Q4	92	96.5	97.4	93	93	95	94.6	95.8
1984 Q1	100	97.2	98.5	95	94	97	95.8	96.5
Q2	106	94.1	99.6	96	95	97	96.5	95.8
Q3	107	93.3	100.6	96	97	98	97.3	96.0
Q4	105	94.4	99.6	98	98	99	98.6	97.0
1985 Q1	101	97.8	100.6	99	100	99	99.2	98.7
Q2	100	101.7	100.0	100	99	100	99.7	100.3
Q3	99	100.6	98.7	100	100	100	100.1	100.2
Q4	99	99.9	100.7	101	101	101	101.0	100.7
1986 Q1	98	101.1	99.2	101	102	102	101.8	101.7
Q2	97	102.2	104.5	104	103	103	103.2	103.2
Q3	97	103.0	106.1	106	105	105	104.8	104.1
Q4	97	103.5	108.2	107	108	105	105.8	105.3
1987 Q1	98	103.7	111.3	108	107	106	106.6	105.9
Q2	98	104.8	109.3	111	113	107	108.9	107.5
Q3	98	106.7	113.0	112	115	110	110.9	109.5
Q4	98	107.8	117.5	114	115	109	111.0	110.2
1988 Q1	97	107.9	122.1	116	118	110	112.5	111.3
Q2	96	109.5	121.5	117	117	111	113.2	112.2
Q3	98	110.3	122.1	119	118	113	114.8	113.4
Q4	98	110.4	126.0	120	121	113	115.6	114.1
1989 Q1	100	109.6	131.7	121	123	114	116.5	114.7
Q2	101	109.1	131.0	122	125	114	116.9	114.7
Q3	102	110.5	128.8	122	127	115	117.7	115.5
Q4	102	110.4	130.2	122	127	115	118.4	115.9
1990 Q1	106	109.9	135.1	124	129	116	119.7	116.8
Q2	108	111.8	133.0	124	128	117	119.8	117.4
Q3	110	108.6	131.1	123	128	117	119.6	116.1
Q4	109	107.0	128.1	121	127	117	119.2	115.2
1991 Q1	110	106.7	125.0	120	123	116	118.0	114.3
Q2	110	105.2	120.8	119	123	116	117.7	113.3
Q3	112	106.2	118.7	119	124	116	117.5	113.5
Q4	111	106.1	116.8	118	125	115	117.2	113.1
1992 Q1	107	105.3	116.2	117	126	115	116.9	112.6
Q2	..	105.0	..	117	..	..	116.9	112.5

1 The latest data for the index of production (series DVIM) are presented in Table 7.1. The figures given in this table are consistent with the figures for the output measure of gross domestic product.

2 Based on the net output of incorporated concerns and the self-employed, using information from the Annual Census of Construction and from the Inland Revenue.

Source: Central Statistical Office

1.5 Personal income, expenditure and saving

£ million

	Personal income before tax					Less United Kingdom taxes on income (pay-ments)	Less Social security contrib-utions	Less Miscell-aneous current deduct-ions	Community Charge	Total personal dispos-able income[2,3,4]	Con-sumers' expend-iture[4]	Balance: personal saving[3]	Saving ratio[5]	Real personal dispos-able income at 1985 prices[6]	Index of real personal dispos-able income (1985 = 100)
	Wages, salaries and forces' pay	Employ-ers' contrib-utions	Current grants from general govern-ment	Other personal income	Total[1]										
	AIJA	AIID	AIIE	AIIF	AIIA	AIIG	AIIH	CFGD	ADBH	AIIJ	AIIK	AAAU	AIIM	CFAG	CFAD
1987	200 143	29 389	52 494	76 738	358 764	43 386	28 642	2 128	-	284 608	264 880	19 728	6.9	261 398	108.3
1988	223 250	32 107	54 087	89 284	398 728	48 290	32 108	2 347	-	315 983	298 796	17 187	5.4	276 362	114.5
1989	248 537	35 048	56 793	101 255	441 633	53 517	33 025	2 441	619	352 031	327 386	24 645	7.0	290 943	120.5
1990	275 441	38 698	62 002	113 991	490 132	61 778	34 651	2 569	8 666	382 468	348 576	33 892	8.9	299 355	124.0
1991	289 918	41 010	71 570	118 868	521 366	63 860	36 670	2 544	8 212	410 080	367 991	42 089	10.3	298 639	123.7

Not seasonally adjusted

	AIJA	AIID	AIIE	AIIF	AIIA	AIIG	AIIH	CFGD	ADBH	AIIJ	AIIK	AAAU	AIIM	CFAG	CFAD
1987 Q1	47 482	7 024	12 703	18 121	85 330	10 522	6 724	516	-	67 568	61 219	6 349	9.4	62 994	104.4
Q2	49 210	7 249	13 084	18 636	88 179	10 079	7 065	523	-	70 512	63 535	6 977	9.9	64 896	107.5
Q3	50 734	7 441	13 140	19 818	91 133	11 138	7 307	538	-	72 150	68 290	3 860	5.3	65 723	108.9
Q4	52 717	7 675	13 567	20 163	94 122	11 647	7 546	551	-	74 378	71 836	2 542	3.4	67 785	112.3
1988 Q1	53 165	7 672	13 293	20 468	94 598	12 231	7 585	577	-	74 205	68 877	5 328	7.2	66 502	110.2
Q2	54 840	7 917	13 265	21 834	97 856	10 793	7 953	584	-	78 526	71 825	6 701	8.5	68 589	113.7
Q3	56 545	8 138	13 638	22 828	101 149	12 119	8 235	591	-	80 204	77 609	2 595	3.2	69 275	114.8
Q4	58 700	8 380	13 891	24 154	105 125	13 147	8 335	595	-	83 048	80 485	2 563	3.1	71 996	119.3
1989 Q1	59 415	8 345	13 450	23 512	104 722	12 566	8 297	603	-	83 256	76 005	7 251	8.7	70 374	116.6
Q2	61 252	8 578	14 220	25 315	109 365	12 346	8 409	610	206	87 794	79 458	8 336	9.5	72 720	120.5
Q3	62 804	8 846	14 351	26 163	112 164	13 700	8 193	635	206	89 430	84 480	4 950	5.5	73 053	121.1
Q4	65 066	9 279	14 772	26 265	115 382	14 905	8 126	593	207	91 551	87 443	4 108	4.5	74 796	124.0
1990 Q1	66 137	9 251	14 616	26 415	116 419	14 878	8 553	659	207	92 122	82 349	9 773	10.6	73 318	121.5
Q2	68 592	9 622	15 417	27 204	120 835	14 339	8 805	665	2 819	94 207	84 759	9 448	10.0	74 221	123.0
Q3	69 815	9 838	15 641	29 748	125 042	16 054	8 569	635	2 820	96 964	89 515	7 449	7.7	75 110	124.5
Q4	70 897	9 987	16 328	30 624	127 836	16 507	8 724	610	2 820	99 175	91 953	7 222	7.3	76 706	127.1
1991 Q1	71 032	9 969	16 427	28 212	125 640	16 106	9 356	654	2 820	96 704	85 830	10 874	11.2	73 157	121.2
Q2	72 174	10 196	17 744	29 565	129 679	15 029	9 203	642	1 797	103 008	89 388	13 620	13.2	74 760	123.9
Q3	73 006	10 359	18 336	30 115	131 816	16 161	8 967	607	1 798	104 283	94 887	9 396	9.0	74 522	123.5
Q4	73 706	10 486	19 063	30 976	134 231	16 564	9 144	641	1 797	106 085	97 886	8 199	7.7	76 200	126.3
1992 Q1	74 274	10 473	19 562	30 736	135 045	18 454	9 818	654	1 799	104 320	90 893	13 427	12.9	73 264	121.4

Seasonally adjusted

	AIJB	AIIR	AIIS	AIIT	AIIQ	AIIU	AIIV	CFGE		AIIW	AIIX	AAUU	AIIZ	CFAH	CFAF
1987 Q1	47 897	7 116	12 851	18 459	86 323	10 464	6 849	516		68 494	63 605	4 889	7.1	63 690	105.5
Q2	49 297	7 233	13 170	18 948	88 648	10 779	7 011	521		70 337	64 990	5 347	7.6	65 109	107.9
Q3	50 682	7 420	13 179	19 437	90 718	11 046	7 259	536		71 877	67 207	4 670	6.5	65 800	109.0
Q4	52 267	7 620	13 294	19 894	93 075	11 097	7 523	555		73 900	69 078	4 822	6.5	66 799	110.7
1988 Q1	53 577	7 762	13 420	20 487	95 246	12 135	7 709	577		74 825	71 787	3 038	4.1	66 944	110.9
Q2	54 937	7 902	13 349	22 331	98 519	11 598	7 896	581		78 444	73 419	5 025	6.4	68 968	114.3
Q3	56 546	8 120	13 668	22 556	100 890	11 967	8 188	589		80 146	75 909	4 237	5.3	69 619	115.4
Q4	58 190	8 323	13 650	23 910	104 073	12 590	8 315	600		82 568	77 681	4 887	5.9	70 831	117.4
1989 Q1	59 853	8 413	13 643	23 871	105 780	12 717	8 393	603		84 067	79 283	4 784	5.7	70 979	117.6
Q2	61 273	8 525	14 315	25 858	109 971	12 996	8 320	607		87 842	81 140	6 702	7.6	73 274	121.4
Q3	62 785	8 835	14 354	25 657	111 631	13 647	8 155	633		88 990	82 399	6 591	7.4	73 127	121.2
Q4	64 626	9 275	14 481	25 869	114 251	14 157	8 157	598		91 132	84 564	6 568	7.2	73 563	121.9
1990 Q1	66 582	9 314	14 831	27 332	118 059	14 779	8 613	658		93 802	85 772	8 030	8.6	74 495	123.5
Q2	68 595	9 566	15 469	27 805	121 435	15 272	8 728	661		93 955	86 630	7 325	7.8	74 510	123.5
Q3	69 766	9 827	15 615	29 019	124 227	16 064	8 544	633		96 166	87 610	8 556	8.9	74 933	124.2
Q4	70 498	9 991	16 087	29 835	126 411	15 663	8 766	617		98 545	88 564	9 981	10.1	75 417	125.0
1991 Q1	71 496	10 025	16 614	29 539	127 674	15 891	9 409	653		98 901	89 425	9 476	9.6	74 663	123.7
Q2	72 153	10 136	17 670	30 408	130 367	16 054	9 127	637		102 752	91 385	11 367	11.1	75 170	124.6
Q3	72 926	10 349	18 423	29 151	130 849	15 793	8 944	606		103 708	92 941	10 767	10.4	74 575	123.6
Q4	73 343	10 500	18 863	29 770	132 476	16 122	9 190	648		104 719	94 240	10 479	10.0	74 231	123.0
1992 Q1	74 749	10 532	19 721	31 788	136 790	17 495	9 871	653		106 972	94 657	12 315	11.5	74 954	124.2

1 Before providing for depreciation and stock appreciation.
2 Equals total personal income before tax *less* payments of taxes on income, social security contributions and other current transfers.
3 Before providing for depreciation, stock appreciation and additions to tax reserves.

4 This series is affected by the abolition of domestic rates and the introduction of the community charge. For details see notes in the UK National Accounts article in the July issue of *Economic Trends*.
5 Personal saving as a percentage of total personal disposable income.
6 Personal disposable income revalued by the implied consumers' expenditure deflator (1985 = 100).

Source: Central Statistical Office

1.6 Consumers' expenditure[1]

£ million

	Durable goods				Other goods								Services		Total
	Cars, motor cycles and other vehicles	Furniture and floor coverings	Other durable goods	Total	Food (household expenditure)	Beer	Other alcoholic drink	Tobacco	Clothing other than footwear	Footwear	Energy products	Other goods	Rent, rates and water charges[2]	Other services[3]	consumers' expenditure[2]
At current prices															
	CCDT	CCDU	CCDV	AIIL	CCDW	CCDX	CCDY	CCDZ	CCEA	CCEB	CCEC	CCED	CCEE	CCEF	AIIK
1987	13 462	5 058	7 749	26 269	34 472	9 398	8 053	7 653	14 599	3 085	18 527	28 850	32 777	81 197	264 880
1988	17 418	5 951	8 565	31 934	36 593	10 039	8 715	7 945	15 736	3 192	19 454	32 575	36 508	96 105	298 796
1989	20 274	6 348	9 216	35 838	39 245	10 676	9 141	8 196	16 533	3 357	20 394	35 285	40 295	108 426	327 386
1990	19 381	6 285	9 324	34 990	41 833	11 745	9 993	8 784	17 157	3 545	22 411	37 875	39 332	120 911	348 576
1991	17 375	6 488	9 734	33 597	44 294	12 775	10 761	9 894	17 388	3 618	24 933	39 745	43 733	127 253	367 991
Not seasonally adjusted															
1989 Q1	5 470	1 667	2 128	9 265	9 149	2 150	1 684	1 998	3 367	686	5 399	7 804	9 658	24 845	76 005
Q2	5 024	1 467	1 925	8 416	9 937	2 686	1 975	2 028	3 770	858	4 793	8 216	10 051	26 728	79 458
Q3	6 701	1 452	2 150	10 303	9 832	2 802	2 096	2 061	3 877	850	4 283	8 397	10 190	29 789	84 480
Q4	3 079	1 762	3 013	7 854	10 327	3 038	3 386	2 109	5 519	963	5 919	10 868	10 396	27 064	87 443
1990 Q1	5 493	1 692	2 180	9 365	9 752	2 269	1 773	2 067	3 512	730	5 883	8 495	10 594	27 909	82 349
Q2	4 657	1 473	1 980	8 110	10 713	2 955	2 164	2 197	3 952	903	5 006	8 968	9 309	30 482	84 759
Q3	6 455	1 432	2 162	10 049	10 506	3 134	2 323	2 240	4 076	911	4 939	9 061	9 569	32 707	89 515
Q4	2 776	1 688	3 002	7 466	10 862	3 387	3 733	2 280	5 617	1 001	6 583	11 351	9 860	29 813	91 953
1991 Q1	4 953	1 713	2 294	8 960	10 342	2 476	1 932	2 228	3 548	741	6 808	8 936	10 155	29 704	85 830
Q2	3 744	1 524	2 042	7 310	11 278	3 111	2 371	2 527	3 965	908	5 808	9 457	10 912	31 741	89 388
Q3	6 036	1 520	2 210	9 766	11 187	3 468	2 493	2 547	4 076	929	5 227	9 585	11 187	34 422	94 887
Q4	2 642	1 731	3 188	7 561	11 487	3 720	3 965	2 592	5 799	1 040	7 090	11 767	11 479	31 386	97 886
1992 Q1	4 616	1 767	2 272	8 655	10 843	2 715	2 096	2 528	3 407	717	7 096	9 336	11 788	31 712	90 893
Revalued at 1985 prices															
	CCBJ	CCBK	CCBL	CCBI	CCBM	CCBN	CCBO	CCBP	CCBQ	CCBR	CCBS	CCCK	CCCL	CCBV	CCBH
1987	11 057	4 735	8 102	23 894	32 358	8 483	7 541	6 763	14 030	2 902	19 618	26 828	28 161	72 701	243 279
1988	12 789	5 373	8 952	27 114	33 127	8 540	7 861	6 780	14 635	2 889	20 454	29 220	28 538	82 172	261 330
1989	14 159	5 477	9 727	29 363	33 717	8 531	7 853	6 797	14 630	2 889	20 250	30 258	28 940	87 347	270 575
1990	12 865	5 130	9 752	27 747	33 315	8 516	7 844	6 821	14 590	2 879	20 563	30 623	29 342	90 588	272 828
1991	10 701	4 992	10 026	25 719	33 632	8 211	7 604	6 703	14 468	2 810	21 234	30 014	29 760	87 833	267 988
Not seasonally adjusted															
1989 Q1	3 907	1 465	2 252	7 624	8 020	1 762	1 478	1 668	3 077	602	5 512	6 826	7 197	20 495	64 261
Q2	3 544	1 266	2 029	6 839	8 605	2 178	1 709	1 690	3 327	744	4 703	7 066	7 222	21 749	65 832
Q3	4 675	1 253	2 273	8 201	8 477	2 225	1 785	1 715	3 458	733	4 273	7 156	7 248	23 755	69 026
Q4	2 033	1 493	3 173	6 699	8 615	2 366	2 881	1 724	4 768	810	5 762	9 210	7 273	21 348	71 456
1990 Q1	3 798	1 421	2 303	7 522	7 890	1 745	1 470	1 683	3 068	609	5 712	7 023	7 297	21 533	65 552
Q2	3 099	1 208	2 063	6 370	8 535	2 170	1 705	1 700	3 358	739	4 700	7 274	7 322	22 917	66 790
Q3	4 257	1 164	2 262	7 683	8 370	2 233	1 791	1 718	3 507	740	4 430	7 284	7 348	24 249	69 353
Q4	1 711	1 337	3 124	6 172	8 520	2 368	2 878	1 720	4 657	791	5 721	9 042	7 375	21 889	71 133
1991 Q1	3 171	1 365	2 420	6 956	7 893	1 702	1 447	1 663	3 043	587	6 034	6 946	7 400	21 276	64 947
Q2	2 329	1 168	2 075	5 572	8 554	2 005	1 667	1 673	3 274	700	4 951	7 106	7 426	21 963	64 891
Q3	3 687	1 164	2 265	7 116	8 531	2 183	1 731	1 682	3 452	725	4 375	7 148	7 452	23 429	67 824
Q4	1 514	1 295	3 266	6 075	8 654	2 321	2 759	1 685	4 699	798	5 874	8 814	7 482	21 165	70 326
1992 Q1	2 741	1 338	2 360	6 439	7 994	1 681	1 429	1 629	2 888	559	5 919	6 840	7 505	20 951	63 834
Seasonally adjusted															
	CCBX	CCBY	CCBZ	CCBW	CCCA	CCCB	CCCC	CCCD	CCCE	CCCF	CCCG	CCCM	CCCN	CCCJ	CAAB
1989 Q1	3 521	1 405	2 378	7 304	8 431	2 118	1 971	1 695	3 663	731	4 815	7 498	7 197	21 512	66 935
Q2	3 653	1 365	2 454	7 472	8 524	2 150	1 969	1 698	3 660	735	5 148	7 483	7 222	21 618	67 679
Q3	3 542	1 345	2 443	7 330	8 348	2 138	1 956	1 703	3 632	715	5 045	7 531	7 248	22 060	67 706
Q4	3 443	1 362	2 452	7 257	8 414	2 125	1 957	1 701	3 675	708	5 242	7 746	7 273	22 157	68 255
1990 Q1	3 446	1 353	2 417	7 216	8 299	2 106	1 962	1 710	3 648	735	4 989	7 695	7 297	22 452	68 109
Q2	3 233	1 304	2 492	7 029	8 444	2 143	1 963	1 708	3 688	730	5 128	7 691	7 322	22 846	68 692
Q3	3 240	1 252	2 422	6 914	8 241	2 144	1 964	1 706	3 675	721	5 260	7 656	7 348	22 628	68 257
Q4	2 946	1 221	2 421	6 588	8 331	2 123	1 955	1 697	3 579	693	5 186	7 581	7 375	22 662	67 770
1991 Q1	2 871	1 295	2 542	6 708	8 304	2 059	1 929	1 690	3 631	708	5 236	7 611	7 400	22 231	67 507
Q2	2 426	1 262	2 517	6 205	8 455	1 980	1 912	1 680	3 600	693	5 473	7 512	7 426	21 916	66 852
Q3	2 794	1 254	2 429	6 477	8 406	2 094	1 891	1 670	3 622	708	5 183	7 520	7 452	21 807	66 830
Q4	2 610	1 181	2 538	6 329	8 467	2 078	1 872	1 663	3 615	701	5 342	7 371	7 482	21 879	66 799
1992 Q1	2 460	1 268	2 475	6 203	8 406	2 035	1 912	1 655	3 449	672	5 161	7 485	7 505	21 842	66 325

1 Estimates are given to the nearest £million but cannot be regarded as accurate to this degree.
2 This series is affected by the abolition of domestic rates and the introduction of the community charge. For details see the UK National Accounts article in the July issue of *Economic Trends*.

3 Including the adjustments for international travel, etc and final expenditure by private non-profit making bodies.

Source: Central Statistical Office

1.7 Value of physical increase in stocks and work in progress

£ million

	All indust-ries	Energy and water supply	Metals	Chemi-cals and man-made fibres	Metal goods, engineer ing and vehicles	Food, drink and tobacco	Text-iles, cloth-ing, footwear and leather	Other manufac-turing	Total[1]	Mater-ials and fuel	Work in progress	Finished goods	Whole-sale[2]	Retail[3]	Other indust-ries
				Manufacturing[1] — Analysis by industry group					Manufacturing[1] — Analysis by type of asset				Distributive trades		
Book value of stocks and work in progress at end Dec-ember 1990[4]	124 216	5 133	2 183	5 056	28 324	6 078	3 084	7 927	52 650	15 964	18 589	18 097	18 869	15 183	32 341
At current prices															
	DHBF	DHBU	DGBR	DGBS	DGBT	DGBU	DGBV	DGBW	DHBA	DHCO	DHDE	DHCT	DHBG	DHBE	DHBW
1987	1 388	-185	-18	60	-661	-65	191	229	-262	112	-252	-123	586	764	485
1988	4 800	-19	-9	124	672	-94	33	255	979	335	164	480	970	795	2 075
1989	3 155	310	56	206	-271	-80	-121	74	-134	-31	-628	524	738	350	1 891
1990	-275	-500	-192	-171	-1 293	53	-218	-554	-2 053	-545	-1 016	-492	-213	157	2 334
1991	-4 705	83	-186	-62	-2 734	-94	-229	-486	-3 789	-1 023	-1 136	-1 628	-1 092	-610	703
Not seasonally adjusted															
1989 Q1	1 580	115	18	73	302	-49	85	68	497	24	61	412	349	-350	969
Q2	2 086	13	24	73	571	-183	57	97	640	37	71	532	-66	412	1 087
Q3	1 352	214	-15	136	-288	70	-170	-63	-329	158	239	-726	654	138	675
Q4	-1 863	-32	29	-76	-856	82	-93	-28	-942	-250	-999	306	-199	150	-840
1990 Q1	132	-295	-139	-55	349	49	29	-99	134	-214	396	-48	365	-327	255
Q2	1 125	-140	1	136	71	-100	88	-2	195	27	-116	284	-290	39	1 321
Q3	43	273	2	-56	-552	199	-170	-61	-633	-43	61	-652	280	252	-129
Q4	-1 575	-338	-56	-196	-1 161	-95	-165	-392	-1 749	-315	-1 357	-76	-568	193	887
1991 Q1	-1 112	-134	-187	23	-152	-10	99	-70	-296	-478	236	-54	-178	-737	233
Q2	-836	137	-55	59	-739	10	88	-75	-712	-266	-368	-77	-418	-127	284
Q3	-702	243	29	4	-768	60	-183	-114	-972	108	19	-1 098	43	250	-266
Q4	-2 055	-163	27	-148	-1 075	-154	-233	-227	-1 809	-387	-1 023	-399	-539	4	452
1992 Q1	-477	-33	-138	-17	-210	67	111	-26	-214	-333	-400	520	-79	26	-177
Revalued at 1985 prices															
Value of stocks and work in progress at end Dec-ember 1990[4]	100763	5 544	2 054	4 228	20 254	5 856	2 379	5 738	40 503	12 805	14 756	12 942	15 512	12 433	26 771
	DGBA	DHBQ	DGBX	DGBY	DGBZ	DGCA	DGCB	DGCC	DHBM	DGAX	DGAY	DGAW	DHBO	DHBN	DHBR
1987	1 158	-210	-20	61	-593	-65	183	213	-221	103	-220	-108	535	722	332
1988	4 031	-108	-5	126	592	-89	32	231	887	315	145	427	844	727	1 681
1989	2 668	252	45	184	-179	-77	-101	106	-22	-31	-439	448	674	299	1 465
1990	-399	-509	-166	-153	-765	70	-164	-455	-1 633	-439	-739	-454	-212	111	1 844
1991	-3 157	205	-162	-17	-1 915	-63	-182	-385	-2 724	-834	-821	-1 071	-823	-494	679
Seasonally adjusted															
1989 Q1	1 613	258	15	57	48	-48	5	16	93	62	-163	193	274	-29	1 017
Q2	885	-85	20	48	128	-158	-33	94	99	-9	-60	168	78	291	502
Q3	1 056	49	-16	128	88	90	-47	-20	223	93	5	125	244	46	494
Q4	-886	30	26	-49	-443	39	-26	16	-437	-177	-221	-38	78	-9	-548
1990 Q1	-31	-185	-119	-55	26	37	-41	-126	-278	-138	80	-220	267	43	122
Q2	328	-151	3	106	-244	-73	-3	-25	-236	19	-207	-48	-142	-36	893
Q3	93	129	-3	-64	9	208	-39	-9	102	-103	-106	311	-118	90	-110
Q4	-789	-302	-47	-140	-556	-102	-81	-295	-1 221	-217	-506	-497	-219	14	939
1991 Q1	-746	103	-134	38	-445	-17	8	-60	-610	-325	-125	-160	-136	-239	136
Q2	-827	219	-52	23	-670	68	-31	-76	-738	-220	-293	-225	-241	-190	123
Q3	-875	-49	33	30	-323	-50	-61	-154	-525	-55	-221	-248	-292	83	-92
Q4	-709	-68	-9	-108	-477	-64	-98	-95	-851	-234	-182	-438	-154	-148	512
1992 Q1	-23	350	-90	-26	-473	64	17	-33	-541	-198	-516	173	-77	382	-137

1 Differences between totals and the sum of constituent parts of manufacturing are due to rounding.
2 Classes 61-63 excluding activity heading 6148 - motor vehicles and acces-sories.
3 Classes 64-65 excluding activity headings 6510 and 6520 - motor vehicles and accessories and filling stations.
4 Seasonally unadjusted stock levels.

Source: Central Statistical Office

1.8 Gross domestic fixed capital formation

£ million

	Private sector[1]	General government[1]	Public corporations[1]	Vehicles, ships and aircraft	Plant and machinery	Other new buildings and works[1]	Dwellings Private	Dwellings Public	Total
At current prices									
	DFDG	AAYE	AAAK	DFEJ	DFCX	DFCT	DFDF	DFDH	DFDC
1987	61 891	7 577	4 609	7 805	27 073	23 925	12 358	2 916	74 077
1988	77 833	6 506	4 619	8 845	31 428	29 828	15 943	2 914	88 958
1989	86 770	9 582	5 490	10 216	36 258	35 292	16 230	3 846	101 842
1990	87 893	12 544	4 846	9 956	36 987	39 736	14 360	4 244	105 283
1991	79 392	12 177	3 584	8 133	34 064	35 656	14 437	2 863	95 153
1989 Q1	20 785	3 265	1 526	2 620	9 427	8 922	3 410	1 197	25 576
Q2	21 247	1 387	1 207	2 369	8 680	7 849	4 294	649	23 841
Q3	21 816	2 113	1 377	2 611	8 580	8 840	4 420	855	25 306
Q4	22 922	2 817	1 380	2 616	9 571	9 681	4 106	1 145	27 119
1990 Q1	21 448	5 271	1 389	2 930	10 114	10 339	2 693	2 032	28 108
Q2	22 522	1 865	938	2 356	8 867	9 210	4 260	632	25 325
Q3	22 144	2 447	1 200	2 323	8 818	9 776	4 111	763	25 791
Q4	21 779	2 961	1 319	2 347	9 188	10 411	3 296	817	26 059
1991 Q1	19 458	4 245	1 296	2 179	9 143	10 020	2 527	1 130	24 999
Q2	19 721	2 095	757	2 086	7 858	8 187	3 925	517	22 573
Q3	20 088	2 785	782	1 723	8 167	8 988	4 210	567	23 655
Q4	20 125	3 052	749	2 145	8 896	8 461	3 775	649	23 926
1992 Q1	17 864	4 939	1 228	2 349	9 066	8 875	2 542	1 199	24 031
Revalued at 1985 prices									
	DFDQ	DFDS	DFCZ	DFEH	DFCY	DFCU	DFDP	DFDR	DFDM
1987	55 807	7 470	4 476	6 648	25 943	21 687	10 734	2 741	67 753
1988	65 614	6 649	4 385	7 130	29 762	24 639	12 568	2 549	76 648
1989	68 907	8 292	4 646	7 676	33 485	26 119	11 559	3 006	81 845
1990	66 248	9 741	3 915	7 046	32 610	27 659	9 489	3 100	79 904
1991	59 289	9 546	3 018	5 436	29 364	25 572	9 386	2 095	71 853
Not seasonally adjusted									
1989 Q1	16 860	2 943	1 346	2 008	8 787	6 928	2 451	975	21 149
Q2	17 078	1 282	1 022	1 794	8 094	5 861	3 119	514	19 382
Q3	17 099	1 802	1 153	1 947	7 889	6 420	3 140	658	20 054
Q4	17 870	2 265	1 125	1 927	8 715	6 910	2 849	859	21 260
1990 Q1	16 350	4 125	1 139	2 115	9 037	7 223	1 737	1 502	21 614
Q2	17 015	1 442	771	1 680	7 785	6 410	2 893	460	19 228
Q3	16 531	1 906	963	1 630	7 694	6 775	2 750	551	19 400
Q4	16 352	2 268	1 042	1 621	8 094	7 251	2 109	587	19 662
1991 Q1	14 548	3 275	1 063	1 489	7 928	7 050	1 606	813	18 886
Q2	14 680	1 645	642	1 404	6 797	5 830	2 561	375	16 967
Q3	14 967	2 202	673	1 138	7 025	6 473	2 786	420	17 842
Q4	15 094	2 424	640	1 405	7 614	6 219	2 433	487	18 158
1992 Q1	13 527	3 936	1 018	1 536	7 732	6 703	1 592	918	18 481
Seasonally adjusted									
	DFEB	DFED	DFDA	DEBP	DEBO	DFCV	DFEA	DFEC	DECU
1989 Q1	17 732	1 784	1 054	1 821	8 364	6 440	3 334	611	20 570
Q2	17 362	1 928	1 217	1 913	8 722	6 386	2 762	724	20 507
Q3	16 914	2 172	1 194	2 000	8 248	6 551	2 715	766	20 280
Q4	16 899	2 408	1 181	1 942	8 151	6 742	2 748	905	20 488
1990 Q1	17 065	2 766	939	1 963	8 636	6 719	2 385	1 067	20 770
Q2	17 339	2 150	918	1 768	8 383	6 966	2 608	682	20 407
Q3	16 282	2 354	973	1 666	7 953	6 882	2 422	686	19 609
Q4	15 562	2 471	1 085	1 649	7 638	7 092	2 074	665	19 118
1991 Q1	15 296	2 115	875	1 354	7 546	6 537	2 298	551	18 286
Q2	14 930	2 317	764	1 480	7 340	6 386	2 277	528	18 011
Q3	14 641	2 579	706	1 178	7 303	6 541	2 409	495	17 926
Q4	14 422	2 535	673	1 424	7 175	6 108	2 402	521	17 630
1992 Q1	14 404	2 608	869	1 440	7 412	6 226	2 212	591	17 881

1 Including transfer costs of land and buildings.

Source: Central Statistical Office

1.8 Gross domestic fixed capital formation
continued

£ million

	Analysis by industry group									
	Extraction of mineral oil and natural gas	All other energy and water supply	Manufact-uring	Distribu-tion, hotels and catering repairs[1]	Transport and communica-tion[1,2]	Financial and business services etc[1]	Other industries and services[1,3]	Dwellings	Transfer cost of land and buildings	Total
At current prices										
	DFDE	DFEK	DFDD	DFDJ	DFDI	DFEL	DFEM	DFDK	DFBH	DFDC
1987	2 047	4 200	10 814	7 687	6 840	11 537	10 518	15 274	4 051	74 077
1988	2 128	4 576	12 281	9 458	7 878	15 102	12 185	18 857	5 456	88 958
1989	2 708	5 252	14 260	9 499	9 586	19 470	..	20 076	4 381	101 842
1990	3 527	6 200	14 816	..	..	..	..	18 604	4 255	105 283
1991	5 116	6 837	12 529	..	..	..	..	17 300	4 161	95 153
Not seasonally adjusted										
1989 Q1	526	1 539	3 122	2 080	2 870	4 763	..	4 607	1 039	25 576
Q2	640	1 038	3 435	2 382	2 492	4 416	..	4 943	1 117	23 841
Q3	757	1 326	3 570	2 388	1 883	5 065	..	5 275	1 133	25 306
Q4	785	1 349	4 133	2 649	2 341	5 226	..	5 251	1 092	27 119
1990 Q1	763	1 791	3 673	..	..	..	..	4 725	988	28 108
Q2	898	1 299	3 611	..	..	..	..	4 892	1 088	25 325
Q3	960	1 524	3 637	..	..	..	..	4 874	1 091	25 791
Q4	906	1 586	3 895	..	..	..	..	4 113	1 088	26 059
1991 Q1	1 047	1 812	3 054	..	..	..	..	3 657	986	24 999
Q2	1 213	1 571	2 994	..	..	..	..	4 442	1 036	22 573
Q3	1 485	1 580	3 190	..	..	..	..	4 777	1 141	23 655
Q4	1 371	1 874	3 291	..	..	..	..	4 424	998	23 926
1992 Q1	1 208	1 981	2 664	..	..	..	..	3 741	703	24 031
Revalued at 1985 prices										
	DFDO	DFEN	DFDN	DFDU	DFDT	DFEO	DFEP	DFDV	DFDW	DFDM
1987	1 928	3 975	10 048	6 995	6 281	10 819	9 879	13 475	3 287	67 753
1988	1 873	4 096	11 198	8 389	6 997	13 786	10 763	15 117	3 596	76 648
1989	2 165	4 347	12 386	7 849	8 116	16 664	..	14 565	2 588	81 845
1990	2 683	4 794	12 154	..	..	..	..	12 589	2 337	79 904
1991	4 027	5 254	10 238	..	..	..	..	11 481	2 248	71 853
Not seasonally adjusted										
1989 Q1	439	1 319	2 801	1 798	2 386	4 095	..	3 426	659	21 149
Q2	518	863	3 005	1 969	2 125	3 874	..	3 633	666	19 382
Q3	601	1 086	3 085	1 965	1 626	4 276	..	3 798	643	20 054
Q4	607	1 079	3 495	2 117	1 979	4 419	..	3 708	620	21 260
1990 Q1	582	1 418	3 072	..	..	..	..	3 239	562	21 614
Q2	682	1 006	2 960	..	..	..	..	3 353	602	19 228
Q3	730	1 165	2 947	..	..	..	..	3 301	584	19 400
Q4	689	1 205	3 175	..	..	..	..	2 696	589	19 662
1991 Q1	809	1 413	2 517	..	..	..	..	2 419	536	18 886
Q2	943	1 207	2 442	..	..	..	..	2 936	560	16 967
Q3	1 174	1 208	2 585	..	..	..	..	3 206	609	17 842
Q4	1 101	1 426	2 694	..	..	..	..	2 920	543	18 158
1992 Q1	980	1 530	2 188	..	..	..	..	2 510	440	18 481
Seasonally adjusted										
	DFDZ	DFEQ	DECV	DFEF	DFEE	DFER	DFES	DFEG	DECX	DECU
1989 Q1	493	1 104	2 864	1 954	2 122	4 198	..	3 945	717	20 570
Q2	502	1 019	3 168	1 960	2 306	4 078	..	3 486	688	20 507
Q3	563	1 121	3 173	1 943	1 756	4 358	..	3 481	590	20 280
Q4	607	1 103	3 181	1 992	1 932	4 030	..	3 653	593	20 488
1990 Q1	643	1 173	3 241	..	..	..	..	3 452	613	20 770
Q2	667	1 176	3 107	..	..	..	..	3 290	622	20 407
Q3	684	1 210	2 905	..	..	..	..	3 108	537	19 609
Q4	689	1 235	2 901	..	..	..	..	2 739	565	19 118
1991 Q1	894	1 168	2 667	..	..	..	..	2 849	585	18 286
Q2	921	1 384	2 555	..	..	..	..	2 805	579	18 011
Q3	1 105	1 230	2 543	..	..	..	..	2 904	562	17 926
Q4	1 107	1 472	2 473	..	..	..	..	2 923	522	17 630
1992 Q1	1 077	1 275	2 333	..	..	..	..	2 803	481	17 881

1 No estimates of an acceptable quality for 1989 and 1990 are available.
2 In this series capital formation in imported ships is included at the time of delivery instead of when the expenditure takes place.
3 Covers agriculture, forestry and fishing construction and other service industries.

Source: Central Statistical Office

1.9 Fixed capital expenditure in manufacturing industry[1]

£ million

	Metals	Mineral products	Chemicals, etc	Mechanical engineering	Electrical engineering	Vehicles	Food	Drink and tobacco
Division, Class or Group	_21,22_	_23,24_	_25,26_	_31,32_	_33, 34,37_	_35,36_	_41 plus 420-423_	_424-429_
At current prices								
	BAAF	BAAI	BAAL	BAAO	BAAR	BAAU	BAAX	BABA
1988	611	852	1 693	1 340	1 371	1 307	1 361	398
1989	700	1 044	2 104	1 672	1 629	1 846	1 388	467
1990	..	3 958	..	..	5 444	..	..	..
1991	..	3 217	..	..	4 739	..	..	..
1988 Q4	157	237	454	414	375	368	364	108
1989 Q1	191	242	412	344	435	348	312	88
Q2	135	259	482	381	373	450	344	133
Q3	174	257	515	431	392	566	356	131
Q4	200	285	695	516	430	482	376	114
1990 Q1	..	945	..	..	1 422	..	..	..
Q2	..	962	..	..	1 310	..	..	..
Q3	..	961	..	..	1 326	..	..	..
Q4	..	1 090	..	..	1 386	..	..	..
1991 Q1	..	761	..	..	1 129	..	..	..
Q2	..	758	..	..	1 198	..	..	..
Q3	..	797	..	..	1 197	..	..	..
Q4	..	901	..	..	1 215	..	..	..
1992 Q1	..	705	..	..	956	..	..	..
Revalued at 1985 prices								
	BAAG	BAAJ	BAAM	BAAP	BAAS	BAAV	BAAY	BABB
1988	558	771	1 538	1 224	1 281	1 234	1 227	356
1989	601	891	1 804	1 458	1 457	1 662	1 203	398
1990	..	3 189	..	..	4 575	..	..	..
1991	..	2 546	..	..	3 971	..	..	..
Seasonally adjusted								
	BAAH	BAAK	BAAN	BAAQ	BAAT	BAAW	BAAZ	BABC
1988 Q4	128	189	364	336	339	321	309	95
1989 Q1	134	215	397	322	371	360	308	83
Q2	150	228	436	374	361	436	303	112
Q3	161	231	455	372	365	470	289	111
Q4	156	217	516	390	360	396	303	92
1990 Q1	..	854	..	..	1 266	..	..	..
Q2	..	820	..	..	1 166	..	..	..
Q3	..	774	..	..	1 068	..	..	..
Q4	..	741	..	..	1 075	..	..	..
1991 Q1	..	658	..	..	988	..	..	..
Q2	..	630	..	..	1 057	..	..	..
Q3	..	644	..	..	967	..	..	..
Q4	..	614	..	..	959	..	..	..
1992 Q1	..	623	..	..	845	..	..	..

1 Totals may not be the exact sums of component items due to rounding.

Source: Central Statistical Office

Analysis by industry according to the Standard Industrial Classification 1980 (including leased assets)

1.9 Fixed capital expenditure in manufacturing industry[1]

continued

£ million

	Analysis by industry SIC 1980 (including leased assets)			Analysis by type of asset			
	Textiles, leather and clothing	Paper, printing and publishing	Other manufacturing industries	New building work	Vehicles	Plant and machinery	Total
Division, Class or Group	43-45	47	46,48,49	2-4	2-4	2-4	

At current prices

	BABD	BABG	BABJ	BABM	BABP	BABS	BABY
1988	559	1 729	1 057	1 528	755	9 998	12 281
1989	503	1 728	1 183	1 964	926	11 370	14 260
1990	..	5 414	..	2 233	877	11 706	14 816
1991	..	4 573	..	1 935	551	10 043	12 529
1988 Q4	138	447	294	450	194	2 713	3 357
1989 Q1	139	356	255	381	235	2 506	3 122
Q2	153	452	273	471	237	2 727	3 435
Q3	110	326	315	514	227	2 829	3 570
Q4	101	594	340	598	227	3 308	4 133
1990 Q1	..	1 306	..	514	260	2 899	3 673
Q2	..	1 339	..	529	206	2 876	3 611
Q3	..	1 350	..	508	214	2 915	3 637
Q4	..	1 419	..	682	197	3 016	3 895
1991 Q1	..	1 164	..	432	195	2 427	3 054
Q2	..	1 038	..	495	92	2 407	2 994
Q3	..	1 196	..	545	138	2 507	3 190
Q4	..	1 175	..	463	126	2 702	3 291
1992 Q1	..	1 001	..	324	152	2 186	2 662

Revalued at 1985 prices

	BABE	BABH	BABK	BABN	BABQ	BABT	BABZ
1988	501	1 551	957	1 358	606	9 234	11 198
1989	428	1 476	1 008	1 587	692	10 107	12 386
1990	..	4 385	..	1 644	595	9 910	12 149
1991	..	3 721	..	1 513	361	8 364	10 238

Seasonally adjusted

	BABF	BABI	BABL	BABO	BABR	BABU	BACA
1988 Q4	125	338	256	355	156	2 285	2 796
1989 Q1	128	313	234	345	168	2 351	2 864
Q2	120	404	246	418	178	2 572	3 168
Q3	96	365	255	422	180	2 571	3 173
Q4	84	394	273	402	166	2 613	3 181
1990 Q1	..	1 120	..	429	163	2 648	3 240
Q2	..	1 120	..	423	147	2 536	3 106
Q3	..	1 062	..	362	140	2 402	2 904
Q4	..	1 083	..	430	145	2 324	2 899
1991 Q1	..	1 021	..	360	124	2 183	2 667
Q2	..	868	..	400	65	2 090	2 555
Q3	..	932	..	408	88	2 047	2 543
Q4	..	900	..	345	84	2 044	2 473
1992 Q1	..	864	..	293	88	1 951	2 332

1 Totals may not be the exact sums of component items due to rounding.

Source: Central Statistical Office

1.10 Fixed capital expenditure of the construction, distribution, road transport and financial sectors (plus shipping)

£ million

	Analysis by industry according to SIC 1980 (including leased assets)							Analysis by type of asset			
		Distribution, etc			Road and misc. transport	Banking, Insurance, Business services and leasing	Total	New building work	Vehicles	Plant and machinery	Shipping
	Construc-tion	Wholesale	Retail and repair	Hotels and catering							
Division or class	5	61-63	64,65,67	66	72, 76,77	8	5,6,8 plus 72, 76,77				74
At current prices											
	BACB	BACE	BACH	BACK	BACN	BALD	BACZ	BADC	BADF	BADI	BADL
1988	1 141	2 973	4 678	1 807	2 533	15 102	28 234	11 028.00	6 362	10 844	136
1989	1 129	2 801	4 667	2 031	2 782	19 470	32 880	14 103.00	6 838	11 939	199
1988 Q1	282	658	855	409	643	3 145	5 992	2 144	1 530	2 318	41
Q2	282	796	1 240	439	599	3 498	6 854	2 778	1 531	2 545	51
Q3	254	667	1 200	499	637	3 742	6 999	2 768	1 607	2 624	10
Q4	323	852	1 383	460	654	4 717	8 389	3 338	1 694	3 357	34
1989 Q1	279	535	1 056	489	721	4 763	7 843	3 213	1 703	2 927	17
Q2	304	680	1 231	471	782	4 416	7 884	3 317	1 607	2 960	71
Q3	318	714	1 127	547	607	5 065	8 378	3 615	1 841	2 922	8
Q4	228	872	1 253	524	672	5 226	8 775	3 958	1 687	3 130	103
Revalued at 1985 prices											
	BACC	BACF	BACI	BACL	BACO	BALE	BADA	BADD	BADG	BADJ	BADM
1988	999	2 665	4 149	1 575	2 181	13 786	25 355	9 456	10 791	5 108	120
1989	922	2 398	3 829	1 622	2 241	16 664	27 676	10 703	11 867	5 106	172
Seasonally adjusted											
	BACD	BACG	BACJ	BACM	BACP	BALF	BADB	BADE	BADH	BADK	BADN
1988 Q1	233	658	876	376	537	2 937	5 617	1 947	2 472	1 198	45
Q2	245	721	1 110	381	543	3 338	6 338	2 380	2 682	1 276	49
Q3	216	599	1 042	415	568	3 538	6 378	2 384	2 699	1 295	8
Q4	305	687	1 121	403	533	3 973	7 022	2 745	2 938	1 339	18
1989 Q1	217	520	1 014	420	570	4 198	6 939	2 700	3 026	1 213	29
Q2	250	591	995	374	627	4 078	6 915	2 551	3 104	1 260	73
Q3	253	627	910	406	518	4 358	7 072	2 693	3 005	1 374	5
Q4	202	660	910	422	526	4 030	6 750	2 759	2 732	1 259	65

Source: Central Statistical Office

2 Population and vital statistics

2.1 Mid-year estimates of resident population

Thousands

	England and Wales			Scotland			Northern Ireland			United Kingdom		
	Males	Females	Persons	Males	Females	Persons	Males	Females	Persons	Males	Females	Persons
	BBAE	BBAF	BBAD	BBAH	BBAI	BBAG	BBAK	BBAL	BBAJ	BBAB	BBAC	DYAY
1974	24 075	25 393	49 468	2 519	2 722	5 241	755	772	1 527	27 349	28 887	56 236
1975	24 091	25 378	49 470	2 516	2 716	5 232	753	770	1 524	27 361	28 865	56 226
1976	24 089	25 370	49 459	2 517	2 716	5 233	754	769	1 524	27 360	28 856	56 216
1977	24 076	25 364	49 440	2 515	2 711	5 226	754	769	1 523	27 345	28 845	56 190
1978	24 067	25 375	49 443	2 509	2 704	5 212	754	770	1 523	27 330	28 848	56 178
1979	24 113	25 395	49 508	2 505	2 699	5 204	755	773	1 528	27 373	28 867	56 240
1980	24 156	25 448	49 603	2 501	2 693	5 194	755	778	1 533	27 411	28 919	56 330
1981	24 160	25 474	49 634	2 495	2 685	5 180	754	783	1 538	27 409	28 943	56 352
1982	24 143	25 459	49 601	2 489	2 677	5 167	754	784	1 538	27 386	28 920	56 306
1983	24 176	25 478	49 654	2 485	2 665	5 150	756	787	1 543	27 417	28 931	56 347
1984	24 244	25 519	49 764	2 484	2 662	5 146	760	791	1 550	27 487	28 972	56 460
1985	24 330	25 594	49 924	2 480	2 656	5 137	763	795	1 558	27 574	29 044	56 618
1986	24 403	25 672	50 075	2 475	2 646	5 121	768	798	1 567	27 647	29 116	56 763
1987	24 493	25 750	50 243	2 471	2 641	5 112	773	802	1 575	27 737	29 193	56 930
1988	24 576	25 817	50 393	2 462	2 632	5 094	774	804	1 578	27 813	29 253	57 065
1989	24 669	25 893	50 562	2 460	2 630	5 091	777	806	1 583	27 907	29 330	57 236
1990	24 766	25 953	50 719	2 467	2 636	5 102	780	809	1 589	28 013	29 398	57 411

Figures may not add due to rounding.

Sources: Office of Population Censuses and Surveys;
General Register Office (Scotland);
General Register Office (Northern Ireland)

2.2 Age distribution of estimated resident population at 30 June 1989

Thousands

	Resident population											
	England and Wales		Wales		Scotland		Northern Ireland[1]		United Kingdom			
	Males	Females	Males	Females	Males	Females	Males	Females	Males	Females	Persons	
0-4	1 713.8	1 632.4	97.2	92.5	166.7	158.6	69.5	65.7	1 950.7	1 857.0	3 807.7	
5-9	1 629.4	1 548.4	93.8	89.0	164.7	157.1	68.2	65.2	1 862.0	1 770.7	3 632.7	
10-14	1 517.1	1 434.1	88.6	83.3	158.1	149.7	64.8	62.4	1 739.3	1 645.2	3 384.5	
15-19	1 830.1	1 739.0	105.1	100.6	190.1	183.5	70.0	63.5	2 091.2	1 987.8	4 079.0	
20-24	2 077.5	2 010.1	113.0	110.6	217.8	208.4	71.8	63.8	2 367.9	2 282.8	4 650.7	
25-29	2 058.9	2 023.2	113.1	114.2	210.8	201.8	64.8	60.6	2 333.5	2 285.1	4 618.7	
30-34	1 761.4	1 737.0	93.4	91.2	184.2	182.1	54.3	55.3	1 998.2	1 972.9	3 971.1	
35-39	1 682.8	1 681.4	92.2	92.6	167.8	168.1	47.5	48.7	1 898.1	1 897.4	3 795.6	
40-44	1 821.8	1 812.7	98.8	99.6	172.6	172.8	47.0	47.9	2 041.1	2 033.4	4 074.5	
45-49	1 466.6	1 454.9	83.0	82.8	144.0	149.1	43.1	44.6	1 652.6	1 647.2	3 299.9	
50-54	1 367.3	1 367.4	77.1	77.6	136.9	145.7	37.7	39.4	1 541.5	1 552.2	3 093.7	
55-59	1 293.7	1 323.7	74.1	77.3	131.2	144.3	34.0	37.2	1 458.8	1 505.4	2 964.2	
60-64	1 245.2	1 333.3	74.2	81.5	123.1	141.1	31.3	36.5	1 399.7	1 510.8	2 910.4	
65-69	1 215.0	1 422.9	73.3	86.2	113.2	142.0	28.0	35.1	1 356.6	1 600.6	2 957.1	
70-74	784.9	1 050.7	48.3	65.4	73.2	106.3	20.6	29.2	878.4	1 185.9	2 064.2	
75-79	648.3	1 022.9	37.1	60.2	59.1	99.6	15.5	25.4	723.1	1 147.8	1 870.9	
80-84	365.7	734.1	20.5	43.0	31.9	70.1	8.5	17.3	405.9	820.9	1 226.8	
85 and over	189.3	565.2	10.6	31.9	15.0	50.3	3.8	11.3	208.1	626.6	834.7	
0-14	4 860.4	4 614.8	279.6	264.7	489.5	465.3	202.5	193.3	5 552.0	5 272.9	10 824.9	
15-64	16 605.4	16 482.8	924.1	928.1	1 678.4	1 696.8	501.5	497.4	18 782.6	18 675.0	37 457.6	
65 and over	3 203.3	4 795.8	189.8	286.7	292.4	468.2	76.4	118.3	3 572.0	5 381.8	8 953.8	
All ages	24 669.1	25 893.4	1 393.5	1 479.6	2 460.4	2 630.3	780.4	809.0	27 906.5	29 329.7	57 236.2	

Figures may not add due to rounding.
1 For Northern Ireland: population at June 1990.

Sources: Office of Population Censuses and Surveys;
General Register Office (Scotland);
General Register Office (Northern Ireland)

2.3 Births and marriages

Thousands

	Live births[1]					Marriages				
	England and Wales		Scotland	Northern Ireland	United Kingdom	England and Wales		Scotland	Northern Ireland	United Kingdom
	Total	Wales				Total	Wales			
	BBCB	BBCC	BBCD	BBCE	BBCA	BBCG	BBCH	BBCI	BBCJ	BBCF
1985	656.4	36.8	66.7	27.6	750.7	346.4	19.1	36.4	10.3	393.1
1986	661.0	37.0	65.8	28.2	755.0	347.9	19.5	35.8	10.2	393.9
1987	681.5	37.8	66.2	27.9	775.6	351.8	19.5	35.8	10.4	397.9
1988	693.6	38.8	66.2	27.8	787.6	348.5	19.3	35.6	10.0	394.1
1989	687.7	38.0	63.5	26.1	777.3	346.7	19.5	35.3	10.0	392.0
1990	706.1	38.9	66.0	26.5	798.6	..	..	34.7	9.6	..
1991[2]	699.2	38.1	67.0	26.3	792.5	..	..	33.8	..	..
1988 Q4	164.6	9.1	15.9	6.3	186.8	67.6	3.9	7.3	1.6	-
1989 Q1	167.0	9.3	15.9	6.5	189.4	48.3	2.9	5.0	1.5	54.7
Q2	176.7	9.7	15.9	6.9	199.5	98.1	5.5	9.9	2.7	110.5
Q3	175.8	9.5	16.0	6.8	198.6	138.6	7.7	13.0	4.3	155.9
Q4	168.2	9.5	15.6	5.9	189.8	61.7	3.4	7.4	1.6	70.7
1990 Q1	168.3	9.2	16.1	6.8	191.3	47.1	2.7	4.7	1.1	52.9
Q2	179.3	9.8	16.3	6.8	202.4	88.4	5.6	10.1	2.9	..
Q3	184.0	10.1	16.9	6.6	207.5	127.1	7.0	12.7	4.0	..
Q4	174.5	9.7	16.6	6.3	197.3	55.4	3.1	7.1	1.6	..
1991 Q1[2]	171.5	9.4	16.4	6.7	194.5	41.4	2.3	4.2	1.1	..
Q2[2]	175.8	9.6	16.6	6.8	199.2	89.4	4.7	9.4	2.7	..
Q3[2]	181.8	9.9	17.3	6.8	205.9	121.5	6.8	13.1	14.0	..
Q4[2]	170.2	9.2	16.7	6.0	192.9	..	..	7.0	..	..
1992 Q1[2]	173.0	9.4	16.5	6.2	195.7	..	..	..	..	..
Q2[2]	..	..	..	6.7	..	..	..	..	..	..

1 Figures for England and Wales relate to date of birth. Figures for Scotland and Northern Ireland relate to date of registration of birth.
2 Provisional.

Sources: Office of Population Censuses and Surveys;
General Register Office (Scotland);
General Register Office (Northern Ireland)

2.4 Deaths registered[1]

Thousands

	Total					Infants under one year				
	England and Wales		Scotland	Northern Ireland	United Kingdom	England and Wales		Scotland	Northern Ireland	United Kingdom
	Total	Wales				Total	Wales			
	BBDB	BBDC	BBDD	BBDE	BBDA	BBDG	BBDH	BBDI	BBDJ	BBDF
1985	590.7	35.5	64.0	16.0	670.6	6.14	0.36	0.62	0.27	7.03
1986	581.2	34.7	63.5	16.1	660.7	6.31	0.35	0.58	0.29	7.18
1987	567.0	33.9	62.0	15.3	644.3	6.27	0.36	0.56	0.24	7.08
1988	571.4	34.0	62.0	15.8	649.2	6.27	0.29	0.54	0.25	7.06
1989	576.9	35.1	65.0	15.8	657.7	5.81	0.30	0.55	0.18	6.54
1990	564.8	34.0	61.5	15.4	641.8	5.56	0.27	0.51	0.20	6.27
1991[2]	570.0	34.1	61.1	15.1	646.2	5.16	0.25	0.47	0.19	5.82
1988 Q4	146.3	8.7	15.9	3.8	166.0	1.61	0.06	0.13	0.06	1.80
1989 Q1	149.5	8.8	16.4	4.0	169.9	1.61	0.07	0.14	0.05	1.80
Q2	136.8	8.6	15.2	3.8	155.8	1.36	0.08	0.14	0.05	1.54
Q3	125.6	7.6	14.1	3.4	143.1	1.26	0.07	0.12	0.04	1.42
Q4	165.0	10.1	19.3	4.6	188.9	1.58	0.08	0.15	0.05	1.78
1990 Q1	156.3	9.4	16.9	4.5	177.8	1.57	0.08	0.15	0.06	1.77
Q2	135.7	8.1	15.1	3.5	154.3	1.35	0.07	0.14	0.05	1.54
Q3	126.3	7.6	13.7	3.5	143.5	1.27	0.06	0.10	0.05	1.43
Q4	146.6	8.9	15.8	3.9	166.3	1.38	0.05	0.12	0.04	1.54
1991 Q1[2]	158.8	9.7	16.3	4.4	179.5	1.39	0.08	0.14	0.05	1.58†
Q2[2]	137.2	8.3	14.9	3.7	155.8	1.33	0.06	0.11	0.05	1.49
Q3[2]	126.6	7.6	13.8	3.2†	143.6	1.19	0.06	0.11	0.05	1.35
Q4[2]	147.5	8.6	16.1	3.7	167.3	1.26	0.06	0.11	0.04	1.41
1992 Q1[2]	156.8	9.4	16.5	4.2	177.6	1.19	0.06†	0.13	0.04†	1.36
Q2[2]	..	..	..	3.5	..	..	..	..	0.04	..

1 Excluding stillbirths.
2 Provisional.

Sources: Office of Population Censuses and Surveys;
General Register Office (Scotland);
General Register Office (Northern Ireland)

3 Employment

3.1 Distribution of the workforce

Thousands

	Not seasonally adjusted							Seasonally adjusted	
			Employees in employment			Self-employed persons (with or without employees)[2]			Employees in employment
	Workforce[1]	Workforce in employment[1]	Males	Females	Total		HM Forces[3]	Workforce[1]	
	DYDB	DYDA	BCAE	BCAF	BCAD	BCAG	BCAH	DYDD	BCAJ
At June									
1987	27 988	25 083	11 698	9 886	21 584	2 869	319	28 077	21 586
1988	28 255	25 914	11 971	10 287	22 258	2 998	316	28 347	22 266
1989	28 427	26 684	11 992	10 668	22 661	3 253	308	28 480	22 670
1990	28 478	26 923	12 071	10 827	22 898	3 298	303	28 530	22 894
1991	28 293	26 052	11 609	10 659	22 268	3 143	297	28 340	22 259
1989 Q2	28 427	26 684	11 992	10 668	22 661	3 253	308	28 480	22 670
Q3	28 505	26 802	12 074	10 689	22 762	3 263	308	28 470	22 735
Q4	28 587	26 948	12 100	10 818	22 918	3 274	306	28 504	22 832
1990 Q1	28 426	26 781	12 037	10 719	22 755	3 284	306	28 483	22 859
Q2	28 478	26 923	12 071	10 827	22 898	3 298	303	28 530	22 894
Q3	28 497	26 823	12 077	10 771	22 848	3 259	303	28 487	22 829
Q4	28 533	26 683	11 932	10 812	22 745	3 220	300	28 450	22 656
1991 Q1	28 375	26 233	11 704	10 644	22 348	3 180	298	28 431	22 454
Q2	28 293	26 052	11 609	10 659	22 268	3 143	297	28 340	22 259
Q3	28 310	25 859	11 535	10 584	22 119	3 104	297	28 310	22 107
Q4	28 263	25 711	11 433	10 568	22 002	3 065	295	28 187	21 919
1992 Q1	28 173	25 466	11 289	10 500	21 790	3 026	293	28 218	21 889

1 The workforce consists of the workforce in employment and the unemployed (claimants); the workforce in employment comprises employees in employment, the self-employed, HM Forces and participants in work-related government training programmes. For more details see the August 1988 edition of *Employment Gazette*.
2 Estimates of the self-employed up to mid-1991 are based on the 1981 census of population and the results of Labour Force Surveys carried out between 1981 and 1991. Figures for periods from September 1991 are projections which assume the rate of decline between June 1990 and June 1991 has continued. The estimates are not seasonally adjusted.
3 HM Forces figures, provided by the Ministry of Defence, represent the total number of UK service personnel, male and female, in HM Regular Forces, wherever serving and including those on release leave. The numbers are not subject to seasonal adjustment.

Sources: Department of Employment;
Department of Economic Development (Northern Ireland)

3.2 Employees in employment: all industries[1]
Great Britain   Industries analysed according to Standard Industrial Classification 1980

Thousands

			1990 Q1	1990 Q2	1990 Q3	1990 Q4	1991 Q1	1991 Q2	1991 Q3	1991 Q4	1992 Q1	1992 Q2
		SIC 1980										
Agriculture, forestry and fishing	DYGE	01-03	272	278	297	268	264	272	294	267	265	..
Production industries												
Coal, oil and natural gas	DYGF	11-14	158	156	154	152	149	148	145	139	132	128
Electricity, gas and water supply	DYGG	15-17	286	285	286	287	286	283	282	277	276	267
Manufacturing industries	DYAW	2-4	5 051	5 039	5 064	4 971	4 811	4 720	4 712	4 643	4 522	4 496
Total production industries	DYCO	1-4	5 495	5 480	5 504	5 410	5 246	5 151	5 139	5 058	4 930	4 891
Construction	DYGS	50	1 050	1 044	1 036	1 011	968	939	910	872	843	..
Service industries												
Wholesale distribution and repairs	DYGT	61-63,67	1 224	1 235	1 236	1 234	1 227	1 217	1 221	1 228	1 200	..
Retail distribution	DYGU	64/65	2 244	2 237	2 235	2 276	2 167	2 143	2 139	2 189	2 119	..
Hotels and catering	DYGV	66	1 187	1 256	1 271	1 233	1 187	1 230	1 219	1 144	1 135	..
Transport	DYGW	71-77	932	930	941	936	920	913	911	915	925	..
Post and telecommunications	DYGX	79	428	431	429	421	415	415	413	404	397	..
Banking, finance and insurance	DYGY	81-85	2 689	2 710	2 716	2 685	2 681	2 658	2 649	2 620	2 615	..
Public administration	DYGZ	91-92	1 909	1 927	1 927	1 920	1 927	1 923	1 921	1 920	1 923	..
Education	DYHA	93	1 801	..	..	..	..	..	..	..	..	..
Medical and other health services, veterinary services	DYHB	95	1 472	..	..	..	..	..	..	..	..	..
Other services	DYHC	94,96-98	1 712	..	..	..	..	..	..	..	..	..
Total service industries	DYCR	6-9	15 409	15 567	15 479	15 521	15 341	15 381	15 253	15 280	15 232	..
Total employees in employment[1]	DYCM	0-9	22 227	22 369	22 317	22 209	21 820	21 743	21 595	21 477	21 271	..
of which:												
Males	DYCA		11 763	11 797	11 802	11 658	11 433	11 340	11 266	11 166	11 025	..
Females	DYCB		10 464	10 572	10 515	10 552	10 387	10 403	10 329	10 311	10 246	..

Note: Quarterly data on above 2 tables relate to March, June, September and December.
1 Excluding private domestic service.

Source: Department of Employment

3.3 Employees in employment: production and construction industries[1]
Great Britain   Industries analysed according to the Standard Industrial Classification 1980

Thousands

	Coal, oil and natural gas extraction and processing	Electricity, gas, other energy and water supply	Manufacturing industries	Metal manufacturing, ore and other mineral extraction	Chemical and man-made fibres	Mechanical engineering	Office machinery, electrical engineering and instruments	Motor vehicles and parts	Other transport equipment
SIC 1980 Divisions or Classes	11-14	15-17	2-4	21-24	25-26	32	33-34,37	35	36
At June									
	DYGF	DYGG	DYAW	DYGH	DYGI	DYGJ	DYGK	DYGL	DYGM
1988	182	296	5 089	356	324	757	737	268	232
1989	167	290	5 080	372	329	763	733	262	228
1990	156	285	5 039	388	324	740	729	244	247
1991	148	283	4 720	347	303	678	691	220	230
1992	128	267	4 496	325	300	647	648	223	202
1991 Jan	153	286	4 910	362	311	718	717	236	242
Feb	152	286	4 864	358	308	706	713	232	240
Mar	149	286	4 811	356	306	698	704	229	238
Apr	150	282	4 783	350	303	696	699	227	236
May	149	284	4 745	347	302	684	696	223	232
Jun	148	283	4 720	347	303	678	691	220	230
Jul	149	283	4 710	345	299	676	687	224	226
Aug	149	282	4 715	342	309	673	688	226	224
Sep	145	282	4 712	345	306	674	686	226	225
Oct	145	280	4 681	338	306	668	683	229	220
Nov	142	278	4 665	335	307	669	683	230	220
Dec	139	277	4 643	336	307	673	676	223	224
1992 Jan	138	278	4 574	328	304	663	668	223	213
Feb	135	275	4 552	326	306	663	663	219	213
Mar	132	276	4 522	326	303	660	656	216	211
Apr	130	275	4 500†	323	300	657	655	217†	209
May	130	271	4 487	318	299	652	657	218	207
Jun	128	267	4 496	325	300	647	648	223	202

	Metal goods nes	Food, drink and tobacco	Textiles, leather, footwear and clothing	Timber, wooden furniture, rubber, plastics etc	Paper products, printing and publishing	Construction	Production and construction industries		
								of which	
							Total	Males	Females
SIC 1980 Divisions or Classes	31	41/42	43-45	46,48-49	47	50			
At June									
	DYGN	DYGO	DYGP	DYGQ	DYGR	DYGS	DYCS	DYCC	DYCH
1988	333	541	546	517	478	1 021	6 587	4 869	1 718
1989	333	530	514	531	487	1 056	6 594	4 862	1 731
1990	320	527	487	546	486	1 044	6 524	4 828	1 722
1991	298	544	439	497	474	939	6 090	..	..
1992	285	496	429	473	468	..	..	..	..
1991 Jan	315	543	462	517	486	..	5 349	..	..
Feb	310	542	459	512	484	..	5 302	..	..
Mar	306	541	451	504	480	..	6 215	..	..
Apr	303	543	446	504	477	..	5 215	..	..
May	299	546	442	500	474	..	5 178	..	..
Jun	298	544	439	497	474	..	6 090	..	..
Jul	297	543	442	498	472	..	5 142	..	..
Aug	296	542	442	501	472	..	5 145	..	..
Sep	297	541	440	498	473	..	6 049	..	..
Oct	294	532	441	499	469	..	5 106	..	..
Nov	292	522	440	496	472	..	5 085	..	..
Dec	293	511	443	486	471	..	5 936	..	..
1992 Jan	290	503	439	474	471	..	5 017	..	..
Feb	288	497	441	470	464	..	4 973	..	..
Mar	283	496	436	471	465	..	..	..	..
Apr	282	495	436	469	457	..	..	..	..
May	281	498	432	467	458	..	..	..	..
Jun	285	496	429	473	468	..	..	..	..

1 Includes Divisions 1-5 of the *Standard Industrial Classification 1980*.

Source: Department of Employment

3.4 Civil Service staff: analysis by ministerial responsibilities[1]

Full-time equivalents (thousands)

		1986	1987	1988	1989	1990	1991	1991 Oct	1992 Apr
Agriculture, Fisheries and Food	BCDA	11.7	11.3	11.1	10.9	10.7	11.0	11.0	10.8
Chancellor of the Exchequer's Departments:									
Customs and Excise	BCDC	25.1	25.8	26.3	26.4	26.9	27.0	26.8	26.4
Inland Revenue	BCDD	69.3	67.8	66.6	67.0	66.0	65.7	67.3	68.9
Department for National Savings	BCDE	7.8	7.7	7.4	7.3	7.0	6.7	6.4	6.3
Treasury and others[2]	BCDF	8.8	8.8	8.3	8.3	9.3	10.1	10.0	10.0
Total	BCDB	111.0	110.1	108.6	109.0	109.2	109.6	110.6	111.6
Education and Science	BCDG	2.4	2.4	2.5	2.5	2.6	2.7	2.7	2.7
Employment[2]	BCDH	55.7	60.5	58.3	55.0	52.4	49.0	52.9	57.1
Energy[3]	BCDI	1.0	1.0	1.0	1.1	1.2	1.2	1.1	1.1
Environment[4]	BCDJ	34.9	34.2	32.9	30.6	29.2	25.8	25.3	23.2
Foreign and Commonwealth	BCDK	9.6	9.5	9.6	9.5	9.5	9.9	9.9	10.0
Health and Social services[8]	BCDO	94.9	97.7	102.3	-	-	-	-	-
Health[5,8,9]	BAKR	-	-	-	10.9	7.5	6.7	6.8	6.9
Home	BCDL	37.5	37.6	39.2	40.8	42.7	44.1	47.8	49.7
Scotland	BCDN	12.9	13.0	11.9	12.3	12.6	12.9	13.1	13.1
Social Security[8]	BAKS	-	-	-	83.4	80.9	79.0	77.8	78.3
Trade and Industry[2]	BCDQ	14.8	14.8	14.6	14.7	13.6	13.4	13.2	12.7
Transport	BCDR	14.7	14.3	14.2	14.2	15.5	15.3	15.2	15.0
Welsh Office	BCDS	2.3	2.3	2.2	2.2	2.3	2.3	2.4	2.4
Other civil departments[6]	BCDT	21.5	25.1	27.8	30.7	31.0	30.9	31.4	31.3
Total civil departments	BCDU	424.9	433.8	436.2	427.9	421.0	413.7	421.2	425.9
Defence	BCDW	169.5	164.0	143.4	141.3	141.4	140.2	140.7	139.5
Total all departments[7]	BCDX	594.4	597.8	579.6	569.2	562.4	553.9	561.9	565.3
of which									
Non-industrials	BCDY	498.2	507.5	506.5	499.8	495.2	490.0	498.7	504.2
Industrials	BCDZ	96.2	90.3	73.1	69.4	67.2	63.9	63.2	61.1

Machinery of Government changes prior to 1 April 1985 are given in the *Annual Supplement of Definitions and Explanatory Notes* published in the January edition of *Monthly Digest*. Figures may not add due to rounding.

1 All annual figures are at 1 April.

2 On 31 July 1989 a new department, the Central Statistical Office was formed, incorporating staff from the Department of Trade and Industry, Cabinet Office and the Department of Employment.

3 Includes the Office of Gas Supply (formed 18 August 1986) and the Office of Electricity Regulation (formed 1 September 1989).

4 Includes Office of Water Supply (formed 1 September 1989).

5 On 1 April 1990 approximately 3000 staff at the Department of Health were transferred to the NHS and therefore are no longer in the manpower count.

6 On 1 October 1986 a new department, the Crown Prosecution Service, was formed. On 20 July 1987 a new department, the Serious Fraud Office, was formed.

7 There were 309 892 males and 243 971 females in the Civil Service on 1 April 1991.

8 With effect from the 25 July 1988, the Department of Health and Social Security was split into the Department of Health and the Department of Social Security.

9 Includes Office of Population Censuses and Surveys.

Source: HM Treasury

3.5 UK Service personnel intake, outflow and strengths

Thousands

	Royal Naval Services[4]			Army			Royal Air Force			All Services		
	Males	Females	Total	Males	Females	Total	Males	Females	Total	Males	Females	Total
Intake[1]												
Financial year												
1987/88	5.6	0.6	6.2	19.9	1.2	21.0	5.7	0.9	6.6	31.2	2.6	33.8
1988/89	5.5	0.7	6.2	19.9	1.5	21.3	5.4	0.9	6.3	30.9	3.0	33.9
1989/90	5.8	0.9	6.7	20.4	1.7	22.1	6.2	1.5	7.7	32.3	4.1	36.4
1990/91	5.7	1.2	6.9	16.0	1.5	17.5	5.1	1.7	6.8	26.8	4.4	31.2
1991/92	5.6	1.0	6.6	15.5	1.6	17.1	3.2	0.9	4.2	24.4	3.5	27.9
Quarter												
1990/91												
Apr-Jun	1.1	0.2	1.3	4.0	0.5	4.5	1.3	0.4	1.8	6.3	1.1	7.5
Jul-Sept	1.7	0.2	1.9	6.5	0.3	6.8	1.3	0.4	1.7	9.5	1.1	10.5
Oct-Dec	1.3	0.3	1.6	2.8	0.4	3.1	1.3	0.4	1.7	5.4	1.0	6.4
Jan-Mar	1.7	0.5	2.2	2.8	0.3	3.1	1.2	0.4	1.6	5.6	1.3	6.9
1991/92												
Apr-Jun	1.2	0.3	1.5	3.1	0.4	3.6	1.1	0.3	1.4	5.5	1.0	6.5
Jul-Sept	1.8	0.3	2.1	5.6	0.4	5.9	0.9	0.3	1.2	8.2	1.0	9.2
Oct-Dec	1.1	0.2	1.3	2.8	0.4	3.3	0.6	0.2	0.8	4.6	0.8	5.4
Jan-Mar	1.4	0.3	1.7	4.0	0.3	4.3	0.7	0.2	0.8	6.1	0.8	6.9
1992/93												
Apr-Jun	0.5	0.1	0.6	2.9	0.3	3.2	0.2	0.1	0.3	3.6	0.5	4.1
Outflow[2]												
Financial year												
1987/88	6.6	0.6	7.2	21.4	1.4	22.7	6.1	0.9	7.0	34.1	2.9	36.9
1988/89	6.5	0.6	7.1	22.8	1.2	24.1	7.2	0.9	8.2	36.6	2.7	39.3
1989/90	7.4	0.7	8.0	23.8	1.3	25.1	8.3	1.1	9.5	39.5	3.1	42.6
1990/91	7.4	0.7	8.1	21.7	1.2	22.8	7.0	1.1	8.1	36.1	3.0	39.1
1991/92	6.1	0.7	6.8	18.3	1.1	19.5	5.6	0.9	6.6	30.1	2.7	32.8
Quarter												
1990/91												
Apr-Jun	1.8	0.2	2.0	5.7	0.3	6.0	1.9	0.3	2.1	9.4	0.8	10.2
Jul-Sept	1.9	0.2	2.1	6.0	0.3	6.3	1.9	0.3	2.2	9.8	0.8	10.6
Oct-Dec	2.0	0.2	2.2	5.2	0.3	5.5	1.6	0.3	1.9	8.8	0.7	9.5
Jan-Mar	1.7	0.2	1.9	4.7	0.3	4.9	1.6	0.3	1.9	8.0	0.7	8.7
1991/92												
Apr-Jun	1.5	0.2	1.7	3.8	0.3	4.1	1.6	0.3	1.9	7.0	0.7	7.7
Jul-Sept	1.7	0.2	1.9	4.7	0.3	5.1	1.6	0.3	1.8	8.0	0.8	8.7
Oct-Dec	1.5	0.2	1.6	4.9	0.3	5.2	1.2	0.2	1.5	7.7	0.6	8.3
Jan-Mar	1.4	0.2	1.6	4.8	0.3	5.1	1.2	0.2	1.4	7.4	0.6	8.1
1992/93												
Apr-Jun	1.2	0.1	1.3	4.6	0.3	4.9	1.5	0.2	1.7	7.2	0.6	7.9
Strength[3]												
1 April												
1987	63.2	3.4	66.5	153.1	6.6	159.7	87.3	6.3	93.6	303.7	16.2	319.8
1988	62.2	3.3	65.4	151.7	6.4	158.1	87.0	6.3	93.3	300.9	15.9	316.9
1989	61.2	3.5	64.7	148.9	6.7	155.6	85.1	6.3	91.4	295.4	16.3	311.6
1990	59.6	3.7	63.2	145.8	7.0	152.8	83.0	6.7	89.7	288.5	17.2	305.7
1991	57.9	4.2	62.1	140.3	7.3	147.6	81.2	7.2	88.4	279.5	18.6	298.1
1992	57.5	4.6	62.1	137.6	7.8	145.4	78.7	7.3	86.0	273.8	19.6	293.4
1990												
1 Apr	59.6	3.7	63.2	145.8	7.0	152.8	83.0	6.7	89.7	288.5	17.2	305.7
1 Jul	58.9	3.7	62.6	144.1	7.2	151.2	82.5	6.8	89.3	285.5	17.6	303.1
1 Oct	58.6	3.7	62.3	144.6	7.2	151.8	82.0	6.9	88.9	285.3	17.7	303.0
1991												
1 Jan	57.9	3.9	61.8	142.4	7.2	149.6	81.6	7.1	88.7	282.1	18.1	300.1
1 Apr	57.9	4.2	62.1	140.3	7.3	147.6	81.2	7.2	88.4	279.5	18.6	298.1
1 Jul	57.8	4.3	62.1	139.8	7.5	147.3	80.6	7.2	87.8	278.3	18.9	297.2
1 Oct	57.9	4.5	62.3	140.4	7.6	148.0	80.0	7.2	87.2	278.4	19.1	297.5
1992												
1 Jan	57.6	4.5	62.0	138.3	7.8	146.0	79.3	7.2	86.5	275.3	19.3	294.6
1 Apr	57.5	4.6	62.1	137.6	7.8	145.4	78.7	7.3	86.0	273.8	19.6	293.4
1 Jul	56.9	4.6	61.5	135.8	7.8	143.6	77.4	7.2	84.5	270.1	19.6	289.6

1 Regard must be taken of the effect of seasonal patterns and differences in planned annual intake levels in any comparisons of quarterly or annual intakes.

2 Some personnel have a liability for Reserve Service. The figures include deaths.

3 The differences between strengths at successive dates may not match the intake and outflow figures for corresponding periods because of delays in recording transfers between the Services and similar occurrences.

4 It has been decided that Royal Marine figures will no longer be shown separately but will be included under the new heading of Royal Naval Services. Also from 1 April 1992, female specialist officers in the Army who have previously been included in male officer numbers will now be included under female totals.

Source: Ministry of Defence

3.6 Local authority staffing[1]

Thousands (Full-time equivalents)[2]

		1990 Q3	1990 Q4	1991 Q1	1991 Q2	1991 Q3	1991 Q4	1992 Q1
England								
Service								
Education: lecturers and teachers	BCHA	469.2	476.1	478.2	476.2	463.7	471.8	474.9
Others	BCHB	354.6	365.4	365.5	363.4	357.1	364.7	366.3
Construction	BCHC	92.7	91.1	87.9	85.7	83.4	81.8	80.2
Transport	BCHD	2.3	1.9	2.1	1.9	1.3	1.5	1.4
Social services	BCHE	237.2	237.7	237.4	235.7	234.9	234.2	233.4
Public libraries and museums	BCHF	33.7	33.1	33.2	33.3	32.8	32.5	32.4
Recreation, parks and baths	BCHG	78.1	74.1	72.9	75.7	76.1	71.7	69.6
Environmental health	BCHH	19.0	18.7	18.6	18.8	19.0	19.2	19.3
Refuse collection and disposal	BCHS	28.7	27.7	27.0	27.1	25.2	24.6	23.9
Housing	BCHT	65.2	65.3	65.0	65.5	65.3	65.3	65.0
Town and country planning	BCHU	23.2	23.1	23.2	23.1	23.2	23.2	23.2
Fire service: Regulars	BAIV	34.4	34.6	34.6	34.5	34.5	34.4	34.4
Others	BAIW	5.8	5.4	5.7	5.7	5.7	5.7	5.8
Other services[3]	BCHM	246.1	246.5	244.4	244.2	245.0	242.4	239.5
Total of above	BCHN	1 690.2	1 700.7	1 695.8	1 690.8	1 667.2	1 673.2	1 669.4
Police service: police (all ranks)	BCHO	120.5	120.6	120.7	120.9	120.8	120.6	120.9
Cadets	BAIX	0.3	0.4	0.4	0.3	0.3	0.4	0.3
Traffic wardens	BAIY	4.5	4.6	4.7	4.7	4.8	4.9	4.9
Civilians	BAIZ	42.7	43.4	43.8	44.0	44.1	44.4	44.7
Magistrates courts	BAJA	9.8	9.9	10.0	9.9	9.9	10.0	10.0
Probation staff: Officers	BAJB	6.6	6.5	6.6	6.6	6.8	6.8	6.8
Others	BAJC	7.0	7.3	7.2	7.2	7.3	7.4	7.5
Total Law and Order	BAJD	191.4	192.7	193.2	193.6	194.0	194.4	195.1
Agency staff	BAJE	1.5	1.5	1.4	1.5	1.1	1.1	1.1
Total(excluding special employment and training measures)	BCHR	1 883.1	1 894.9	1 890.4	1 885.9	1 862.3	1 868.7	1 865.7

		1990 Q2	1990 Q3	1990 Q4	1991 Q1	1991 Q2	1991 Q3	1991 Q4
Wales								
Service								
Education: lecturers and teachers	BCGA	32.0	31.5	31.9	32.3	32.3	31.9	32.1
Others	BCGB	22.3	23.0	23.6	23.4	23.3	23.0	23.5
Construction	BCGC	7.4	7.5	7.4	7.2	7.0	6.9	6.8
Transport	BCGD	-	-	0.1	-	-	-	-
Social services	BCGE	15.3	15.3	15.1	15.3	15.3	15.7	15.7
Public libraries and museums	BCGF	1.6	1.6	1.6	1.7	1.7	1.7	1.7
Recreation, parks and baths	BCGG	5.8	5.7	5.4	5.3	5.9	5.9	5.4
Environmental health	BCGH	1.4	1.4	1.3	1.3	1.4	1.4	1.4
Refuse collection and disposal	BCGI	1.6	1.6	1.6	1.7	1.7	1.6	1.6
Housing	BCGJ	2.8	2.9	2.9	2.9	2.9	2.9	3.0
Town and country planning	BCGK	1.5	1.6	1.6	1.6	1.6	1.7	1.7
Fire service: Regulars	BAKT	1.8	1.8	1.8	1.8	1.8	1.8	1.8
Others	BAKU	0.3	0.4	0.4	0.4	0.4	0.4	0.4
Other services[3]	BCGM	19.0	19.1	18.9	18.8	18.9	18.9	18.8
Total of above	BCGN	112.9	113.4	113.6	113.8	114.2	113.9	114.0
Police service: police (all ranks)	BCGO	6.5	6.5	6.5	6.5	6.6	6.6	6.6
Cadets	BAKV	-	-	-	-	-	-	-
Traffic wardens	BAKW	0.2	0.2	0.2	0.2	0.2	0.2	0.2
Civilians	BAKX	2.0	2.0	2.0	2.1	2.1	2.1	2.0
Magistrates courts	BAKY	0.6	0.6	0.6	0.6	0.6	0.6	0.6
Probation staff: officers	BAKZ	0.4	0.4	0.4	0.4	0.4	0.4	0.4
Others	BALA	0.3	0.3	0.3	0.3	0.3	0.4	0.4
Total Law and Order	BALB	10.1	10.1	10.1	10.2	10.2	10.2	10.2
Agency staff	BALC	-	-	-	-	-	-	-
Total (excluding special employment and training measures)	BCGR	122.9	123.5	123.8	123.9	124.4	124.2	124.3

1 Figures are based on surveys undertaken on behalf of central and local government by the Local Government Management Board (LGMB) and the National Joint Council for Local Authority Services (Scottish Councils).
2 Based on the following factors to convert part-time employees to approximate full-time equivalents: for teachers and lecturers in further education, 0.11; teachers in primary and secondary education and all other non-manual employees, 0.53; manual employees, 0.41.
3 Including central services departments (eg engineers and treasurers) and all services not shown separately.

Sources: Department of the Environment;
Joint Staffing Watch;
Welsh Office

3.6 Local authority staffing[1]

continued

Thousands (Full-time equivalents)[2]

		1990 Q2	1990 Q3	1990 Q4	1991 Q1	1991 Q2	1991 Q3	1991 Q4
Scotland								
Service								
Education: lecturers and teachers[3]	BCMA	59.7	58.3	60.1	60.1	59.4	58.7	59.7
Others[4,5]	BCMB	29.5	28.3	28.7	27.9	27.7	27.6	27.7
Construction	BCMC	14.0	13.5	13.5	13.3	13.5	13.1	12.8
Transport	BCMD	0.7	0.8	0.7	0.7	0.8	0.8	0.8
Social services	BCME	36.2	36.0	35.9	36.3	36.2	36.5	36.7
Public libraries and museums	BCMF	4.4	4.5	4.4	4.4	4.4	4.6	4.4
Recreation, leisure and tourism	BCMG	13.8	13.8	12.5	12.3	13.6	13.1	11.9
Environmental health	BCMH	2.3	2.5	2.5	2.4	2.5	2.5	2.5
Cleansing	BCMI	8.4	8.3	8.0	7.8	8.2	8.2	7.9
Housing	BCMJ	7.3	7.5	7.2	7.3	7.3	7.3	7.2
Physical planning	BCMK	2.0	2.0	2.0	2.0	2.0	2.0	2.1
Fire service	BCML	5.1	5.1	5.1	5.2	4.7	5.2	4.6
Other services[5,6]	BCMM	53.7	55.3	55.2	56.7	56.8	57.9	57.5
Total of above	BCMN	237.3	235.7	236.0	236.4	237.5	237.4	236.1
Police service: police (all ranks)	BCMO	13.7	13.8	13.8	13.9	13.9	13.8	13.9
Others[7]	BCMP	4.7	4.7	4.6	4.6	4.6	4.6	4.7
Administration of district courts	BCMQ	0.2	0.2	0.1	0.2	0.2	0.2	0.2
Total (excluding special employment measures) and training	BCMR	255.8	254.2	254.6	255.0	256.2	256.1	254.8

For footnote 1 see previous page.

2 Based on the following factors to convert part-time employees to approximate full-time equivalents: for lecturers and teachers, 0.40; non-manual staff (excluding teachers), 0.58; manual employees, 0.46.

3 Includes only those part-time staff employed in vocational further education (ie courses of an academic nature or those leading to a qualification).

4 Includes school-crossing patrols.

5 Figures for recent quarters show a drop in numbers employed in Education (other than teachers and lecturers) and a rise in numbers employed in Other Services. This is almost certainly due to the introduction of competitive tendering to school cleaning services.

6 A contributing factor to the rise in Other Services is the community charge. Including central services departments (eg engineers and finance) and all services not shown separately.

7 Includes civilian employees of police forces and traffic wardens.

Sources: Department of the Environment;
Joint Staffing Watch;
Welsh Office;
Scottish Development Department;
Scottish Joint Staffing Watch.

3.7 Number of workers employed in agriculture[1,2]

Thousands

	Regular workers					Seasonal or casual workers			All workers		
	Whole-time		Part-time								
	Male	Female	Male	Female	Total	Male	Female	Total	Male	Female	Total
	BAMY	BAMZ	BANA	BANB	BANC	BAND	BANE	BANF	BANG	BANH	BANI
1985 Jun	141.6	15.1	31.5	29.8	218.0	58.1	39.1	97.2	231.1	84.1	315.2
1985 Dec	139.6	16.9	30.7	30.2	217.4	59.8	36.5	96.4	230.1	83.7	313.7
1986 Jun	134.1	14.8	32.2	29.1	210.3	57.2	38.1	95.3	223.5	82.1	305.5
1986 Dec	132.7	16.3	29.7	29.6	208.3	58.5	36.9	95.4	220.9	82.7	303.6
1987 Jun	127.4	14.5	31.4	28.8	202.1	55.9	37.7	93.5	214.7	81.0	295.7
1987 Dec	125.5	17.1	31.6	29.3	203.6	59.6	36.1	95.8	216.8	82.5	299.3
1988 Jun	120.7	14.5	31.3	29.0	195.5	56.2	36.7	92.8	208.2	80.2	288.4
1988 Dec	122.2	16.3	31.1	28.9	198.5	56.2	32.0	88.3	209.5	77.2	286.7
1989 Jun	114.6	15.1	30.6	27.7	188.1	54.0	34.3	88.3	199.2	77.1	276.3
1989 Dec	114.4	16.9	29.3	27.9	188.5	51.6	31.3	82.9	195.3	76.1	271.4
1990 Jun	109.7	15.5	31.5	28.1	184.8	55.6	34.9	90.5	196.7	78.6	275.3
1990 Dec	106.5	17.8	30.0	27.2	181.5	52.4	26.4	78.7	188.9	71.4	260.3
1991 Jun	104.6	14.9	31.1	27.6	178.3	53.8	32.8	86.6	189.6	75.3	264.9
1991 Dec	102.0	17.2	32.1	27.0	178.3	55.1	26.6	81.7	189.2	70.8	260.0

1 Figures exclude farmers, partners, directors and their spouses, salaried managers, school children and most trainees.

2 Including estimates for minor holdings in England and Wales.

Source: Agricultural Departments

3.8 Overtime and short-time worked by operatives in manufacturing industries[1]
Great Britain

Thousands

	Operatives working overtime			Operatives on short-time							
		Hours of overtime worked		Stood off for whole week		Working part of week			Total		
	Number of operatives	Total	Average	Number of operatives	Total number of hours lost	Number of operatives	Hours lost		Number of operatives	Hours lost	
							Total	Average		Total	Average
	BCIA	BCIB	BCIC	BCIG	BCIH	BCII	BCIJ	BCIK	BCID	BCIE	BCIF
1990 Apr	1 331	12 578	9.4	4	160	22	197	9.2	26	358	13.9
May	1 322	12 269	9.2	5	203	12	110	9.2	17	313	18.4
Jun	1 335	12 469	9.3	5	177	8	80	9.4	13	256	20.1
Jul	1 314	12 440	9.4	6	231	8	67	8.8	14	299	21.9
Aug	1 257	12 012	9.5	9	338	5	46	9.0	14	385	28.2
Sep	1 331	12 868	9.6	15	603	4	31	8.3	19	633	32.6
Oct	1 364	13 022	9.5	8	315	9	83	9.4	16	398	24.3
Nov	1 355	12 513	9.2	7	285	18	159	8.8	26	445	17.3
Dec	1 297	12 343	9.5	7	262	20	172	8.8	27	433	16.3
1991 Jan	1 097	9 804	9.0	11	432	28	288	10.0	39	720	18.5
Feb	1 061	9 224	8.6	10	394	55	522	9.4	65	915	14.0
Mar	1 060	9 493	8.9	11	420	94	834	9.0	104	1 254	12.0
Apr	1 052	9 209	8.7	10	385	88	840	9.7	98	1 225	12.6
May	1 053	9 359	8.9	11	432	61	543	9.1	72	975	13.6
Jun	1 048	9 633	9.2	7	280	48	454	9.4	56	733	13.2
Jul	1 111	10 388	9.3	6	214	48	425	8.8	54	639	11.9
Aug	1 028	9 605	9.3	12	455	43	388	9.1	55	843	15.4
Sep	1 055	9 774	9.3	9	328	47	414	8.7	56	743	13.3
Oct	1 142	10 782	9.4	3	116	45	378	8.4	48	494	10.3
Nov	1 140	10 524	9.2	5	201	42	409	9.7	47	610	12.9
Dec	1 104	10 497	9.5	7	285	35	357	10.3	42	642	15.2
1992 Jan	982	8 768	8.9	15	567	48	442	9.1	63	1 009	16.0
Feb	1 091	9 745	8.9	2	71	62	610	9.9	64	681	10.7
Mar	1 023	9 348	9.1	8	288	60	556†	9.2	68	844†	12.5
Apr[2]	1 091	10 036†	9.2	5	201	50	501†	10.0	55	702†	12.7
May[2]	1 136	10 945	9.6	3	103	31	277	8.8	34	380	11.2
Jun[2]	1 038	9 679	9.3	5	185	34	314	9.2	39	500	12.9

1 Divisions 2-4 of the *Standard Industrial Classification 1980.*
2 Provisional.

Source: Department of Employment

3.9 Unemployed in United Kingdom[1]
Analysis by duration of unemployment

Thousands

| | Males | | | | Females | | | |
	Up to 26 weeks	Over 26 and up to 52 weeks	Over 52 weeks	Total	Up to 26 weeks	Over 26 and up to 52 weeks	Over 52 weeks	Total
	BCNA	BCNB	BCNC	BCND	BCNE	BCNF	BCNG	BCNH
1987 Q4	718.7	289.6	895.4	1 903.6	417.3	153.6	276.9	847.8
1988 Q1	758.1	288.3	846.3	1 892.7	416.9	158.2	254.3	829.5
Q2	662.9	310.6	792.2	1 765.7	360.3	173.0	237.0	770.3
Q3	599.0	278.0	729.3	1 606.3	346.0	155.5	218.9	720.4
Q4	568.5	233.4	682.3	1 484.2	304.5	127.0	203.2	634.6
1989 Q1	615.9	221.7	635.6	1 473.2	298.3	117.0	185.9	601.1
Q2	542.9	230.8	577.1	1 350.8	251.1	114.6	167.1	532.8
Q3	518.4	219.1	524.1	1 261.6	258.5	100.8	150.4	509.8
Q4	511.0	193.2	477.2	1 181.3	235.9	82.4	136.2	454.5
1990 Q1	593.0	192.9	453.3	1 239.3	245.3	78.2	124.3	447.7
Q2	569.2	203.5	425.5	1 198.2	233.7	80.2	114.2	428.1
Q3	577.4	207.9	406.8	1 192.1	248.9	75.8	106.8	431.5
Q4	624.4	215.8	404.3	1 244.4	249.0	73.7	103.5	426.2
1991 Q1	809.5	250.3	421.0	1 480.8	292.0	83.1	103.8	479.0
Q2	907.4	313.2	447.6	1 668.2	324.1	98.7	107.5	530.2
Q3	921.8	380.3	480.3	1 782.4	361.7	111.6	111.9	585.2
Q4	880.1	426.2	533.4	1 839.7	343.9	121.8	120.6	586.2
1992 Q1	976.1	454.8	614.4	2 045.4	360.1	135.9	132.5	628.5
Q2	951.2	454.9	694.0	2 100.1	346.3	143.3	146.9	636.5

Figures shown are at January, April, July and October respectively.
1 These figures have been affected by benefit regulations for under 18 year olds introduced in September 1988.

Source: Department of Employment

3.10 Unemployment

Thousands

	United Kingdom						Great Britain	
	Not seasonally adjusted[1,2]		Seasonally adjusted[4,5]				Seasonally adjusted[4,5]	
	Total	Percentage rate [3]	Males	Females	Total	Percentage rate [3]	Total	Percentage rate [3]
	BCJA	BCJB	DPAE	DPAF	BCJD	BCJE	DPAG	DPAJ
1986	3 289.1	11.8	2 139.0	959.0	3 097.9	11.1	2 975.3	11.0
1987	2 963.5[†]	10.6	1 955.3	851.3	2 806.5	10.0	2 684.5	9.8
1988	2 426.0	8.4	1 588.1	686.8	2 274.9	8.1	2 161.7	7.9
1989	1 841.3	6.3	1 277.4	507.0	1 784.4	6.3	1 678.8	6.1
1990	1 651.9	5.8	1 231.3	431.4	1 622.7	5.8	1 565.5	5.6
1991	2 237.9	8.1	1 734.6	552.8	2 287.4	8.1	2 187.0	7.9
1989 Jun	1 743.1	6.1	1 275.7	509.5	1 785.2	6.3	1 679.4	6.1
Jul	1 771.4	6.2	1 261.9	498.7	1 760.6	6.2	1 655.4	6.0
Aug	1 741.1	6.1	1 242.9	481.4	1 724.3	6.1	1 619.7	5.8
Sep	1 702.9	6.0	1 225.6	468.7	1 694.3	6.0	1 590.9	5.7
Oct	1 635.8	5.8	1 219.9	462.1	1 682.0	5.9	1 579.3	5.7
Nov	1 612.4	5.7	1 206.0	453.0	1 659.0	5.8	1 557.7	5.6
Dec	1 639.0	5.8	1 196.4	443.7	1 640.1	5.8	1 539.6	5.6
1990 Jan	1 687.0	5.9	1 183.0	436.6	1 619.6	5.7	1 520.3	5.5
Feb	1 675.7	5.9	1 183.9	432.6	1 616.5	5.7	1 517.6	5.5
Mar	1 646.6	5.8	1 171.0	426.0	1 597.0	5.6	1 498.8	5.4
Apr	1 626.3	5.7	1 169.8	426.2	1 596.0	5.6	1 498.1	5.4
May	1 578.5	5.5	1 177.7	422.7	1 600.4	5.6	1 502.8	5.4
Jun	1 555.6	5.5	1 188.8	422.2	1 611.0	5.7	1 514.2	5.5
Jul	1 623.6	5.7	1 204.6	419.3	1 623.9	5.7	1 527.2	5.5
Aug	1 657.8	5.8	1 228.4	423.4	1 651.8	5.8	1 556.1	5.6
Sep	1 673.9	5.9	1 255.1	426.6	1 681.7	5.9	1 585.9	5.7
Oct	1 670.6	5.9	1 288.8	434.8	1 723.6	6.1	1 627.9	5.9
Nov	1 728.1	6.1	1 331.2	446.0	1 777.2	6.2	1 680.7	6.1
Dec	1 850.4	6.5	1 393.0	460.1	1 853.1	6.5	1 755.9	6.3
1991 Jan	1 959.7	6.9	1 425.6	468.0	1 893.6	6.7	1 796.2	6.5
Feb	2 045.4	7.2	1 499.5	486.2	1 985.7	7.0	1 888.0	6.9
Mar	2 142.1	7.6	1 579.3	509.9	2 089.2	7.4	1 990.5	7.2
Apr	2 198.5	7.8	1 639.3	527.3	2 166.6	7.7	2 067.4	7.5
May	2 213.8	7.8	1 690.6	541.6	2 232.2	7.9	2 132.8	7.7
Jun	2 241.0	7.9	1 739.0	553.9	2 292.9	8.1	2 192.9	8.0
Jul	2 367.5	8.4	1 791.1	571.4	2 362.5	8.4	2 261.7	8.2
Aug	2 435.1	8.6	1 835.5	587.0	2 422.5	8.6	2 320.7	8.4
Sep	2 450.7	8.7	1 864.5	593.6	2 458.1	8.7	2 356.1	8.6
Oct	2 426.0	8.6	1 883.4	593.7	2 477.1	8.8	2 374.6	8.6
Nov	2 471.8	8.7	1 919.6	598.1	2 517.7	8.9	2 414.8	8.8
Dec	2 551.7	9.0	1 948.0	603.2	2 551.2	9.0	2 448.2	8.9
1992 Jan	2 673.9	9.5	1 990.2	616.9	2 607.1	9.2	2 503.3	9.1
Feb	2 710.5	9.6	2 022.4	622.5	2 644.9	9.4	2 541.0	9.2
Mar	2 707.5	9.6	2 030.3	622.4	2 652.7	9.4	2 548.2	9.3
Apr	2 736.5	9.7	2 065.9	629.4	2 695.3	9.5	2 590.8	9.4
May	2 707.9	9.6	2 084.2	631.5	2 715.7	9.6	2 610.5	9.5
Jun	2 678.2	9.5	2 089.7[†]	634.6[†]	2 724.3[†]	9.6	2 618.1[†]	9.5
Jul	2 774.0	9.8	2 108.8	644.6	2 753.4	9.7	2 646.3	9.6

1 Unadjusted figures for 1988 were affected by the benefit regulations for those aged under 18 introduced in September 1988, most of whom are no longer eligible for Income Support. This reduced the UK unadjusted total by about 90 000 on average, with most of this effect having taken place over the two months to October 1988.

2 The unadjusted unemployment figures between September 1989 and March 1990 are affected by the change in the conditions of the Redundant Mineworkers Payment Scheme. An estimated 15 500 men left the count as a result of this change.

3 Percentage rates have been calculated by expressing the number of unemployed claimants as a percentage of the estimated total workforce (the sum of unemployed claimants, employees in employment, self-employed, HM Forces and participants on work related government

training programmes) at mid-1991 for 1991 and 1992 figures and at the corresponding mid-year estimates for earlier years.

4 The seasonally adjusted series relate only to claimants aged 18 or over, in order to maintain the consistent series, available back to 1971 (1974 for the regions - see p.660 of the December 1990 *Employment Gazette* for the list of discontinuities taken into account).

5 The latest national and regional seasonally adjusted unemployment figures are provisional and can be subject to revision in the following month.

Sources: Department of Employment;
Department of Economic Development (Northern Ireland)

3.11 Unemployment[1]
Analysis by standard regions

Thousands, seasonally adjusted[3]

	North	Yorkshire and Humberside	East Midlands	East Anglia	South East	South West	West Midlands	North West	Wales	Scotland	Northern Ireland
	DPAW	DPAX	DPAY	DPAZ	DPBA	DPBB	DPBC	DPBD	DPBE	DPBF	DPBG
1985	219.4	279.8	186.3	75.2	728.5	190.6	326.9	420.1	167.7	320.9	112.7
1986	219.9	291.7	189.1	78.8	750.2	195.8	327.6	422.3	168.3	331.7	122.6
1987	201.3	266.4	171.6	69.4	657.8	172.3	292.1	383.8	148.1	321.8	122.1
1988	171.0	220.9	137.3	50.4	495.8	133.7	229.7	320.8	123.9	278.2	113.2
1989	140.0	175.2	104.7	35.2	366.9	98.0	167.9	261.9	96.0	233.2	105.6
1990	122.7	161.1	99.3	37.4	372.1	97.2	152.6	234.7	86.2	202.1	97.2
1991	143.4	206.9	141.7	59.0	637.8	160.8	218.4	286.6	113.0	219.4	100.5
1990 Jul	120.7	157.6	96.9	36.4	358.2	94.6	148.1	230.0	84.7	199.7	96.7
Aug	121.7	159.4	99.4	37.7	372.7	97.8	150.9	231.6	86.0	199.0	95.7
Sep	122.8	161.4	101.3	39.0	388.0	100.8	152.7	233.9	86.7	199.2	95.8
Oct	124.2	165.3	104.1	40.9	406.8	105.1	156.4	237.6	88.9	198.7	95.7
Nov	127.2	169.4	107.4	42.9	427.9	111.0	161.4	242.7	91.3	199.6	96.5
Dec	129.4	175.3	112.0	45.4	459.0	119.5	168.3	250.0	94.6	202.3	97.2
1991 Jan	129.9	178.0	115.3	46.7	477.4	124.7	173.0	252.2	96.4	202.6	97.4
Feb	132.5	184.7	121.1	50.3	515.9	134.4	182.8	259.8	100.5	205.8	97.7
Mar	135.2	191.4	128.7	53.2	561.7	143.7	195.1	266.9	104.8	209.6	98.7
Apr	140.0	199.2	133.3	55.2	586.9	149.3	206.0	274.8	108.6	214.4	99.2
May	142.6	204.3	137.7	57.4	610.6	154.5	212.7	281.8	111.8	219.1	99.4
Jun	144.1	208.8	141.8	58.9	636.2	160.1	219.3	287.3	114.2	221.9	100.0
Jul	147.0	213.8	146.6	61.0	663.4	166.6	226.8	293.6	117.1	225.6	100.8
Aug	148.9	218.3	150.8	62.6	688.7	171.7	233.0	300.1	119.3	227.0	101.8
Sep	149.9	220.0	153.2	63.9	706.4	176.1	237.8	302.8	120.0	225.7	102.0
Oct	149.6	220.4	154.4	64.3	717.6	178.6	240.1	304.0	119.9	225.7	102.5
Nov	150.0	221.5	157.5	66.3	736.3	182.9	245.0	307.1	121.0	227.1	102.9
Dec	151.0	222.6	160.5	67.8	752.6	186.7	249.0	308.4	121.8	227.9	103.0
1992 Jan	152.2	225.9	164.1	70.5	776.2	192.4	254.4	313.4	123.3	230.9	103.8
Feb	152.7	228.3	166.8	72.4	796.0	195.8	259.0	314.9	123.6	231.5	103.9
Mar	152.1	228.6	167.1	73.1	803.4	196.9	259.0	314.2	122.5	231.3	104.5
Apr	153.6	230.7	170.0	74.8	820.0	201.9	263.2	319.2	123.6	233.9	104.5
May	153.5	231.9	171.8	75.2	829.7	203.3	265.6	319.9	124.2	235.2	105.2
Jun	154.3†	232.3	171.6	75.7†	833.7†	204.1†	265.6	319.6	124.6†	236.5†	106.2†
Jul	155.5	233.8	173.3	76.8	845.3	207.5	267.5	321.0	125.5	239.9	107.1

Unemployment rate[2]											
June	11.1	9.7	8.7	7.4	9.2	9.0	10.5	10.5	9.6	9.4	14.5

Note: Seasonally adjusted series takes account of past discontinuities, to be consistent with the current coverage at the count. To maintain a consistent assessment, the seasonally adjusted series relates only to claimants aged 18 and over.

1 The latest national and regional seasonally adjusted unemployment figures are provisional and can be subject to revision in the following month.

2 Percentage rates have been calculated by expressing the number of unemployed claimants as a percentage of the estimated total workforce (the sum of unemployed claimants, employees in employment, self-employed,

HM Forces and participants on work related government training programmes at mid-1991 for 1991 and 1992 figures and at the corresponding mid-year estimates for earlier years.

3 The seasonally adjusted series relate only to claimants aged 18 or over, in order to maintain the consistent series, available back to 1971 (1974 for the regions - see p.660 of the December 1990 *Employment Gazette* for the list of discontinuities taken into account.

Sources: Department of Employment;
Department of Economic Development (Northern Ireland)

3.12 Vacancies at Jobcentres and career offices[1]
Analysis by standard regions

Thousands

	South East	Greater London[2]	East Anglia	South West	West Midlands	East Midlands	Yorkshire and Humberside	North West	North	Wales	Scotland	Great Britain	Northern Ireland[3]	United Kingdom
Total vacancies at Jobcentres: not seasonally adjusted														
	BCRA	BCRB	BCRC	BCRD	BCRE	BCRF	BCRG	BCRH	BCRI	BCRJ	BCRK	BCRL	BCRM	BCOM
1988	95.1	32.2	9.7	20.4	24.1	13.8	15.5	23.9	11.4	12.0	20.0	245.9	1.9	247.8
1989	71.7	23.6	8.3	18.5	20.5	12.9	13.3	24.4	10.7	13.8	21.7	215.8	2.6	218.4
1990	47.6	14.8	5.4	13.9	14.6	10.5	11.7	21.1	10.7	12.2	21.6	169.1	3.4	172.5
1991	28.8	8.2	3.2	9.9	8.2	7.1	7.9	15.8	6.6	8.1	18.3	113.8	3.0	116.9
1991 Aug	28.3	7.2	3.1	8.9	7.0	6.5	7.3	14.4	5.9	7.2	16.3	104.7	2.9	107.7
Sep	33.8	9.2	3.7	10.2	8.8	8.2	8.5	17.2	6.7	8.0	18.6	123.9	3.3	127.2
Oct	34.3	9.3	3.8	10.3	9.3	8.7	9.1	17.1	6.9	8.0	19.6	127.0	2.9	129.9
Nov	30.6	8.3	3.3	8.8	8.0	7.6	8.0	15.5	6.5	7.6	18.2	114.2	2.9	117.0
Dec	26.7	7.3	2.9	7.2	7.1	6.6	6.8	13.5	5.4	7.0	15.9	99.0	2.8	101.7
1992 Jan	24.2	7.0	2.6	6.6	6.3	5.8	6.3	12.4	5.0	6.6	14.4	90.1	2.6	92.7
Feb	25.6	7.0	2.9	7.3	6.4	6.1	6.6	12.7	5.4	7.1	15.8	95.8	2.7	98.5
Mar	27.6	7.2	3.1	8.6	6.8	6.9	6.9	13.1	5.5	7.8	16.9	103.3	2.9	106.3
Apr	29.7	8.1	3.5	9.8	7.4	7.1	7.3	14.3	5.9	9.0	20.1	114.0	3.0	117.0
May	30.1	8.3	3.9	10.8	7.6	7.6	7.8	14.9	6.3	9.7	20.7	119.4	3.2	122.6
Jun	32.2	8.5	4.0	10.9	8.0	8.2	8.4	15.2	7.2	9.9	20.9	124.9†	3.2	128.2†
Jul	30.2	7.7	3.6	9.1	7.1	7.5	7.7	13.9	6.5	9.1	18.4	113.3	3.1	116.4
Seasonally adjusted[3]														
	BCQA	BCQB	BCQC	BCQD	BCQE	BCQF	BCQG	BCQH	BCQI	BCQJ	BCQK	BCQL	BCQM	DPCB
1991 Aug	28.1	8.3	2.8	8.5	7.6	6.6	7.0	14.3	5.6	6.4	15.6	102.4	4.2	106.6
Sep	28.6	8.0	2.7	8.4	6.9	6.7	6.7	14.0	6.0	6.4	15.9	102.2	4.3	106.5
Oct	23.6	4.4	2.8	9.2	6.1	7.0	7.0	13.3	6.1	7.1	17.3	99.6	3.9	103.5
Nov	27.1	6.2	3.1	9.6	6.0	6.9	7.2	13.9	6.8	7.9	17.4	105.9	3.8	109.7
Dec	32.8	8.2	3.8	10.5	8.1	7.6	8.0	16.0	6.6	9.1	17.3	119.7	3.8	123.9
1992 Jan	33.3	9.4	3.7	10.0	7.7	7.1	7.9	15.4	6.7	8.4	17.9	118.0	4.0	122.0
Feb	33.5	9.2	4.0	10.5	7.9	7.4	8.1	15.4	6.5	8.6	18.7	120.5	3.8	124.3
Mar	34.4	9.1	4.0	10.5	8.6	8.1	8.2	15.0	6.3	9.1	19.0	123.3	4.2	127.5
Apr	31.1	8.7	3.6	8.5	8.1	7.3	7.8	14.6	5.6	9.2	19.9	115.7	3.9	119.6
May	27.5	8.1	3.6	8.0	7.8	7.3	7.7	14.2	5.6	8.9	20.0	110.5	4.1	114.6
Jun	25.7	7.5	3.1	7.1	7.5	7.5	7.4	13.7	5.9	8.2	19.4	105.4	4.0	109.5
Jul	27.8	8.1	3.2	7.6	7.3	7.5	7.7	14.3	5.7	7.9	17.6	106.6	4.2	110.8
Vacancies at careers offices: not seasonally adjusted														
	BCSA	BCSB	BCSC	BCSD	BCSE	BCSF	BCSG	BCSH	BCSI	BCSJ	BCSK	BCSL	BCSM	BCSN
1988	16.0	8.2	0.9	1.6	1.8	1.3	1.1	1.3	0.4	0.3	0.5	25.2	1.0	26.3
1989	14.5	7.6	1.0	1.5	2.7	1.5	1.2	1.4	0.5	0.4	0.8	25.5	1.3	26.8
1990	9.4	4.9	0.6	1.1	2.3	1.0	1.1	1.5	0.5	0.2	1.1	18.8	0.6	19.4
1991	3.5	2.0	0.3	0.5	1.4	0.4	0.6	0.8	0.3	0.1	0.7	8.7	0.3	9.0
1991 Aug	3.9	2.2	0.3	0.5	1.5	0.4	0.6	0.8	0.3	0.1	0.7	9.1	0.2	9.3
Sep	3.8	2.1	0.3	0.5	1.4	0.4	0.6	0.8	0.4	0.1	0.6	8.8	0.3	9.1
Oct	2.6	1.3	0.3	0.4	1.3	0.4	0.5	0.6	0.3	0.1	0.6	7.2	0.3	7.5
Nov	2.2	1.3	0.3	0.4	1.2	0.2	0.4	0.5	0.2	0.1	0.6	6.1	0.3	7.4
Dec	2.1	1.3	0.2	0.3	1.1	0.2	0.3	0.5	0.2	0.1	0.4	5.4	0.3	5.7
1992 Jan	2.0	1.1	0.1	0.4	1.1	0.2	0.3	0.5	0.2	0.1	0.5	5.3	0.3	5.6
Feb	2.1	1.2	0.2	0.3	0.9	0.2	0.3	0.5	0.3	0.1	0.4	5.4	0.3	5.7
Mar	2.0	1.1	0.3	0.3	1.4	0.2	0.4	0.5	0.3	0.1	0.6	6.1	0.3	6.4
Apr	2.0	0.9	0.3	0.4	1.4	0.2	0.5	0.5	0.3	0.1	0.5	6.2	0.3	6.5
May	2.3	1.1	0.4	0.4	1.5	0.3	0.6	0.6	0.3	0.1	0.6	7.1	0.3	7.4
Jun	5.1	3.1	0.4	0.4	1.6	0.5	0.5	0.8	0.3	0.1	0.7	10.4	0.4	10.8
Jul	4.8	3.0	0.4	0.5	1.4	0.4	0.5	0.6	0.3	0.1	0.7	9.7	0.3	10.1

1 About one third of all vacancies are notified to Jobcentres. These could include some that are suitable for young persons and similarly vacancies notified to careers offices could include some for adults. Because of possible duplication the two series should not be added together. The figures represent only the number of vacancies notified by employers and remaining unfilled on the day of the count.

2 Included in South East.

3 Excluding vacancies on government programmes (except vacancies on Enterprise Ulster and Action for Community Employment (ACE) which are included in the seasonally adjusted figures for Northern Ireland). Note that Community Programme vacancies handled by Jobcentres were excluded from the seasonally adjusted series when the coverage was revised in September 1985. The coverage of the seasonally adjusted series is therefore not affected by the cessation of C.P. vacancies with the introduction of Employment Training in September 1988. Figures on the current basis are available back to 1980. For further details see page 143 of the October 1985 *Employment Gazette*.

Source: Department of Employment

3.13 Industrial stoppages[1]

Thousands

	Workers beginning involvement in period in any dispute	Total working days lost[2]						
		All industries and services	Coal, coke, mineral oil and natural gas	Metals, engineering and vehicles	Textiles, footwear and clothing	Construction	Transport and communication	All other industries and services
SIC 1980		*All classes*	*11-14*	*21-22,31-37*	*43,45*	*50*	*71-79*	*All other classes*
	BCPI	BCPJ	BCPK	BCPL	BCPM	BCPN	BCPO	BCPP
1987	884	3 546	217	458	50	22	1 705	1 095
1988	759	3 702	222	1 456	90	17	1 490	428
1989	727	4 128	52	655	16	128	625	2 652
1990	285	1 903	94	953	24	14	177	641
1991	175	761	29	181	1	14	60	476
1988 Jun	34	306	3	230	34	2	20	17
Jul	18	349	2	283	4	1	24	35
Aug	135	431	2	280	1	1	134	14
Sep	161	1 115	6	30	5	1	1 036	37
Oct	26	53	1	26	-	1	6	19
Nov	134	183	5	27	4	-	21	126
Dec	12	38	9	6	1	-	15	6
1989 Jan	13	42	4	9	1	1	17	11
Feb	26	64	2	16	5	6	16	19
Mar	26	80	4	36	-	6	-	34
Apr	37	106	6	29	-	22	20	29
May	32	184	2	76	5	15	38	48
Jun	76	259	6	21	2	20	154	57
Jul	389	2 424	10	22	2	29	339	2 022
Aug	6	99	4	22	1	-	15	58
Sep	26	71	4	16	-	14	5	32
Oct	61	162	3	38	-	9	2	110
Nov	26	341	8	228	-	5	8	92
Dec	8	297	1	143	-	-	12	141
1990 Jan	45	443	1	273	1	-	3	165
Feb	24	515	5	347	2	-	8	154
Mar	19	236	13	104	17	4	26	73
Apr	53	112	4	56	1	1	7	42
May	23	131	2	77	-	-	25	26
Jun	20	150	5	45	1	1	60	38
Jul	16	55	9	10	1	-	13	21
Aug	25	67	36	5	1	1	6	19
Sep	15	35	5	8	-	1	1	19
Oct	18	54	5	10	-	-	9	29
Nov	18	65	6	11	-	5	16	26
Dec	9	40	3	5	-	-	4	28
1991 Jan	7	44	5	2	-	4	2	32
Feb	14	36	4	3	-	-	4	25
Mar	40	55	1	4	-	3	2	46
Apr	12	105	-	11	-	2	2	90
May	20	105	2	50	-	-	32	21
Jun	7	53	-	32	-	1	4	16
Jul	10	57	1	13	-	1	13	28
Aug	10	64	12	6	-	-	-	46
Sep	11	78	1	28	-	4	-	44
Oct	17	84	4	24	-	-	-	55
Nov	12	46	-	3	-	-	1	42
Dec	15	34	-	3	-	-	-	31
1992 Jan	18	55†	1	13†	-	-	1	40†
Feb	5	24	1	10	-	-	-	12
Mar	10	30	1	3	1	-	-	24
Apr	8†	25	4	8	-	-	-	12
May	8	25	-	3	-	1	7	14
Jun	6	25	-	10	-	-	-	16

1 Excludes stoppages involving fewer than 10 workers or lasting less than one day except any in which the total number of working days lost exceeded 100. There may be some under-recording of small or short stoppages; this would have much more effect on the total stoppages than on working days lost. The figures for 1992 are provisional.

2 The figures of working days lost relate to the total working days lost within each of the periods shown as a result of stoppages *in progress* in that period, whether the stoppages began in that period or earlier.

Source: Department of Employment

4 Social services

4.1 National insurance and child benefit
Great Britain

	Persons in receipt of unemployment benefit[2]	Weekly averages New claims for Unemployment benefit[3]	Weekly averages New claims for Sickness and invalidity benefits[4]	At end of period Retirement pensioners[5]	At end of period Widows receiving pensions or widowed mothers' allowances[6]	Families receiving benefits	Children in families receiving benefits
	BDAD	BDAC	BDAA	BDAE	BDAF	BDAG	BDAH
1987	783	91.9	19.1	9 303	347	6 712	12 015
1988	607	75.2	19.0[9]	9 315	354	6 706	12 021
1989	364	65.4	19.9	9 318[7]	350	6 695	12 024
1990	318	71.0	20.0	9 381	334	6 732	12 121
1991 Feb	477	94.0	23.4	-	-	6 761[8]	12 185[8]
Mar	-	88.1	20.5	9 368	331	6 783[8]	12 233[8]
Apr	-	84.4	21.5	-	..	6 798[8]	12 264[8]
May	555	75.0	20.1	-	..	6 818[8]	12 312[8]
Jun	-	84.3	20.6	-	..	6 832[8]	12 343[8]
Jul	-	101.1	21.7	-	..	6 836[8]	12 357[8]
Aug	608	86.0	19.3	-	..	6 843[8]	12 379[8]
Sep	-	92.6	21.5	9 407	..	6 739[8]	12 147[8]
Oct	-	90.4	22.6	..	..	6 758[8]	12 190[8]
Nov	626	91.2	21.7	..	..	6 778[8]	12 232[8]
Dec	-	71.1	17.6	..	..	6 802[8]	12 284[8]
1992 Jan	-	107.4	23.8	..	..	6 804[8]	12 287[8]
Feb	695	88.7	22.9	..	..	6 815[8]	12 313[8]
Mar	..	83.4	23.0	..	..	6 813[8]	12 312[8]
Apr	..	81.7	20.0	..	..	6 828[8]	12 348[8]
May	..	73.7	18.5	..	..	6 834[8]	12 361[8]
Jun	..	85.3	21.1	..	..	6 856[8]	12 415[8]

1 Includes overseas cases.
2 Yearly figures are averages of quarterly figures. Quarterly figures relate to the Thursday following the first Monday in the month.
3 Excluding claims made under the emergency benefit procedure. Figures for individual months are averages of the four or five weeks starting on the first Monday of each month.
4 From 6 April 1983 Statutory sick pay was introduced to cover the first 8 weeks of incapacity. From 6 April 1986 the period was extended to 28 weeks. From April 1988 reporting periods will be calendar months instead of all weeks (ending on Tuesday) in each month.

5 Excluding pensioners in receipt of non-contributory retirement pension awarded under National Insurance Acts 1970 and 1971 and cases where graduated pension only was awarded.
6 Including a diminishing number of widows with pensions of £1.50 a week derived from the old Contributory Pensions Acts.
7 Figures include approx. 1.12m cases converted to Pension Strategy Project (PSP) and 7700 new awards taken on by Pension Strategy Computer System (PSCS).
8 Provisional.
9 Until April 1988 data held for 4 week periods. Claims received in early January 1988 calculated from the figure availiable for the 4 weeks ending 12:1:88.

Source: Department of Social Security

4.2 Family income supplement / family credit
Great Britain

At last Tuesday of first month of quarter, thousands

	Families receiving family income supplement / family credit Two-parent families	One-parent families	All families		Families receiving family income supplement / family credit Two-parent families	One-parent families	All families
Family Income Supplement							
				1988 Q3	-	-	283[2]
	BDBB	BDBC	BDBA	Q4	-	-	282[2]
1986 Q1	117	82	199				
Q2	118	83	200				
Q3	128	88	215	1989 Q1	-	-	279[2]
Q4	131	90	221	Q2	177	108	286
				Q3	195	118	313
1987 Q1	127	90	217	Q4	192	122	314
Q2	128	92	220				
Q3	129	94	225	1990 Q1	180	119	299
Q4	130	95	224	Q2	192	121	314
				Q3	200	126	326
1988 Q1	126	94	223	Q4	197	129	326
				1991 Q1	189	126	315
				Q2	210	131	341
				Q3	222	133	355
				Q4	214	135	349
Family Credit[1]				1992 Q1	211	135	346

Note: Source: 10% sample to Qtr 1 of 1988, 5% sample from Qtr 2 of 1988.

1 1988 quarter two to 1989 quarter one, no split available.
2 Estimate.

Source: Department of Social Security

4.3 Income Support
Great Britain

In a week in the month shown, thousands

| | Elderly aged 60 or over | Unemployed | | | With disability premium | With lone parent premium not in other groups | Others | Total number of Income Support recipients |
		With contributory benefit	Without contributory benefit	Total				
	BALZ	BAMA	BAMB	BAMC	BAMD	BAME	BAMF	BAMG
1988 Nov	1 659	122	1 102	1 224	273	703	400	4 260
1989 Feb	1 649	122	1 110	1 232	286	746	441	4 354
May	1 557	99	1 011	1 110	291	741	465	4 164
Aug	1 605	89	1 084	1 173	298	757	474	4 308
Nov	1 729	82	955	1 036	305	749	465	4 284
1990 Feb	1 712	104	1 014	1 118	317	748	458	4 353
May	1 628	50	944	994	318	767	479	4 186
Aug	1 610	57	1 090	1 147	339	785	444	4 325
Nov	1 562	58	1 018	1 076	354	790	477	4 259
1991 Feb	1 575	81	1 168	1 249	359	817	477	4 477
May	1 502	90	1 221	1 311	355	856	500	4 524
Aug	1 489	103	1 354	1 457	362	883	503	4 694
Nov	1 504	109	1 404	1 513	372	899	535	4 823
1992 Feb	1 497	115	1 545	1 660	381	913	581	5 030

Source: Department of Social Security

4.4 Family practitioner services

Thousands

| | England and Wales | | | | Scotland | | | |
| | | Dental services | Ophthalmic services[5] | | | Dental services | Ophthalmic services | |
	Pharmaceutical services Prescriptions dispensed by chemists etc[1]	Completed courses of adult[2] treatment and cases of occasional treatment	Sight tests paid for[5],[6]	Pairs of NHS glasses dispensed/ vouchers issued[3],[5]	Pharmaceutical services Prescriptions dispensed by chemists etc[4]	Completed courses of treatment and cases of occasional treatment[2]	Sight tests paid for[6]	Pairs of NHS glasses dispensed/ vouchers issued[3]
	BDDA	BDDB	BDDC	BDDD	BDDE	BDDF	BDDG	BDDH
1987	361 330	23 561[7]	11 742	2 684	38 343	2 989	1 022	338
1988	373 608	25 292[7]	..	..	39 505	3 055	1 141	322
1989	379 646	24 001[7]	..	..	41 016	3 144	716	313
1990	388 900	23 889[7]	..	..	..	2 861	417	320
1991	..	24 441[7]	..	..	..	2 463	477	374
1988 Q3	90 819	-	2 903	564	9 654	738	247	70
Q4	96 737	-	-	-	10 026	750	300	76
1989 Q1	92 309	-	7 117	1 178	9 861	820	337	81
Q2	95 135	-	-	-	10 311	788	194	83
Q3	91 863	-	3 550	1 227	9 938	743	87	73
Q4	100 339	-	-	-	10 906	793	98	76
1990 Q1	97 120	-	2 022	1 196	10 509	757	96	74
Q2	96 404	-	-	-	10 599	794	107	82
Q3	94 506	-	2 156	1 278	10 258	766	102	79
Q4	100 769	5 897[8]	-	-	11 054	545	111	85
1991 Q1	100 054	5 638	2 269	1 330	10 815	621	112	79
Q2	99 604	6 018	-	-	10 954	579	126	106
Q3	100 991	6 286	2 573†	1 496†	10 925	642	116	93
Q4	106 589	6 499	-	-	11 613	621	123	96
1992 Q1	105 843	6 797	2 739	1 552	11 324	638	131	98
Q2	..	6 744	..	..	..	642	..	..

1 Includes drug stores and appliance contractors.
2 Number scheduled in respect of the stated period.
3 From July 1986 this related to the number of voucher claims submitted.
4 Includes prescriptions dispensed by chemists and appliance suppliers. Excludes prescriptions dispensed by dispensing doctors and stock orders .
5 From October 1988, data on Ophthalmic services in England and Wales are collected six monthly.

6 From April 1989 NHS sight tests were made available only to children, people on low income, users of certain complex lenses, persons registered blind or partially sighted, diabetic and glaucoma sufferers and persons aged over 40 who are relatives of glaucoma sufferers.
7 The data refer to financial years rather than calendar years.
8 A new dental contract was introduced on 1 October 1990.

Sources: Department of Health;
Common Services Agency for the Scottish Health Service

5 Law enforcement

5.1 Notifiable offences recorded by the police
England and Wales

Thousands

	Violence against the person	Sexual offences	Burglary	Robbery	Theft and handling stolen goods	Fraud and forgery	Criminal damage	Other	Total
	BEAB	BEAC	BEAD	BEAE	BEAF	BEAG	BEAH	BEAI	BEAA
1985	121.7	21.4	866.7	27.5	1 884.1	134.8	539.0	16.7	3 611.8
1986	125.5	22.7	931.6	30.0	2 003.9	133.4	583.6	16.7	3 847.4
1987	141.0	25.2	900.1	32.6	2 052.0	133.0	589.0	19.3	3 892.2
1988	158.2	26.5	817.8	31.4	1 931.3	133.9	593.9	22.7	3 715.8
1989	177.0	29.7	825.9	33.2	2 012.8	134.5	630.1	27.6	3 870.7
1990	184.7	29.0	1 006.8	36.2	2 374.4	147.9	733.4	31.1	4 543.6
1991	190.3	29.4	1 219.5	45.3	2 761.1	174.7	821.1	34.6	5 276.2
1987 Q4	38.0	6.6	229.5	8.6	529.7	34.9	151.0	5.7	1 003.9
1988 Q1	35.5	6.3	229.6	7.9	499.5	35.4	151.4	5.5	971.2
Q2	39.1	6.7	198.0	7.5	484.6	34.1	150.1	5.6	925.7
Q3	40.9	7.2	184.0	8.0	468.1	32.5	141.1	5.5	887.4
Q4	42.7	6.3	206.1	8.1	479.1	31.8	151.4	6.1	931.6
1989 Q1	39.3	7.0	213.3	8.2	479.6	32.1	156.8	6.0	942.2
Q2	45.2	7.5	192.7	7.8	499.1	32.8	156.0	6.6	947.8
Q3	48.3	8.0	192.3	8.0	505.2	35.4	152.5	7.3	957.0
Q4	44.2	7.2	227.7	9.1	528.8	34.2	164.8	7.8	1 023.8
1990 Q1	41.0	6.6	252.3	8.4	555.2	34.7	175.4	7.2	1 080.9
Q2	47.0	7.4	231.6	8.4	586.3	34.4	188.6	7.8	1 111.3
Q3	49.5	7.9	233.4	8.9	590.5	37.3	175.0	7.7	1 110.3
Q4	47.2	7.2	289.5	10.5	642.4	41.4	194.4	8.4	1 241.0
1991 Q1	41.6	6.6	298.9	9.6	649.3	41.4	195.6	8.2	1 251.2
Q2	48.1	7.6	292.0	10.7	701.1	44.1	214.0	8.5	1 326.2
Q3	52.3	8.1	289.3	11.8	703.8	44.9	198.0	8.9	1 317.2
Q4	48.3	7.1	339.2	13.2	706.9	44.4	213.6	9.0	1 381.6
1992 Q1	45.5	7.2	345.9	12.0	701.7	42.4	223.8	9.9	1 388.3

Source: Home Office

5.2 Crimes and offences recorded by the police
Scotland

Thousands

	Non-sexual crimes of violence	Crimes of indecency	Crimes of dishonesty	Fire raising, vandalism etc	Other crimes	Motor vehicle offences	Miscellaneous offences	Total crimes and offences (monthly)	Total crimes and offences (annual)
	BEBC	BEBD	BEBE	BEBF	BEBG	BEBI	BEBH	BEBB	BEBA
1985	15.3	5.8	344.0	79.8	19.3	230.3	119.2	813.6	800.4
1986	15.7	5.4	342.5	78.9	21.4	238.1	120.4	823.5	822.4
1987	18.5	5.2	356.7	76.6	24.4	249.6	127.2	858.3	858.2
1988	18.0	5.1	344.7	73.5	28.6	248.6	124.9	843.5	855.6
1989	18.5	5.7	354.2	78.6	34.0	277.8	124.8	893.6	902.0
1990	18.6	6.0	386.2	86.2	39.6	294.1	127.2	957.9	959.1
1991	21.4	5.8	426.6	89.0	44.2	300.9	121.4	1 009.1	1 020.7
1987 Q4	4.9	1.2	91.8	19.1	6.6	63.9	32.5	220.0	..
1988 Q1	4.4	1.3	85.3	18.4	6.0	64.0	30.2	209.6	..
Q2	4.4	1.3	83.6	18.2	6.9	61.3	31.3	207.1	..
Q3	4.5	1.3	85.3	17.6	7.8	58.3	31.6	206.4	..
Q4	4.6	1.2	90.4	19.3	7.9	65.0	31.9	220.3	..
1989 Q1	4.4	1.2	84.9	19.0	7.1	69.7	27.7	214.0	..
Q2	4.9	1.4	88.1	20.0	8.6	71.2	33.0	227.2	..
Q3	4.7	1.6	89.4	19.2	8.3	64.6	32.4	220.2	..
Q4	4.5	1.5	91.8	20.5	10.0	72.2	31.7	232.1	..
1990 Q1	4.5	1.5	94.6	21.6	9.1	72.5	30.3	234.0	..
Q2	4.5	1.7	92.5	21.4	9.8	75.0	32.8	237.7	..
Q3	4.8	1.5	96.2	20.7	10.0	71.6	32.6	237.5	..
Q4	4.8	1.4	102.9	22.5	10.7	75.0	31.5	248.7	..
1991 Q1	4.7	1.3	97.6	21.9	10.0	77.9	28.3	241.7	..
Q2	5.2	1.6	107.6	23.2	11.1	79.2	31.0	258.9	..
Q3	5.7	1.6	111.4	21.8	11.8	73.3	32.3	257.8	..
Q4	5.8	1.3	110.0	22.1	11.3	70.5	29.8	250.7	..
1992 Q1	5.7	1.5	105.2	22.7	11.3	78.6	28.9	253.9	..

Components may not add to totals due to separate rounding.

Source: The Scottish Office Home and Health Department

6 Agriculture, food, drinks and tobacco

6.1 Land use and crop areas[1]
Area at the June Census

Thousand hectares

		1986	1987	1988	1989	1990	1991
Agricultural land							
Total crops	BFAA	5 239	5 272	5 255	5 137	5 013	4 956
Bare fallow	BFAB	48	42	58	65	64	64
All grasses	BFAC	6 801	6 802	6 773	6 784	6 843	6 848
Sole right rough grazing	BFAD	4 829	4 791	4 759	4 736	4 706	4 674
All other land on agricultural holdings, including woodland	BFAE	543	554	570	623	680	712[2]
Total area on agricultural holdings	BFAF	17 460	17 461	17 415	17 345	17 307	17 254
Common rough grazing (estimated)	BFAG	1 216	1 216	1 236	1 236	1 236	1 233
Total agricultural land	BFAH	18 676	18 677	18 651	18 581	18 542	18 487
Crops							
Cereals (excluding maize and triticale)							
Wheat	BFAK	1 997	1 994	1 886	2 083	2 013	1 980
Barley (winter and spring)	BFAL	1 916	1 831	1 879	1 652	1 516	1 393
Oats	BFAM	97	98	120	118	107	103
Mixed corn	BFAN	7	6	5	5	4	4
Rye	BFAO	7	7	7	7	8	9
Total	BFAJ	4 024	3 937	3 898	3 866	3 648	3 489
Rape grown for oilseed	BFAP	299	388	347	321	390	440
Sugar beet, not for stockfeeding	BFAQ	205	202	201	197	194	196
Potatoes	BFAR	178	178	180	174	177	177
Fodder crops	BFAS	298	345	393	336	342	336
Horticultural crops (excluding mushrooms)	BFAV	214	200	209	208	208	204
Orchards: commercial	BFBG	36	35	35	33	32	32
non-commercial	BFBH	2	2	2	2	2	2

For further information refer to section 6 of the *Supplement of Definitions and Explanatory Notes* published in the January edition of *Monthly Digest*.
1 Figures include estimates for minor holdings in England and Wales but not for Scotland and Northern Ireland.
2 Includes land officially designated under Set-Aside scheme.

Source: Agricultural Departments

6.2 Crops: yields and production

		Yields per hectare (tonnes)						Production (thousand tonnes)				
		1987	1988	1989	1990	1991		1987	1988	1989	1990	1991
Agricultural crops												
Wheat	BFBJ	5.99	6.23	6.74	6.97[†]	7.25	BADO	11 940	11 751	14 033	14 033	14 363
Barley (winter and spring)	BFBK	5.04	4.67	4.88[†]	5.22	5.47	BADP	9 229	8 778	8 073	7 911[†]	7 627
Oats	BFBO	4.57	4.55	4.46	4.96[†]	5.04	BADQ	454	548	529	530	523
Sugar beet	BFBL	39.91	41.30	41.80	41.13	..	BADR	7 990	8 150	8 115	7 900	..
Potatoes	BFBM	37.60	38.10	35.70	36.40	..	BADS	6 697	6 890	6 250	6 473	..

		1986/87	1987/88	1988/89	1989/90	1990/91		1986/87	1987/88	1988/89	1989/90	1990/91
Horticultural crops												
Field vegetables												
Brussels sprouts	BFBR	14.7	15.1	15.2	14.0	12.4	BADT	167.8	173.2	164.5	133.8	102.7
Cabbage, inc. savoy and spring greens	BFBS	30.2	30.1	31.8	31.1	29.6	BADU	687.8	698.0	744.1	718.1	665.8
Cauliflowers	BFBT	20.3	21.4	21.8	20.3	17.8	BADV	359.5	369.8	372.1	359.7	308.1
Carrots	BFBU	42.8	38.2	42.8	37.5	35.4	BADW	634.6	548.6	674.8	586.7	550.1
Turnips and swedes	BFBV	34.8	33.8	35.3	30.2	25.3	BADX	162.8	160.5	165.0	134.3	126.0
Beetroot	BFBW	36.9	38.3	37.9	36.7	35.5	BADY	94.6	103.6	105.4	96.9	95.8
Onions dry bulb	BFBX	33.3	39.6	37.9	32.1	31.4	BADZ	247.4	298.1	298.9	225.2	224.7
Peas green for market (in pod weight)	BFBY	8.7	8.4	9.1	7.9	7.5	BAEA	19.8	13.7	14.4	9.6	9.7
Peas green for processing (shelled weight)	BFBZ	5.1	4.6	4.6	4.5	4.8	BAEB	238.6	229.1	234.1	236.4	260.5
Lettuce	BFCA	29.8	30.8	31.5	31.3	29.2	BAEC	157.5	189.8	222.3	207.6	206.4
Protected crops												
Tomatoes	BFCB	185.9	198.4	213.8	228.3	243.6	BAED	131.4	123.4	130.8	136.7	138.8
Cucumbers	BFCC	333.7	372.7	380.9	366.1	389.0	BAEE	75.7	80.9	86.8	87.5	89.9
Lettuce	BFBP	31.6	31.7	32.4	32.5	31.4	BAEF	49.8	46.7	48.2	47.5	45.7
Fruit												
Dessert apples	BAEG	11.7	11.5	9.5	18.5	12.0	BFCD	163.3	164.8	134.1	252.7	158.6
Cooking apples	BAEH	15.6	13.9	15.8	23.4	18.8	BFCE	139.4	123.3	134.3	194.8	151.9
Soft fruit	BAEI	..	..	..	..	..	BFCF	108.7	107.1	103.8	96.0	93.6
Pears	BAEJ	12.2	16.5	8.2	11.5	10.1	BFBQ	46.6	66.4	32.3	43.1	36.7

For further information refer to section 6 of the *Supplement of Definitions and Explanatory Notes* published in the January edition of *Monthly Digest*.

Source: Agricultural Departments

6.3 Livestock[1]

Thousands

		1987 Jun	1987 Dec	1988 Jun	1988 Dec	1989 Jun	1989 Dec	1990 Jun	1990 Dec	1991 Jun	1991 Dec
Cattle and calves											
Dairy herd	BFCH	3 042	3 052	2 912	2 976	2 865	2 933	2 847	2 890	2 770	2 779
Beef herd	BFCI	1 345	1 366	1 375	1 432	1 495	1 547	1 599	1 635	1 666	1 662
Heifers in calf (first calf)	BFCJ	775	612	834	697	793	664	757	673	733	644
Bulls for service	BFCK	74	72	75	75	78	78	82	79	81	78
All other cattle and calves	BFCL	6 934	6 760	6 688	6 729	6 744	6 700	6 774	6 566	6 616	6 461
Total cattle and calves	BFCG	12 170	11 862	11 844	11 909	11 975	11 922	12 059	11 843	11 866	11 623
Sheep and lambs											
Ewes kept for breeding	BFCN	14 836	17 407	15 521	18 108	16 205	18 760	16 760	19 075	16 944	18 864
Rams kept for service	BFCO	437	487	461	505	490	525	500	525	503	532
Lambs under one year old	BFCP	19 381	9 258	20 596	9 665	21 564	9 347	22 023	9 510	21 942	8 515
All other sheep and lambs	BFCY	4 102	722	4 430	825	4 728	1 046	4 515	1 037	4 232	1 021
Total sheep and lambs	BFCM	38 756	27 873	41 007	29 103	42 988	29 678	43 799	30 147	43 621	28 932
Pigs											
Sows and gilts for breeding	BFCR	901	901	878	829	831	838	854	855	874	869
Boars being used for service	BFCS	44	45	43	41	42	42	43	44	45	44
Barren sows for fattening	BFCT	11	14	12	10	10	11	10	10	10	10
All other pigs	BFCU	6 987	6 956	7 049	6 746	6 627	6 493	6 542	6 471	6 668	6 596
Total pigs	BFCQ	7 943	7 915	7 982	7 627	7 509	7 383	7 449	7 380	7 596	7 519
Poultry											
Ducks and geese	BFCW	1 768	1 553	1 848	1 941	2 110	2 794	2 217	2 102	2 191	2 041
Total fowls	BFCV	128 801	127 006	130 998	128 159	120 351	117 690	124 615	118 449	127 228	118 748

1 Figures include estimates for minor holdings in England and Wales but not for Scotland and Northern Ireland. For further details refer to the *Supplement of Definitions and Explanatory Notes* in the January edition of *Monthly Digest*.

Source: Agricultural Departments

6.4 Animals slaughtered and meat produced
Monthly averages or totals for four or five week periods

	Animals slaughtered (thousands)							Meat produced (thousand tonnes)				
	Steers, heifers and young bulls	Cows and adult bulls	Calves	Ewes and rams	Other sheep and lambs	Sows and boars	Other pigs	Beef and veal	Mutton and lamb	Pork	Offal	Total
	BFHA	BFHB	BFHC	BFHD	BFHE	BFHF	BAKP	BFHK	BFHL	BFHM	BFHN	BFHJ
1986	257	65	6	117	1 172	28	1 272	88.5	24.1	62.2	12.9	188.2
1987[1]	261	76	6	128	1 186	28	1 289	93.1	24.6	65.3	14.0	197.2
1988	222	56	3	127	1 300	32	1 284	78.8	26.8	66.3	13.0	185.0
1989	227	58	2	147	1 488	28	1 182	81.5	30.5	60.5	13.5	186.0
1990	236	54	4	153	1 515	27	1 157	83.5	30.8	62.0	13.8	190.0
1991 Mar	231	51	4	137	1 277	29	1 056	81.7	26.7	57.5	12.9	178.8
Apr	263	63	4	162	1 223	34	1 308	92.4	26.9	70.9	14.4	204.6
May	204	49	2	118	1 038	25	1 014	72.1	21.9	53.9	11.3	159.3
Jun	215	53	2	126	1 474	26	1 076	76.1	29.7	57.6	12.8	176.2
Jul	224	62	5	135	2 020	34	1 328	80.4	39.7	73.4	15.0	208.6
Aug	197	52	5	120	1 669	26	1 069	71.3	32.7	58.4	12.8	175.2
Sep	220	60	7	129	1 917	30	1 137	79.7	36.9	63.8	14.2	194.6
Oct	303	82	6	165	2 302	38	1 413	110.0	44.2	79.9	18.4	252.5
Nov	262	76	4	137	1 796	34	1 187	96.8	34.7	66.7	15.6	213.8
Dec	215	53	4	128	1 430	28	1 114	76.8	28.3	62.7	12.8	180.5
1992 Jan	249	70	4	136	1 320	39	1 319	93.7	27.8	74.2	14.7	210.5
Feb	215	52	2	110	973	32	1 087	77.6	21.0	60.9	11.9	171.4
Mar	211	47	2	106	989	31	1 067	75.7	21.3	60.4	11.7	169.1
Apr	256	56	2	129	1 241	34	1 255	90.9	26.6	70.3	14.2	202.0
May	183	42	2	98	989	26	1 001	65.3	20.8	55.7	10.6	152.3
Jun	185	43	2	123	1 306	27	1 025	66.2	26.7	69.1	11.4	173.4

1 53 week year.

Source: Ministry of Agriculture, Fisheries and Food

6.5 Cereals and cereal products
Monthly averages or totals for four or five week periods

Thousand tonnes

	Wheat and flour						Oats				Barley				
	Sales of home-grown wheat for food	Wheat milled Home-produced	Imported	Stocks (including flour as wheat)	Flour produced	Flour disposals	Sales of home-grown oats for milling	Oats milled	Products of oat-milling	Stocks	Sales of home-grown barley for food[1]	Disposals for food and brewing	Stocks	Breakfast cereals:[2] production	Biscuits: production
	BFDA	BFDB	BFDC	BFDD	BFDE	BFDF	BFDG	BFDH	BFDI	BFDJ	BFDK	BFDL	BFDM	BFDN	BFDO
1985	301	301	95	1 033	304	303	13	12	7	36	374	395	975	21	58
1986	272	257	146	1 263	308	305	13	13	8	37	473	472	1 143	20	59
1987	322	318	87	918	319	313	14	13	8	27	394	397	795	22	58
1988	284	281	147	952	333	325	16	15	9	35	382	399	845	23	..
1989	352	347	73	918	328	328	20	19	11	43	410	416	1 043	23	..
1991 Feb	365	321	40	889	289	293	15	20	11	31	370	414	971	23	..
Mar	358	336	42	894	303	311	16	17	10	29	263	331	919	27	..
Apr	418	387	50	878	354	351	14	18	10	24	359	438	801	25	..
May	335	314	43	876	290	293	15	16	9	24	219	314	519	22	..
Jun	370	384	47	827	321	319	14	15	9	22	99	203	504	28	..
Jul[3]	361	400	54	716	365	361	16	18	10	19	43	155	385	22	..
Aug[3]	246	307	55	650	291	298	15	16	9	19	516	243	664	21	..
Sep[3]	304	335	58	618	311	315	24	17	9	28	650	378	943	27	..
Oct[3]	392	406	67	614	379	371	26	20	12	35	288	266	961	26	..
Nov[3]	363	341	55	625	316	320	20	21	12	34	261	306	918	23	..
Dec[3]	329	365	53	647	285	291	17	18	11	34	351	405	864	24	..
1992 Jan[3]	374	364	62	658	341	341	21	23	13	30	282	327	828	22	..
Feb[3]	337	309	51	671	289	296	20	19	11	31	328	357	805	23	..
Mar[3]	319	327	55	656	305	306	15	17	9	28	394	460	746	28	..
Apr[3]	365	366	61	639	345	352	13	18	10	25	242	327	665	23	..
May[3]	339	317	50	663	292	293	15	17	10	22	222	316	572	24	..

1 Including quantities used for brewing, malting and distilling.
2 Other than oatmeal and oatmeal flakes.
3 Provisional.

Source: Ministry of Agriculture, Fisheries and Food

6.6 Production of compound feedingstuffs
Monthly averages

Thousand tonnes

	Cattle feed	Calf feed	Pig feed	Poultry feed	Other compounds	Total
	BFFB	BFFC	BFFD	BFFE	BFFF	BFFA
1986	375.0	33.6	183.3	288.8	53.3	934.0
1987	319.2	29.1	182.7	299.4	56.1	886.4
1988	313.3	28.7	182.6	307.8	62.2	894.6
1989	321.9	28.3	177.8	292.8	64.3	885.0
1990	321.8	26.5	186.5	309.4	69.0	913.1
1989 Q1	372.5	33.8	169.2	287.4	115.5	978.4
Q2	256.7	22.8	174.5	286.4	54.3	794.7
Q3	272.0	21.8	180.0	295.6	36.7	806.0
Q4	386.2	34.7	187.5	301.9	50.7	960.8
1990 Q1	397.5	32.9	176.7	294.4	129.5	1 031.0
Q2	253.8	19.9	184.6	317.0	51.4	826.7
Q3	272.4	21.1	193.9	332.0	40.6	859.8
Q4	372.4	32.7	204.3	336.1	59.7	1 005.2
1991 Q1	374.5	29.4	187.6	310.1	141.4	1 043.1
Q2	255.2	20.1	194.4	332.5	61.9	864.0
Q3	253.4	16.1	202.5	327.1	30.5	829.7
Q4	362.4	24.7	208.7	321.8	54.7	972.4
1992 Q1	378.8	20.8	196.5	304.3	142.8	1 043.0

Source: Ministry of Agriculture, Fisheries and Food

6.7 Potatoes, sugar and jam
Monthly averages, calendar months or totals for four or five week periods

Thousand tonnes

	Potatoes				Sugar (as refined)						
	Movement into human consumption in the United Kingdom				Quota production from home-grown sugar beet	Disposals			Syrup and treacle: production	Glucose: production	Jam and marmalade: production
	From home crop	Imports[4]	Exports	Stocks[1,2]		Total[3]	For food in the United Kingdom	Stocks			
	BFGA	BFGB	BFGC	BFGD	BFGF	BFGG	BFGH	BFGI	BFGJ	BFGK	BFGL
1986	459	68	13	3 111	112.1	188.3	185.7	907.9	4.3	39.3	14.5
1987	456	64	13	3 168	106.4	191.5	189.7	899.1	4.4	37.6	14.6
1988	463	60	8	3 347	109.1	193.0	191.7	978.4	4.4	41.6	14.5
1989	414	81	12	2 933	86.5	196.2	194.7	860.0	4.3	45.2	15.1
1990	410	..	..	..	..	..	..	..	..	..	..
1991 Mar	413	62	21	-	-	210.7	210.5	760.6	4.2	46.8	..
Apr	399	81	18	-	-	170.5	168.5	696.6	5.3	49.6	..
May	376	100	14	-	-	188.0	187.6	600.4	3.1	48.6	..
Jun	282[†]	120	10	-	-	229.5	224.7	507.1	4.4	53.0	..
Jul	369	77	5	-	-	184.2	179.9	398.3	4.8	42.8	..
Aug	382	65	8	-	-	205.2	201.5	305.8	3.6	46.0	..
Sep	457	48	5	-	12.3	184.8	173.9	228.4	4.0	50.6	..
Oct	508	51	13	4 266	292.2	184.8	180.8	414.1	5.5	52.3	..
Nov	447	53	26	3 589	306.1	236.5	233.4	614.3	4.9	49.1	..
Dec	421	55	27	-	295.4	171.7	166.8	824.1	3.1	32.4	..
1992 Jan	419	70	21	2 752	195.2	162.0	156.7	979.4	4.4	42.6	..
Feb	423	77	19	2 019	..	177.7[†]	171.5	1 084.8	3.9	42.3	..
Mar	426	81	20	..	..	175.5[†]	173.5[†]	803.9	4.2	53.1	..
Apr	386	..	..	..	..	204.6	197.7	717.3	4.4	41.5	..
May	328	..	..	..	..	175.9	172.9	607.4	3.4	47.5	..
Jun	..	..	..	..	..	..	..	..	3.6	52.0	..

For further information refer to Section 6 of the *Supplement of Definitions and Explanatory Notes* in the January edition of *Monthly Digest*.
1 Changes in stocks differ from movements into human consumption due to wastage when dressing potatoes on producers'/merchants' premises.

2 Estimate of end - December stocks based on Potato Marketing returns.
3 From January 1984, total UK consumption by food and other industries (including sugar used in the chemical industry).
4 Excludes Channel Isles exports to G.B.

Sources: Ministry of Agriculture, Fisheries and Food;
Central Statistical Office

6.8 Production of bacon, ham and canned meat and meat stocks in cold storage
Monthly averages or totals for four or five week periods   Monthly averages or end of period stocks

Thousand tonnes

	Bacon and ham			Meat stocks in cold storage				
	Production	Disposals (including for canning)	Canned meat: production	Beef and veal	Mutton and lamb	Pork	Offal	Total
	BAKQ	BFIC	BFID	BFIF	BFIG	BFIH	BFII	BFIE
1987	16.6	38.2	7.8	84.3	26.6	7.1	12.5	130.5
1988	16.6	37.9	7.2	78.3	20.7	10.4	12.0	121.4
1989	16.2	37.9	9.8[†]	55.7	15.8	8.8	11.5	91.8
1990	15.0	36.8	8.9	..	..	..	..	..
1991	14.6	35.8	12.1	..	..	..	..	..
1991 Feb	12.8	33.2	11.8[†]	116.0	25.7	11.9	9.9	163.5
Mar	13.0	34.6	-	125.0	23.8	10.8	9.0	168.6
Apr	17.2	38.6	-	129.7	22.4	10.2	9.6	171.8
May	14.2	36.5	12.0	137.6	19.1	10.4	7.9	175.0
Jun	14.5	35.5	-	142.6	17.1	9.6	7.5	176.8
Jul	16.5	35.4	-	144.8	21.5	11.7	8.3	186.3
Aug	13.6	34.1	11.9	142.2	23.9	11.5	9.3	186.9
Sep	13.6	32.5	-	145.2	22.4	11.1	9.4	188.0
Oct	16.6	39.1	-	156.2	21.4	10.8	9.6	198.0
Nov	14.5	37.1	12.6	163.1	18.7	10.9	9.6	202.3
Dec	12.7	32.7	-	170.4	20.5	11.2	9.9	212.0
1992 Jan	16.8	36.2	-	164.3	21.2	10.5	10.9	206.9
Feb	13.2	31.8	-	167.1	17.2	9.0	8.6	201.8
Mar	12.9	30.1	11.4	173.0	16.2	9.9	9.2	208.2
Apr	15.7	37.0	-	169.0	13.1	9.0	8.1	199.2
May	12.6	33.5	-	165.1	15.8	8.8	8.6	198.3
Jun	13.3	-	-	168.9	16.3	9.4	8.7	203.3

Sources: Ministry of Agriculture, Fisheries and Food;
Central Statistical Office

6.9 Fish, oils and fats
Monthly averages, calendar months or totals for four or five week periods; stocks: end of period

Thousand tonnes

	Fresh, frozen and cured fish				Oilseeds and nuts			Vegetable oil Crude oil equivalent		Marine oil Crude oil equivalent				
		Disposals										Margar-ine: produc-tion	Solid cooking fat	Other table spreads
			For food in the United Kingdom				Stocks: crude oil equiv-alent							
	UK landings	Total (landed weight)	Landed weight	Filleted weight	Crushed	Crude oil produced		Disposals	Stocks[1]	Usage[2]	Stocks[3]			
	BFJA	BFJB	BFJC	BFJD	BFJE	BFJF	BFJG	BFJJ	BFJK	BFJL	BFJM	BFJN	BFJO	BFJP
1985	57.1	95.5	59.3	24.7	101.1	35.4	37.2	86.0	71.5	16.3	42.3	31.5	9.0	-
1986	51.9	51.9	59.3	24.7	106.1	35.9	38.5	99.6	74.5	14.9	22.4	32.0	8.7	6.3
1987	65.9	97.7	69.8	29.1	127.2	46.7	36.2	117.6	95.0	13.9	15.9	32.6	8.9	6.1
1988	-	..	..	..	155.9	55.0	25.8	129.6	86.3	10.7	12.0	31.3	8.6	8.0
1989	66.6	..	..	..	143.7	49.1	24.0	124.5	86.2	11.8	10.7	30.6	11.6	10.1
1991 Apr	23.1	-	-	-	148.1	47.0	35.3	123.5	93.7	11.6	8.2	32.2	11.9	9.4
May	36.0	64.7	37.8	16.6	140.2	43.6	18.2	160.8	77.6	11.4	9.3	28.1	8.9	9.8
Jun	29.0	-	-	-	· 105.4	31.8	6.5	116.7	72.5	7.8	11.2	25.9	8.8	9.6
Jul	49.5	-	-	-	57.8	14.3	13.5	132.5	76.1	10.2	11.6	32.2	9.0	9.6
Aug	86.6	195.3	78.5	37.7	123.2	46.6	20.1	146.8	79.6	8.6	13.0	25.3	7.5	7.7
Sep	45.8	-	-	-	162.4	64.0	19.9	138.0	80.7	9.9	12.4	29.3	9.6	10.1
Oct	50.2	-	-	-	138.9	56.8	20.3	160.5	75.0	11.9	11.8	36.6	11.0	8.9
Nov	51.4	109.9	71.9	30.0	146.4	52.4	18.9	143.5	74.8	10.5	10.5	32.2	9.6	10.1
Dec	59.0	-	-	-	157.2	59.7	27.9	136.2	83.5	9.0	8.6	26.3	8.7	8.9
1992 Jan	84.3	-	-	-	150.9	51.7	21.9	142.7[†]	85.1[†]	9.4	12.9	29.3	9.8	8.7
Feb	59.9	79.0	49.7	20.7	155.6	55.4	29.5	131.6	94.0	8.3	11.9	28.3	7.4	10.4
Mar	27.0	..	..	..	174.5	64.3	26.8	151.4	92.3	8.9	12.0	28.7	9.0	10.0
Apr	30.6	..	..	..	157.8	54.4	27.4	165.4	80.6	9.9	10.6	34.1	10.0	9.4
May	32.7	..	..	..	148.8	53.3	34.6	113.4	94.5	8.6	9.0	29.0	8.6	10.5

1 Comprising stocks of crude and refined oils held by seed crushers, oil refiners and manufacturers of margarine, solid cooking fat and other table spreads.
2 For the manufacture of margarine, solid cooking fat and other table spreads only.

3 Including quantities held by seed crushers, hardeners, and refiners of oil, and manufacturers of margarine.

Source: Ministry of Agriculture, Fisheries and Food

6.10 Milk, milk products and eggs
Monthly averages or calendar months; stocks: end of period

	Million litres			Thousand tonnes										Supply of hen eggs for human consump-tion (million dozen)[1,2]
				Condensed and evaporated milk		Milk powder				Butter		Cheese		
						Full-cream		Skimmed						
	Liquid milk	Milk for manufac-ture	Total milk dis-posals	Pro-duction	Stocks	Pro-duction	Stocks	Pro-duction	Stocks	Pro-duction	Stocks	Pro-duction	Stocks	
	BFKB	BFKC	BFKA	BFKH	BFKI	BFKJ	BFKK	BFKL	BFKM	BFKD	BFKE	BFKF	BFKG	BFKN
1985	576	679	1 272	15.0	8.4	5.1	3.3	20.1	22.6	16.8	221.7	21.3	115.2	77.3
1986	572	699	1 288	14.5	6.5	4.7	2.2	22.3	18.7	18.5	256.9	21.4	123.5	74.1
1987	569	647	1 219	15.0	9.0	7.8	4.5	16.1	18.4	14.7	157.9	22.0	112.6	73.1
1988	568	619	1 187	15.3	10.3	8.7	6.5	11.4	21.7	11.6	51.6	24.8	145.6	72.5
1989	567	598	1 165	17.3	14.9	8.0	6.5	11.1	20.7	10.8	33.0	23.3	135.8	64.1
1991 Apr	552	660	1 214	16.5	11.3	4.2	3.3	12.6	13.36	11.0	54.70	31.6	137.9	-
May	572	748	1 321	16.5	10.4	5.0	2.4	15.7	18.15	13.3	58.50	35.9	147.8	71.0
Jun	555	626	1 182	17.9	11.2	6.6	2.9	11.5	17.97	9.7	57.70	30.0	161.1	-
Jul	560	570	1 131	16.2	10.0	6.4	3.9	8.8	17.41	8.8	58.20	24.6	154.0	-
Aug	555	531	1 088	15.3	10.1	5.9	4.2	9.4	16.11	8.5	57.20	21.8	151.3	71.6
Sep	558	488	1 047	17.7	10.1	5.8	1.9	8.8	11.80	7.5	54.50	19.9	146.4	-
Oct	589	492	1 082	16.2	8.0	6.4	2.2	6.8	10.51	6.6	44.00	21.3	139.7	-
Nov	571	471	1 043	17.3	8.5	7.1	2.5	6.6	9.22	6.4	40.70	18.8	130.7	68.7
Dec	567	546	1 113	16.1	9.4	8.1	4.2	11.2	11.15	6.9	41.60	21.2	124.6	-
1992 Jan	561	585	1 146	14.1	9.3	5.3	4.9	8.4	8.31	8.6	42.20	29.1	125.4	-
Feb	539	543	1 083	15.8	8.5	5.1	3.5	8.1	7.63	8.2	42.30	21.1	123.8	67.2
Mar	580	599	1 180	19.1	8.7	7.0	2.9	8.6	5.11	8.7	44.00	25.8	126.6	-
Apr	548	621[†]	1 170[†]	17.6	8.3	6.7	2.3	9.3	7.43	9.3	50.00	26.3	130.8	-
May	559	706	1 265	17.1	8.9	7.0	2.2	11.5	9.83	9.7	48.30	32.0	139.7	68.7
Jun	548	577	1 126	17.5	10.6	7.9	3.1	6.1	7.49	6.5	..	29.3	..	..

For further information refer to section 6 of the *Supplement of Definitions and Explanatory Notes* in the January edition of *Monthly Digest*.
1 Includes first and second quality eggs broken out.

2 This series has been revised as a result of changes in survey methodology and grossing up procedures.

Source: Ministry of Agriculture, Fisheries and Food

6.11 Canned fruit, vegetables and soups, cocoa, chocolate, tea, coffee and soft drinks
Monthly averages, calendar months or totals for four or five week periods; stocks: end of period

	Thousand tonnes														Million litres	
	Canned and bottled fruit		Canned vegetables		Soups: pro-duction[2]	Cocoa beans: pro-duction[3]	Chocolate and sugar confectionery			Tea		Raw coffee		Soft drinks	
	Pro-duction	Stocks[1]	Pro-duction	Stocks[1]			Pro-duction	Dis-posals	Stocks[1]	Dis-posals[4]	Stocks	Dis-posals	Stocks	Concen-trated: sales	Unconcen-trated: sales
	BFLA	BFLB	BFLC	BFLD	BFLE	BFLF	BFLG	BFLH	BFLI	BFLJ	BFLK	BFLL	BFLM	BFLN	BFLO
1987	3.4	13.2	60.2	153.2	27.4	7.9	70.00	73.60	63.1	13.1	51.1	9.4	8.40	46.5	309.4
1988	3.0	7.9	58.4	106.6	26.2	8.4	75.55	66.56	..	13.6	50.2	8.5	8.30	47.2	302.3
1989	2.9	9.3	61.3	134.5	..	9.6	67.27	74.80	..	13.5	51.4	8.2	7.20	46.2	342.7
1990	..	..	..	..	..	10.4	70.68	80.39	..	12.1	48.4	8.7	11.30	46.5	359.6
1991	..	..	..	..	..	12.4	..	..	..	12.6	42.8	8.4	10.10	..	..
1991 Jan	..	..	..	..	..	-	56.52	65.60	..	-	-	-	-	-	-
Feb	..	..	..	..	..	11.0	65.37	73.60	..	12.6	43.6	8.6	9.7	36.6	282.4
Mar	..	..	..	..	..	-	73.57†	82.77†	..	-	-	-	-		
Apr	..	..	..	..	..	-	65.00	74.28	..	-	-	-	-	..	..
May	..	..	..	..	..	12.0	64.98	75.10	..	.13.0	43.3	8.8	9.3	..	..
Jun	..	..	..	..	..	-	60.36	71.37	..	-	-	-	-		
Jul	..	..	..	..	..	-	60.95	73.09	..					..	..
Aug	..	..	..	..	..	14.0	65.61	75.82	..	11.5	44.0	7.8	10.0		
Sep	..	..	..	..	..	-	78.80	92.32	..	-	-	-	-	..	..
Oct	..	..	..	..	..	-	92.27	106.83	..	-	-	-	-	..	..
Nov	..	..	..	..	..	12.5	85.74	98.94	..	13.5	42.8	8.6	10.1	..	..
Dec	..	..	..	..	..	..	74.94	85.30	..	-	-	-	-		
1992 Jan	..	..	..	..	..	..	63.05	73.46	..	-	-	-	-	..	..
Feb	..	..	..	..	..	..	79.27	88.91	..	12.3	42.2	9.1	9.0	..	..
Mar	..	..	..	..	..	..	83.56	94.61	..	..	..	..	..	..	..
Apr	..	..	..	..	..	..	72.45	82.87	..	..	..	..	..	..	..

1 Manufacturers' stocks only.
2 Canned and powdered soups.
3 Quantity of beans ground.
4 Excluding exports.

Sources: Ministry of Agriculture, Fisheries and Food;
Central Statistical Office

6.12 Tobacco products
Monthly averages or calendar months

	Released for home consumption										
	Thousand million			Million kilogrammes							Total tobacco products other than cigarettes
	Cigarettes			Home-produced				Imported			
	Home produced	Imported	Total	Cigars	Other tobacco products		Total	Cigars	Other tobacco products[1]	Total	
					Hand-rolling	Other[1]					
	BFMB	BFMC	BFMA	BFMF	BFMG	BFMH	BFME	BFMJ	BFMK	BFMI	BFMD
1986	6.90	0.98	7.92	0.19	0.40	0.23	0.82	0.016	0.005	0.021	0.84
1987	7.50	0.98	8.47	0.20	0.40	0.22	0.82	0.016	0.007	0.022	0.84
1988	7.30	0.78	8.11	0.20	0.38	0.20	0.77	0.017	0.008	0.025	0.80
1989	7.40	0.70	8.00	0.19	0.36	0.19	0.74	0.015	0.011	0.026	0.76
1990	7.27	0.86	8.13	0.18	0.34	0.18	0.70	0.013	0.011	0.024	0.72
1991 Aug	7.18	0.75	7.93	0.17	0.36	0.17	0.70	0.010	0.014	0.024	0.72
Sep	6.81	0.71	7.52	0.17	0.32	0.16	0.65	0.010	0.015	0.025	0.68
Oct	13.80	1.49	15.29	0.26	0.60	0.29	1.15	0.016	0.018	0.034	1.18
Nov	3.18	0.99	4.17	0.34	0.13	0.09	0.56	0.017	0.014	0.031	0.59
Dec	9.66	1.08	10.74	0.09	0.33	0.16	0.58	0.010	0.016	0.026	0.61
1992 Jan	2.97	0.26	3.23	0.06	0.25	0.12	0.43	0.009	0.012	0.021	0.45
Feb	9.79	0.67	10.46	0.12	0.38	0.18	0.68	0.008	0.018	0.026	0.71
Mar	10.77†	1.88†	12.65†	0.14	0.42	0.16	0.72	0.019	0.017	0.036	0.76
Apr	1.68†	0.14†	1.82†	0.12	0.18	0.14	0.44	0.005	0.011	0.016	0.46
May	4.12	0.31	4.43	0.14	0.29	0.14	0.57	0.008	0.014	0.022	0.59
Jun	..	..	..	0.16	0.32	0.16	0.64	..	..	..	..

1 Excluding snuff.

Source: HM Customs and Excise

6.13 Alcoholic drink
Monthly averages or calendar months

		Thousand hectolitres									Thousand hectolitres of alcohol		
		Released for home consumption									Released for home consumption		
		Beer			Wine of fresh grapes						Spirits		
					Still								
	Beer pro-duction[1]	Home produced[2]	Imported	Total	Not exceeding 15%[3,4]	15% or more[3]	Total sparkling	Total	Made wine	Cider and perry	Home produced whisky	Other[5]	Spirits: total pro-duction[6]
	BFNK	BFNM	BFNN	BFNL	BFNO	BFNP	BFNS	BFNT	BFNV	BFNW	BFNX	BFNY	BFNZ
1984	5 009	4 937	237	5 173	346.0	85.2	18.6	449.8	41.0	271.6	36.2	39.9	235.3
1985	4 971	4 869	256	5 126	377.1	71.8	21.5	470.3	44.8	264.5	38.4	42.7	244.9
1986	4 953	4 826	275	5 101	421.8	46.6	23.4	491.8	44.0	269.4	38.0	42.6	247.0
1987	4 991	4 877	288	5 165	456.2	40.8	26.3	523.2	46.8	268.9	37.2	44.6	261.3
1988	5 012	4 909	363	5 272	473.3	37.6	29.3	540.2	49.5	258.5	37.6	48.5	297.4
1989	5 001	4 890	378	5 268	489.3	33.9	32.7	555.8	49.2	271.9	35.9	47.6	350.9
1990	4 971	4 836	422	5 257	491.1	31.5	30.4	552.4	58.8	305.5	34.5	47.2	389.7
1988 Oct	4 942	4 850	412	5 262	619.2	57.3	38.3	714.8	51.3	314.7	51.4	63.6	-
Nov	5 778	5 671	473	6 144	787.1	87.9	50.8	925.9	81.4	320.8	85.6	101.1	1 075.7
Dec	4 469	4 364	385	4 749	596.8	67.0	47.5	711.4	75.6	283.6	52.8	65.2	-
1989 Jan	4 233	4 137	353	4 490	271.4	18.0	23.3	312.7	26.7	158.0	14.1	23.5	-
Feb	4 456	4 360	264	4 624	302.5	20.2	19.7	342.3	48.2	217.6	23.8	36.6	1 042.9
Mar	4 742	4 634	334	4 968	429.0	30.3	25.8	485.1	63.5	208.1	38.3	52.7	
Apr	4 633	4 539	329	4 868	423.7	20.3	23.8	467.8	38.8	243.3	21.3	24.3	
May	5 139	5 029	401	5 430	466.7	21.8	28.3	516.8	38.4	253.5	27.6	35.2	1 145.0
Jun	5 792	5 652	438	6 090	531.8	22.2	37.6	591.6	46.9	312.3	29.1	40.0	-
Jul	5 267	5 139	376	5 515	488.7	21.9	34.2	544.8	34.9	357.8	29.7	43.8	-
Aug	5 622	5 514	376	5 890	484.0	22.8	29.3	536.0	39.9	374.6	32.9	42.4	864.6
Sep	5 132	5 024	375	5 399	462.4	27.7	28.0	518.1	39.6	201.4	30.7	41.6	-
Oct	5 177	5 058	422	5 480	600.1	59.0	37.0	696.1	56.3	316.6	49.7	64.8	-
Nov	5 723	5 611	522	6 133	798.4	80.9	56.3	935.6	86.3	345.1	84.0	102.3	1 159.0
Dec	4 099	3 982	343	4 325	612.7	61.4	48.7	722.7	71.1	274.0	49.0	63.7	-
1990 Jan	4 124	4 029	321	4 350	270.0	16.1	20.1	306.2	39.9	189.8	12.8	24.9	-
Feb	3 997	3 886	288	4 174	320.5	18.0	19.7	358.1	43.9	260.3	23.3	30.3	1 150.2
Mar	5 028	4 912	389	5 301	413.1	22.1	22.2	457.3	66.5	255.8	34.4	51.2	-
Apr	4 786	4 652	324	4 976	438.8	22.4	25.2	486.3	41.7	273.8	22.6	31.0	-
May	5 756	5 591	436	6 027	534.4	24.9	31.2	590.5	47.2	309.7	28.1	41.4	1 243.1
Jun	5 508	5 345	477	5 822	476.2	21.8	28.3	526.3	68.1	301.2	28.8	40.1	-
Jul	5 052	4 897	447	5 344	523.8	23.4	31.1	578.3	57.9	400.4	29.3	39.9	-
Aug	5 578	5 430	482	5 912	458.1	18.1	25.4	501.7	48.2	327.9	23.3	35.4	961.3
Sep	4 808	4 687	420	5 106	422.4	22.8	25.7	470.9	44.6	334.7	27.5	38.6	-
Oct	5 435	5 295	480	5 775	639.2	45.4	36.6	720.2	81.6	349.5	46.0	59.5	-
Nov	5 689	5 539	597	6 136	799.1	76.6	53.7	929.5	88.5	344.4	81.2	98.5	1 321.3
Dec	3 892	3 763	406	4 168	597.0	66.6	46.1	709.7	77.9	318.9	56.1	75.4	-
1991 Jan	4 000	3 887	329	4 216	257.0	13.9	16.5	287.4	30.5	202.8	12.7	22.8	-
Feb	3 940	3 843	299	4 142	295.5	16.5	13.5	325.5	40.3	274.3	20.2	28.2	1 054.4
Mar	4 686	4 566	351	4 918	481.4	26.9	21.3	529.6	57.6	289.4	44.9	55.2	-
Apr	4 987	4 828	418	5 247	460.3	19.6	19.9	499.7	41.5	282.2	15.7	25.7	-
May	5 252	5 100	451	5 551	492.4	22.0	23.6	538.0	41.8	241.4	22.9	33.3	1 248.9
Jun	4 808	4 627	466	5 093	482.7	20.1	28.9	531.7	48.5	291.7	26.6	35.1	-
Jul	5 203	5 022	484	5 506	522.9	23.5	26.2	572.4	56.9	375.4	27.2	39.1	-
Aug	4 953	4 781	498	5 279	471.2	24.9	21.4	517.6	56.1	320.0	26.4	39.2	961.4
Sep	4 915	4 769	491	5 260	470.9	19.5	21.8	512.2	63.9	344.1	26.0	37.8	-
Oct	5 571	5 406	551	5 958	659.6	45.8	35.6	741.0	81.3	229.8	39.7	56.4	-
Nov	5 221	5 055	570	5 624	771.2	58.6	43.7	873.5	107.2	498.1	68.8	86.1	1 211.1
Dec	3 823	3 631	421	4 052	614.8	65.5	43.9	724.2	75.8	363.3	51.4	87.9	-
1992 Jan	3 712	3 613	318	3 931	273.9	15.3	13.6	302.8	41.0	452.3	10.4	20.9	-
Feb	3 954	3 845	319	4 164	332.0	16.9	12.3	361.3	40.9	219.1	22.5	28.5	1 064.5
Mar	4 586	4 453	434	4 887	475.4	21.6	17.7	514.7	71.0	440.4	35.1	44.5	-
Apr	4 697	4 542	430	4 971	480.6	20.6	18.1	519.3	51.7	348.3	19.6	28.4	-
May	4 953	4 777	463	5 240	503.2	19.1	21.8	544.1	53.0	292.7	21.3	34.3	-

1 The figures relating to both home production and releases for home consumption take account of brewing at high gravity with the addition of some brewing liquor after fermentation.
2 Home produced figures are beer production less exports.
3 Percentage alcohol by volume.
4 For the period April 1984 to July 1985 the middle band included wine of a strength of exactly 15 per cent.

5 Includes imported spirits.
6 A small quantity of molasses spirit is used in beverage spirit production. See Section 9 of the *Supplement of Definitions and Explanatory Notes* in the January edition of *Monthly Digest*.

Source: HM Customs and Excise

7 Production, output and costs

7.1 Output of the production industries

					Summary					
						Manufacturing industries				
	Total production industries	Energy and water supply	Total manufac- turing industries	Metals	Other minerals and mineral[2] products	Chemicals and man-made fibres	Engineering and allied industries	Food, drink and tobacco	Textiles, footwear, clothing and leather	Other manufac- turing
Class[3]	DIV 1-4	DIV 1	DIV 2-4	21-22	23-24	25-26	31-37	41-42	43-45	46-49
Weights	*1000*	*309*	*691*	*26*	*35*	*71*	*295*	*91*	*47*	*126*
	DVIM	DVIN	DVIS	DVIT	DVIU	DVIV	DVIY	DVJE	DVJH	DVJK
1985	100.0	100.0	100.0	100.0	100.0	100.0	100.0	100.0	100.0	100.0
1986	102.4	105.0	101.3	100.3	101.3	101.8	100.2	100.8	100.7	104.5
1987	105.7	103.9	106.6	108.6	106.8	109.0	103.7	103.2	103.7	115.0
1988	109.5	99.3	114.1	122.3	117.3	114.2	112.3	104.7	102.0	126.6
1989	109.9	89.6	118.9	124.7	120.1	119.4	119.9	105.6	98.3	132.3
1990	109.3	88.9	118.4	121.3	113.4	118.3	119.8	106.3	95.9	133.2
1991	106.0	92.3	112.2	110.0	103.0	121.5	111.0	106.1	87.7	126.1
Seasonally adjusted										
1987 Q1	103.7	105.2	103.0	103.1	101.0	105.9	99.8	102.4	101.9	110.0
Q2	104.8	102.9	105.6	107.8	106.1	106.8	102.6	103.0	103.8	114.1
Q3	106.7	103.6	108.1	110.3	109.6	111.0	105.3	103.3	105.3	116.6
Q4	107.8	103.8	109.6	113.1	110.4	112.2	106.9	104.3	103.8	119.2
1988 Q1	107.9	101.1	110.9	118.5	116.9	111.1	108.0	103.6	103.5	122.3
Q2	109.5	102.9	112.4	120.7	115.0	112.5	110.8	104.7	100.8	123.8
Q3	110.3	98.8	115.5	124.2	116.6	116.2	113.6	105.7	102.0	129.4
Q4	110.4	94.5	117.4	125.8	120.7	117.0	117.0	104.9	101.5	131.0
1989 Q1	109.6	89.1	118.7	130.7	121.9	118.7	118.9	104.6	99.8	132.4
Q2	109.1	87.1	118.9	122.1	122.2	118.3	119.7	105.8	99.2	132.6
Q3	110.5	90.8	119.2	122.6	119.8	120.4	121.1	105.6	97.3	131.4
Q4	110.4	91.4	118.9	123.3	116.4	120.1	120.0	106.1	96.8	132.7
1990 Q1	109.9	88.5	119.5	120.1	116.0	120.6	120.3	106.3	98.6	134.8
Q2	111.8	92.5	120.4	125.8	114.9	119.8	122.5	106.1	97.4	135.3
Q3	108.6	86.0	118.7	123.2	113.2	118.3	120.2	107.0	94.9	133.3
Q4	107.0	88.8	115.1	116.1	109.6	114.4	116.3	105.9	92.6	129.3
1991 Q1	106.7	91.7	113.4	110.1	104.1	118.1	114.0	106.5	89.3	126.6
Q2	105.2	89.1	112.4	110.1	103.0	120.3	111.6	106.3	87.9	126.3
Q3	106.2	92.7	112.2	110.9	104.2	123.8	110.3	106.0	87.6	126.3
Q4	106.1	95.7	110.7	109.0	100.6	123.7	108.0	105.7	86.2	125.3
1992 Q1	105.3[†]	92.4	111.1[†]	109.8	100.1	123.4[†]	107.9	106.9[†]	86.4[†]	127.2[†]
Q2	105.0	90.4	111.6	108.6	100.5	121.7	108.6	108.0	86.8	128.2
1990 Nov	106.7	89.7	114.4	118	110	114	115	106	92	129
Dec	106.1	86.8	114.8	116	108	113	117	105	92	128
1991 Jan	105.9	86.4	114.6	110	105	118	116	107	90	127
Feb	107.1	94.8	112.7	108	103	117	113	105	89	126
Mar	107.1	93.9	113.0	112	104	119	113	107	89	127
Apr	104.3	85.9	112.4	108	102	121	112	106	88	126
May	104.1	85.7	112.2	110	103	120	112	107	87	126
Jun	107.3	95.6	112.5	112	104	121	111	106	88	127
Jul	107.2	93.9	113.2	111	105	124	112	106	88	126
Aug	105.5	91.1	111.9	112	104	123	110	106	88	127
Sep	105.9	93.1	111.6	110	103	124	109	106	87	126
Oct	106.3	97.1	110.5	109	101	124	107	106	87	125
Nov	106.1	95.4	110.8	110	101	123	109	104	87	125
Dec	105.8	94.7	110.7	108	100	123	108	107	85	126
1992 Jan	104.7[†]	92.9	110.0[†]	108	99	123[†]	107	106	85	126[†]
Feb	106.0	93.8	111.4	110	101	123	108	107	87	127
Mar	105.2	90.6	111.8	111	100	124	109[†]	107	87	128
Apr	105.7	92.1	111.8	108	100	122	110[†]	107	86	128
May	104.6	89.7[†]	111.3	110	100[†]	122	108	108[†]	87	128
Jun	104.8	89.5	111.5	108	101	122	108	109	87	128

Note: The figures contain, where appropriate, an adjustment for stock changes.

2 Mainly building materials.

3 Industries are grouped according to the *Standard Industrial Classification 1980.*

Source: Central Statistical Office

7.1 Output of the production industries
continued

				Detailed analysis			Chemicals and man-made fibres	
		Energy and water supply						
	Coal and coke	Extraction of mineral oil and natural gas	Mineral oil processing	Other energy and water supply[1]	Metals	Other minerals and mineral products[2]	Chemicals	Man-made fibres
Class[3]	11-12	13	14	15-17	21-22	23-24	25	26
Weights	36	180	12	81	26	35	69	2
	DVIO	DVIP	DVIQ	DVIR	DVIT	DVIU	DVIW	DVIX
1985	100.0	100.0	100.0	100.0	100.0	100.0	100.0	100.0
1986	114.2	101.2	100.9	109.9	100.3	101.3	101.7	103.6
1987	110.8	98.6	102.1	112.9	108.6	106.8	109.0	109.9
1988	109.9	90.1	109.4	113.8	122.3	117.3	114.4	107.8
1989	105.8	73.4	112.0	115.0	124.7	120.1	119.5	114.8
1990	97.4	73.4	111.1	116.4	121.3	113.4	118.3	117.2
1991	99.5	75.0	115.6	124.2	110.0	103.0	121.5	120.2
Seasonally adjusted [4]								
1987 Q1	111.1	100.6	95.8	114.4	103.1	101.0	105.7	111.9
Q2	110.0	97.6	100.3	112.0	107.8	106.1	106.6	111.4
Q3	111.6	99.0	104.2	110.1	110.3	109.6	111.1	108.1
Q4	110.3	97.2	108.2	115.0	113.1	110.4	112.3	108.2
1988 Q1	103.9	96.5	108.4	108.9	118.5	116.9	111.2	108.0
Q2	110.7	96.6	108.4	112.8	120.7	115.0	112.6	106.8
Q3	114.1	85.7	107.9	119.7	124.2	116.6	116.6	103.1
Q4	110.9	81.4	112.8	113.7	125.8	120.7	117.1	113.3
1989 Q1	113.3	72.2	115.3	111.9	130.7	121.9	119.1	104.6
Q2	109.5	66.6	108.2	119.6	122.1	122.2	118.6	110.6
Q3	101.4	76.5	111.5	114.8	122.6	119.8	120.3	122.6
Q4	99.2	78.2	113.0	114.0	123.3	116.4	120.1	121.5
1990 Q1	96.6	75.6	113.6	109.9	120.1	116.0	120.6	120.2
Q2	97.6	80.2	114.2	114.1	125.8	114.9	119.8	118.7
Q3	96.9	67.6	109.9	118.4	123.2	113.2	118.4	117.8
Q4	98.7	70.1	106.9	123.1	116.1	109.6	114.4	111.9
1991 Q1	101.3	74.5	110.2	122.9	110.1	104.1	118.2	112.8
Q2	100.8	68.0	115.5	126.8	110.1	103.0	120.3	121.6
Q3	97.6	77.7	117.8	120.1	110.9	104.2	123.9	121.1
Q4	98.3	79.6	118.8	126.9	109.0	100.6	123.6	125.1
1992 Q1	96.9	76.4	115.4	122.5	109.8	100.1	123.4[†]	120.9
Q2	91.8	73.1	111.4	125.1	108.6	100.5	121.7	122.3
1990 Nov	100	71	113	124	118	110	114	112
Dec	96	67	103	124	116	108	113	108
1991 Jan	101	65	117	122	110	105	118	111
Feb	102	77	106	130	108	103	117	112
Mar	101	81	107	116	112	104	119	115
Apr	99	64	115	124	108	102	121	120
May	102	62	116	126	110	103	119	123
Jun	101	78	115	130	112	104	121	123
Jul	100	78	118	122	111	105	124	121
Aug	93	76	118	119	112	104	123	120
Sep	100	78	118	119	110	103	124	122
Oct	101	81	123	128	109	101	124	125
Nov	99	79	116	127	110	101	123	126
Dec	95	79	118	125	108	100	123	125
1992 Jan	96	78	110	121	108	99	123[†]	122
Feb	97	78	116	124	110	101	123	121
Mar	97	73	120	122	111	100	124	120
Apr	93	75	112	127	108	100	122	119[†]
May	91	72	108	126	110	100[†]	122	123
Jun	91	73	114	122	108	101	121	124

1 Electricity and gas sent out, water supply and nuclear fuel production.
2 Mainly building materials.
3 Industries are grouped according to the *Standard Industrial Classification 1980*.
4 Unadjusted data may be obtained from the Central Statistical Office at the address shown inside the front cover of this publication.

Source: Central Statistical Office

43

7.1 Output of the production industries

continued

Detailed analysis (continued)

	Engineering and allied industries					Food, drink and tobacco		Textiles, footwear, clothing and leather		Other manufacturing	
	Metal goods nes	Mechanical engineering	Elect. and instrument engineering	Motor vehicles and parts	Other transport equipment	Food	Drink and tobacco	Textiles	Clothing, footwear and leather	Paper, printing and publishing	All other manufacturing[1]
Class[2]	31	32	33-34, 37	35	36	411-423	424-429	43	44-45	47	46, 48-49
Weights	37	85	98	38	37	66	25	22	25	71	55
	DVIZ	DVJA	DVJB	DVJC	DVJD	DVJF	DVJG	DVJI	DVJJ	DVJL	DVJM
1985	100.0	100.0	100.0	100.0	100.0	100.0	100.0	100.0	100.0	100.0	100.0
1986	99.4	96.5	100.6	96.9	111.9	101.3	99.6	100.2	101.0	104.2	105.0
1987	103.4	96.8	106.3	103.9	112.6	103.2	103.3	104.6	103.0	114.4	115.7
1988	111.5	105.3	117.9	119.1	107.8	105.1	103.6	101.8	102.1	125.2	128.5
1989	113.5	109.7	126.2	125.3	127.7	105.1	106.9	96.9	99.5	132.0	132.6
1990	110.8	112.3	125.4	121.6	129.7	105.5	108.6	92.4	98.9	133.9	132.3
1991	99.5	100.2	121.7	111.2	118.8	105.8	106.9	85.5	89.6	128.6	123.0
Seasonally adjusted [3]											
1987 Q1	100.8	93.5	105.2	95.6	103.7	102.8	101.4	102.3	101.6	109.3	110.8
Q2	102.1	95.8	103.2	101.7	118.0	103.4	101.7	103.8	103.8	114.2	113.9
Q3	104.2	98.5	106.8	106.5	117.0	103.5	103.1	106.9	104.0	116.0	117.3
Q4	106.2	99.4	110.0	111.9	111.9	103.3	106.8	105.3	102.6	118.0	120.8
1988 Q1	109.1	101.7	113.2	109.5	106.0	103.8	102.9	103.5	103.5	120.3	124.8
Q2	109.7	102.7	117.5	120.9	102.2	104.9	104.1	100.2	101.3	122.6	125.3
Q3	113.0	106.9	118.2	123.3	107.1	106.7	102.9	102.1	102.0	128.0	131.2
Q4	114.2	109.8	122.5	122.6	115.8	105.0	104.7	101.6	101.4	129.7	132.8
1989 Q1	114.8	111.0	122.5	127.3	122.7	105.1	103.4	99.9	99.8	131.1	134.0
Q2	113.8	107.5	124.9	127.1	132.5	105.5	106.5	99.3	99.2	131.3	134.3
Q3	113.1	109.1	128.6	126.8	131.0	104.5	108.7	95.3	99.1	131.6	131.2
Q4	112.2	111.3	128.7	120.1	124.4	105.1	108.8	93.3	99.8	134.0	131.0
1990 Q1	113.3	113.3	127.9	116.4	127.6	106.1	106.9	94.0	102.6	135.1	134.4
Q2	112.7	115.6	128.4	123.5	131.4	104.5	110.3	93.9	100.5	135.8	134.7
Q3	111.0	112.2	125.0	124.4	130.7	106.3	109.0	91.9	97.5	134.1	132.3
Q4	106.3	108.2	120.1	122.1	129.0	105.0	108.4	89.7	95.0	130.5	127.7
1991 Q1	101.6	104.0	123.4	114.5	123.7	106.2	107.2	85.8	92.2	128.5	124.2
Q2	99.3	100.5	123.3	112.6	117.5	106.1	107.0	85.5	89.8	128.5	123.5
Q3	99.6	99.2	121.3	110.4	117.4	105.8	106.6	85.2	89.5	128.8	123.0
Q4	97.6	97.1	118.8	107.2	116.4	105.2	106.8	85.4	86.9	128.4	121.3
1992 Q1	97.4[†]	95.8[†]	118.0[†]	111.7	115.4[†]	106.9[†]	106.7[†]	85.3[†]	87.3[†]	128.9[†]	124.9[†]
Q2	97.3	95.8	119.6	114.8	114.1	107.2	110.1	84.4	88.8	130.9	124.7
1990 Nov	105	107	119	119	125	105	110	89	94	130	127
Dec	106	106	121	120	136	105	106	89	94	129	126
1991 Jan	103	105	125	119	127	107	107	87	92	129	125
Feb	101	103	123	113	125	105	106	86	92	128	123
Mar	101	104	122	112	120	106	109	84	92	129	124
Apr	100	102	123	113	118	105	109	85	90	128	124
May	99	100	123	116	117	107	107	85	90	128	123
Jun	99	100	124	110	118	107	105	86	90	129	124
Jul	100	100	122	119	119	106	106	85	90	129	124
Aug	100	100	121	102	117	106	106	85	90	129	123
Sep	98	98	121	110	116	105	107	85	88	129	122
Oct	98	96	118	106	115	105	111	85	88	128	121
Nov	98	99	119	107	117	104	103	86	87	128	122
Dec	96	96	119	109	118	107	106	85	86	129	122
1992 Jan	97	94	117	107	116	106	106	84	86	129	124
Feb	98	96	119	113	115	108	106[†]	85	88	129[†]	125
Mar	98	97	118	116	115	107	108	87[†]	87	129	126
Apr	98[†]	95[†]	121[†]	116[†]	116[†]	107	108	85	87[†]	130	126
May	97	95	120	112	114	108[†]	110	84	89	131	124[†]
Jun	98	97	118	116	112	107	113	84	90	132	124

1 Including timber, furniture, rubber and plastics.
2 Industries are grouped according to the *Standard Industrial Classification 1980*.

3 Unadjusted data may be obtained from the Central Statistical Office at the address shown inside the front cover of this publication.

Source: Central Statistical Office

7.1 Output of the production industries

continued

Average 1985 = 100

	Consumer goods industries						Investment goods industries					Intermediate goods industries	
	Total consumer goods	Cars, etc	Other durables	Clothing and footwear etc	Food, drink and tobacco[1]	Other	Total investment goods	Electrical	Transport	Other	Total inter-mediate goods	Fuels	Materials
Weights[2]	243	21	26	27	84	85	195	59	56	80	562	299	263
	DVJP	DVJQ	DVJR	DVJS	DVJT	DVJU	DVJV	DVJW	DVJX	DVJY	DVJZ	DVKA	DVKB
1985	100.0	100.0	100.0	100.0	100.0	100.0	100.0	100.0	100.0	100.0	100.0	100.0	100.0
1986	101.2	95.0	103.2	100.2	100.6	102.9	100.6	98.4	107.0	97.7	103.6	105.1	102.0
1987	106.4	103.7	108.3	101.2	103.4	111.1	103.0	103.5	109.5	98.0	106.4	104.0	109.2
1988	112.0	118.1	120.3	98.8	104.4	119.7	111.1	115.9	111.9	107.0	107.9	99.2	117.7
1989	114.5	125.4	119.1	95.4	105.7	125.5	120.4	125.9	126.3	112.2	104.2	89.1	121.3
1990	114.0	118.8	115.3	93.6	106.3	126.8	121.6	125.0	127.4	114.9	103.1	88.5	119.6
1991	109.6	106.0	107.4	85.9	106.2	122.1	114.4	125.4	116.9	104.5	101.6	91.9	112.7
Seasonally adjusted [3]													
1987 Q1	103.2	95.9	102.7	100.4	102.4	106.9	99.0	102.5	100.3	95.5	105.5	105.3	105.7
Q2	105.4	102.3	105.5	101.9	102.8	109.8	102.1	99.4	111.9	97.2	105.4	103.0	108.2
Q3	107.8	106.8	111.4	102.1	103.6	112.8	104.8	103.8	113.2	99.5	106.9	103.7	110.6
Q4	109.3	109.8	113.6	100.6	104.8	115.0	106.1	108.1	112.8	99.8	107.8	103.9	112.2
1988 Q1	109.2	106.3	116.5	100.6	103.3	116.3	106.5	109.3	108.3	103.2	107.7	101.1	115.3
Q2	111.1	121.0	118.3	98.3	104.7	117.0	109.2	116.5	108.5	104.3	108.9	102.9	115.7
Q3	113.7	122.1	123.2	98.5	105.2	122.0	112.2	116.3	113.1	108.5	108.2	98.6	119.0
Q4	114.0	123.0	123.1	97.9	104.6	123.4	116.5	121.4	117.6	112.1	106.7	94.3	120.8
1989 Q1	114.6	126.5	124.2	96.3	104.9	124.2	119.1	121.8	124.1	113.5	104.1	88.6	121.7
Q2	114.9	126.8	121.1	95.6	105.8	125.2	119.8	122.9	130.3	110.0	102.9	86.6	121.5
Q3	114.5	127.5	116.2	94.8	105.6	126.0	122.0	130.2	128.7	111.2	104.7	90.4	121.0
Q4	114.2	120.6	115.0	94.8	106.3	126.4	120.9	128.9	122.0	114.1	105.1	91.0	121.1
1990 Q1	114.7	113.9	118.2	96.6	106.1	128.2	122.1	128.5	124.4	115.8	103.6	88.1	121.3
Q2	115.2	120.2	116.5	94.9	106.2	128.9	124.7	129.4	129.5	117.8	105.9	92.1	121.5
Q3	114.2	120.4	114.8	92.4	106.9	126.8	121.9	123.6	129.4	115.4	101.6	85.5	120.0
Q4	112.1	120.8	111.8	90.7	105.9	123.0	117.5	118.5	126.5	110.5	101.2	88.3	115.8
1991 Q1	110.3	109.9	108.7	89.1	106.7	121.3	117.1	125.6	121.4	107.9	101.5	91.3	113.1
Q2	109.9	109.4	109.3	86.5	106.3	121.4	114.8	127.3	116.0	104.6	99.8	88.6	112.6
Q3	109.4	102.6	107.4	85.2	106.0	122.8	114.0	125.2	116.6	103.9	102.2	92.4	113.3
Q4	108.7	102.1	104.1	83.0	105.7	122.9	111.6	123.4	113.7	101.4	103.0	95.5	111.6
1992 Q1	110.1[†]	107.3[†]	105.0[†]	84.8[†]	106.9[†]	123.8[†]	110.5	119.6[†]	115.3[†]	100.5	101.4[†]	92.0	112.2[†]
Q2	110.9	112.0	103.3	85.3	108.0	124.3	111.0	122.0	114.6	100.5	100.4	90.0	112.3
1990 Nov	111.4	116	111	90	106	122	115.5	116	123	110	101.7	89	116
Dec	111.1	118	112	90	105	122	118.8	121	130	109	99.6	86	115
1991 Jan	110.8	115	109	89	107	121	119.1	128	125	109	99.1	86	114
Feb	109.5	108	108	89	106	121	116.8	125	122	107	102.8	94	112
Mar	110.6	107	109	89	107	122	115.6	124	118	108	102.6	94	113
Apr	109.9	109	110	87	106	122	115.0	127	117	105	98.1	85	113
May	109.9	114	109	86	106	120	114.7	128	116	104	97.9	85	112
Jun	109.9	106	109	86	106	122	114.6	128	115	104	103.6	95	113
Jul	110.5	113	109	86	106	123	115.3	126	120	104	103.0	94	114
Aug	108.5	92	108	86	106	123	113.9	125	115	105	101.4	91	113
Sep	109.1	102	106	84	106	123	112.8	124	115	102	102.1	93	113
Oct	108.7	100	104	83	106	123	110.6	122	112	101	103.8	97	112
Nov	107.9	102	105	83	104	122	112.6	124	114	103	103.0	95	112
Dec	109.4	105	104	82	107	124	111.5	124	115	100	102.2	94	111
1992 Jan	109.0[†]	101	105[†]	84[†]	106	123[†]	109.9	119	114	100	101.1[†]	92	111
Feb	110.6	109	106	86	107	124	110.6	120	115	100	102.4	93	113
Mar	110.7	112	104	85	107	124	111.1	119[†]	117[†]	101	100.8	90	113
Apr	110.4	113[†]	104	85	107	124	112.2[†]	124	117	100	101.5	92	113
May	111.0	111	102	86	108[†]	125	110.5	122	113	100	99.8	89[†]	112
Jun	111.3	112	104	85	109	124	110.4	120	114	101	100.0	89	112

1 This does not include certain activities classified to intermediate goods industries: materials.
2 These sum to the total of 1 000 for the production industries.

3 Unadjusted data may be obtained from the Central Statistical Office at the address shown inside the front cover of this publication.

Source: Central Statistical Office

7.1 Output of the production industries
continued

Average 1985 = 100

	Total production industries	Energy and water supply	Total manufac-turing industries	Metals	Other minerals and mineral products[1]	Chemicals and man-made fibres	Engineering and allied industries	Food, drink and tobacco	Textiles, footwear, clothing and leather	Other manufac-turing
Class[2]	DIV 1-4	DIV 1	DIV 2-4	21-22	23-24	25-26	31-37	41-42	43-45	46-49
Weights	1000	309	691	26	35	71	295	91	47	126
	DVIM	DVIN	DVIS	DVIT	DVIU	DVIV	DVIY	DVJE	DVJH	DVJK
1985	100.0	100.0	100.0	100.0	100.0	100.0	100.0	100.0	100.0	100.0
1986	102.4	105.0	101.3	100.3	101.3	101.8	100.2	100.8	100.7	104.5
1987	105.7	103.9	106.6	108.6	106.8	109.0	103.7	103.2	103.7	115.0
1988	109.5	99.3	114.1	122.3	117.3	114.2	112.3	104.7	102.0	126.6
1989	109.9	89.6	118.9	124.7	120.1	119.4	119.9	105.6	98.3	132.3
1990	109.3	88.9	118.4	121.3	113.4	118.3	119.8	106.3	95.9	133.2
1991	106.0	92.3	112.2	110.0	103.0	121.5	111.0	106.1	87.7	126.1
Not seasonally adjusted [3]										
	DVLQ	DVLR	DVLW	DVLX	DVLY	DVLZ	DVMC	DVMI	DVML	DVMO
1987 Q1	109.6	118.0	105.9	109.8	99.6	109.0	105.1	101.5	103.3	110.8
Q2	102.0	96.2	104.6	110.4	108.3	108.5	100.7	100.9	100.7	113.2
Q3	100.0	91.9	103.6	101.1	109.3	107.1	99.4	100.4	100.9	114.0
Q4	111.3	109.4	112.2	112.9	110.0	111.3	109.4	110.1	109.9	121.8
1988 Q1	113.5	112.8	113.8	125.4	115.7	114.3	113.5	102.6	105.3	122.7
Q2	107.1	96.7	111.7	123.7	118.3	114.5	109.2	102.8	98.0	123.0
Q3	103.6	87.4	110.9	113.8	116.6	111.7	107.6	102.8	97.8	126.7
Q4	114.2	100.4	120.3	125.1	120.1	116.1	120.0	112.2	107.4	133.2
1989 Q1	114.0	99.2	120.6	134.4	119.8	121.3	123.3	102.7	99.8	131.8
Q2	107.3	81.4	118.8	129.5	125.6	121.0	118.5	103.8	98.2	132.6
Q3	103.9	80.5	114.4	113.0	119.1	115.0	114.5	102.8	93.4	128.9
Q4	114.4	97.2	122.0	122.4	115.6	119.3	124.2	112.1	102.2	134.7
1990 Q1	115.0	99.2	122.1	127.4	113.9	124.1	125.3	104.2	100.7	135.4
Q2	109.2	86.1	119.5	129.3	117.9	121.7	120.7	104.1	93.9	134.7
Q3	102.2	75.9	114.0	114.4	112.8	113.5	113.6	104.2	90.6	131.0
Q4	110.5	94.6	117.6	114.1	109.1	113.7	118.7	113.2	97.4	131.3
1991 Q1	111.3	103.6	114.7	116.4	101.2	120.7	116.7	104.4	90.8	126.2
Q2	103.1	81.9	112.5	113.6	106.4	123.1	111.1	104.2	86.4	127.0
Q3	100.1	82.5	107.9	102.9	103.9	119.1	104.6	103.1	82.8	124.2
Q4	109.5	101.2	113.2	107.9	100.0	122.6	110.8	112.7	89.5	127.2
1992 Q1	110.4†	104.1	113.2†	115.5†	98.1†	126.5†	111.9†	104.4	88.9	127.9†
Q2	102.0	83.9	110.1	112.1	103.5	124.1	107.6	97.5	84.2	128.4
1990 Nov	115.3	97.6	123.1	125	116	118	122	119	105	141
Dec	103.9	95.4	107.6	97	95	102	115	106	82	110
1991 Jan	104.1	99.1	106.4	106	97	115	106	99	84	118
Feb	114.6	110.0	116.7	118	103	123	119	104	95	129
Mar	115.0	101.6	121.0	125	103	125	125	110	93	132
Apr	104.1	87.1	111.7	110	105	125	110	103	86	126
May	100.3	79.9	109.4	106	104	120	108	103	83	123
Jun	104.9	78.7	116.6	125	110	124	116	107	90	132
Jul	98.2	81.7	105.6	101	102	117	104	101	77	119
Aug	94.6	80.3	100.9	93	98	113	96	100	79	117
Sep	107.4	85.4	117.2	114	112	127	114	109	92	136
Oct	110.4	97.7	116.0	115	106	130	109	115	95	135
Nov	114.2	102.6	119.3	118	106	127	116	116	98	137
Dec	103.9	103.2	104.1	91	88	111	107	106	76	109
1992 Jan	102.9†	105.3	101.8†	103	92	119†	97†	97	79	117
Feb	113.2	107.8	115.6	120	100	129	114	105	93	130†
Mar	115.1	99.1	122.3	124	101	131	124	111	95	137
Apr	103.7	92.7	108.7	109	101†	125	105	102†	81	125
May	100.0	84.1†	107.1	106	103	122	104	94	83†	126
Jun	102.4	75.1	114.7	122	107	125	114	97	89	134

Note: The figures contain, where appropriate, an adjustment for stock changes.
1 Mainly building materials.

2 Industries are grouped according to the Standard Industrial Classification 1980.
3 Includes adjustments to standardise the length of months.

Source: Central Statistical Office

7.2 Employment and output per head[1]

1985 = 100

| | Whole economy[2] | Total production industries | Total manufacturing industries | Manufacturing industries | | | | | | | Construction |
| | | | | Metals | Other minerals and mineral products | Chemicals and man-made fibres | Engineering and allied industries | Food, drink and tobacco | Textiles, footwear, clothing and leather | Other manufacturing | |
Class		DIV 1-4	DIV 2-4	21-22	23-24	25-26	31-37	41-42	43-45	46-49	DIV 5
Employed labour force [3]											
	DMBC	DMBK	DMBD	DMBL	DMBM	DMBN	DMBO	DMBP	DMBQ	DMBR	DMBS
1985	100.0	100.0	100.0	100.0	100.0	100.0	100.0	100.0	100.0	100.0	100.0
1986	100.1	97.3	97.9	89.1	94.0	97.1	97.5	97.4	100.1	100.7	99.6
1987	101.9	96.1	97.0	82.3	90.2	94.8	96.2	96.5	99.3	103.3	104.4
1988	105.2	96.7	98.2	77.7	90.5	96.2	97.6	95.9	100.0	106.3	110.8
1989	107.8	96.6	98.5	83.0	93.8	97.7	97.6	94.1	95.6	109.4	121.0
1990	108.5	95.4	97.3	87.8	94.7	95.9	95.8	94.0	90.5	109.9	121.9
1991	105.5	90.6	92.3	77.0	88.4	90.9	90.0	95.0	84.1	105.5	110.3
Seasonally adjusted											
1988 Q3	105.7	96.7	98.3	77.2	90.5	96.5	97.7	95.6	99.7	106.7	111.3
Q4	106.3	96.9	98.4	76.6	90.8	97.3	98.1	96.0	99.3	108.0	113.8
1989 Q1	107.1	96.9	98.6	74.6	90.5	97.5	98.3	95.2	98.3	108.4	116.5
Q2	107.6	96.7	98.5	79.2	92.6	97.5	97.7	94.1	96.4	108.8	119.9
Q3	108.0	96.6	98.5	87.5	95.3	97.8	97.2	93.7	94.5	110.0	123.2
Q4	108.4	96.3	98.3	90.6	96.7	98.2	97.1	93.6	93.3	110.6	124.1
1990 Q1	108.6	96.1	98.1	90.0	96.1	97.1	96.6	93.3	92.2	110.2	123.8
Q2	108.8	95.8	97.6	88.9	95.0	96.1	96.0	93.2	91.3	110.2	123.1
Q3	108.6	95.4	97.3	87.6	94.1	95.8	95.8	94.0	90.1	110.1	121.6
Q4	107.8	94.2	96.3	84.6	93.5	94.6	94.8	95.6	88.5	109.2	119.2
1991 Q1	106.9	92.7	94.6	80.0	91.3	92.0	92.6	96.7	86.2	107.2	115.7
Q2	105.9	91.1	92.8	77.3	88.8	90.3	90.2	96.4	84.0	105.6	112.0
Q3	105.1	89.9	91.3	76.2	87.0	90.3	88.9	94.9	83.0	105.0	108.5
Q4	104.2	88.8	90.3	74.4	86.4	91.0	88.3	91.8	83.3	104.3	105.1
1992 Q1	103.7	87.6	89.2	72.8	84.2	90.5	86.7	90.0	83.1	103.0	102.0
Q2	..	86.8	88.4	72.5	82.7	89.5	85.4	88.9	82.2	102.7	..
Output per person employed											
	DMBE	CAIW	DMBF	DMBT	DMBU	DMBV	DMBW	DMBX	DMBY	DMBZ	DMCA
1985	100.0	100.0	100.0	100.0	100.0	100.0	100.0	100.0	100.0	100.0	100.0
1986	103.5	105.3	103.5	112.6	107.8	104.9	102.8	103.5	100.5	103.8	104.9
1987	106.3	110.1	109.8	131.8	118.3	114.9	107.7	107.0	104.4	111.3	108.0
1988	107.2	113.2	116.2	157.2	129.5	118.7	115.1	109.2	102.0	119.1	111.0
1989	106.9	113.7	120.8	151.2	128.1	122.1	122.9	112.1	102.8	120.9	107.9
1990	107.3	114.6	121.7	138.1	119.7	123.3	125.0	113.1	105.9	121.1	108.1
1991	107.6	117.0	121.6	142.8	116.5	133.7	123.3	111.8	104.3	119.5	109.1
Seasonally adjusted											
1988 Q3	107.3	114.0	117.5	160.6	128.8	120.5	116.2	110.5	102.3	121.3	109.7
Q4	107.4	113.9	119.3	164.1	132.9	120.3	119.2	109.4	102.2	121.4	110.7
1989 Q1	107.1	113.1	120.5	174.9	134.6	121.8	120.9	109.9	101.5	122.1	113.0
Q2	106.6	112.8	120.8	153.9	131.9	121.3	122.6	112.5	103.0	121.8	109.3
Q3	107.0	114.4	121.1	139.9	125.6	123.1	124.6	112.8	103.1	119.5	104.5
Q4	106.9	114.6	120.9	136.0	120.3	122.3	123.6	113.4	103.8	120.0	104.9
1990 Q1	107.6	114.4	121.8	133.3	120.7	124.2	124.5	114.0	107.0	122.4	109.2
Q2	107.9	116.7	123.4	141.3	120.9	124.6	127.6	113.9	106.7	122.8	108.0
Q3	106.9	113.9	122.0	140.5	120.3	123.6	125.4	113.8	105.4	121.1	107.8
Q4	106.9	113.5	119.6	137.1	117.1	120.9	122.6	110.8	104.6	118.3	107.5
1991 Q1	106.9	115.1	119.9	137.6	114.0	128.4	123.0	110.1	103.6	118.1	108.0
Q2	107.0	115.4	121.1	142.2	115.9	133.2	123.7	110.3	104.6	119.6	107.8
Q3	108.0	118.2	122.9	145.4	119.7	137.2	124.1	111.7	105.5	120.3	109.4
Q4	108.6	119.5	122.6	146.3	116.3	135.9	122.4	115.2	103.5	120.1	111.2
1992 Q1	108.6	120.2[†]	124.6	150.7	118.8[†]	136.4[†]	124.4	118.7[†]	103.9[†]	123.4[†]	114.0
Q2	..	121.1	126.2	149.5	121.5	136.0	127.2	121.5	105.5	124.8	..

1 Output per head is the ratio of the output index numbers published in Table 7.1 and the employed labour force. A monthly series for total manufacturing industries is presented in Table 7.3.
2 Based on Gross Domestic Product at factor cost.
3 Comprises employees in employment, self-employed and HM Forces.

Sources: Central Statistical Office; Department of Employment

7.3 Productivity and unit labour costs

1985=100

	Whole economy			Manufacturing industry		
	Implied GDP deflator[1]	Labour costs per unit of output	Wages & salaries per unit of output[2]	Wages & salaries per unit of output[3]	Output per person per hour	Output per person employed[4]
	DJCM	DJDP	DJDO	DMBG	DMBH	DMBF
1984	94.8	96.1	95.0	94.5	97.5	97.0
1985	100.0	100.0	100.0	100.0	100.0	100.0
1986	102.7	104.7	105.2	104.0	103.8	103.5
1987	107.9	109.3	110.2	105.9	109.4	109.8
1988	114.9	117.2	118.4	108.6	115.3	116.2
1989	123.6	128.1	129.8	113.6	120.2	120.8
1990	133.8	140.6	142.6	123.4	121.6	121.7
1991	142.3	151.5	153.5	133.5	123.1	121.6
1987 Q2	106.8	108.5	109.4	105.4	108.6	109.1
Q3	108.5	109.5	110.5	105.5	110.7	111.2
Q4	110.6	112.3	113.3	106.9	111.7	112.4
1988 Q1	111.3	113.9	115.0	107.9	112.5	113.3
Q2	113.1	115.8	117.0	108.8	113.8	114.6
Q3	116.2	118.1	119.4	108.2	116.7	117.5
Q4	118.6	120.8	122.3	109.4	118.1	119.3
1989 Q1	121.2	123.6	125.4	110.4	119.4	120.5
Q2	122.7	126.5	128.6	112.4	120.0	120.8
Q3	124.3	129.2	131.0	114.5	120.5	121.1
Q4	126.3	133.0	134.3	117.0	120.7	120.9
1990 Q1	129.1	135.3	137.4	119.0	121.5	121.8
Q2	132.7	138.8	140.8	120.2	123.1	123.4
Q3	135.9	142.8	144.8	124.7	121.8	122.0
Q4	137.6	145.4	147.3	129.5	120.0	119.6
1991 Q1	139.2	148.4	150.5	131.7	121.4	119.9
Q2	142.0	151.1	153.2	132.8	122.9	121.1
Q3	143.4	152.5	154.4	133.3	124.2	122.9
Q4	144.6	153.9	155.8	136.2	123.8	122.6
1992 Q1	146.8	157.0	159.3	137.6[†]	125.5[†]	124.6
Q2	..	..	..	135.1	126.3	126.2
1989 Oct	..	..	..	116.7	120.3	120.6
Nov	..	..	..	117.4	120.3	120.5
Dec	..	..	..	116.9	121.7	121.6
1990 Jan	..	..	..	118.4	120.9	121.1
Feb	..	..	..	119.2	121.1	121.4
Mar	..	..	..	119.5	122.6	123.0
Apr	..	..	..	118.4	123.3	123.8
May	..	..	..	119.9	123.5	123.6
Jun	..	..	..	122.1	122.5	122.8
Jul	..	..	..	122.7	122.7	122.9
Aug	..	..	..	124.6	121.9	122.0
Sep	..	..	..	126.8	120.8	121.0
Oct	..	..	..	127.9	120.3	120.1
Nov	..	..	..	130.6	119.2	118.7
Dec	..	..	..	130.1	120.6	120.1
1991 Jan	..	..	..	130.5	121.3	120.3
Feb	..	..	..	132.7	120.9	119.0
Mar	..	..	..	131.9	122.1	120.3
Apr	..	..	..	133.1	122.3	120.3
May	..	..	..	132.8	122.7	120.9
Jun	..	..	..	132.6	123.6	122.1
Jul	..	..	..	131.2	124.5	123.6
Aug	..	..	..	134.3	124.0	122.7
Sep	..	..	..	134.5	124.3	122.5
Oct	..	..	..	136.4	123.1	121.9
Nov	..	..	..	136.1	124.1	122.8
Dec	..	..	..	136.2	124.2	123.0
1992 Jan	..	..	..	137.2[†]	124.3[†]	123.0[†]
Feb	..	..	..	136.4	125.6	124.8
Mar	..	..	..	139.2	126.7	125.8
Apr	..	..	..	133.2	126.5	126.2
May	..	..	..	136.3	125.4	126.0
Jun	..	..	..	135.8	127.0	126.3

1 Based on expenditure data. At factor cost. Also known as the Index of total home costs.
2 The method of calculating whole economy unit wage costs can be found in the Employment Gazette, May 1986.
3 Series based on output and employment series in Tables 7.1 and 7.2 and earnings from Table 18.10.
4 Quarterly series also in Table 7.2.

Sources: Department of Employment; Central Statistical Office

8 Energy

8.1 Inland energy consumption: primary fuel input basis

Million tonnes of oil or oil equivalent

| | Not seasonally adjusted | | | | | | | Seasonally adjusted (annual rates)[7] | | | | | | |
| | | | | Primary electricity | | | | | | | Primary electricity | | | |
	Coal[1]	Petro-leum[2]	Natural gas[3]	Nuclear	Natural flow hydro[5]	Net imports	Total	Coal[1,4]	Petro-leum[2,4]	Natural gas[3,4]	Nuclear	Natural flow hydro[5]	Net imports[6]	Total
	BHBB	BHBC	BHBD	BHBE	BHBF	BHBM	BHBA	BHBH	BHBI	BHBJ	BHBK	BHBL	BHBN	BHBG
1987	68.3	64.3	50.5	11.7	1.2	2.8	198.9	67.2	63.5	49.6	11.7	1.2	2.8	196.1
1988	65.9	68.3	47.9	13.5	1.4	3.1	200.1	65.9	68.3	49.7	13.5	1.4	3.1	201.9
1989	63.6†	69.5	47.4	15.4	1.4†	3.0	200.2†	64.5†	70.2†	50.5	15.4	1.4†	3.0	204.9†
1990	63.8†	71.3†	49.0†	14.2†	1.6†	2.9	202.7†	65.0†	73.3†	52.4†	14.2†	1.6†	2.9	209.3†
1991	63.3	71.1†	52.8†	15.2†	1.4	3.9	207.7	63.1	70.8	52.7†	15.2†	1.4	3.9	207.0
1991 Mar*	6.6	6.4	5.9	1.5	0.2	0.4	21.0	65.7	66.3	52.9	14.6	1.3	4.1	205.0
Apr	4.9	5.4	4.3	1.1	0.2	0.3	16.2	64.2	72.6	50.5	13.9	1.3	4.1	206.6†
May	4.8	5.5	3.4	1.0	0.1	0.3	15.0	66.9	75.9	54.5	11.8	1.3	4.1	213.6†
Jun*	5.4	6.6	3.3	1.2	0.1	0.3	16.8	62.6	69.3	53.8	14.1	1.3	2.8	203.9
Jul	4.1	5.5	1.9	1.1	0.1	0.3	12.9	61.8	79.2	51.4	16.2	1.3	3.7	213.6
Aug	3.8	5.3	1.8	1.2	0.1	0.3	12.4	63.2	74.5	47.6	16.5	1.3	4.1	207.3
Sep*	5.2	6.6	2.6	1.3	0.1	0.4	16.3	63.6	68.9	49.4	14.4	1.3	4.1	201.7
Oct	4.8	5.5	3.7	1.3	0.1	0.3	15.7	63.8	71.3	50.7	17.3	1.3	4.1	208.5
Nov	5.3	5.6	5.3	1.1	0.2	0.3	17.7	61.2	70.8	53.1	15.5	1.3	4.1	206.0
Dec*	6.6	7.0	7.2	1.4	0.2	0.4	22.8	62.3	65.4	54.3	14.8	1.4	4.1	202.3
1992 Jan	5.3	5.5	6.0	1.4	0.2	0.3	18.7	60.2	71.4	51.9	15.3	1.4	4.2	204.4
Feb	5.5	5.6	6.1	1.4	0.1	0.3	19.0	60.8	72.7	52.5	14.6	1.4	4.2	206.1
Mar*	6.1	6.9	6.3	1.8	0.2	0.4	21.7	59.5	69.8†	54.4†	19.0	1.4	4.1	208.2
Apr	4.7	5.5	4.3	1.3	0.1	0.3	16.2	61.4	74.2†	53.9†	17.7	1.4	4.1	212.7
May[8]	4.2	5.1	3.1	1.3	0.1	0.3	14.1	60.1	71.8	53.9	16.5	1.5	4.1	207.8

1 Consumption by fuel producers *plus* disposals (including imports) to final users *plus* (for annual unadjusted figures only) net foreign trade and stock change in other solid fuels. See also footnotes 6 and 7 to Table 8.4.

2 Inland deliveries for energy use *plus* refinery fuel and losses *minus* the differences between deliveries to and actual consumption at power stations and gasworks.

3 Including non-energy use and excluding gas flared or re-injected.

4 Also temperature corrected.

5 Excludes generation from pumped storage stations.

6 Not seasonally adjusted.

7 For hydro the estimated annual out-turn.

8 Provisional.

Source: Department of Trade and Industry

CENTRAL STATISTICAL OFFICE

Economic Trends

Price £11.50 net

Central Statistical Office publications are published by HMSO.
They are obtainable from HMSO bookshops and through booksellers.

8.2 Supply and use of fuels

Million therms

		1990	1991	1990 Q2	1990 Q3	1990 Q4	1991 Q1	1991 Q2	1991 Q3	1991 Q4	1992[12] Q1
Primary fuels and equivalents											
Production of primary fuels											
Coal	BHCA	22 723[†]	23 363	5 740	5 572	5 545	6 044[†]	6 068	5 479	5 771	5 756
Petroleum[1]	BHCB	39 830[†]	39 732	10 416	9 074	9 819	10 123	8 276	10 331	10 999	10 466
Natural gas[2]	BHCC	18 044[†]	20 086	3 711	2 421	5 846	7 111	4 337[†]	2 425	6 214	6 987
Primary electricity[3]	BHCD	6 156[†]	6 467	1 400	1 359	1 647	1 858[†]	1 408	1 526	1 676	2 049
Total	BHCE	86 753[†]	89 648	21 267	18 426	22 857	25 135[†]	20 089	19 761	24 660	25 257
Arrivals											
Petroleum[4]	BHCF	27 528[†]	29 006	6 964	7 245	5 987	6 844[†]	7 849	7 194	7 118	6 876
Other	BHCG	8 054[†]	9 702	1 930	1 757	2 455	2 745[†]	2 404	2 146	2 405	2 779
Shipments	BHCH	32 090	32 726[†]	8 298	7 185	7 820	7 605[†]	7 469	8 549	9 103	8 295
Bunkers											
Stock change[5]	BHCI	1 059[†]	1 039	287	276	246	214	298	283	243	249
Solid fuels	BHCJ	391	-1 477[†]	-583	-562	349	429[†]	-947	-1 100	140	-65
Crude petroleum	BHCK	218[†]	-94	190	-57	387	-360[†]	184	139	-57	146
Petroleum products	BHCL	211[†]	16	-120	-148	123	-125[†]	153	-74	62	-15
Natural gas	BHCM	43[†]	-102	-50	-59	120	289	-300	-114	23	123
Non-energy use	BHCN	3 968	4 337	951	1 027	917	1 010	1 108	1 141	1 078	1 076
Statistical difference[6]	BHCO	-371[†]	-548	-240	-15	-234	-216[†]	-123	-115	-91	-369
Total primary energy input[7]	BHCP	85 710[†]	88 049	19 822	18 099	23 061	25 912[†]	20 434	17 864	23 837	25 277
Conversion losses, etc[8]	BHCQ	27 098[†]	27 598	6 307[†]	5 959	6 779	8 014	6 436	5 978	7 171	7 803
Final consumption by fuel[9]											
Coal	BHCR	3 071[†]	3 258	816[†]	689	717	1 026	782	713	738	908
Other solid fuel[10]	BHCS	2 278[†]	2 158	586	552[†]	548	578	559	494	528	543
Coke oven gas	BHCT	289	272	72[†]	72	70	72	70	66	64	67
Gas[11]	BHCU	18 504[†]	19 936	3 618[†]	2 484	6 111	7 203	4 176	2 287	6 270	6 813
Electricity	BHCV	9 366[†]	9 590	2 159[†]	2 039	2 565	2 718	2 231	2 053	2 587	2 716
Petroleum	BHCW	25 104[†]	25 235	6 263[†]	6 304	6 171	6 301	6 179	6 274	6 480	6 426
Total all fuels	BHCX	58 612[†]	60 451	13 515[†]	12 140	16 182	17 898	13 998	11 886	16 666	17 474

1 Crude petroleum and natural gas liquids. Annual data include extend well-test production.
2 Excluding gas flared or re-injected.
3 Nuclear, natural flow hydro and generation at wind stations.
4 Crude petroleum, process oils and petroleum products.
5 Stock rises are indicated with a (-).
6 Supply greater than recorded demand (-).
7 Thermal equivalent of total inland energy consumption in Table 8.1.

8 Losses in conversion and distribution and used by fuel industries.
9 Deliveries, except for gas, electricity and iron and steel industry use of solid fuels.
10 Coke and other manufactured solid fuels.
11 Includes colliery methane. Also includes non-energy use of natural gas.
12 1992 Q1 figures are provisional.

Source: Department of Trade and Industry

8.2 Supply and use of fuels
continued

Million therms

		1990	1991	1990 Q2	1990 Q3	1990 Q4	1991 Q1	1991 Q2	1991 Q3	1991 Q4	1992[6] Q1
Final consumption by user[1]											
Iron and steel industry											
Coal	BHTA	3[†]	2	1	1	1	1	1	-	1	1
Other solid fuel[2]	BHTB	1 704[†]	1 633	437[†]	410	424	427	422	373	412	418
Coke oven gas	BHTC	270	253	67	69[†]	67	65	64	63	61	60
Gas[3]	BHTD	461[†]	404	115[†]	93	122	127	108	74	94	116
Electricity	BHTE	310[†]	306	79[†]	73	77	80	78	72	77	80
Petroleum	BHTF	294[†]	296	86[†]	91	45	65	84	71	74	74
Total	BHTG	3 042[†]	2 895	785[†]	737	736	764	757	653	718	748
Other industries											
Coal	BHTH	1 406[†]	1 311	375[†]	326	319	411	315	289	296	346
Other solid fuel[2]	BHTI	59[†]	48	18[†]	15	19	15	6	12	18	21
Coke oven gas	BHTJ	19	19	5[†]	3	3	7	6	3	3	7
Gas[3]	BHTK	4 795[†]	4 687	1 096[†]	953	1 433	1 415	1 101	888	1 282	1 221
Electricity	BHTL	3 125[†]	3 091	769[†]	746	811	818	747	749	777	774
Petroleum	BHTM	2 944[†]	3 215	726[†]	670	704	927	764	695	829	893
Total	BHTN	12 348[†]	12 373	2 989[†]	2 712	3 289	3 593	2 939	2 636	3 205	3 263
Transport sector											
Coal	BHTO	-[†]	-	-	-	-	-[†]	-	-	-	-
Electricity[4]	BHTP	180[†]	180	45[†]	45	45	45	45	45	45	45
Petroleum	BHTQ	19 126	18 864[†]	4 856	4 968	4 687	4 406	4 708	4 969	4 781	4 560
Total	BHTR	19 306[†]	19 044	4 900[†]	5 013	4 732	4 452	4 753	5 013	4 826	4 605
Domestic sector											
Coal	BHTS	1 331[†]	1 646	361	306	320	524[†]	403	370	352	469
Other solid fuel[2]	BHTT	405[†]	396	102[†]	100	85	111	107	94	83	90
Gas[3]	BHTU	10 250[†]	11 395	1 827	1 098	3 584	4 332	2 253	996	3 814	4 208
Electricity	BHTV	3 200	3 347[†]	689[†]	605	940	1 045	743	603	956	1 044
Petroleum	BHTW	989	1 092	203	217	267	339	228	200	325	343
Total	BHTX	16 191[†]	17 876	3 182[†]	2 326	5 196	6 351	3 733	2 263	5 529	6 154
Other final users[5]											
Coal	BHTY	315	299[†]	79	56	76	90	63	54	89	92
Other solid fuel[2]	BHTZ	109[†]	81	29[†]	27	21	25	24	15	15	14
Gas[3]	BHNA	2 998	3 450[†]	580	340	972	1 329	714	329	1 080	1 268
Electricity	BHNB	2 552	2 665[†]	577[†]	570	691	730	619	584	732	773
Petroleum	BHNC	1 750	1 769[†]	393	360	468	564	395	339	471[†]	556
Total	BHND	7 726[†]	8 264	1 657[†]	1 352	2 229	2 738	1 816	1 321	2 388	2 703
Total final users	BHNE	58 612[†]	60 451	13 515[†]	12 140	16 182	17 898	13 998	11 886	16 666	17 474

1 Deliveries, except for gas, electricity and iron and steel industry use of solid fuels.
2 Coke and other manufactured solid fuels.
3 Includes colliery methane, also includes non-energy use of natural gas.

4 Includes use in transport related premises, eg. airports and warehouses etc.
5 Mainly public administration, commerce and agriculture.
6 1992 Q1 figures are provisional.

Source: Department of Trade and Industry

8.3 Coal supply and colliery manpower and productivity at BCC mines

	Thousand tonnes						BCC mines			
	Coal supply							Tonnes		
	Production							Average output[4] per manshift worked		
							Wage earners on colliery books (thousands)		Underground	
	Deep-mined	Opencast	Total[1]	Net imports	Import[2]	Export[3]		Overall	Total	Production[5]
	BHDC	BHDD	BHDB	BHDE	BHDF	BHDG	BHGA	BHGH	BHGI	BHGJ
1987	85 957	15 786	104 533	7 428	9 781	2 353	102	3.59	4.42	15.81
1988	83 762	17 899	104 066	9 864	11 685	1 822	86	3.97	4.85	18.25
1989	79 628	18 657	101 135	10 088	12 137	2 049	66	4.33	5.21	20.41
1990	72 899	18 134	94 397	12 250	14 783	2 533	59	4.53	5.40	21.86
1991	73 357	18 620	96 144	17 819	19 491	1 672	49	5.11	6.08	24.66
1991 May*	6 013	1 584	8 078	1 395	1 529	134	56	5.3	6.4	25.6
Jun*	7 312	1 931	9 743	1 739	1 904	165	56	5.4	6.4	25.8
Jul	5 611	1 410	7 404	1 590	1 700	110	56	5.2	6.2	24.7
Aug*	4 480	1 321	6 061	1 133	1 255	121	55	4.7	5.6	22.6
Sep*	6 729	1 966	9 107	1 648	1 821	172	54	5.1	6.1	23.7
Oct	5 931	1 688	7 962	1 329	1 451	123	53	5.3	6.3	25.3
Nov*	6 052	1 542	7 912	1 574	1 647	73	51	5.4	6.3	26.9
Dec*	5 965	1 491	7 903	1 353	1 503	150	49	5.1	6.0	26.9
1992 Jan	4 844†	1 116	6 300	2 145	2 205	59	48	5.3	6.3	28.1
Feb	5 923†	1 603	7 789†	1 621	1 699	79	46	5.7	6.8	29.0
Mar*	7 637	2 070†	10 083†	1 987†	2 037†	50	44	6.2	7.3	30.2
Apr	5 036	1 195†	6 588	1 340	1 437	97	41	6.0	7.0	29.0
May[6]	5 171	1 619	7 176	1 918	1 975	57	41	6.1	7.1	28.1

1 Including an estimate for slurry, etc, recovered and disposed of otherwise than by the British Coal Corporation (BCC).
2 As recorded in the *Overseas Trade Statistics of the United Kingdom*.
3 Shipments as recorded by BCC; the figures may differ from those published in OTS.
4 Saleable deep-mined revenue coal.
5 Output from production faces divided by production manshifts.
6 Provisional.

Source: Department of Trade and Industry

8.4 Inland use and stocks of coal
Stocks: end of period[1]

Thousand tonnes

	Inland use									
	Fuel producers (consumption)				Final users[6]					
		Secondary				Domestic				
	Primary: collieries	Power stations[2]	Coke ovens	Other conversion industries[3]	Industry[4]	House coal[4,5]	Other[7]	Miscellaneous[8]	Total inland consumption	Stocks[9]
	BHEB	BHEC	BHED	BHEE	BHEF	BHEG	BHEH	BHEI	BHEA	BHEJ
1987	235	87 960†	10 859	2 052	6 204†	5 685	1 475	1 425	115 894	33 246†
1988	196	84 258	10 902	2 006	6 291	5 112	1 469	1 265	111 498	36 166
1989	146	82 586	10 792	1 717	5 565	4 344	1 368	1 066	107 581	39 244
1990	117	84 547	10 852	1 544	5 367	3 372	1 250	1 211	108 256	37 760
1991	119	84 017	10 011	1 501	4 997	3 953	1 744	1 139	107 492	43 321
1991 May	10	6 167†	797	123	397†	342	176	84	8 096	37 902†
Jun*	8	7 016	988	141	425	379	142	75	9 173	39 930
Jul	5	5 112	766	113	360	332	177	61	6 925	41 584
Aug*	6	4 844	751	121	345	261	125	56	6 508	42 486
Sep*	7	6 945	947	136	396	252	129	92	8 904	44 009
Oct	8	6 309	766	117	369	323	160	91	8 142	44 954
Nov	10	7 395	755	112	355	189	142	115	9 073	45 229
Dec*	15	9 305	919	127	403	236	160	138	11 302	43 321
1992 Jan	9	7 017	751	105	484	568	123	104	9 160	42 191
Feb	11	7 517	758	99	402	375†	106	118	9 384	42 043
Mar*	10	8 308	926	103	425	335†	94	131	10 331†	43 295
Apr	7	6 341	757†	103	289	273	93	72	7 934	43 397
May[10]	5	5 466	755	99	341	340	93	63	7 164	44 717

1 Stocks at end of period, Great Britain only.
2 Coal-fired power stations belonging to major electricity generating companies.
3 Low temperature carbonisation and patent fuel plants.
4 Includes estimated proportion of total imports.
5 Including miners' coal.
6 Disposals by collieries and opencast sites.
7 Anthracite, dry steam coal and imported naturally smokeless fuels.
8 Includes public administration and commerce.
9 Excluding distributed stocks held in merchants' yards, etc, mainly for the domestic market and stocks held by the industrial sector.
10 Provisional.

Source: Department of Trade and Industry

8.5 Sources of supply and gas sent out by the gas supply system

Million therms

	Natural gas supply			
	Source			
	Indigenous	Imported	Gas input[1,2]	Gas sent out
	BHHB	BHHC	BHHA	BHHD
1987	15 904	4 416	20 319	19 935
1988	15 314	3 897	19 211	18 783
1989	15 095	3 882	18 976	18 748
1990	16 674	2 730	19 404	19 382
1991	18 818[4]	2 426[4]	21 245[†]	20 949[†]
1991 Apr	1 616	236	1 852	1 716
May	1 252	222	1 473	1 371[†]
Jun*	1 190	210	1 401	1 331
Jul	671	104	775	711
Aug	604	97	701	653
Sep*	883	149	1 032	947
Oct	1 349	161	1 510	1 453
Nov	1 893[4]	220[4]	2 113	2 082
Dec*	2 610[4]	260[4]	2 870	2 882
1992 Jan	2 134[4]	217[4]	2 351	2 389
Feb	2 154[4]	231[4]	2 385	2 467
Mar*	2 335[4]	228[4]	2 563	2 539
Apr	1 547[4]	186[4]	1 733	1 733
May[3]	1 088[4]	132[4]	1 220	1 170

1 Figures include third party carriage gas.
2 Figures differ from Gas sent out because of stock changes and the inclusion of small quantities of Substitute Natural Gas and Town Gas in Gas sent out. They include gas put to storage, but to avoid double counting, exclude gas withdrawn from storage to the system. The figures also differ from total consumption (expressed as oil equivalent in Table 8.1) because they exclude producers' own use and losses.
3 Provisional.
4 Estimates.

Source: Department of Trade and Industry

8.6 Fuel used by and electricity production and availability from the electricity supply industry[1]

	Million tonnes of oil or oil equivalent					Terawatt hours						
	Fuel used							Electricity supplied by type of plant				
	Coal[2]	Oil[2,3]	Nuclear electricity	Hydro-electricity	Total[4]	Electricity generated	Own use[5]	Conventional Steam plant[6]	Nuclear	Other[7]	Total	Total Electricity available[8]
	FTAJ	FTAK	FTAL	FTAM	FTAN	BHJF	BHJJ	FTAB	FTAC	FTAD	BHJK	BHJL
1987	50.70	4.81	10.55	1.06	67.12	282.75[†]	20.85	214.84	43.95	3.12	261.90	279.12
1988	48.51	5.39	12.41	1.27	67.59	288.51	21.58	211.50	51.70	3.73	266.93	285.16[†]
1989	47.39	5.52	14.24	1.22	68.38	292.90	21.19	208.68	59.31	3.73	271.71	290.84
1990	48.56	6.69	13.20	1.34	69.80	298.50	20.52	218.96	54.96	4.06	277.98	295.28
1991[9]	48.25	5.73	14.23[†]	1.17	69.39[†]	301.18	20.53[†]	217.95	59.27[†]	3.43[†]	280.65[†]	302.41
1991 Jun*	4.01	0.64	1.11	0.04	5.81	25.10	1.70	18.66	4.64	0.10	23.40	25.23
Jul	2.93	0.49	1.04	0.05	4.50	19.31	1.33	13.52	4.32	0.14	17.98	19.58
Aug	2.77	0.38	1.11	0.05	4.32	18.62	1.32	12.53	4.64	0.14	17.31	19.02
Sep*	3.98	0.38	1.26	0.07	5.70	24.46	1.68	17.35	5.24	0.19	22.78	24.99
Oct	3.62	0.35	1.21	0.12	5.30	23.08	1.53	16.15	5.04	0.37	21.56	23.27
Nov	4.26	0.44	1.07	0.14	5.91	25.69	1.70	19.08	4.47	0.44	23.98	25.76
Dec*	5.36	0.56	1.35	0.17	7.44	32.45	2.17	24.14	5.63	0.52	30.28	32.67
1992 Jan	4.04	0.47	1.34	0.15	6.00	26.23[†]	1.78[†]	18.40	5.57	0.48	24.45	26.42
Feb	4.33	0.47	1.31	0.11	6.22	27.15	1.78	19.55	5.44	0.38	25.37	27.29[†]
Mar*	4.87[†]	0.50[†]	1.72	0.19	7.28[†]	24.32	6.21	16.50[†]	5.71[†]	0.39[†]	18.11[†]	31.46
Apr	3.55	0.37	1.22	0.12	5.26	23.47	1.64	16.39	5.07	0.37	21.84	23.66
May[9]	3.13	0.34	1.23	0.11	4.80	20.98	1.54	14.00	5.12	0.33	19.45	21.17

1 Fuel used and electricity generated by major generating companies (National Power, PowerGen, Nuclear Electric, National Grid Company, Scottish Power, Scottish Hydro-Electric, Scottish Nuclear, Northern Ireland Electricity service, Midlands Electricity and South Western Electricity), and electricity available through the grid in England and Wales and from Distribution Companies in Scotland and Northern Ireland.
2 Including quantities used in the production of steam for sale.
3 Including oil used in gas turbine and diesel plant and for lighting up coal-fired boilers and Orimulsion.
4 Including wind power and refuse derived fuel.
5 Used in works and for pumping at pumped storage stations.
6 Coal Oil (including Orimulsion) and mixed or dual-fired (including gas).
7 Including gas turbine, diesel, wind and hydro-electric plant.
8 Including net imports and purchases from outside sources mainly UKAEA and British Nuclear Fuels plc, and net of supplies direct from generators to final consumers.
9 Provisional.

Source: Department of Trade and Industry

8.7 Sales by the gas and public electricity supply systems

	Gas: million therms						Electricity: TWh				
	Power stations[1]	Iron and steel industry	Other industries	Domestic	Other[2]	Total	Industrial[3]	Commercial[4]	Domestic	Other[5]	Total
	BHIB	BHIC	BHID	BHIE	BHIF	BHIA	FTAE	FTAF	FTAG	FTAH	FTAI
1987	357†	465†	5 057†	10 500†	2 990	19 373†	90.77	64.18	93.25	7.98	256.19
1988	381	446	4 560	10 254	2 996	18 639†	94.13	67.31	92.36	7.99	261.79
1989	395	467	4 654	9 914	2 919	18 349	96.26†	70.29†	92.27	7.90	266.72†
1990	396	461	4 821	10 250	2 999†	18 928	98.17†	70.96†	93.79†	8.40†	271.32†
1991	467	404	4 576	11 395	3 450	20 294	96.87	74.58	98.10†	8.20	277.75
1988 Q1	21	138	1 524	4 096	1 166	6 945	24.66	18.68	28.58	2.10	74.03
Q2	20	109	1 127	1 810	590	3 655	23.10	15.44	19.69	1.74	59.98
Q3	20	89	928	1 128	349	2 514	22.16	15.20	17.80	1.84	57.00
Q4	22	113	1 276	3 221	891	5 523	24.21	17.98	26.28	2.31	70.79
1989 Q1	21	124	1 372	3 766	1 072	6 355	24.80	19.09	28.04	2.10	74.04
Q2	20	120	1 216	1 881	606	3 844	24.08	16.69	20.19	1.75	62.71
Q3	19	98	960	962	308	2 346	23.09	15.95	17.20	1.85	58.09
Q4	21	130	1 417	3 305	933	5 805	24.29	18.55	26.84	2.21	71.88
1990 Q1	143†	131†	1 435†	3 742	1 106	6 558	25.02†	19.68†	28.30†	2.32	75.32†
Q2	80	115	1 065	1 827	580	3 666	24.32	16.26	20.21	1.81†	62.59
Q3	75	93	920	1 098	340	2 525	23.43	16.01	17.73	1.87	59.04
Q4	99	122	1 400	3 584	972	6 178	25.40	19.01	27.56	2.41	74.37
1991 Q1	161	127	1 370	4 332	1 329	7 318	25.66	20.41	30.64	2.16	78.86
Q2	88	108	1 048	2 253	714	4 211	23.51	17.53	21.76	1.78	64.59
Q3	86	74	871	996	329	2 357	23.48	16.37	17.68	1.91	59.44
Q4	131	94	1 289	3 814	1 080	6 408	24.21	20.27	28.02	2.36	74.86
1992 Q1	158	116	1 270	4 208	1 268	7 019	24.81	21.01	30.61	2.31	78.75

1 Power stations belonging to major generating companies and transport undertakings.
2 Public administration, commerce and agriculture.
3 Manufacturing industry, construction, energy and water supply industries.
4 Commercial premises, transport and other service sector consumers.
5 Agriculture, public lighting and combined domestic/commercial premises.

Source: Department of Trade and Industry

8.8 Indigenous production, refinery receipts, arrivals and shipments of oil[1]

	Million tonnes			Thousand tonnes									
	Indigenous oil production			Foreign trade[6]									
				Refinery receipts			Crude oil and NGLs		Process oils		Petroleum products		
	Crude oil	NGLs	Total[2]	Indigenous[3]	Other[4]	Net foreign arrivals[5]	Arrivals	Shipments	Arrivals	Shipments	Arrivals	Shipments	Bunkers[7]
	BHMB	BHML	BHMA	BHMC	BHMD	BHME	BHMF	BHMG	BHMM	BHMH	BHMI	BHMJ	BHMK
1987	117.7†	5.7	123.4†	38 794	939	40 630	31 713	80 273	9 827	883	8 570	17 056	1 668
1988	109.5	5.0	114.5	40 582	730	42 613	34 495	70 274	9 777	1 658	9 219	17 176	1 831
1989	87.4	4.4	91.8	39 585	904	48 351	38 676	49 328	10 824	1 134	9 479	17 873	2 396
1990	88.0	3.6	91.6	37 754	916	51 065	42 074	54 131	10 636	1 769	11 005	18 002	2 538
1991	86.8	4.4	91.3	35 932	772	55 819	45 800	52 565	11 284	1 237	10 140	20 677	2 486
1991 Apr	6.1	0.3	6.4	2 112	37	5 114	4 094	4 267	1 058	38	657	1 707	240
May	5.8	0.3	6.1	2 341	45	5 091	4 016	3 453	1 108	34	796	2 034	240
Jun	6.2	0.3	6.4	2 480	51	5 519	4 603	3 586	1 090	174	763	1 638	230
Jul	7.5	0.4	7.9	2 941	99	4 696	3 618	4 497	1 083	5	686	1 881	239
Aug	7.6	0.4	7.9	3 637	70	4 677	3 445	4 062	1 268	35	812	1 956	232
Sep	7.6	0.4	7.9	2 976	49	4 661	3 856	4 950	912	137	947	1 963	206
Oct	8.2	0.5	8.7	3 829	81	4 260	3 213	4 538	1 174	123	769	1 988	223
Nov	7.6	0.5	8.1	3 210	31	4 386	3 584	4 495	985	178	977	1 794	188
Dec	8.0	0.5	8.5	2 670	85	4 818	4 272	5 505	707	161	823	1 991	173
1992 Jan	8.0	0.5	8.5	2 984	13	4 160	3 497	5 037	947	284	797	1 580	198
Feb	7.4	0.5	7.9	3 528	66	3 638	2 892	4 025	823	76	896	1 379	160
Mar	7.2†	0.5	7.6†	2 518	85	5 202	4 402	4 544	859	59	809	1 925	236
Apr	7.3†	0.4	7.7†	2 922	48	4 652	3 938	4 810	736	22	873	1 788	218†
May[8]	7.1	0.4	7.5	2 554	96	4 954	4 044	4 014	1 007	96	831	1 968	234

1 The term indigenous is used in this table for convenience to include oil from the UK Continental Shelf as well as the small amounts produced on the mainland.
2 Crude oil *plus* condensates and petroleum gases derived at onshore treatment plants.
3 Crude oil *plus* NGLs.
4 Mainly recycled products (backflows to refineries).
5 Total arrivals *less* refinery shipments of crude oil, NGLs and process oils (ie partly refined products).
6 Foreign trade as recorded by the petroleum industry and may differ from figures published in the *Overseas Trade Statistics*.
7 International marine bunkers.
8 Provisional.

Source: Department of Trade and Industry

8.9 Deliveries of petroleum products for inland consumption

Thousand tonnes

	Butane and propane[1]	Naphtha (LDF) and Middle Distillate Feedstock[2]	Motor Spirit Total	of which: Unleaded	Aviation turbine fuel	Kerosene Burning oil Premier	Standard domestic	Gas/diesel oil Derv fuel	Other	Fuel oil	Lubricat-ing oils	Bitumen	Total[3]
	BHOB	BHOC	BHOD	BHON	BHOE	BHOF	BHOG	BHOI	BHOJ	BHOK	BHOL	BHOM	BHOA
1987	1 838	3 504†	22 184	18	5 815	100	1 390	8 469	8 608	9 935	828	2 162	67 701
1988	1 912	3 866	23 249	258	6 200	68	1 415	9 370	8 456	11 865	849	2 342	72 317
1989	1 893	3 932	23 924	4 648	6 564	55	1 417	10 118	8 323	11 125	839	2 423	73 028
1990	1 969	3 477	24 312	8 255	6 589	41	1 526	10 652	8 046	11 997	822	2 491	73 943
1991	2 273	3 898	24 021	9 868	6 176	46	1 779	10 694	8 031	11 948	759	2 514	74 506
1991 Mar	150	360	2 051	802	418	3	128	891	653	1 019	60	224	6 160
Apr	248	293	2 011	810	428	3	146	896	689	921	65	201	6 078
May	195	317	2 128	866	516	3	113	907	620	1 083	67	246	6 370
Jun	176	294	1 924	791	550	1	100	854	517	1 095	65	249	5 989
Jul	204	338	2 153	892	652	1	83	926	570	939	68	244	6 403
Aug	191	264	2 100	871	636	1	96	868	605	1 073	58	253	6 349
Sep	175	278	1 957	828	614	4	118	896	563	894	63	229	5 969
Oct	183	319	2 088	896	559	4	165	987	676	929	69	250	6 468
Nov	177	351	1 981	857	505	5	171	927	708	827	70	222	6 164
Dec	155	317	2 010	867	458	5	219	838	687	1 036	50	129	6 145
1992 Jan	158	356	1 898	832	471	7	216	875	804	1 152	71	156	6 444
Feb	158	312	1 843	818	457	5	192	853	703	983	66	176	5 990
Mar	135	317	2 005	908	532	4	183	951	692	1 017	65	222	6 372
Apr	170†	350	2 044†	937	515†	3	161†	914†	676†	982†	62†	186	6 269†
May[4]	135	302	2 014	929	581	1	94	885	544	763	63	223	5 809

1 Including amounts for petro-chemicals.
2 Now mainly petro-chemical feedstock. Prior to the October 1986 issue of the *Monthly Digest*, Middle Distillate Feedstock was included in the Gas/Diesel (Other) column.

3 Including other petroleum gases, aviation spirit, wide-cut gasoline, industrial and white spirits, petroleum wax, non-domestic standard burning oil and miscellaneous products, but excluding refinery fuel.
4 Provisional.

Source: Department of Trade and Industry

9 Chemicals

9.1 Fertilisers

Thousand tonnes

	Deliveries to UK agriculture[1]				
	N(nitrogen)				
	Straight[2] Monthly averages or calendar months	Compounds[2] Quarterly averages or totals for quarters	P_2O_5 phosphate[2] Quarterly averages or totals for quarters	K_2O potash[2] Quarterly averages or totals for quarters	Compounds[3] Monthly averages or calendar months
	BIAD	BIAE	BIAF	BIAG	BIAH
1984	71.5	119.0	98.6	116.1	256.9
1985	75.3	117.7	101.0	119.2	263.9
1986	74.0	112.4	91.6	109.5	248.1
1987	81.2	122.0	98.3	121.2	267.9
1988	66.5	122.8	89.5	113.0	262.6
1989	59.2	121.6	82.6	104.8	254.8
1990	56.5	126.3	76.8	101.5	248.8
1988 Jul	33.5	82.0	84.0	111.0	177.0
Aug	52.2	-	-	-	266.1
Sep	40.5	-	-	-	224.1
Oct	50.4	54.0	74.0	84.0	142.3
Nov	75.2	-	-	-	135.5
Dec	95.4	-	-	-	208.4
1989 Jan	72.1	144.0	81.0	99.0	221.9
Feb	66.8	-	-	-	366.6
Mar	70.4	-	-	-	436.2
Apr	60.5	210.0	96.0	134.0	369.7
May	35.2	-	-	-	310.7
Jun	21.0	-	-	-	178.1
Jul	77.3	-	-	-	185.1
Aug	47.6	85.0[4]	120.0[4]	149.0[4]	231.8
Sep	30.0	-	-	-	208.5
Oct	37.6	-	-	-	140.5
Nov	108.7	88.0	61.0	72.0	231.2
Dec	83.4	-	-	-	177.1
1990 Jan	60.0	-	-	-	211.6
Feb	65.0	190.0	101.0	129.0	296.3
Mar	90.7	-	-	-	536.0
Apr	59.8	-	-	-	296.6
May	26.8	148.9	49.5	93.7	276.3
Jun	18.7	-	-	-	169.6
Jul	30.1	-	-	-	161.2
Aug	51.9	53.1	94.2	109.2	217.7
Sep	60.3	-	-	-	209.3
Oct	90.0	-	-	-	178.5
Nov	73.1	113.1	62.6	74.2	260.9
Dec	51.7	-	-	-	171.0
1991 Jan	41.4	-	-	-	167.1
Feb	48.8	143.3	72.7	89.6	222.9
Mar	72.1	-	-	-	393.6
Apr	56.8	-	-	-	357.3
May	27.3	152.6	48.9	92.4	255.0
Jun	23.7	-	-	-	147.0
Jul	36.8	-	-	-	104.4
Aug	39.1	44.8	68.5	80.2	144.2
Sep	59.7	-	-	-	183.5
Oct	80.8	-	-	-	116.7
Nov	66.2	63.8	43.0	49.4	147.0
Dec	42.5	-	-	-	129.9
1992 Jan	40.3	-	-	-	165.4
Feb	71.3	142.6	77.6	93.2	266.1
Mar	60.1	..	..	..	367.5
Apr	46.9	..	..	..	267.4
May	22.9	..	..	..	231.4
Jun	19.3	..	..	..	133.1

1 Until 1989 years ended 31 May, thereafter 30 June.
2 Nutrient content.
3 Total weight of compound fertilisers.
4 Figures relate to four month period June-September 1989.

Sources: Department of Trade and Industry;
HM Customs and Excise;
Fertiliser Manufacturers Association

9.2 Sulphur and sulphuric acid
Production and consumption: monthly averages or calendar months; stocks: end of period

Thousand tonnes

	Sulphur and other materials used for sulphuric acid manufacture				Sulphuric acid (as 100 per cent acid)	
	Consumption		Stocks			
	Sulphur	Zinc concentrates	Sulphur	Zinc concentrates	Production	Consumption
	BIBA	BIBC	BIBD	BIBH	BIBF	BIBG
1984	69.0	20.3	39.1	-	221.2	232.2
1985	64.6	19.8	34.3	-	212.9	222.2
1986	59.4	20.2	29.5	48.6	194.1	206.6
1987	54.8	18.4	21.5	43.7	181.7	181.4
1988	59.1	16.3	23.5	27.3	188.1	187.9
1989	55.0	18.1	18.2	31.7	179.7	178.9
1990	49.6	21.3	19.2	35.0	166.4	165.8
1987 Sep	55.9	18.8	21.3	17.6	183.0	187.8
Oct	62.0	18.6	16.8	40.1	199.1	197.9
Nov	53.8	17.8	20.8	23.5	178.2	183.1
Dec	60.0	18.5	21.1	26.5	193.9	186.8
1988 Jan	70.0	18.2	18.2	18.0	197.6	187.4
Feb	58.6	15.5	21.3	39.4	190.3	189.0
Mar	60.6	19.9	28.3	38.3	196.2	196.0
Apr	55.3	20.6	25.5	25.5	182.4	186.2
May	57.9	18.2	23.3	21.7	192.8	191.4
Jun	58.1	20.2	22.3	28.4	186.9	185.0
Jul	55.1	19.7	24.9	28.0	183.0	196.2
Aug	56.8	19.8	24.3	18.1	186.0	177.8
Sep	55.6	9.6	22.2	14.6	172.2	195.6
Oct	60.9	0.3	25.4	38.9	183.1	180.4
Nov	55.3	15.8	23.8	30.4	179.6	177.8
Dec	65.0	17.8	22.3	26.3	207.4	192.0
1989 Jan	56.1	16.6	20.1	23.4	183.6	180.7
Feb	56.0	15.8	18.8	33.7	181.2	174.9
Mar	58.4	17.0	16.7	30.1	188.7	186.1
Apr	52.8	12.8	19.9	29.7	169.3	178.0
May	58.6	15.3	18.0	26.0	188.9	186.6
Jun	52.4	19.7	16.8	18.5	172.7	155.6
Jul	46.8	18.7	20.0	37.8	156.1	163.4
Aug	50.8	17.6	17.3	39.7	167.8	181.8
Sep	54.8	21.0	19.3	47.7	179.0	184.2
Oct	59.5	22.4	15.5	39.7	196.0	201.9
Nov	57.8	19.1	17.9	26.0	189.0	176.4
Dec	55.9	20.8	18.4	27.9	184.2	177.6
1990 Jan	55.0	23.7	21.3	27.2	189.9	182.2
Feb	49.5	21.4	18.8	23.7	164.2	158.0
Mar	53.1	24.5	18.9	15.3	178.1	176.8
Apr	50.9	21.8	18.9	24.1	172.5	179.5
May	46.8	18.3	18.0	32.3	155.8	157.8
Jun	47.6	17.4	23.9	41.8	156.6	171.1
Jul	47.8	20.4	22.7	45.1	160.8	165.6
Aug	42.9	19.6	21.2	53.0	145.4	132.5
Sep	49.1	22.9	17.5	47.9	164.1	192.9
Oct	49.4	27.8	16.8	28.2	166.5	157.2
Nov	50.0	20.5	18.5	35.6	168.1	159.4
Dec	52.5	16.9	13.7	45.5	174.2	156.5
1991 Jan	54.0	15.7	16.2	37.3	174.9	163.2
Feb	45.5	16.3	16.8	44.7	150.5	156.3
Mar	49.6	20.1	18.4	36.9	173.4	186.8
Apr	42.8	21.8	18.2	33.4	143.4	148.4
May	49.5	24.6	16.1	19.7	161.3	154.9
Jun	39.6	19.9	17.9	23.0	144.2	166.1
Jul	46.3	22.1	16.4	23.3	151.2	143.5
Aug	39.9	24.4	15.9	32.3	132.4	118.9
Sep	41.3	18.5	15.4	28.1	151.8	176.4
Oct	48.0	14.8	16.7	41.2	153.6	160.6
Nov	46.0	22.0	14.9	24.8	149.9	135.3
Dec	45.3	21.1	14.5	19.9	165.1	163.0
1992 Jan	45.9	21.4	16.6	23.8	151.1	153.1
Feb	46.4	16.1	15.4	20.6	148.4	143.6
Mar	43.9	21.1	14.0	31.6	157.5	160.9
Apr	47.0	20.8	12.5	37.4	153.6	144.0

Sources: Department of Trade and Industry;
National Sulphuric Acid Association

9.3 Dyestuffs and pigments: paints and varnish
Sales by manufactures

Quarterly averages or totals for quarters

	Dyestuffs and pigments:[1] thousand tonnes							Paint and varnish:[2] million litres				
	Finished synthetic dyestuffs	Synthetic organic pigments	Inorganic pigment colours	Ochres and mineral products	Titanium dioxide	White lead	Vegetable tanning and dyeing products	Emulsion paints and other aqueous paints	Cellulose based paints, varnishes and lacquers	Varnishes, lacquers, and stains (other than cellulose)	Other[3]	Total
	BICA	BICB	BICC	BICD	BICE	BICF	BICG	BICI	BICJ	BICK	BICL	BICH
1985	10.72	..	3.05	..	54.78	..	..	61.8	6.7	2.6	73.6	144.7
1986	11.49	..	2.94	..	57.49	..	..	64.5	7.9	2.8	74.8	150.0
1987	12.84	..	3.03	..	63.89	..	..	73.9	8.8	2.5	79.4	164.6
1988	13.47	..	3.24	..	66.57	..	..	73.1	9.2	2.7	84.7	169.1
1989	..	..	..	..	..	..	..	71.8	8.5	2.4	85.0	167.6
1990	..	..	..	..	..	..	..	64.9	7.3	1.6	71.0	144.7
1991	..	..	..	..	..	..	..	63.7	7.4	0.9	66.9	138.5
1981 Q1	9.95	2.66	3.34	..	44.60	..	-	52.3	8.3	2.0	71.6	134.2
Q2	11.41	2.62	3.38	..	43.22	..	-	49.8	8.6	2.4	77.6	138.4
Q3	10.87	2.61	3.26	..	43.17	..	-	50.0	8.4	2.5	81.9	142.8
1981 Q4	10.51	2.63	3.25	..	38.60	..	-	42.2	7.0	2.0	66.3	117.5
1982 Q1	10.98	2.44	3.51	..	48.26	..	-	56.6	6.6	2.0	68.3	133.5
Q2	11.56	2.74	3.18	..	40.75	..	-	52.5	7.2	2.7	80.9	143.3
Q3	9.75	2.15	2.66	..	40.32	..	-	54.3	6.6	2.6	75.7	139.2
Q4	10.08	2.52	2.53	..	43.01	..	-	46.1	5.9	2.2	60.9	115.0
1983 Q1	10.49	2.80	3.47	..	50.87	..	-	61.1	6.9	2.3	67.7	138.1
Q2	10.59	2.82	3.38	..	52.26	..	-	55.5	7.7	2.6	75.4	141.2
Q3	10.52	2.88	3.38	..	43.59	..	-	55.1	7.4	2.7	81.5	146.7
Q4	10.49	3.43	3.42	..	48.16	..	-	45.8	6.9	2.4	65.8	120.9
1984 Q1	11.63	..	3.17	..	53.92	..	-	57.3	7.3	2.3	73.9	140.8
Q2	11.27	..	3.45	..	53.40	..	-	59.4	8.0	2.6	79.1	149.1
Q3	9.75	..	3.01	..	49.67	..	-	58.6	7.6	2.7	79.7	148.6
Q4	10.60	..	3.21	..	49.00	..	-	52.6	6.4	2.1	61.2	122.3
1985 Q1	11.04	..	3.16	..	56.22	..	-	61.0	6.5	2.4	72.8	142.7
Q2	10.68	..	3.06	..	56.59	..	-	65.0	7.0	2.8	79.1	153.9
Q3	10.04	..	2.90	..	53.81	..	-	64.9	6.9	2.8	77.2	151.8
Q4	11.13	..	3.08	..	52.52	..	-	56.5	6.4	2.2	65.2	130.3
1986 Q1	11.52	..	2.79	..	57.03	..	-	62.1	7.6	2.4	67.5	139.6
Q2	11.79	..	2.85	..	58.08	..	-	68.1	8.2	2.9	80.8	160.0
Q3	11.09	..	2.82	..	55.39	..	-	66.0	8.6	3.1	80.9	158.6
Q4	11.58	..	3.30	..	59.45	..	-	61.6	7.3	2.7	70.1	141.7
1987 Q1	12.93	..	3.47	..	64.71	..	0.35	67.2	7.9	2.5	71.3	148.9
Q2	12.96	..	3.06	..	62.49	..	0.40	77.3	9.8	2.7	83.9	173.7
Q3	12.15	..	2.90	..	58.86	..	0.37	82.0	8.8	2.6	87.5	180.9
Q4	13.31	..	2.74	..	69.52	..	0.34	69.3	8.8	2.0	74.7	154.8
1988 Q1	13.92	..	3.27	..	69.82	..	0.36	73.1	8.8	2.5	79.9	164.3
Q2	13.98	..	3.34	..	66.60	..	0.36	76.2	10.3	2.8	89.0	178.3
Q3	12.58	..	3.18	..	63.36	..	0.24	77.0	9.3	3.0	89.3	178.6
Q4	13.38	..	3.16	..	66.51	..	0.32	66.1	7.7	2.3	78.9	155.0
1989 Q1	13.67	..	3.91	..	65.53	..	0.32	71.1	8.0	1.8	71.4[4]	152.2
Q2	15.35	..	3.55	..	69.29	..	0.30	70.2	9.3	1.5	76.7	157.8
Q3	..	..	..	..	..	..	..	70.1	7.4	0.9	75.3	153.7
Q4	..	..	..	..	..	..	..	60.7	5.8	1.8	63.2	131.5
1990 Q1	..	..	..	..	..	..	..	67.3	7.5	1.3	69.6	145.7
Q2	..	..	..	..	..	..	..	68.0	9.1	1.3	77.6	155.9
Q3	..	..	..	..	..	..	..	66.1	7.1	2.0	73.4	148.5
Q4	..	..	..	..	..	..	..	58.5	5.4	1.6	63.5	128.9
1991 Q1	..	..	..	..	..	..	..	63.1†	6.9	0.9	59.7†	130.6†
Q2	..	..	..	..	..	..	..	68.6	8.7	1.0	72.3	150.5
Q3	..	..	..	..	..	..	..	67.2	7.4†	0.9	73.5	149.0
Q4	..	..	..	..	..	..	..	58.4	6.9	0.9	58.7	124.9
1992 Q1	..	..	..	..	..	..	..	66.4	8.0	1.4	59.3	135.1

1 Figures relate to sales by manufacturers in the United Kingdom employing 25 or more persons, and from 1st quarter 1981 those employing 100 or more persons.

2 Figures relate to sales by manufacturers in the United Kingdom employing 50 or more persons, and from 1st quarter 1989 those employing 100 or more persons.

3 Figures from 1st quarter 1986 include other marine paints; an equivalent figure for 4th quarter 1985 is 71.0.

4 Figures from 1st quarter 1989 exclude marine paints, (approximately 6 million litres per quarter) and certain miscellaneous paints, (approximately 4 million litres per quarter).

Source: Central Statistical Office

9.4 Production of selected organic chemicals[1]

Tonnes: quarterly averages or totals for quarters

| | Acyclic (single chemicals)[2] | | | Cyclic (single chemicals)[2] | | Formaldehyde[6] | Acetone |
	Ethylene	Propylene	Butadiene	Benzene[3,5]	Toluene[4]		
	BIFA	BIFB	BIFC	BIFD	BIFE	BIFF	BIFG
1985	361 629	243 307	74 408	199 135	41 209	30 917	36 699
1986	435 025	216 043	48 217	213 193	8 267	25 804	30 794
1987	449 464	218 731	57 856	227 888	15 888	28 370	29 464
1988	501 310	212 618	59 919	218 192	26 997	27 905	31 865
1989	493 840	199 211	56 476	256 213	..	19 917	32 582
1990	374 525	187 816	49 536	175 741	..	10 712	32 116
1991	448 730	208 564	49 379	217 424	..	14 906	31 328
1981 Q3	283 729	184 931	42 758	155 133	43 217	25 765	29 725
Q4	356 540	217 496	59 875	140 317	48 132	30 713	31 717
1982 Q1	281 582	207 905	50 993	158 815	40 286	30 765	34 338
Q2	278 157	194 977	55 638	139 393	27 649	28 846	33 778
Q3	276 904	208 088	65 002	136 982	-	22 500	28 530
Q4	278 757	213 203	57 166	134 264	52 237	25 043	38 612
1983 Q1	271 500	194 397	50 004	172 856	35 842	25 074	33 887
Q2	314 706	217 036	63 433	184 648	-	24 540	31 932
Q3	294 210	220 367	64 865	193 780	-	21 402	31 972
Q4	274 230	200 104	59 376	174 575	-	26 785	23 963
1984 Q1	350 505	250 842	66 968	203 924	45 916	27 167	42 852
Q2	277 241	208 954	56 383	170 677	25 289	27 146	34 293
Q3	336 413	251 490	62 748	180 617	-	23 140	41 850
Q4	360 117	264 496	73 123	199 445	25 674	26 134	42 457
1985 Q1	343 085	236 787	70 099	199 564	30 413	26 349	33 041
Q2	364 715	219 685	68 815	188 353	42 669	34 625	40 952
Q3	378 244	260 567	84 327	191 638	44 521	27 648	37 195
Q4	360 470	256 187	74 390	216 986	47 233	35 045	35 607
1986 Q1	336 082	208 797	48 963	217 879	33 067	25 547	31 170
Q2	429 851	201 045	56 656	231 942	-	26 039	31 392
Q3	480 421	225 700	43 217	205 506	-	24 856	32 019
Q4	493 746	228 628	44 031	197 445	-	26 772	28 596
1987 Q1	482 256	197 313	58 105	220 297	-	26 669	28 004
Q2	357 405	206 021	43 122	193 881	-	31 437	31 804
Q3	467 991	228 860	63 752	260 755	31 896	26 514	26 776
Q4	490 203	242 731	66 446	236 620	31 654	28 859	31 270
1988 Q1	496 349	261 812	59 695	243 883	-	25 989	33 918
Q2	518 986	204 521	62 250	160 164	34 385	30 671	29 829
Q3	492 626	185 685	59 259	237 516	47 087	25 798	29 312
Q4	497 277	198 452	58 470	231 203	26 517	29 160	34 400
1989 Q1	515 744	200 848	58 826	310 417	-	24 843	35 400
Q2	499 075	156 553	58 462	237 683	-	18 069	29 544
Q3	472 414	162 923	51 280	198 626	..	16 516[7]	33 700
Q4	488 125	276 521	57 337	278 127	..	20 238[7]	31 683
1990 Q1	485 536	216 281	60 520	209 313	..	11 846	31 834
Q2	320 325	147 516	37 928	161 661	..	11 649	33 261
Q3	346 593	198 469	58 008	159 834	..	9 339	39 676
Q4	345 646	188 997	41 686	172 154	..	10 012	23 691
1991 Q1	452 424	207 747	38 685	222 627	..	15 922	26 987
Q2	398 473	204 989	55 361	203 042	..	15 912	33 819
Q3	472 243	220 216	54 036	207 583	..	14 089	32 660
Q4	471 778	201 304	49 432	236 445	..	13 702	31 844

1 Figures relate to sales by UK manufacturers employing 100 or more persons from 1990 Q1 replacing the previous employment level of 50.
2 Hydrocarbons (other than products of coal tar distillation, benzole refining and wood carbonisation).
3 Including that obtained by dealkylation of toluene.
4 Including that used in the production of benzene.
5 Includes hydrocarbon benzene from 1985 Q4. A comparable figure for 1985 Q3 is 210 108.
6 Including paraformaldehyde (expressed as 100 per cent formaldehyde).
7 Estimated.

Source: Central Statistical Office

10.1 Iron and steel
Weekly averages   Stocks: end of period

Thousand tonnes

	Iron ore		Pig iron			Scrap[4]		Crude steel: production	Net home and export deliveries	Finished steel products			Iron castings: production
											Stocks		
	Production	Consumption of imported iron ore[1]	Production in blast furnaces[2]	Steel-making consumption	Total stocks[3]	Consumption in steel-making	Total stocks			At producers works[5]	Consumers'	Stock-holders'	
	BJAA	BJAB	BJAC	BJAD	BJAE	BJAF	BJAG	BJAH	BJAI	BJAJ	BJAK	BJAL	BJAM
1985	5	290	201	195	152	135	438	302	251	3 233	1 640	1 250	23.2
1986	6	275	188	185	103	128	552	283	253	2 743	1 376	1 199	20.9
1987	5	332	228	225	94	133	582	329	283	2 900	2 680	1 250	21.2
1988	4	380	253	250	91	148	382	364	321	2 943	2 710	1 230	22.0
1989	1	365	246	246	49	151	467	360	325	2 874	2 930	1 230	21.4
1990	1	351	240	234	67	139	430	343	309	2 809	2 640	1 050	28.0
1991 Apr	1.0	373	249	245	35	118	368	334	280	2 479	-	-	20.2
May	1.0	381	255	250	47	116	348	338	276	2 660	-	-	13.5
Jun	1.0	373	244	240	64	126	361	336	264	2 577	2 270	800	21.8
Jul	1.0	334	218	213	68	89	367	278	253	2 587	-	-	14.6
Aug	1.0	302	199	193	70	108	318	275	237	2 684	-	-	17.2
Sep	1.0	366	244	241	62	126	312	340	300	2 775	2 210	780	18.8
Oct	1.0	366	252	247	48	105	311	346	300	2 801	-	-	19.7
Nov	1.0	371	247	242	43	125	349	339	316	2 757	-	-	23.4
Dec	1.0	313	211	204	44	94	365	275	249	2 754	2 240	840	16.5
1992 Jan	1.0	338	230	222	61	116	332	305	274	2 767	..	-	18.7
Feb	1.0	373	246	242	64	132	293	343	317	2 666	..	-	23.8
Mar	1.0	356	240	236	56	131	308	337	370	2 477	..	890	26.3
Apr	1.0	369	244	240	56	125	290	337	283	2 537	..	..	18.2
May	..	..	..	239	..	121	..	330	..	..	..	..	..

1 Including manganese ore.
2 Includes blast furnace ferro-alloys.
3 Includes blast furnace ferro-alloys, but excludes iron foundries and refined iron works.
4 Excludes iron foundries and refined iron works.
5 Stocks of ingots, semi-finished and finished steel.

*Sources: Department of Trade and Industry;
Iron and Steel Statistics Bureau*

10.2 Supplies and deliveries of steel
Weekly averages

Thousand tonnes (crude steel equivalent)

	Supply from home sources				Total	Imports[3]	Exports[3]	Net home disposals
	Crude steel production		Producers' stock changes[1]	Re-usable material[2]				
	Total	of which: alloy						
	BJBA	BJBB	BJBC	BJBD	BJBE	BJBF	BJBG	BJBH
1985	302.3	23.5	11.5	1.6	292.4	93.8	115.7	270.5
1986	283.2	21.9	-13.3	1.6	298.1	104.5	126.3	276.3
1987[4]	328.6	23.9	3.8	2.0	326.8	108.2	153.4	281.6
1988	364.4	25.8	1.1	1.5	364.8	114.4	142.1	337.1
1989	360.4	26.3	-1.7	1.3	363.4	120.2	144.0	339.6
1990	343.1	23.1	1.3	1.5	343.3	114.7	147.4	310.6
1989 Q1	387.0	28.5	0.6	1.4	387.8	135.0	134.8	388.0
Q2	373.4	26.1	-7.8	1.3	382.5	124.1	161.6	345.0
Q3	338.2	21.5	13.7	1.2	325.7	113.1	129.3	309.5
Q4	342.5	25.1	-13.2	1.4	357.1	108.6	150.4	315.3
1990 Q1	358.2	26.0	-31.4	1.3	390.9	109.5	148.4	352.0
Q2	362.1	24.2	0.4	1.4	363.0	112.6	153.5	322.1
Q3	328.4	21.7	9.5	1.5	340.6	117.3	138.7	319.2
Q4	323.3	20.3	-9.9	1.6	334.8	119.5	149.2	305.1
1991 Q1	313.5	20.4	40.6	1.0	273.9	130.5	151.1	253.3
Q2	335.8	19.4	-26.4	1.4	363.6	119.9	184.8	298.7
Q3	295.9	16.8	-11.6	1.5	309.0	110.9	163.2	256.7
Q4	322.1	18.7	1.6	1.6	322.1	116.3	171.4	267.0

1 Increases in stock are shown as + and decreases in stock (ie deliveries from stock) as -.
2 Currently mainly old rails for re-rolling.
3 Derived from HM Customs statistics.
4 53-week period.

*Sources: Department of Trade and Industry;
Iron and Steel Statistics Bureau*

10.3 Copper and aluminium
Monthly averages or calendar months; stocks: end of period[1]

Thousand tonnes

	Copper							Aluminium					
	Production		Home consumption			Production[2]		Production		Despatches to customers			
	Primary refined	Secondary refined	Primary and secondary refined	Scrap (metal content)	Stocks refined	Semi-manu-factures	Castings and miscellan-eous uses	Primary[3]	Secondary[4]	Primary[3]	Secondary	Wrought including foil stock	Castings
	BJDA	BJDB	BJDC	BJDD	BJDE	BJDF	BJDG	BJDH	BJDI	BJDJ	BJDK	BJDL	BJDM
1985	5.3	5.1	28.9	11.0	37.6	41.2	4.1	22.9	10.6	36.3	10.6	-	6.0
1986	5.2	5.3	28.3	11.3	31.6	40.6	4.1	23.0	9.7	37.6	10.0	-	5.2
1987	4.5	5.7	27.3	11.5	11.7	39.8	4.1	24.5	9.7	38.5	-	-	-
1988	4.1	6.2	27.3	11.0	13.8	39.3	4.1	25.0	8.8	45.1	-	-	-
1989	4.1	5.9	27.1	10.8	-	38.8	4.0	24.8	9.1	43.8	-	-	-
1990	3.9	6.2	27.0	10.5	-	38.3	4.0	24.1	10.0	43.4	-	28.4	-
1991 Jul	0.6	4.4	22.4	9.8	9.5	32.5	4.1	24.4	11.3	28.9	8.5	24.9	..
Aug	-	4.9	18.4	9.0	11.5	28.0	4.1	24.0	10.0	37.0	6.6	25.3	..
Sep	0.4	3.9	22.5	10.0	10.0	33.1	4.0	26.1	10.6	37.2	7.7	28.3	..
Oct	0.9	3.3	23.0	11.3	8.3	34.9	4.2	24.3	12.1	31.3	8.7	30.1	..
Nov	0.6	3.9	21.2	10.9	9.3	33.1	4.0	20.7	11.8	37.4	9.6	28.4	..
Dec	1.0	3.4	17.0	10.4	9.3	27.9	4.0	21.5	8.9	25.1	6.9	15.5	..
1992 Jan	0.9	2.7	27.1	6.6	8.5	37.7	..	19.4	10.6	35.5	9.3	34.7	..
Feb	2.1	1.4	25.9	7.5	8.6	37.6	..	21.3	11.8	48.6	9.8	29.2	..
Mar	0.9	2.9	26.2	10.3	9.8	41.2	..	19.4	11.5	61.8	9.4	33.2	..
Apr	..	..	..	..	..	..	..	19.3	9.8	51.7	8.3	37.9	..
May	..	..	..	..	..	..	..	21.8	7.1	52.2	6.2	31.3	..
Jun	..	..	..	..	..	..	..	19.4	10.4	48.4	8.4	31.3	..

1 End of period stocks (monthly) are as published in *World Metal Statistics Consumers' Stocks*, but annual totals are arrived at by the addition of LME (UK owned) stocks.
2 Copper and copper alloys.
3 Including the pure content of primary alloys.
4 Including the primary content used in the production of secondary metal.

Sources: Department of Trade and Industry;
World Bureau of Metal Statistics;
Aluminium Federation

10.4 Lead, tin and zinc
Monthly averages or calendar months; stocks: end of period[1]

Thousand tonnes

	Lead					Tin				Zinc			
		Home consumption		Stocks				Exports			Home consumption		
	Production of refined[2]	Refined lead[3]	Scrap (metal content)[4]	Bullion	Refined lead[5]	Home consump-tion	Imports refined tin[3]	and re-ex-ports[3]	Stocks[5]	Slab production	Slab	Other (metal content)[6]	Stocks: slab[5]
	BJEA	BJEB	BJEC	BJED	BJEE	BJEF	BJEG	BJEH	BJEI	BJEJ	BJEK	BJEL	BJEM
1985	27.27	22.85	2.42	13.44	57.01	0.79	0.33	0.61	19.37	6.20	14.5	4.90	15.9
1986	27.39	23.51	2.26	16.15	46.79	0.81	0.35	1.13	11.94	7.20	15.2	4.50	15.0
1987	28.91	23.96	3.05	26.07	27.16	0.82	0.24	1.23	6.80	6.80	15.7	4.40	14.0
1988	31.15	25.21	3.08	18.59	26.74	0.85	0.17	1.16	0.98	6.30	16.0	4.30	13.0
1989	29.17	25.11	2.92	16.96	25.70	0.85	0.39	0.45	2.23	6.60	16.2	4.10	13.9
1990	27.45	25.13	2.71	17.98	22.34	0.86	0.32	0.47	1.81	7.00	15.7	4.40	12.0
1991 May	16.82	21.67	2.18	4.12	26.56	0.85	0.32	0.36	1.40	8.8	13.9	4.1	11.6
Jun	23.29	23.63	3.24	8.62	24.10	0.84	0.36	0.50	1.36	10.0	14.0	3.9	11.7
Jul	24.13	22.72	2.55	7.70	23.88	0.84	0.46	0.22	1.42	8.4	12.8	4.0	11.9
Aug	19.25	20.48	2.58	10.26	23.83	0.85	0.38	0.18	1.45	7.4	13.3	3.8	11.8
Sep	23.64	22.91	4.41	24.18	21.98	0.86	0.48	0.04	1.43	8.8	14.6	4.1	11.4
Oct	27.56	23.36	3.46	23.38	21.79	0.87	0.53	0.04	1.40	9.0	15.5	4.1	11.3
Nov	28.78	23.76	2.82	25.11	20.50	0.86	0.43	-	1.39	8.0	15.0	4.5	10.4
Dec	28.03	20.68	2.66	22.36	21.57	0.84	0.50	0.03	1.37	9.9	13.9	4.0	11.1
1992 Jan	30.59	24.75	2.80	20.14	22.39	0.85	0.73	0.06	1.40	8.2	15.1	4.6	11.3
Feb	27.39	22.77	3.07	17.62	23.37	0.84	0.87	0.03	1.35	8.1	14.6	4.5	11.8
Mar	25.41	21.93	3.30	17.74	23.32	0.85	0.86	0.03	1.29	9.4	14.8	4.3	12.0
Apr	28.26	20.49	3.01	15.69	25.20	0.86	..	..	1.20	7.4	15.8	4.4	11.9

1 End of period stocks (monthly) are as published in *World Metal Statistics Consumers' Stocks*, but annual totals are arrived at by the addition of LME (UK-owned) stocks.
2 Lead reclaimed from secondary scrap metal, and lead refined from bullion and domestic ore, including antimonial lead.
3 Including toll transactions. Figures of home consumption of lead comprise imported primary, secondary, English refined and antimonial lead.
4 Excluding secondary.
5 Stocks held by consumers and LME warehouses.
6 Including scrap.

Sources: Department of Trade and Industry;
World Bureau of Metal Statistics

10.5 Metal goods, engineering and vehicle industries
Total sales of UK based manufacturers[1]
Standard Industrial Classification 1980

£ million

Activity heading Product group		1988	1989	1990	1991	1991 Q2	1991 Q3	1991 Q4	1992 Q1	1992 Q2
Division 3										
Class 31: Manufacture of metal goods not elsewhere specified[2]										
3120 Forging, pressing and stamping	BJFB	1 364	1 434	1 214	917	247	196	196	235	216
3137 Bolts, nuts, washers, rivets, springs and non-precision chains	BJFC	758	828	863	817	207	193	198	217	205
3142 Metal doors, windows, etc	BJFD	897	956	1 043	986	251	245	240	204	198
3161 Hand tools and implements	BJFE	246	267	346	311	79	73	80	78	76
3162 Cutlery, spoons, forks and similar tableware; razors	BJFF	157	185	234	308	77	77	84	77	81
3163 Metal storage vessels (mainly non-industrial)	BJFG	78	97	108	94	25	21	23	22	19
3164 Packaging products of metal	BJFH	1 913	1 976	2 236	2 122	550	551	542	495	562
3165 Domestic heating and cooking appliances (non-electrical)	BJFI	411	400	433	419	102	99	121	108	89
3166 Metal furniture and safes	BJFJ	795	870	968	917	219	233	229	250†	242
3167 Domestic utensils of metal	BJFK	263	220	228	201	48	50	57	50	44
3169 Miscellaneous finished metal products	BJFL	3 474	3 829	4 033	4 044	1 018	1 007	1 004	1 069†	1 028
Total	BJFA	10 354	11 061	11 705	11 136	2 822	2 745	2 775†	2 805	2 758
Mechanical engineering[3]										
Class 32 :										
3204 Fabricated constructional steelwork	BJFN	2 038	2 432	2 535	2 531	664	630	654	603	617
3205 Boilers and process plant fabrications	BJFO	1 760	1 948	2 160	2 308	566	611	592	573	535
3211 Agricultural machinery	BJFP	349	342	378	369	99	104	75	92†	96
3212 Wheeled tractors	BJFQ	1 166	1 109	1 183	865	230	193	207	262	309
3221 Metal-working machine tools	BJFR	1 148	1 286	1 415	1 141	291	267	272	268†	247
3222 Engineers' small tools	BJFS	908	992	1 044	1 024	258	245	252	266	267
3230 Textile machinery	BJFT	421	399	457	404	97	96	114	117	116
3244 Food, drink and tobacco processing machinery; packaging and bottling machinery	BJFU	807	858	960	912	229	212	279	220	260
3245 Chemical industry machinery; furnaces and kilns; gas, water and waste treatment plant	BJFV	578	580	682	696	161	175	180	170	176
3251 Mining machinery	BJFW	753	832	780	712	166	177	171	152	147
3254 Construction and earth moving equipment	BJFX	1 606	1 811	1 946	1 700	462	405	421	364	396
3255 Mechanical lifting and handling equipment	BJFY	2 179	2 396	2 650	2 612	636	648	689	646†	673
3261 Precision chains and other mechanical power transmission equipment	BJFZ	993	1 037	1 128	1 071	262	260	259	257	250
3262 Ball, needle and roller bearings	BJOA	481	522	566	514	133	118	123	134	130
3275 Machinery for working wood, rubber, plastics, leather and making paper, glass, bricks and similar materials; laundry and dry cleaning	BJOB	636	781	710	630	160	154	176	132	142
3276 Printing, bookbinding and paper goods machinery	BJOC	909	924	952	815	187	208	219	210	205
3281 Industrial (including marine) engines	BJOD	1 093	1 233	1 448	1 422	383	327	373	350	367
3283 Compressors and fluid power equipment	BJOE	1 131	1 241	1 322	1 270	324	313	306	336	318
3284 Refrigerating, space-heating, ventilating and air conditioning equipment	BJOF	1 540	1 779	2 347	2 415	597	601	615	572†	549
3285 Scales, weighing machinery and portable power tools	BJOG	582	589	561	577	140	127	154	159	145
3286 Miscellaneous industrial and commercial machinery	BJOH	1 172	1 261	1 264	1 257	308	272	333	330	318
3287 Pumps	BJOI	682	813	892	911	220	233	245	230	224
3288 Industrial valves	BJOJ	608	704	665	645	162	162	164	217	204
3289 Miscellaneous mechanical marine and precision engineering	BJOK	2 102	2 461	3 032	2 871	728	684	706	746†	747
3290 Ordnance, small arms and ammunition	BJOL	1 157	1 123	1 170	1 022	220	233	303	229	227
Total	BJFM	26 798	29 453	32 247	30 691	7 682	7 454	7 881	7 631†	7 666
Manufacture of office machinery and data processing equipment										
Class 33:										
3301 Office machinery	BJON	403	460	483	445	112	108	106	116	105
3302 Electronic data processing equipment	BJOO	6 438	7 412	7 815	8 081	1 971	1 745	2 424	1 888	1 962
Total	BJOM	6 841	7 872	8 298	8 526	2 083	1 853	2 530	2 004	2 067
Electrical and electronic engineering[4]										
Class 34:										
3410 Insulated wires and cables	BJOQ	1 748	2 100	2 176	1 815	458	413	409	480	449
3420 Basic electrical equipment	BJOR	3 243	3 590	4 176	4 422	1 090	1 111	1 113	1 114	1 088
3432 Batteries and accumulators	BJOS	523	534	588	601	141	140	175	133	130
3433 Alarms and signalling equipment	BJOT	474	581	680	742	176	191	184	202	151
3434 Electrical equipment for motor vehicles, cycles and aircraft	BJOU	805	973	982	956	255	224	228	235	232
3435 Miscellaneous electrical equipment for industrial use	BJOV	502	512	551	493	135	116	111	118	112
3441 Telegraph and telephone apparatus and equipment	BJOW	2 279	2 577	2 395	2 354	570	578	566	479	457
3442 Electrical instruments and control systems	BJOX	1 805	2 005	1 959	1 926	444	484	487	542	480
3443 Radio and electronic capital goods	BJOY	3 735	3 847	3 887	3 984	878	984	956	1 162	823
3444 Components other than active components, mainly for electronic equipment	BJOZ	1 441	1 583	1 829	1 758	445	423	432	480	473
3452 Vinyl records and pre-recorded tapes	BJPA	492	512	493	513	94	115	196	109	105
3453 Active components and electronic sub-assemblies	BJPB	2 133	2 290	2 483	2 346	603	591	574	626	602
3454 Electronic consumer goods and miscellaneous equipment	BJPC	1 914	2 063	2 380	2 082	453	525	615	415	389
3460 Domestic-type electric appliances	BJPD	1 966	1 938	1 803	1 815	434	440	496	430	395
3470 Electric lamps and other electric lighting equipment	BJPE	1 065	1 244	1 307	1 128	259	274	304	321	291
Total	BJOP	24 125	26 349	27 687	26 935	6 435	6 610	6 847	6 845	6 176

See footnotes on next page.

Source: Central Statistical Office

10.5
continued

Metal goods, engineering and vehicle industries
Total sales of UK based manufacturers[1]
Standard Industrial Classification 1980

£ million

Activity heading Product group		1988	1989	1990	1991	1991 Q2	1991 Q3	1991 Q4	1992 Q1	1992 Q2
Manufacture of motor vehicles and parts thereof										
Class 35:										
3510 Motor vehicles and their engines	BJPG	10 928	12 049	12 002	12 170	3 029	2 952	2 935	3 131	-
3521 and Motor vehicle bodies and vehicle parts	BJPH	4 431	4 906	5 249	5 317	1 380	1 223	1 333	1 446	1 429
3530										
3522/3 Trailers, semi-trailers and caravans	BJPI	924	1 055	1 049	1 021	271	222	246	276	253
Total	BJPF	16 283	18 011	18 300	18 508	4 680	4 397	4 514	4 853	-
Manufacture of other transport equipment[5]										
Class 36:										
3620 Railway and tramway vehicles	BJPK	740	708	811	799	181	193	175	203	183
3640 Aerospace equipment manufacturing, repairing and modification	BJPL	7 891	11 015	12 176	11 532	3 198	2 507	3 388	2 624[†]	3 124
3650 Baby carriages and wheelchairs	BJPM	102	110	140	145	44	36	28	35	34
Total	BJPJ	8 732	11 833	13 127	12 476	3 422	2 737	3 591	2 861[†]	3 340
Instrument engineering										
Class 37:										
3710 Measuring, checking and precision instruments and apparatus	BJPO	1 685	1 841	1 925	1 909	475	473	482	517	502
3720 Medical and surgical equipment and orthopaedic appliances	BJPP	645	705	864	903	223	223	232	249	231
3731 Spectacles and unmounted lenses	BJPQ	221	196	226	282	77	72	64	73	68
3732 Optical precision instruments	BJPR	338	331	356	294	68	65	72	62	54
3733 Photographic and cinematographic equipment	BJPS	397	378	365	514	124	127	135	130	132
3740 Clocks, watches and other timing devices	BJPT	90	89	111	123	28	29	35	39	29
Total	BJPN	3 375	3 540	3 848	4 025	995	989	1 020	1 070	1 016

1 These figures represent the total sales of UK based manufacturers. Estimates for establishments which fall below the employment cut-off of the Monthly Sales Inquiry are included.
2 Excluding ferrous and non-ferrous metal foundries AH 3111/2, and heat and surface treatment of metals, including sintering AH 3138.
3 Excluding process engineering contractors AH 3246.
4 Excluding electrical equipment installation AH 3480.
5 Excluding shipbuilding and repairing AH 3610, and cycles and motor cycles AH 3633/4.

Source: Central Statistical Office

10.6

Mechanical, instrument and electrical engineering industries
Seasonally adjusted volume index numbers of sales

1985 average monthly sales=100

	Combined engineering			Mechanical engineering			Instrument and electrical engineering [1]		
	Total	Home	Export	Total	Home	Export	Total	Home	Export
	FEAJ	BJGB	BJGC	BJGD	BJGE	BJGF	BJGG	BJGH	BJGI
1987	104	102	106	98	98	98	109	106	114
1988	115	112	120	106	107	104	122	116	135
1989	121	116	132	110	110	109	131	121	152
1990	124	117	138	113	111	116	133	121	158
1991	116	107	136	101	99	104	129	113	165
1990 Nov	119	111	135	108	108	109	128	114	157
Dec	120	113	137	106	105	109	132	119	163
1991 Jan	118	109	136	102	102	102	131	115	165
Feb	117	110	132	102	100	105	129	117	156
Mar	119	111	137	105	103	110	131	117	163
Apr	113	105	130	99	97	102	125	111	155
May	114	105	134	100	99	102	127	110	163
Jun	121	111	142	105	104	109	134	117	172
Jul	113	103	133	98	98	99	124	107	164
Aug	117	106	140	103	101	107	129	111	169
Sep	116	105	139	99	96	104	131	113	171
Oct	109	101	128	97	96	100	120	105	153
Nov	116	105	141	101	98	107	129	110	171
Dec	119	107	145	98	95	104	137	117	183
1992 Jan	107	97	127	92	89	99	119	105	152
Feb	113	102	137	96	92	103	128	110	167
Mar	116	104	140	100	96	108	128	111	168
Apr	110	97	137	93	89	100	124	103	170
May	111	98	139	95	91	102[†]	124	103	171
Jun	114	103	137	101	98	109	124	107	161

1 Classes 33, 34 and 37 of the *Standard Industrial Classification (revised) 1980*.

Source: Central Statistical Office

10.7 Mechanical, instrument and electrical engineering industries
Seasonally adjusted volume index numbers of orders on hand[1]

Average 1985=100

	Combined engineering			Mechanical engineering			Instrument and electrical engineering [2]		
	Total	Home	Export	Total	Home	Export	Total	Home	Export
	DKCJ	FEAV	FEAX	BJHD	BJHE	BJHF	BJHG	BJHH	BJHI
1987	100	103	96	96	99	89	104	105	101
1988	107	109	104	97	102	86	116	115	116
1989	120	120	121	105	106	104	131	130	131
1990	113	110	117	94	95	94	127	123	133
1991	103	97	112	80	81	80	119	110	132
1991 Feb	106	105	107	90	91	90	118	117	119
Mar	104	103	107	88	88	88	116	114	119
Apr	104	102	107	87	88	86	116	113	121
May	102	100	106	86	88	84	114	110	120
Jun	102	98	107	85	86	83	114	108	122
Jul	103	101	107	87	91	80	115	108	124
Aug	104	101	108	87	91	80	116	110	126
Sep	102	99	109	83	84	81	117	110	127
Oct	103	99	109	82	84	79	118	111	129
Nov	104	99	111	83	83	81	119	111	131
Dec	103	97	112	80	81	80	119	110	132
1992 Jan	102	97	111	79	78	82	119	112	130
Feb	103	95	116[†]	80	78	84	120	110	136
Mar	102	95	115	78[†]	76	80	121	110	138
Apr	103	95	115	76	74	81	122	112	137
May	101	93	115	78	73	88	118	108[†]	132
Jun	101	93	114	78	71	90	118	109	130

1 End of period.
2 Classes 33, 34, 37 of the *Standard Industrial Classification (revised 1980)*.

Source: Central Statistical Office

10.8 Mechanical, instrument and electrical engineering industries
Seasonally adjusted volume index numbers of new orders[1]

1985 average monthly sales=100

	Combined engineering			Mechanical engineering			Instrument and electrical engineering[2]		
	Total	Home	Export	Total	Home	Export	Total	Home	Export
	FEAL	FEAN	FEAP	BJID	BJIE	BJIF	BJIG	BJIH	BJII
1987	105	105	106	100	102	96	110	108	115
1988	119	115	125	107	109	102	128	121	145
1989	128	121	142	114	112	118	139	129	163
1990	120	112	136	107	106	111	130	118	159
1991	111	100	133	94	92	97	125	107	165
1991 Feb	102	97	113	90	92	87	112	101	137
Mar	107	95	132	91	89	96	120	100	165
Apr	111	100	134	94	97	90	124	102	173
May	105[†]	97	125	95	97	90	114	96	156
Jun	118	102	150	100	97	107	132	107	189
Jul	121	115	133	109	124	81	130[†]	109	179
Aug	121	109	146	101	100	104	138	117	184
Sep	108	90	147	77	60	110[†]	135	115	179
Oct	114	105	131	94	96	89	130	113	168
Nov	119	102	155	102	94	118	133	109	187
Dec	113	97	148	85	78[†]	98	137	112	193
1992 Jan	104	95	122	87	75	112	117	112[†]	131
Feb	118	94	169	99	90	118	134	98	216
Mar	112	101	136	85	87	82	134	111	185
Apr	111	100	135	85[†]	76	104	132	118	163[†]
May	102	84	141[†]	107	86	149	98	82	134
Jun	111	102	131	98	89	116	123	113	145

1 Net of cancellations.
2 Classes 33, 34 and 37 of the *Standard Industrial Classification (revised 1980)*.

Source: Central Statistical Office

10.9 Passenger cars [1]
Monthly totals are for four or five week periods

Number

	Total production					Production for export					Sales:[2] £ million	
	1000c.c and under	Over 1000c.c and not over 1600c.c	Over 1600c.c and not over 2800c.c	Over 2800c.c	Total	1000c.c and under	Over 1000c.c and not over 1600c.c	Over 1600c.c and not over 2800c.c	Over 2800c.c	Total	Passenger cars	Commercial vehicles
	BJKC	BJKD	BJKE	BJKF	BJKB	BJKH	BJKI	BJKJ	BJKK	BJKG	BJKL	BJKM
1986	162 090	665 093	134 802	56 977	1 018 962	51 150	71 635	20 522	44 249	187 556	5 025.8	1 491.6
1987	153 214	718 046	205 067	66 356	1 142 683	45 801	76 956	53 841	49 599	226 197	6 866.2	1 803.2
1988[3]	129 446	764 289	260 231	72 869	1 226 835	38 572	79 864	45 155	50 279	213 870	7 215.8	2 621.7
1989	133 135	716 784	375 309	73 854	1 299 082	41 969	89 073	99 604	50 083	280 729	8 188.2	2 752.9
1990	93 039	809 219	325 116	68 236	1 295 610	39 305	188 053	128 987	49 424	405 769	8 436.8[4]	2 258.2
1991	26 621	830 530	338 877	40 872	1 236 900	8 630	377 689	187 763	31 303	605 385	8 441.6	2 206.4
1991 Jun*	4 841	85 218	30 020	4 998	125 077	666	33 116	16 448	3 481	53 711	..	..
Jul	3 335	70 671	25 560	2 441	102 007	412	24 154	12 082	1 942	38 590	..	..
Aug*	654	37 498	15 514	3 722	57 388	417	18 893	8 143	3 117	30 570	..	..
Sep	791	61 620	24 441	3 761	90 613	554	28 670	16 049	3 220	48 493	..	..
Oct	24	65 426	29 106	2 574	97 130	19	30 646	17 750	2 107	50 522	..	..
Nov*	1 388	80 207	31 786	2 995	116 376	1 063	39 239	17 605	2 204	60 111	..	..
Dec	987	52 395	23 559	2 071	79 012	477	26 562	14 114	1 243	42 396	..	..
1992 Jan	873	59 928	31 028	3 416	95 245	350	22 953	15 842	2 347	41 492	..	..
Feb	626	73 434	36 968	3 164	114 192	272	28 528	16 103	2 227	47 130	..	..
Mar*	685	83 677	46 410	3 109	133 881	-	33 933	19 601	2 113	55 647	..	..
Apr	6	69 061	38 083	1 752	108 902	-	27 008	15 623	1 181	43 812	..	..
May	-	68 266	34 409	2 649	105 324	-	24 481	13 639	1 793	39 913	..	..
Jun	-	82 517	42 995	3 691	129 203	-	21 755	17 097	1 566	40 418	..	..

1 Including chassis delivered as such by manufacturers. Taxi-cabs are included.
2 Annual totals are the sum of calendar quarters.
3 53 weeks.
4 Excludes passenger cars with three wheels.

Source: Central Statistical Office

10.10 Commercial motor vehicles
Monthly totals are for four or five week periods

Number

	Total production						Production for export					
	Light Commercial vehicles	Gross Vehicle Weight Trucks		Motive units	Buses, coaches and mini-buses	Total	Light Commercial vehicles	Gross Vehicle Weight Trucks		Motive units	Buses, coaches and mini-buses	Total
		Under 7.5 tonnes	Over 7.5 tonnes					Under 7.5 tonnes	Over 7.5 tonnes			
	BJLC	BJLD	BJLE	BJLF	BJLG	BJLB	BJLI	BJLJ	BJLK	BJLL	BJLM	BJLH
1987	188 858	15 697	22 834	5 343	13 996	246 728	44 833	2 273	6 317	437	6 876	60 736
1988[1]	250 053	19 732	24 887	6 171	16 500	317 343	68 954	1 823	6 319	238	7 113	84 447
1989	267 135	17 687	21 083	5 827	14 858	326 590	82 584	2 109	5 013	235	5 562	95 503
1990	230 510	10 515	13 674	3 327	12 320	270 346	83 651	[2]	6 654	[2]	5 403	95 708
1991	184 005	8 833	11 766	2 700	9 837	217 141	95 264	[2]	8 465	[2]	5 360	109 089
1991 Jun*	15 564	624	1 160	178	888	18 414	7 125	168	711	58	496	8 558
Jul	13 956	588	969	226	576	16 315	6 502	160	494	57	346	7 559
Aug*	6 604	539	895	128	191	8 357	3 304	[2]	734	[2]	38	4 076
Sep	13 881	703	929	199	688	16 400	6 280	[2]	716	[2]	460	7 456
Oct	16 667	906	1 106	301	1 085	20 065	8 947	[2]	783	[2]	419	10 149
Nov*	23 516	1 216	1 310	258	1 506	27 806	13 566	[2]	955	[2]	898	15 419
Dec	14 194	667	676	199	1 022	16 758	8 799	[2]	378	[2]	631	9 808
1992 Jan	14 138	652	592	194	822	16 398	8 795	114	121	31	612	9 673
Feb	19 052	695	640	240	625	21 252	12 172	222	185	31	346	12 956
Mar*	25 847	913	975	246	1 213	29 194	15 341	248	330	14	614	16 547
Apr	19 797	859	1 011	214	660	22 541	11 558	232	432	7	298	12 527
May	19 510	792	937	213	654	22 106	11 266	235	327	11	328	12 167
Jun	24 337	945	1 204	262	686	27 434	12 539	180	419	12	213	13 363

1 53 weeks.
2 Included in series BJLK.

Source: Central Statistical Office

10.11 Merchant shipbuilding:[1] vessels of 100 gross tonnes and over[2]

	Orders on hand at end of period[3]								Completions[3]			
	Not yet laid down				Under construction				Total		Export[4]	
	Total		Export[4]		Total		Export[4]					
	Number	Thousand gross tonnes	Number	Thousand gross tonnes	Number	Thousand gross tonnes	Number	Thousand gross tonnes	Number	Thousand gross tonnes	Number	Thousand gross tonnes
	BJNA	BJNB	BJNC	BJND	BJNE	BJNF	BJNG	BJNH	BJNI	BJNJ	BJNK	BJNL
1986	42	132	26	96	32	293	5	44	48	106	5	29
1987	29	163	18	94	36	142	13	66	43	247	10	53
1988	13	31	-	-	43	233	18	123	41	31	5	4
1989	23	446	7	428	32	252	12	121	43	106	12	78
1990	21	302	11	285	36	355	14	276	37	133	8	51
1991	20	774	8	275	27	389	14	325	31	110	10	83
1988 Q4	13	31	-	-	43	233	18	123	10	4	1	2
1989 Q1	19	94	2	70	39	237	14	108	13	27	4	17
Q2	10	51	4	36	42	262	12	128	12	25	4	17
Q3	13	283	7	272	34	218	9	85	11	51	4	45
Q4	23	446	7	428	32	252	12	121	7	3	-	-
1990 Q1	19	449	9	436	31	160	8	75	13	105	6	49
Q2	25	378	11	365	32	243	8	153	9	8	1	-
Q3	26	387	13	371	33	275	10	190	7	9	1	2
Q4	21	302	11	288	36	353	14	276	8	11	-	-
1991 Q1	17	293	9	283	36	358	15	280	5	6	1	2
Q2	11	283	6	279	31	323	14	250	13	49	4	37
Q3	16	664	3	162	26	427	16	365	9	13	2	3
Q4	20	774	8	275	27	389	14	325	4	42	3	41
1992 Q1	22	776	8	274	22	305	10	242	8	89	4	84

| | New orders[3] | | | | Modifications and cancellations[5] | | | | Net new orders[3] | | | |
| | Total | | Export[4] | | Total | | Export[4] | | Total | | Export[4] | |
	Number	Thousand gross tonnes	Number	Thousand gross tonnes	Number[6]	Thousand gross tonnes	Number[6]	Thousand gross tonnes	Number	Thousand gross tonnes	Number	Thousand gross tonnes
	BJNM	BJNN	BJNO	BJNP	BJNQ	BJNR	BJNS	BJNT	BJNU	BJNV	BJNW	BJNX
1987	37	163	10	112	3	-37	2	-38	34	126	8	74
1988	41	26	1	1	9	-34	9	-34	32	-9	8	-34
1989	42	534	13	500	-	5	-	4	42	538	13	504
1990	35	42	14	67	..	1	..	1	35	93	14	68
1991	21	613	6	114	..	5	..	1	21	615	6	112
1988 Q4	11	6	-	-	-	-	-	-	11	6	-	-
1989 Q1	15	92	2	70	-	2	-	2	15	94	2	71
Q2	6	5	4	2	-	2	-	1	6	7	4	3
Q3	6	238	4	237	-	1	-	1	6	239	4	238
Q4	15	199	3	192	-	-	-	-	15	199	3	192
1990 Q1	8	16	4	11	-	1	-	1	8	17	4	12
Q2	12	19	3	7	-	-	-	-	12	19	3	7
Q3	9	50	5	45	-	-	-	-	9	50	5	45
Q4	6	7	2	4	-	-	-	-	6	7	2	4
1991 Q1	1	-	-	-	-	-1	-	-	1	-	-	-
Q2	2	-	-	-	-	3	-	3	2	3	-	-
Q3	9	499	-	-	-	-1	-	-2	9	498	-	-2
Q4	9	114	6	114	-	-	-	-	9	114	6	114
1992 Q1	5	6	-	-	-	-	-	-	5	6	-	-

1 Includes naval vessels registered as merchant ships.
2 Gross tonnes is a constructed measure of the volume of all the enclosed spaces in a vessel except those occupied by engines, bunkers and crew.
3 The total tonnage specified on ordering vessels differs slightly from total actual measured tonnage on completion.
4 Vessels are shown for export if they are for other than UK registration.

5 Modifications include alterations of 500 gross tonnes or more to the tonnage and the country of registration of vessels already on order.
6 Cancellations only.
7 Modifications and cancellations exceed new orders for the period.

Source: Department of Trade and Industry

11 Textiles and other manufactures

11.1 Index numbers of textile and clothing industries
Standard Industrial Classification 1980

1985=100, seasonally adjusted

	Textile industry (production)							
	Man-made fibres	All textiles[1]	Woollen and worsted industry	Spinning and doubling on cotton system	Weaving of cotton, silk and man-made fibres	Hosiery and other knitted goods	Textile finishing	Carpets and other textile floor coverings
Activity heading	2600	43	4310	4321	4322	4360	4370	4380
	BKAA	BKAB	BKAC	BKAD	BKAE	BKAF	BKAG	BKAH
1987	109.9	104.6	107.0	100.0	101.4	101.6	115.8	106.3
1988	107.8	101.8	103.9	92.0	97.1	96.1	106.1	114.4
1989	114.5	96.8	94.8	79.1	95.4	93.1	103.0	109.0
1990	117.2	91.8†	87.1†	70.1	95.1	85.5†	108.1†	101.3†
1991	120.0	85.3	80.0	55.1	84.7	83.9	101.9	92.3
1990 Q1	122.2†	93.3†	90.5†	74.5	96.9	86.6†	107.3†	102.8†
Q2	118.1	93.8	90.0	75.1	95.4	88.7	109.1	102.9
Q3	117.1	91.0	87.3	65.8	94.6	85.8	101.4	99.2
Q4	111.6	89.1	80.8	65.1	93.4	81.0	114.6	100.1
1991 Q1	113.1	87.7	76.6	59.4	87.8	90.2	107.7	91.0
Q2	122.5	84.9	79.3	55.1	90.5	84.1	92.9	95.3
Q3	118.7	83.4	82.3	51.0	77.4	80.7	97.7	90.2
Q4	125.9	85.3	82.0	55.0	83.3	80.3	109.2	92.5
1992 Q1	121.5	85.2	84.1	47.4	75.0	83.6	105.3	96.0
Q2	123.0	84.5	87.3	49.7	73.4	81.5	102.5	93.5

	Clothing industry (production)						
	All clothing, hats and gloves[2]	Weather-proof outerwear	Men's and boys' tailored outerwear	Women's and girls' tailored outerwear	Work clothing and men's and boys' jeans	Men's and boys' shirts, underwear and nightwear	Women's and girls' light outerwear, lingerie and infants' wear
Activity heading	453	4531	4532	4533	4534	4535	4536
	BKAI	BKAJ	BKAK	BKAL	BKAM	BKAN	BKAO
1987	99.8	110.9	107.3	99.3	104.5	102.5	95.3
1988	99.4	109.7	105.8	89.3	112.4	109.4	93.9
1989	96.9	92.3	97.9	82.0	111.6	111.9	94.8
1990	98.1†	86.7†	95.1†	89.0†	127.3†	116.8†	92.6†
1991	88.4	83.5	87.1	87.2	106.0	113.1	80.2
1990 Q1	101.4†	91.8†	94.6†	95.5†	120.0†	120.8†	98.5†
Q2	100.1	89.7	96.8	91.9	122.8	123.5	94.6
Q3	96.9	81.0	93.8	89.7	130.0	117.0	89.7
Q4	93.9	84.4	95.2	79.1	136.6	106.0	87.5
1991 Q1	92.3	79.4	91.9	89.5	106.4	124.4	82.7
Q2	88.9	89.4	91.6	87.5	99.4	111.0	81.4
Q3	87.8	84.4	86.6	82.1	104.9	114.7	80.1
Q4	84.4	81.0	78.2	89.7	113.3	102.5	76.4
1992 Q1	87.1	78.5	78.2	86.2	110.4	109.5	83.9
Q2	90.3	80.9	88.3	95.6	122.3	110.4	83.1

1 In addition to the sectors listed, this includes throwing, texturing, etc of continuous filament yarn; spinning and weaving of flax, hemp and ramie; jute and polypropylene yarns and fabrics, and miscellaneous textiles (ie lace; rope, twine and net; narrow fabrics and other miscellaneous textiles).

2 In addition to the sectors listed, this includes hats, caps and millinery; gloves, other dress industries (ie swimwear and foundation garments; umbrellas and miscellaneous industries).

Source: Central Statistical Office

11.2 Cotton
Stocks: end of period

			Thousand tonnes						Million metres	
			Yarn production[1]						Woven cloth production[1]	
			Single yarn[2]							
	Raw cotton home consumption for cotton spinning	Stocks	Cotton (excluding waste yarns)	Cotton waste yarns	Spun man-made fibres and mixture yarns[3]	Total	Doubled yarn	Cotton	Man-made fibres and mixtures[4]
	BKCA	BKCB	BKCD	BKCE	BKCF	BKCC	BKCG	BKCH	BKCI
1987	51.09	4	0.80	0.17	1.04	2.02	0.60	4.7	5.0
1988	43.22	4	0.68	0.16	0.98	1.82	0.60	4.2	4.9
1989	38.50	3	0.55	0.15	0.83	1.52	0.58	4.0	5.0
1990	28.29	1	0.43	0.14	0.72	1.30	0.50	3.2	5.0
1991	18.86	1	0.24	0.15	0.60	0.99	0.45	3.0	4.5
1991 Jun	1.55	1	0.24	0.16	0.60	1.00	0.44	3.0	4.8
Jul	1.04	2	0.13	0.10	0.36	0.59	0.34	1.8	2.7
Aug	1.58	1	0.23	0.17	0.59	0.99	0.42	3.0	4.4
Sep	1.35	1	0.16	0.13	0.53	0.82	0.39	2.6	4.1
Oct	1.58	1	0.22	0.17	0.70	1.08	0.46	3.3	4.8
Nov	1.38	1	0.19	0.17	0.66	1.02	0.48	3.3	4.9
Dec	1.00	1	0.15	0.13	0.48	0.77	0.41	2.5	3.5
1992 Jan	0.79	1	0.14	0.15	0.52	0.81	0.40	2.5	4.2
Feb	0.81	1	0.19	0.19	0.64	1.02	0.48	3.3	4.8
Mar	0.90	1	0.21	0.17	0.63	1.01	0.46	3.4	5.0
Apr	..	..	0.13	0.12	0.49	0.74	0.41	2.6	4.4
May	..	..	0.17	0.17	0.60	0.94	0.40	2.5	4.5

1 Weekly averages.
2 Spun in the cotton industry.

3 Including other waste yarn.
4 Including synthetic fibres.

Source: Department of Trade and Industry

11.3 Man-made fibre and wool
Monthly averages or calendar months

		Thousand tonnes						Million square metres			
	Man-made fibre (rayon, nylon, etc)							Woven wool and mixture fabrics			
	Production										
	Continuous filament yarn (single)	Staple fibre	Total	Other fibres:[1] consumption	Wool tops: production	Woollen yarn	Worsted yarn: deliveries	Woollen	Worsted	Total	Blankets
	BKDB	BKDC	BKDA	BKBA	BKBB	BKBC	BKBD	BKBF	BKBG	BKBE	BKBH
1986	8.40	15.60	24.00	2.76	3.39	6.10	6.25	3.93	3.84	7.76	0.58
1987	8.25	14.80	23.06	2.85	3.35	6.40	6.61	4.00	3.53	7.53	0.56
1988	8.77	14.57	23.34	2.74	3.29	6.52	6.15	3.97	3.45	7.42	0.60
1989	9.04	13.67	22.71	2.51	2.94	6.24	5.42	3.80	3.32	7.12	0.59
1990	8.47	14.28	22.77	2.17	2.56	6.06	4.88	3.52	3.06	6.58	0.61
1991	7.72	14.56	22.28	1.87	2.62	5.51	4.36	3.25	2.76	6.00	0.52
1991 Jun	8.00	13.91	21.91	1.88	2.49	5.66	4.47	3.39	2.83	6.22	0.50
Jul	7.36	14.39	21.75	1.57	2.82	4.69	4.20	3.11	2.73	5.84	0.38
Aug	5.55	12.65	18.20	1.79	1.89	5.48	3.82	3.02	2.40	5.42	0.43
Sep	7.35	13.89	21.24	1.79	2.91	5.45	4.62	3.27	2.71	5.98	0.41
Oct	8.88	18.14	27.02	2.13	3.09	6.41	4.93	3.37	3.31	6.68	0.51
Nov	7.97	15.26	23.23	2.06	3.44	5.98	4.68	3.33	2.97	6.30	0.54
Dec	7.47	12.75	20.22	1.65	2.29	4.96	3.93	2.96	2.45	5.41	0.48
1992 Jan	8.08	14.75	22.83	2.00	3.63	5.97	4.51	3.20	2.99	6.19	0.48
Feb	8.03	13.71	21.74	1.92	2.95	5.68	4.51	2.87	2.85	5.72	0.49
Mar	8.34	14.19	22.53	2.07	3.13	6.16	4.92	3.29	3.06	6.35	0.53
Apr	8.57	13.95	22.52	1.77	2.80	5.79	4.09	3.04	2.83	5.87	0.47
May	8.62	14.07	22.69	..	..	..	..	..	..	..	..
Jun	7.99	14.12	22.11	..	..	..	..	..	..	..	..

1 All fibres (other than virgin wool) used in woollen spinning and felting and hair used in the making of tops.

Source: Department of Trade and Industry

11.4 Hosiery and other knitted goods[1]
Quarterly sales

Millions

	Underwear[2]			Pullovers, jumpers, cardigans, etc[2]			Socks and stockings (pairs)				
	Men's	Women's	Children's and infants'	Men's	Women's	Children's and infants'	Men's	Women's full-length stockings	Women's tights and pantihose	Women's ankle socks and 3/4-hose	Children's and infants' socks, 3/4-hose and stockings
	BALN	BALP	BALQ	BALR	BALS	BALT	BALU	BALV	BALW	BALX	BALY
1986	50.8	39.6	18.1	318.2	259.9	61.00	96.1	21.8	168.6	15.5	49.8
1987	50.6	52.2	16.9	331.6	271.6	59.40	89.5	21.9	178.9	19.3	52.3
1988	42.4	45.1	19.8	313.8	284.7	61.60	96.2	29.8	203.1	21.9	56.3
1989	37.9	42.6	23.4	259.9	241.4	46.40	81.5	34.4	200.6	19.9	52.6
1990	37.5	54.4	21.5	250.1	208.6	34.30	86.0	33.2	187.1	19.4	51.8
1991	34.7	62.4	18.3	258.5	210.1	27.60	96.2	45.4	200.7	21.4	47.5
1989 Q4	10.5	23.0	7.1	79.1	68.9	11.8	27.0	13.3	67.2	6.3	12.5
1990 Q1	6.7	10.9	4.6	40.7	43.9	6.3	19.2	8.6	46.9	3.9	14.3
Q2	9.6	12.6	5.3	46.2	40.7	7.3	16.7	6.1	39.2	3.4	11.3
Q3	9.7	14.9	5.5	80.7	64.6	10.8	21.0	6.9	36.6	4.7	12.2
Q4	11.5	16.0	6.1	81.5	59.6	9.9	29.0	11.6	64.4	7.4	14.0
1991 Q1	7.9	13.0	6.0	42.7†	41.9	5.4	20.9	12.0	43.4	5.0	12.7
Q2	6.0†	12.9†	3.1	46.1	39.2†	4.7†	19.4	10.0	45.2	4.8	11.2
Q3	8.1	17.0	4.6	82.6	60.1	8.2	22.9	11.4	35.8	4.3	11.7
Q4	13.6	19.6	4.6	85.9	66.8	8.9	31.8†	12.0	76.2	7.3	12.3†
1992 Q1	7.1	14.9	4.8	42.4	46.4	5.7	21.0	6.5	48.6	6.0	13.2

1 Manufacturers' sales by establishments employing 25 or more persons.
2 Including garments made-up from knitted fabrics of all types by establishments engaged in knitting, except those engaged in warp knitting.

Source: Central Statistical Office

11.5 Manufacturers' sales of footwear[1]
Quarterly averages and quarterly totals

Million pairs

	With leather uppers					With uppers other than of leather	Slippers, etc	Plastic protective footwear	Safety footwear (all types)	Total
	Men's	Women's	Children's	Sports shoes	Total					
	BKFC	BKFD	BKFE	BKFF	BKFB	BKFG	BKFH	BKFJ	BKFK	BKFA
1987	3.8	5.4	4.0	0.7	13.8	9.4	5.7	1.1	1.4	31.5
1988	4.1	4.8	3.8	0.6	13.3	10.2	4.4	0.9	1.4	30.1
1989	3.4	4.2	3.3	0.5	11.4	7.8	3.7	0.8	1.1	24.8
1990	3.2	3.8	3.1	0.3	10.5	7.4	3.2	0.7	1.1	22.9
1991	2.6	4.0	3.2	0.1	9.9	4.7	1.9	0.3	1.4	17.9
1987 Q3	3.5	5.6	4.3	0.7	14.1	8.8	7.2	1.5	1.3	32.9
Q4	4.2	5.2	3.3	0.6	13.3	9.7	8.6	1.4	1.6	34.6
1988 Q1	4.5	5.6	4.3	0.7	15.1	11.2	2.2	0.7	1.5	30.7
Q2	3.8	4.5	4.0	0.7	13.0	9.5	2.5	0.4	1.3	26.7
Q3	4.0	4.6	4.0	0.6	13.2	10.7	6.2	1.2	1.3	32.6
Q4	4.1	4.4	3.0	0.5	12.0	9.2	6.6	1.2	1.5	30.5
1989 Q1	3.8	5.1	3.9	0.8	13.6	10.7	2.2	0.5	1.4	28.4
Q2	3.4	4.4	3.8	0.7	12.3	8.8	3.1	0.6	1.4	26.2
Q3	3.6	5.1	3.9	0.6	13.2	9.1	5.3	1.0	1.2	29.8
Q4	3.5	4.1	2.7	0.3	10.6	7.2	5.6	1.1	1.2	25.7
1990 Q1	3.5	4.9	3.8	0.4	12.6	8.1	2.0	0.5	1.1	24.3
Q2	3.3	3.3	2.9	0.4	9.9	6.8	2.0	0.4	1.1	20.2
Q3	2.9	3.6	3.5	0.5	10.5	7.3	4.5	0.9	1.0	24.2
Q4	2.9	3.6	2.2	0.1	8.8	7.5	4.4	0.9	1.2	22.8
1991 Q1	2.8	4.6	3.7	0.1	11.2	6.0	1.2	0.4	1.1	19.9
Q2	2.6	4.0	3.0	0.1	9.7	3.8	1.4	0.3	1.2	16.3
Q3	2.8	3.6	3.7	0.2	10.4	4.3	3.4	0.2	1.1	19.4
Q4	2.2	3.8	2.3	0.1	8.4	4.7	1.5	0.3	1.1	15.9

1 The figures relate to sales by establishments employing 50 or more persons.

Source: Central Statistical Office

11.6 Manufacturers' sales of floorcoverings
Quarterly averages or totals for quarters

Thousand square metres

| | Carpets and rugs of all types | | Woven carpets | | | | Tufted carpets | |
| | | | Faced with yarn containing 50% or more by weight of wool | | Faced with all other yarn | | | |
	Total[1,2]	of which for export	Total[2]	of which for export	Total[2]	of which for export	Total	of which for export
	BKMA	BKMB	BKMC	BKMD	BKME	BKMF	BKMG	BKMH
1986	37 774	5 316	3 833	772	1 140	253	28 790	3 425
1987	40 425	5 374	3 857	748	1 070	272	30 758	3 382
1988	42 214	5 470	4 212	930	992	298	31 494	3 103
1989	39 558	5 250	4 528	1 198	725	227	29 018	2 521
1990	38 213	6 309	4 339	1 253	551	233	28 289	2 890
1991	37 925	6 472	4 186	1 580	491	233	28 270	3 378
1982 Q3	32 068	3 512	3 061	602	1 763	251	24 701	1 885
Q4	37 648	4 491	3 449	639	2 168	296	29 159	2 579
1983 Q1	34 836	3 949	3 268	638	1 855	225	26 280	2 159
Q2	36 967	3 897	3 033	644	1 948	259	29 091	2 028
Q3	35 028	3 806	3 057	682	1 835	222	26 960	2 103
Q4	40 313	4 281	3 642	780	2 113	405	31 195	2 252
1984 Q1	33 429	4 255	3 321	750	1 849	244	24 727	1 936
Q2	32 844	4 406	3 135	741	1 460	323	25 034	2 488
Q3	34 167	3 838	3 284	622	1 571	294	26 034	2 080
Q4	41 088	5 140	3 960	695	1 861	408	32 190	2 975
1985 Q1	36 042	5 120	3 428	719	1 366	309	27 303	3 268
Q2	37 236	5 572	3 564	881	1 324	251	28 694	3 664
Q3	36 715	4 571	3 558	799	1 189	219	28 238	2 560
Q4	40 243	5 488	4 144	918	1 427	323	30 844	3 244
1986 Q1	35 061	4 673	3 499	741	1 120	256	26 475	2 834
Q2	37 063	6 322	3 751	736	1 040	241	28 523	4 581
Q3	36 687	4 816	3 814	750	1 071	260	27 863	2 973
Q4	42 271	5 454	4 268	862	1 310	257	32 298	3 314
1987 Q1	37 041	5 029	3 469	783	901	192	28 082	3 038
Q2	39 532	5 419	3 617	713	1 059	220	30 377	3 517
Q3	39 690	5 064	3 892	676	1 084	231	30 082	3 289
Q4	45 398	5 982	4 448	819	1 234	444	34 489	3 682
1988 Q1	40 349	5 467	4 177	1 089	1 095	347	29 540	3 056
Q2	41 715	5 526	4 028	882	995	309	31 303	3 279
Q3	41 537	5 338	4 081	793	962	272	31 174	3 114
Q4	45 252	5 549	4 559	957	917	264	33 960	2 962
1989 Q1	40 829	5 364	4 474	1 066	869	222	29 965	2 684
Q2	38 540	4 599	4 434	1 049	764	227	27 787	2 140
Q3	37 577	4 856	4 463	1 229	522	233	27 416	2 263
Q4	41 288	6 183	4 737	1 452	745	226	30 906	2 998
1990 Q1	39 779	7 070	4 499	2 717	802	172	28 663	2 548
Q2	37 343	6 295	4 202	1 629	467	189	27 806	3 097
Q3	37 504	5 709	4 115	1 067	410	289	27 538	2 894
Q4	38 225	6 164	4 538	1 135	528	281	29 148	3 020
1991 Q1	32 941	5 078	3 650	893	388	228	24 447	2 689
Q2	34 030	5 923	3 446	791	266	203	26 524	3 773
Q3	35 365	6 145	3 240	806	293	240	27 282	4 130
Q4	38 018	6 826	3 913	906	287	242	30 069	4 069
1992 Q1	35 207	6 428	3 729	869	187	290	26 669	4 034

1 Includes needleloom carpets.
2 Excludes spool Axminster for 1982 Q1 and Q2.

Source: Central Statistical Office

12 Construction

12.1 Value and volume of output[1]
Great Britain

£ million

	Value of output												Volume of output: 1985=100 seasonally adjusted
	New work						Repair and maintenance						
	New housing for		Other new work for				Housing		Other work for		Total repair and maintenance	Total all work	
				Private sector									
	Public sector	Private sector	Public sector	Industrial	Commercial	Total new work	Public	Private	Public sector	Private sector			
	BLAC	BLAD	BLAE	BLAF	BLAG	BLAB	BLBK	BLBL	BLAJ	BLAK	BLAH	FGAY	FEAQ
1987	933	5 812	3 870	3 204	5 247	19 066	3 462	4 898	4 042	3 112	15 515	34 580	111.4
1988	922	7 547	4 318	4 023	6 610	23 420	3 791	5 536	4 251	3 547	17 125	40 546	119.5
1989	979	7 088	5 095	4 936	9 217	27 315	4 109	6 101	4 635	4 014	18 859	46 174	124.5
1990	965	5 919	5 837	5 243	10 390	28 354	4 386	6 324	5 044	4 360	20 113	48 467	125.7
1991	810	4 846	5 772	5 314	8 224	24 967	3 964	5 804	4 807	4 168	18 743	43 709	114.5
1988 Q3	235	1 890	1 143	1 046	1 778	6 092	945	1 461	1 042	898	4 346	10 439	118.0
Q4	216	1 838	1 161	1 170	1 912	6 297	969	1 448	1 060	948	4 424	10 721	120.9
1989 Q1	241	1 792	1 140	1 162	2 040	6 376	1 061	1 435	1 144	956	4 595	10 971	125.9
Q2	250	1 858	1 243	1 274	2 212	6 838	954	1 511	1 110	1 025	4 600	11 437	125.2
Q3	237	1 854	1 327	1 228	2 449	7 094	1 010	1 617	1 171	995	4 792	11 886	122.6
Q4	251	1 584	1 385	1 272	2 515	7 007	1 084	1 539	1 211	1 039	4 873	11 880	124.5
1990 Q1	264	1 511	1 359	1 238	2 484	6 856	1 155	1 564	1 288	1 077	5 084	11 940	129.1
Q2	242	1 505	1 437	1 347	2 661	7 191	1 119	1 557	1 187	1 066	4 929	12 121	127.0
Q3	247	1 486	1 597	1 312	2 742	7 384	1 090	1 624	1 306	1 085	5 106	12 490	124.7
Q4	213	1 417	1 444	1 346	2 503	6 923	1 021	1 579	1 262	1 132	4 994	11 917	122.1
1991 Q1	207	1 114	1 469	1 252	2 227	6 269	1 058	1 418	1 280	1 071	4 826	11 095	118.9
Q2	192	1 294	1 394	1 310	2 158	6 348	941	1 389	1 174	1 114	4 617	10 965	115.1
Q3	197	1 226	1 466	1 444	2 006	6 338	1 020	1 540	1 205	980	4 746	11 084	112.9
Q4	215	1 211	1 444	1 309	1 834	6 012	945	1 457	1 149	1 003	4 554	10 566	111.1
1992 Q1[2]	260	1 159	1 366	1 167	1 572	5 523	1 022	1 266	1 249	971	4 508	10 032	110.4

1 Classified to construction in the *Standard Industrial Classification 1980*. Estimates of unrecorded output by small firms and self-employed workers, and output by the public sector's direct labour department are included.
2 Provisional.

Source: Department of the Environment

12.2 Value of new orders obtained by contractors for new work[1]
Great Britain

£ million

	New housing			Other new work						
	Public and housing association	Private	All new housing	From public sector[2]	From private sector			All other new work	Total value of new orders
					Industrial	Commercial	Total		
	BLBC	BLBD	FGAU	BLBF	FGAS	BLBI	BLBG	BLBE	FHAA
1987	903	6 441	7 344	4 513	3 660[3]	6 602	10 262[3]	14 775	22 119
1988	882	7 894	8 776	5 116	3 128	9 278	12 407	17 523	26 299
1989	872	6 497	7 369	6 205	3 377	10 191	13 568	19 773	27 142
1990	683	4 856	5 539	5 146	3 736	8 071	11 807	16 953	22 492
1991	875	4 552	5 427	4 767	3 452	5 811	9 263	14 030	19 457
1988 Q3	189	2 081	2 270	1 164	718	2 326	3 044	4 208	6 479
Q4	230	1 947	2 177	1 347	832	2 480	3 312	4 659	6 836
1989 Q1	219	1 818	2 037	1 372	796	2 789	3 584	4 957	6 994
Q2	213	1 908	2 121	1 758	941	2 769	3 709	5 467	7 588
Q3	179	1 464	1 643	1 501	876	2 341	3 218	4 719	6 362
Q4	261	1 307	1 568	1 573	765	2 292	3 057	4 630	6 198
1990 Q1	244	1 336	1 580	1 411	983	2 166	3 149	4 560	6 139
Q2	152	1 403	1 555	1 226	1 122	2 339	3 461	4 687	6 242
Q3	153	1 168	1 321	1 333	848	1 863	2 711	4 044	5 363
Q4	134	949	1 083	1 177	784	1 703	2 487	3 664	4 748
1991 Q1	181	1 102	1 283	1 205	701	1 507	2 208	3 413	4 697
Q2	213	1 310	1 523	1 140	1 186	1 606	2 792	3 932	5 454
Q3	216	1 213	1 429	1 139	856	1 381	2 237	3 376	4 805
Q4	266	926	1 192	1 283	709	1 317	2 026	3 309	4 501
1992 Q1	365	1 008	1 373	1 082	947	1 516	2 463	3 545	4 919

1 Including the value of speculative building when work starts on site.
2 Excluding open cast coal orders in accordance with the *Standard Industrial Classification 1980*.
3 Orders include the Channel Tunnel project.

Source: Department of the Environment

12.3 Building materials and components
Great Britain

Production: monthly averages or calendar months; stocks: end of period

	Building bricks		Fibre cement products: production (000 tonnes)	Concrete building blocks (000 sq m)	Concrete roofing tiles		Ready mixed concrete:[1] production (000 cu m)	Slate[2]		Sand and gravel: sales (000 tonnes)
	Production (millions)	Stocks (millions)			Production (000 sq m of roof covered)	Stocks (000 sq m of roof covered)		Production (tonnes)	Stocks (tonnes)	
	BLDA	BLDB	BLDU	BLDM	BLDN	BLDO	BLDP	BLDQ	BLDR	BLDS
1984	334	512	21.2	6 804	2 890	5 250	1 734	6 914	5 888	8 134
1985	342	718	21.0	6 204	2 323	4 135	1 801	5 710	8 921	8 286
1986	331	501	18.1	7 263	2 570	3 945	1 795	6 143	6 458	8 608
1987	352	329	17.1	8 083	2 892	4 245	2 030	7 979	7 442	9 195
1988	390	281	20.9	9 169	3 235	4 091	2 404	6 110	4 601	10 677
1989	388	965	18.4	9 000	2 982	5 861	2 466	6 998	6 594	10 511
1990	317	1 350	19.6	7 596	2 626	7 183	2 232	8 125	8 648	9 414
1991	268	1 473	11.1	6 219	2 197	6 371	1 835	7 913	15 007	7 911
1990 Nov	301	1 274	19.9	7 167	2 453	7 183	2 022	8 738	8 648	8 511
Dec	263	1 350	-	4 678	-	-	-	-	-	-
1991 Jan	226	1 390	-	5 544	-	-	-	-	-	-
Feb	263	1 467	13.3	5 191	2 264	8 627	1 697	7 589	11 954	6 927
Mar	320	1 487	-	6 835	-	-	-	-	-	-
Apr	266	1 470	-	6 170	-	-	-	-	-	-
May	278	1 441	10.1	6 788	2 215	8 592	1 995	7 625	13 278	8 663
Jun	300	1 426	-	7 604	-	-	-	-	-	-
Jul	263	1 403	-	6 814	-	-	-	-	-	-
Aug	225	1 361	10.5	6 080	2 017	6 137	1 955	8 156	16 168	8 698
Sep	302	1 362	-	6 990	-	-	-	-	-	-
Oct	268	1 365	-	6 412	-	-	-	-	-	-
Nov	271	1 419	10.7	6 236	2 291	6 371	1 693	8 280	15 007	7 357
Dec	230	1 473	-	3 967	-	-	-	-	-	-
1992 Jan	212	1 476	-	5 637	-	-	-	-	-	-
Feb	243	1 488	11.6	5 736	2 063	7 139	1 714	6 977	17 588	6 900[†]
Mar	292	1 493	..	6 876	..	..	..	..	..	..
Apr	267[†]	1 520[†]	..	5 229[3]	..	..	..	..	..	..
May	248	1 487	..	5 297[3]	..	..	..	..	..	..
Jun	285[3]	1 477[3]	..	7 101[3]	..	..	..	..	..	..

1 United Kingdom.
2 Excluding slate residue used as fill.

3 Provisional.

Sources: Department of the Environment;
Central Statistical Office

12.4 Permanent dwellings started, under construction and completed

Number

	Started				Under construction at end of period				Completed			
	Private enterprise	Housing associations	Local authorities, new towns and government departments	All dwellings	Private enterprise	Housing associations	Local authorities, new towns and government departments	All dwellings	Private enterprise	Housing associations	Local authorities, new towns and government departments	All dwellings
England												
	BLHC	BLHM	BAEP	BLHA	BLHG	BLHN	BAET	BLHE	BLHK	BLHO	BAEX	BLHI
1985[1]	144 325	10 387	18 787	173 499	193 565	18 194	25 300	237 059	135 449	11 368	23 314	170 131
1986	158 369	11 076	16 962	186 407	203 756	18 818	22 593	245 167	148 178	10 452	19 669	178 299
1987[1]	174 707	9 682	16 044	200 433	217 566	17 977	21 926	257 469	160 858	10 568	16 705	188 131
1988	195 295	10 627	13 193	219 115	239 109	18 520	19 050	276 679	173 752	10 084	16 069	199 905
1989	141 881	11 018	12 945	165 844	229 445	19 876	17 409	266 730	151 537	9 646	14 610	175 793
1990	110 437	13 734	6 350	130 521	210 974	20 576	9 844	241 394	130 084	13 045	13 866	156 995
1991	111 735	15 720	2 656	130 111	198 165	21 238	4 697	224 100	124 551	14 977	7 877	147 405
1990 Q1	28 924	3 309	2 356	34 589	225 151	20 533	16 368	262 052	33 267	2 652	3 348	39 267
Q2[1]	29 835	4 044	1 554	35 433	224 846	21 375	14 359	260 580	30 140	3 202	3 563	36 905
Q3[1]	27 824	3 620	1 273	32 717	220 961	21 893	11 582	254 436	31 698	3 113	4 050	38 861
Q4[1]	23 854	2 761	1 167	27 782	210 974	20 576	9 844	241 394	34 979	4 078	2 905	41 962
1991 Q1[1]	25 484	2 925	1 142	29 551	206 639	19 806	8 746	235 191	29 848	3 646	2 260	35 754
Q2	30 963	4 156	698	35 817	207 733	19 866	7 145	234 744	29 869	4 042	2 353	36 264
Q3	31 294	4 305	467	36 066	207 437	20 286	5 793	233 516	31 590	3 885	1 819	37 294
Q4	23 994	4 334	349	28 677	198 165	21 238	4 697	224 100	33 244	3 404	1 445	38 093
1992 Q1	26 940[†]	7 098[†]	416[†]	34 454[†]	193 992[†]	24 505[†]	4 015[†]	222 512[†]	31 055[†]	3 978[†]	1 009[†]	36 042[†]
Q2	28 438	6 886	212	35 536	194 877	27 166	3 570	225 613	27 553	4 225	657	32 435

1 Transfers of dwellings under construction between tenures in this period.

Source: Department of the Environment

12.4 Permanent dwellings started, under construction and completed

continued

Number

	Started				Under construction at end of period				Completed			
	Private enterprise	Housing associations	Local authorities, new towns and government departments[1]	All dwellings	Private enterprise	Housing associations	Local authorities, new towns and government departments[1]	All dwellings	Private enterprise	Housing associations	Local authorities, new towns and government departments[1]	All dwellings
Wales	BLIC	BLIM	BAEQ	BLIA	BLIG	BLIN	BAEU	BLIE	BLIK	BLIO	BAEY	BLII
1985	7 217	579	893	8 689	10 389	714	960	12 063	6 540	607	1 075	8 222
1986	7 111	507	743	8 361	10 474	687	833	11 994	7 026	534	870	8 430
1987	8 741	1 014	911	10 666	11 240	1 234	932	13 406	7 975	467	812	9 254
1988[2]	10 727	1 564	722	13 013	12 432	2 090	860	15 382	9 535	708	794	11 037
1989	9 970	1 568	501	12 039	13 281	2 016	731	16 028	9 121	1 642	630	11 393
1990	7 630	2 213	340	10 183	13 149	2 577	563	16 289	7 708	1 652	562	9 922
1991	6 810	2 396	185	9 391	12 498	2 564	332	15 394	7 461	2 409	416	10 286
1990 Q1	1 971	542	99	2 612	13 231	2 154	568	15 953	2 021	404	262	2 687
Q2	2 131	701	57	2 889	13 289	2 446	428	16 163	2 073	409	197	2 679
Q3	1 911	423	115	2 449	13 677	2 419	533	16 619	1 479	450	64	1 993
Q4	1 617	547	69	2 233	13 149	2 577	563	16 289	2 135	389	39	2 563
1991 Q1	1 599	575	46	2 220	12 815	2 746	516	16 077	1 933	406	93	2 432
Q2	1 982	652	30	2 664	12 994	2 858	436	16 288	1 803	540	110	2 453
Q3	1 862	606	43	2 511	13 286	2 622	338	16 246	1 570	842	141	2 553
Q4	1 367	563	66	1 996	12 498	2 564	332	15 394	2 155	621	72	2 848
1992 Q1	1 554	777	33	2 364	12 075	2 916	327	15 318	1 977	425	38	2 440
Q2	1 596	628	-	2 224	12 088	3 011	266	15 365	1 583	533	61	2 177
Scotland	BLFC	BLFM	BAER	BLFA	BLFG	BLFN	BAEV	BLFE	BLFK	BLFO	BAEZ	BLFI
1985	14 115	1 487	2 266	17 868	13 339	2 221	2 393	17 953	14 435	1 148	2 828	18 411
1986	14 610	1 414	2 651	18 675	13 079	2 169	2 743	17 991	14 870	1 466	2 301	18 637
1987[2]	13 087[†]	1 988	3 012	18 087[†]	12 271	2 988	3 121	18 380	13 904[†]	1 169	2 634	17 707[†]
1988[2]	15 046	2 068[†]	2 417[†]	19 531	13 164	3 726	2 712	19 602	14 179	1 278	2 815	18 272
1989	18 168	2 748	1 773	22 689	15 262	4 745	2 137	22 144	16 287	1 620	2 265[†]	20 172
1990	16 898	2 111	1 671	20 014	15 672	5 206	1 807	22 685	16 551	1 430[†]	2 005	19 986
1991	16 227	3 499	957	20 683	16 067	6 785	1 212	24 064	15 984	1 920	1 546	19 450
1990 Q1	4 556[†]	856[†]	794	6 206[†]	15 636	5 351	2 244	23 231	4 189[†]	236[†]	658[†]	5 083[†]
Q2	4 962	227	388[†]	5 577	16 367	5 054	2 190	23 611	4 214	175[†]	432	4 821
Q3	4 124	309	203	4 636	16 298	4 962	1 944	23 204	4 200	273	489	4 962
Q4	3 256	719	286	3 595	15 672	5 206	1 807	22 685	3 948	746	426	5 120
1991 Q1	4 812	2 005	359	7 176	17 443	6 539	1 795	25 777	3 044	672	371	4 087
Q2	4 110	455	216	4 781	17 643	6 391	1 675	25 709	4 026	603	336	4 965
Q3	3 312	534	183	4 029	17 087	6 600	1 466	25 153	3 947	325	406	4 678
Q4	3 993	505	199	4 697	16 067	6 785	1 212	24 064	4 967	320	433	5 720
1992 Q1	3 852	896	418	5 166	16 857[†]	7 442[†]	1 337[†]	25 636[†]	3 062	239	293	3 594
Q2	3 900	600	250	4 750	16 757	7 742	1 187	25 686	4 000	300	400	4 700
Northern Ireland	BLGC	BLGM	BAES	BLGA	BLGG	BLGN	BAEW	BLGE	BLGK	BLGO	BAFA	BLGI
1985[2]	7 199	370	2 353	9 922	12 931	577	2 011	15 519	6 940	626	3 235	10 801
1986[2]	7 114	629	1 920	9 663	12 963	733	1 351	15 047	7 082	483	2 580	10 145
1987[2]	7 418	725	1 605	9 748	12 930	912	1 192	15 034	7 451	546	1 764	9 761
1988	7 228	572	2 061	9 861	12 647	769	1 538	14 954	7 511	715	1 715	9 941
1989	6 763	498	940	8 201	11 499	582	770	12 851	7 911	685	1 708	10 304
1990	5 704	764	1 059	7 527	11 040	896	515	12 451	6 163	450	1 314	7 927
1991	5 531	791	1 136	7 458	11 407	909	695	13 012	5 164	778	955	6 898
1989 Q4	1 375	104	203	1 682	11 499	582	770	12 851	1 864	103	521	2 488
1990 Q1	1 346	266	90	1 702	11 183	809	647	12 639	1 662	39	213	1 914
Q2	1 615	75	497	2 187	11 423	718	692	12 833	1 375	166	452	1 993
Q3	1 545	181	314	2 040	11 691	712	769	13 172	1 277	187	237	1 701
Q4	1 198	242	158	1 598	11 040	896	515	12 451	1 849	58	412	2 319
1991 Q1	1 185	197	125	1 507	11 015	967	401	12 383	1 210	126	238	1 575
Q2	1 604	197	518	2 319	11 204	1 003	505	12 713	1 415	161	414	1 990
Q3	1 497	301	284	2 082	11 551	1 078	654	13 284	1 150	226	135	1 511
Q4	1 245	96	209	1 550	11 407	909	695	13 012	1 389	265	168	1 822
1992 Q1	1 442	144	143	1 729	11 250	892	584	12 727	1 599	161	254	2 014

1 Includes housebuilding for the Scottish Special Housing Association and the Northern Ireland Housing Executive.

2 Under construction figures are not strictly comparable with those of earlier periods.

Sources: Welsh Office;
Scottish Development Department;
Department of the Environment (Northern Ireland)

13 Transport

13.1 Road vehicles in Great Britain: new registrations by taxation class

Thousands

	All vehicles								Of which body-type cars		
	Private and light goods[1]		Motor cycles, scooters and mopeds	Goods vehicles[1]	Public transport vehicles	Agricultural tractors[2]	Other vehicles[3]	Total	Total	Percent company	Percent imported
	Private cars	Other vehicles									
	BMAA	BMAE	BMAD	BMAZ	BMAG	BMAH	BMAY	BMAX	BMAJ	BMAV	BMAC
1985	1 804.0	224.9	125.8	51.8	6.8	40.1	55.4	2 309.3	1 842.1	45	57
1986	1 839.3	231.3	106.4	51.5	8.9	34.8	61.5	2 333.7	1 883.2	46	54
1987	1 962.7	248.3	90.8	54.0	8.7	37.7	70.1	2 473.9	2 016.2	48	50
1988	2 154.7	282.4	90.1	63.4	9.2	45.6	78.6	2 723.5	2 210.3	51	55
1989	2 241.2	293.6	97.3	64.7	8.0	42.5	81.4	2 828.9	2 304.4	51	55
1990	1 942.3	237.6	94.4	44.0	7.4	34.2	78.4	2 438.4	2 005.1	52	56
1991 Feb	119.0	14.2	4.3	2.3	0.4	1.8	5.3	147.1	123.3	56	50
Mar	166.0	18.9	7.2	3.0	0.6	2.4	6.7	204.3	171.0	54	54
Apr	116.0	15.6	8.1	2.3	0.5	2.9	6.2	152.0	121.4	60	55
May	113.7	14.2	7.8	2.2	0.5	2.4	6.3	147.0	119.0	60	55
Jun	94.0	12.8	6.8	2.3	0.3	1.9	5.9	123.9	98.8	61	78
Jul	33.5	8.2	4.2	1.1	0.2	1.3	3.6	52.1	36.1	64	49
Aug	358.3	24.9	14.1	3.5	0.7	4.8	14.5	420.8	371.5	37	58
Sep	121.0	15.2	7.1	2.4	0.4	2.1	6.6	154.4	126.1	50	54
Oct	99.0	11.3	5.1	2.7	0.4	2.1	5.5	125.7	103.0	53	57
Nov	98.0	11.4	4.2	2.2	0.4	1.6	5.9	123.7	102.9	55	52
Dec	59.3	9.1	2.9	1.9	0.3	1.0	4.8	79.3	63.2	56	48
1992 Jan	146.0	13.9	3.8	2.1	0.4	1.7	5.8	173.7	151.0	58	52
Feb	105.0	13.3	4.1	2.1	0.7	1.8	6.2	133.1	110.2	56	53
Mar	137.7	16.1	5.6	3.0	0.6	2.4	6.5	171.8	142.9	54	56
Apr	129.5	14.0	6.4	2.2	0.5	2.5	7.0	162.2	135.2	55	55
May	116.6	13.6	6.8	2.0	0.5	2.4	6.4	148.3	121.9	58	55
Jun	97.6	13.6	6.7	2.4	0.3	1.9	6.9	129.4	103.4	58	57

1 For the period up to Oct 1990 retrospective counts within these taxation classes have been estimated. See notes and definitions - Taxation Class Changes.
2 Includes trench diggers, mobile cranes etc but excludes agricultural tractors on exempt licences.
3 Includes crown and exempt vehicles, three-wheelers, pedestrian controlled vehicles, general haulage and showmen's tractors.

Source: Department of Transport

13.2 Motor vehicles currently licensed

Thousands

	Private and light goods		Motor-cycles, scooters and mopeds	Public transport vehicles[2]	Goods vehicles[1,3]	Agricultural tractors[4]	Other vehicles[5]	Crown and exempt vehicles	All vehicles
	Private cars[1]	Other vehicles[1]							
	BMBJ	BMBK	BMBB	BMBE	BMBD	BMBC	BMBF	BMBL	BMBI
1982	15 303	1 585	1 370	111	477	371	91	454	19 762
1983	15 543	1 709	1 290	113	496	376	86	621[6]	20 209
1984	16 055	1 770	1 225	116	497	375	82	670	20 765
1985	16 453	1 804	1 148	120	486	374	77	695	21 157
1986	16 981	1 879	1 065	125	484	371	72	720	21 699
1987	17 421	1 952	978	129	484	374	68	744	22 152
1988	18 432	2 095	912	132	503	383	83	761	23 302
1989	19 248	2 199	875	122	505	384	77	785	24 196
1990	19 742	2 247	833	115	482	376	71	807	24 673
1991	19 737	2 215	750	109	449	346	65	840	24 511

1 For years up to 1990 retrospective counts within these new taxation classes have been estimated. See notes and definitions on taxation class changes.
2 Includes taxis.
3 Includes agricultural vans and lorries and showmen's goods vehicles licensed to draw trailers.
4 Includes combine harvesters, mowing machines, digging machines, mobile cranes and works trucks.
5 Includes three-wheelers, pedestrian controlled vehicles and showmen's haulage.
6 Includes old vehicles exempt from tax converted for the first time to the DVLA system.

Source: Department of Transport

13.3 Index numbers of road traffic and goods transport by road

Average 1977=100

| | Index of vehicle kilometres travelled on roads in Great Britain[1] | | | | | | | | Index of tonne-kilo-metres of road goods transport[4,5,6] |
| | Motor traffic | | | | | Other goods vehicles | | | |
	All motor traffic	Motorcycles etc	Cars and taxis	Buses and coaches	Light vans[2]	Total	Articulated[3]	Pedal cycles	
	BMCA	BMCB	BMCC	BMCD	BMCE	BMCF	BMCG	BMCH	BMCI
1984	123	131	126	119	111	104	119	105	101
1985	125	119	129	113	114	106	121	100	104
1986	132	114	136	114	120	109	124	90	106
1987	142	108	147	126	131	120	144	95	114
1988	152	97	157	134	145	129	158	86	131
1989	165	96	171	140	160	137	174	86	139
1990	166	90	173	142	161	134	171	87	137
1991[7]	163	91	170	154	163	131	160	96	-
1989 Q2	168	108	174	147	165	141	176	97	140
Q3	176	119	183	154	165	140	177	117	139
Q4	162	81	168	131	157	135	174	62	138
1990 Q1	155	73	159	138	158	139	177	65	140
Q2	175	102	184	146	163	134	166	101	138
Q3	174	108	182	149	163	134	170	110	137
Q4	161	76	167	135	161	131	172	71	134
1991 Q1[7]	149	76	154	138	156	126	161	62	131
Q2[7]	169	98	175	162	170	136	167	99	134
Q3[7]	176	118	183	164	174	137	160	134	132
Q4[7]	159	72	167	153	153	124	151	91	127
1992 Q1[7]	151	70	158	128	144	120	142	73	125†

1 All indices have been revised.
2 Not over 30 cwt. unladen weight.
3 Includes vehicles with drawbar trailers.
4 The figures for road goods transport are estimated from a continuing sample enquiry.
5 The quarterly figures relate to 13-week periods and not three calendar months.
6 Revised to exclude estimates of work done by vehicles under 3.5 tonnes gross vehicle weight.
7 Index of vehicle kilometres is provisional for 1991-1992.

Source: Department of Transport

13.4 Road casualties in Great Britain

Number

| | Total casualties | | Severity | | | All severities | | | |
	All ages	Under 15 years	Killed	Seriously injured	Slightly injured	Pedestrians	Pedal cyclists	Motor cyclists and their passengers[1]	Other drivers and their passengers
	BMDA	BMDB	BMDC	BMDD	BMDE	BMDF	BMDG	BMDH	BMDI
1985	317 524	43 644	5 165	70 980	241 379	61 390	26 998	56 591	172 545
1986	321 451	41 426	5 382	68 752	247 317	60 875	26 129	52 280	182 167
1987	311 473	40 013	5 125	64 293	242 055	57 453	26 194	45 801	182 025
1988	322 305	41 050	5 052	63 491	253 762	58 843	25 849	42 836	194 777
1989	341 592	43 041	5 373	63 158	273 061	60 080	28 513	42 630	210 369
1990	341 141	43 853	5 217	60 441	275 483	60 230	26 422	39 042	215 447
1991[2]	311 269	40 571	4 568	51 605†	255 096	53 992	24 803	30 736	202 738
1988 Q4	86 885	9 658	1 475	16 807	68 603	16 242	6 129	10 865	53 649
1989 Q1	77 828	9 364	1 232	14 571	62 025	14 897	5 854	9 027	48 050
Q2	83 305	11 865	1 186	15 324	66 795	14 871	7 660	11 202	49 572
Q3	87 747	12 209	1 422	16 390	69 935	14 126	8 800	12 122	52 699
Q4	92 712	9 603	1 533	16 873	74 306	16 186	6 199	10 279	60 048
1990 Q1	81 015	9 700	1 278	14 712	65 025	15 904	5 609	8 614	50 888
Q2	84 522	12 341	1 254	14 763	68 505	14 661	7 188	10 299	52 374
Q3	87 051	12 537	1 267	15 595	70 189	14 263	7 804	10 991	53 993
Q4	88 553	9 275	1 418	15 371	71 764	15 402	5 821	9 138	58 192
1991 Q1[2]	70 217	8 178	969	11 746	57 502	12 817	4 643	6 040	46 717
Q2[2]	77 702	11 676	1 047	12 921	63 734	13 638	6 586	8 178	49 300
Q3[2]	81 667	12 149	1 203	13 580	66 884	13 276	8 304	9 248	50 839
Q4[2]	81 683	8 568	1 349	13 358†	66 976	14 261	5 270	7 270	55 882

1 Includes riders and passengers of mopeds, motor scooters and combinations.
2 Provisional.

Sources: Department of Transport;
Scottish Development Department;
Welsh Office

13.5 Local (stage) bus services: vehicle kilometres and passenger journeys
Great Britain

Millions

	London[1]	English metropolitan areas	English shire counties	England	Scotland	Wales	All Great Britain	All outside London	All outside London and English metropolitan areas
Vehicle kilometres									
	BAJO	BAJP	BAJQ	BAJR	BAJS	BAJT	BAJU	BAJV	BAJW
1983[2]	264	582	875	1 721	290	106	2 117	1 853	1 271
1984[2]	268	584	882	1 734	286	105	2 125	1 857	1 273
1985/86	273	575	848	1 696	285	95	2 076	1 803	1 228
1986/87	278	558	928	1 764	302	94	2 160	1 882	1 324
1987/88	276	617	1 014	1 908	329	105	2 341	2 065	1 447
1988/89	285	634	1 023	1 943	325	118	2 386	2 101	1 466
1989/90	292	654	1 041	1 987	335	120	2 442	2 151	1 496
1990/91	304	649	1 035	1 988	333	123	2 444	2 140	1 491
Passenger journeys									
	BAJX	BAJY	BAJZ	BAKA	BAKB	BAKC	BAKD	BAKE	BAKF
1983[2]	1 087	2 011	1 629	4 727	680	180	5 587	4 500	2 489
1984[2]	1 162	2 047	1 604	4 813	669	168	5 650	4 488	2 441
1985/86	1 152	2 069	1 587	4 807	671	163	5 641	4 489	2 420
1986/87	1 164	1 811	1 572	4 547	644	152	5 343	4 179	2 368
1987/88	1 240	1 733	1 545	4 518	647	156	5 321	4 081	2 347
1988/89	1 240	1 695	1 499	4 434	647	161	5 242	4 001	2 307
1989/90	1 207	1 649	1 466	4 322	613	153	5 088	3 881	2 232
1990/91	1 197	1 528	1 396	4 121	583	147	4 851	3 654	2 126

1 Passenger journey statistics for London may not be consistent with those published by London Regional Transport.

2 Estimates by area for 1983 and 1984 are derived from a number of sources and may be less reliable than those for later years.

Source: Department of Transport

13.6 Local (stage) bus services: fare indices
Great Britain

1985=100

	London	English metropolitan areas	English shire counties	England	Scotland	Wales[1]	All Great Britain	All outside London	All outside London and English metropolitan areas
	BAKG	BAKH	BAKI	BAKJ	BAKK	BAKL	BAKM	BAKN	BAKO
1983	100.0	99.4	88.8	94.1	94.4	89.5	93.7	92.8	90.2
1984	91.6	98.6	94.8	95.3	98.3	96.3	95.8	96.5	95.7
1985/86[2]	101.8	100.4	101.3	101.1	100.2	101.1	100.9	100.8	101.0
1986/87[2]	107.8	127.0	106.4	112.6	103.7	105.5	111.0	111.7	105.6
1987/88[2]	113.1	137.9	111.9	119.3	107.8	..	117.2	118.1	110.7
1988/89[2]	125.3	146.7	117.6	127.0	112.2	..	124.3	124.2	115.9
1989/90[2]	138.2	158.7	127.3	137.8	117.9	..	134.3	133.6	124.7
1990/91[2]	152.5	176.4	140.5	152.1	126.9	..	147.8	147.0	136.9
1987 Q4	110.2	138.7	112.4	119.2	107.8		117.1	118.5	111.0
1988 Q1	121.7	141.8	113.8	123.0	109.1	..	120.5	120.3	112.4
Q2	121.7	143.1	115.1	124.1	110.7	..	121.7	121.7	113.7
Q3	121.7	146.1	116.6	125.7	112.1	..	123.2	123.5	115.2
Q4	121.7	148.4	118.3	127.2	112.3	..	124.5	125.0	116.5
1989 Q1	136.1	149.1	120.3	131.1	113.7	..	127.9	126.5	118.4†
Q2	136.1	153.9	123.4	133.9	115.8	..	130.7	129.8	121.2
Q3	136.1	159.1	126.2	136.9	117.6	..	133.5	133.1	123.7
Q4	136.1	160.0	128.5	138.3	118.6	..	134.8	134.6	125.6
1990 Q1	144.6	161.9	131.2	141.9	119.6	..	138.1	136.9	128.1
Q2	148.8	166.1	135.6	146.1	122.6	..	142.0	140.9	132.1
Q3	148.8	171.4	137.9	148.8	124.5	..	144.6	143.9	134.2
Q4	148.8	181.4	142.8	154.0	128.7	..	149.7	149.8	139.0
1991 Q1	163.4	186.7	145.6†	159.5	131.9	..	154.8	153.3	142.1
Q2	163.8	191.5	148.1	162.1†	134.3	..	157.4	156.3	144.6
Q3	164.0	194.6	150.3	164.1†	136.1	..	159.3†	158.6	146.6
Q4[3]	164.0	199.6	153.0	166.8	136.3	..	161.6	161.3	148.7
1992 Q1[3]	176.0	201.5	154.3	170.3	139.8	..	165.0	163.1	150.6

1 Figures for Wales since 1986/87 are omitted because insufficient data are available.

2 Due to rounding financial year data may differ from that published by the Department of Transport.

3 Provisional.

Source: Department of Transport

13.7 British Rail and London Underground

Millions

	British Rail: passenger kilometres			London Underground: passenger journeys[3]		
	Ordinary fares	Season tickets	Total	Full and reduced fares	Season tickets	Total
	BMGB	BMGD	BMGA	BMGF	BMGG	BMGE
1985	21 585	8 099	29 684	341	391	732
1986	21 948	9 036	30 984	355	414	769
1987	22 607	9 711	32 318	373	425	798
1988	23 276	11 137	34 412	363	452	815
1989	22 629	10 766	33 394	380	385	765
1990	23 463	10 762	34 226	399	376	775
1991[4]	21 894	9 940	31 834	368	383	751
1988 Q3	6 318	2 571	8 889	96	112	208
Q4	5 835	2 962	8 797	94	116	210
1989 Q1	5 324	2 853	8 177	85	114	199
Q2[1]	5 459	2 682	8 141	85	95	180
Q3[2]	5 864	2 378	8 242	97	91	189
Q4	5 983	2 852	8 834	101	100	201
1990 Q1	5 444	2 986	8 430	96	99	195
Q2	5 868	2 526	8 394	101	94	195
Q3	6 327	2 400	8 726	105	95	200
Q4	5 825	2 851	8 675	102	96	198
1991 Q1	4 784	2 612	7 396	90	92	182
Q2	5 446	2 502	7 948	93	97	190
Q3	6 084	2 264	8 349	95	93	189
Q4	5 567	2 651	8 216	94	96	190
1992 Q1	4 931	2 614	7 545	86	97	182
Q2	..	..	..	90	90	180

1 NUR Industrial action on 2 days (BR only).
2 NUR Industrial action on 4 days (BR only).
3 From 1985 LRT annual figures relate to financial years.
4 Provisional.

Source: Department of Transport

13.8 British Rail: freight traffic

	British Rail [1]				
	Freight lifted: million tonnes				Net tonne kilometres: millions[2]
	Coal and coke	Metals including iron and steel	Other traffic	Total	
	BMHB	BMHC	BMHD	BMHA	BMHE
1985	65.9	14.1	40.5	122.0	15 370
1986	79.7	16.8	43.2	139.6	16 473
1987	77.7	19.1	44.2	141.0	17 297
1988	78.8	20.5	50.1	149.5	18 184
1989	76.5	19.7	49.6	145.8	17 295
1990	74.9	18.4	47.8	141.1	15 829
1991[5]	74.8	17.3	42.7	134.8	-
1988 Q2	19.3	5.3	12.1	36.8	4 480
Q3	18.1	4.5	12.8	35.4	4 382
Q4	20.9	5.4	12.8	39.1	4 729
1989 Q1	20.9	5.4	12.6	38.8	4 798
Q2[3]	18.8	5.2	12.5	36.5	4 229
Q3[4]	17.3	4.7	12.0	34.0	4 103
Q4	19.5	4.4	12.6	36.5	4 165
1990 Q1	20.2	4.6	12.3	37.1	3 468
Q2	18.6	4.9	12.4	35.9	4 235
Q3	18.1	4.6	11.7	34.4	4 118
Q4	18.1	4.3	11.2	33.6	4 008
1991 Q1	20.0	4.2	10.6	34.8	3 829
Q2	18.8	4.8	10.8	34.4	..
Q3	17.8	4.0	10.7	32.5	..
Q4[5]	18.2	4.3	10.6	33.1	..
1992 Q1	20.2	4.7	10.8	35.7	..

1 Freight train traffic only.
2 Freightliner traffic omitted from 1989 Q1.
3 NUR Industrial action on 2 days.
4 Industrial action on 4 days.

5 Provisional.

Source: Department of Transport

13.9 UK airlines:[1] aircraft kilometres flown, passengers and cargo uplifted
Tonne-kilometres and seat kilometres used

Monthly averages or calendar months: thousands or tonnes

	All services			Domestic services			International services		
	Aircraft kilometres flown (000's)	Passengers uplifted (000's)	Cargo uplifted (tonnes)[2]	Aircraft kilometres flown (000's)	Passengers uplifted (000's)	Cargo uplifted (tonnes)[2]	Aircraft kilometres flown (000's)	Passengers uplifted	Cargo uplifted (tonnes)[2]
	BMIA	BMIB	BMIC	BMID	BMIE	BMIF	BMIG	BMIH	BMII
1985	30 955	2 068.7	30 003	5 772	747.7	3 842	25 183	1 321.0	26 161
1986	32 067	2 083.1	31 330	5 932	756.8	3 962	26 136	1 326.3	27 368
1987	33 802	2 374.7	33 780	6 127	837.4	4 235	27 675	1 537.3	29 546
1988	36 562	2 603.7	35 669	6 446	933.2	4 064	30 117	1 670.5	31 606
1989	40 472	2 931.0	37 786	7 100	1 019.2	3 888	33 372	1 911.8	33 898
1990	43 653	3 196.0	40 461	7 207	1 057.5	3 818	36 446	2 138.5	36 643
1991	41 475	2 882.7	38 885	7 169	970.8	3 145	34 306	1 911.9	35 740
1987 Sep	36 082	2 807.7	34 548	6 817	1 013.4	4 249	29 265	1 794.3	30 299
Oct	35 919	2 654.8	36 758	6 403	931.9	4 363	29 516	1 723.0	32 394
Nov	33 190	2 191.2	35 963	5 555	787.4	4 291	27 635	1 403.9	31 672
Dec	33 001	2 126.5	35 957	5 469	751.3	4 114	27 532	1 375.2	31 844
1988 Jan	34 189	2 063.4	33 757	5 413	707.5	3 977	28 776	1 355.8	29 781
Feb	32 145	2 015.4	35 736	5 346	721.4	4 331	26 799	1 294.0	31 405
Mar	35 196	2 457.6	39 310	5 977	879.6	4 691	29 219	1 578.0	34 618
Apr	35 995	2 494.0	36 675	6 244	887.1	3 942	29 750	1 606.9	32 733
May	38 315	2 650.8	38 176	6 855	989.3	4 658	31 459	1 661.5	33 518
Jun	37 647	2 791.5	35 612	6 986	1 015.8	4 524	30 679	1 775.7	31 088
Jul	39 364	3 025.2	34 098	7 369	1 085.7	3 634	31 996	1 939.6	30 464
Aug	38 873	3 018.2	32 186	7 338	1 082.5	3 682	31 535	1 935.7	28 504
Sep	37 998	3 033.2	32 872	6 977	1 102.0	3 481	31 021	1 931.2	29 391
Oct	38 345	2 892.9	36 493	6 737	1 026.3	3 894	31 608	1 866.5	32 599
Nov	35 338	2 426.0	36 113	6 131	871.2	4 040	29 207	1 554.7	32 075
Dec	35 333	2 376.2	37 005	5 981	829.9	3 912	29 352	1 546.3	33 093
1989 Jan	37 256	2 335.0	33 839	6 188	778.0	3 341	31 068	1 557.0	30 499
Feb	33 347	2 216.2	35 149	5 629	764.4	3 588	27 718	1 451.7	31 561
Mar	38 050	2 715.4	38 895	6 604	947.6	3 822	31 447	1 767.7	35 073
Apr	38 470	2 777.1	37 177	6 786	980.2	3 625	31 684	1 797.4	33 552
May	41 743	2 974.1	37 457	7 568	1 063.5	4 030	34 176	1 910.6	33 428
Jun	41 935	3 116.7	37 472	7 727	1 105.2	4 125	34 207	2 011.4	33 347
Jul	44 139	3 357.4	38 126	8 108	1 170.1	4 095	36 031	2 187.3	34 032
Aug	43 494	3 325.4	36 094	8 087	1 156.9	4 146	35 407	2 168.5	31 948
Sep	43 270	3 405.2	37 892	7 800	1 196.2	4 085	35 470	2 209.0	33 807
Oct	43 934	3 302.1	40 943	7 627	1 138.5	3 975	36 307	2 163.6	36 968
Nov	40 126	2 817.1	39 550	6 783	967.7	3 940	33 343	1 849.4	35 609
Dec	39 193	2 643.8	39 072	6 270	867.8	3 592	35 923	1 776.0	35 480
1990 Jan	41 256	2 641.3	36 017	6 882	875.8	3 551	34 286	1 765.5	32 466
Feb	37 538	2 556.9	36 871	6 220	848.7	3 514	31 318	1 708.2	33 357
Mar	42 615	3 076.2	43 163	7 154	1 030.3	4 015	35 461	2 045.9	39 149
Apr	43 576	3 278.0	38 874	7 423	1 104.0	3 520	36 153	2 174.0	35 355
May	45 837	3 382.0	40 061	7 643	1 080.1	3 993	38 194	2 237.0	36 070
Jun	45 199	3 510.2	40 534	7 506	1 147.7	4 914	37 694	2 362.5	35 621
Jul	47 397	3 774.2	41 697	7 895	1 213.5	3 783	39 502	2 560.7	37 914
Aug	47 425	3 729.5	39 534	8 106	1 215.4	3 793	39 319	2 512.0	35 742
Sep	46 200	3 679.2	41 657	7 556	1 211.5	3 884	38 644	2 467.7	37 773
Oct	46 599	3 497.5	44 427	7 518	1 134.7	4 053	39 081	2 362.8	40 374
Nov	40 671	2 759.4	42 159	6 579	959.5	3 460	34 092	1 799.9	38 699
Dec	39 826	2 615.9	41 256	6 005	854.8	3 451	33 281	1 761.1	37 805
1991 Jan	40 328	2 289.3	35 205	6 442	763.0	3 006	33 886	1 526.3	32 199
Feb	30 364	1 852.8	32 868	5 182	688.6	2 592	25 182	1 164.2	30 276
Mar	36 996	2 655.3	38 592	6 118	913.9	3 145	30 878	1 741.4	35 447
Apr	40 662	2 791.7	37 267	7 282	969.6	3 214	33 380	1 822.1	34 053
May	42 950	3 061.2	38 646	7 758	1 075.9	3 190	35 192	1 985.3	35 456
Jun	43 224	3 162.9	40 322	7 550	1 067.1	3 000	35 674	2 095.8	37 322
Jul	45 433	3 347.2	38 639	7 994	1 102.5	3 034	37 439	2 244.7	35 605
Aug	45 000	3 402.4	37 440	8 013	1 136.4	3 088	36 987	2 266.0	34 352
Sep	44 440	3 384.3	39 529	7 847	1 137.4	3 126	36 593	2 246.9	36 403
Oct	45 076	3 256.8	42 735	7 945	1 063.1	3 345	37 131	2 193.7	39 390
Nov	42 090	2 728.0	43 252	7 150	896.1	3 114	34 940	1 831.9	40 138
Dec	40 979	2 655.0	41 550	6 587	831.0	3 300	34 392	1 824.0	38 250
1992 Jan	42 938	2 606.7	36 975	7 052	803.1	2 880	35 886	1 803.6	34 095
Feb	39 940	2 563.8	39 776	6 699	800.2	2 941	33 241	1 763.5	36 835
Mar	43 961	2 985.4	43 140	7 411	925.9	3 258	36 550	2 059.6	39 882

1 Scheduled services only. All kilometre statistics are based on standard (Great Circle) distance.
2 Including weight of freight mail, excess baggage and diplomatic bags, but excluding passengers' and crews' permitted baggage.

Source: Civil Aviation Authority

13.9
UK airlines:[1] aircraft kilometres flown, passengers and cargo uplifted
Tonne-kilometres and seat kilometres used

continued

Monthly averages or calendar months: thousands or tonnes

	All services (thousand tonne-kilometres)				Domestic services (thousand tonne-kilometres)				International services (thousand tonne-kilometres)			
	Mail	Freight[2]	Passenger	Seat kilometres used (millions)	Mail	Freight[2]	Passenger	Seat kilometres used (millions)	Mail	Freight[2]	Passenger	Seat kilometres used (millions)
	BMIJ	BMIK	BMIL	BMIM	BMIN	BMIO	BMIP	BMIQ	BMIR	BMIS	BMIT	BMIU
1985	16 916	131 427	393 046	4 300.2	497	845	23 648	291.2	16 419	130 581	369 398	4 009.0
1986	16 611	141 510	392 415	4 283.5	495	873	24 127	297.3	16 115	140 637	368 288	3 986.2
1987	16 898	157 109	458 047	4 989.3	537	888	26 538	327.1	16 361	156 221	431 508	4 662.2
1988	14 356	166 127	483 230	5 249.7	524	839	29 607	365.2	13 831	165 288	453 624	4 884.5
1989	13 524	183 864	550 407	5 849.7	591	745	32 664	397.3	12 934	183 119	517 744	5 452.4
1990	14 052	199 062	622 134	6 631.6	631	723	34 336	418.4	13 421	198 340	587 798	6 213.2
1991	15 217	198 326	583 994	6 218.0	617	562	31 861	388.6	14 600	197 764	552 134	5 829.3
1987 Sep	15 783	162 573	530 971	5 790.6	571	865	31 424	386.5	15 212	161 708	499 547	5 404.1
Oct	16 748	175 479	498 305	5 434.9	571	911	29 232	360.8	16 178	174 568	469 073	5 074.1
Nov	20 130	165 837	406 252	4 424.5	562	900	25 167	312.5	19 568	164 937	381 085	4 112.0
Dec	20 869	164 656	427 677	4 610.9	569	853	24 512	301.8	20 300	163 803	403 164	4 309.2
1988 Jan	16 398	155 885	434 879	4 695.2	551	802	23 041	284.0	15 847	155 083	411 838	4 411.2
Feb	14 764	167 084	374 236	4 068.4	495	969	23 042	286.4	14 269	166 114	351 194	3 782.0
Mar	15 940	182 452	456 746	4 980.9	557	981	27 933	346.0	15 383	181 471	428 813	4 634.9
Apr	13 899	174 070	452 388	4 946.5	519	840	27 966	345.1	13 380	173 230	424 423	4 601.3
May	13 741	179 547	461 680	5 048.1	476	1 106	30 889	381.7	13 265	178 441	430 792	4 666.5
Jun	12 551	160 709	501 102	5 458.2	642	844	31 876	393.8	11 909	159 864	469 226	5 064.4
Jul	13 240	159 719	573 159	6 231.3	477	722	34 552	424.7	12 763	158 997	538 607	5 806.6
Aug	12 135	152 744	576 045	6 252.9	478	743	33 976	416.5	11 657	152 001	542 069	5 836.4
Sep	9 143	156 721	541 294	5 887.0	347	790	34 509	424.7	8 795	155 930	506 785	5 462.3
Oct	14 544	170 878	525 236	5 709.2	543	775	32 390	399.3	14 001	170 103	492 846	5 309.9
Nov	15 635	167 166	440 651	4 773.6	588	791	28 034	347.4	15 047	166 376	412 618	4 426.3
Dec	20 278	166 549	461 342	4 945.3	616	703	27 070	333.0	19 661	165 845	434 272	4 612.3
1989 Jan	14 027	158 968	476 961	5 142.2	488	621	25 535	314.6	13 539	158 348	451 426	4 827.6
Feb	13 224	164 792	416 799	4 461.6	514	694	24 782	303.4	12 711	164 098	392 017	4 158.3
Mar	14 272	187 381	503 268	5 387.8	540	751	30 477	371.1	13 731	186 630	472 791	5 016.8
Apr	12 247	183 058	520 296	5 478.8	590	840	31 576	382.0	11 657	182 218	488 720	5 096.8
May	11 580	183 138	544 445	5 737.6	602	763	34 501	417.0	10 979	182 376	509 944	5 320.6
Jun	11 857	181 914	578 581	6 092.3	611	785	36 041	434.4	11 245	181 129	542 540	5 657.8
Jul	11 477	188 521	641 618	6 736.6	588	760	38 351	461.1	10 889	187 761	603 266	6 275.5
Aug	11 857	179 825	643 665	6 867.8	596	813	36 750	446.6	11 261	179 012	606 915	6 421.2
Sep	11 956	184 812	630 753	6 741.3	635	797	38 014	463.4	11 321	184 015	592 739	6 277.9
Oct	12 899	205 289	608 316	6 494.2	606	785	36 171	443.9	12 293	204 504	572 145	6 090.3
Nov	15 999	191 577	519 614	5 528.6	662	744	31 416	386.4	15 337	190 834	488 197	5 142.1
Dec	20 921	187 317	520 856	5 491.6	665	702	29 095	352.6	2 026	186 615	491 761	5 139.0
1990 Jan	12 728	172 764	540 195	5 725.7	560	687	29 604	361.2	12 168	172 076	510 591	5 364.6
Feb	12 628	176 944	477 632	5 097.3	555	673	27 880	341.8	12 073	176 272	449 752	4 755.5
Mar	14 451	206 093	574 463	6 158.0	669	759	33 414	409.4	13 782	205 333	541 049	5 748.6
Apr	12 380	191 930	590 545	6 337.3	577	666	35 208	429.5	11 803	191 263	555 336	5 907.8
May	12 793	192 582	623 618	6 675.7	614	794	36 565	447.5	12 179	191 787	587 053	6 228.3
Jun	12 956	191 650	682 381	7 284.2	616	793	37 042	451.7	12 339	190 858	645 338	6 832.5
Jul	12 658	211 795	749 512	7 984.9	580	805	39 891	483.8	12 078	210 990	709 620	7 501.2
Aug	12 443	203 077	753 488	8 017.3	589	759	39 393	477.7	11 854	202 318	714 096	7 539.6
Sep	13 231	212 345	714 897	7 624.6	656	769	38 714	470.5	12 575	211 576	676 183	7 154.1
Oct	14 541	223 103	661 159	7 076.9	691	799	36 319	442.6	13 850	222 304	624 840	6 634.3
Nov	16 865	205 694	539 618	5 741.5	703	624	31 213	383.2	16 162	205 070	508 405	5 358.3
Dec	20 956	200 934	561 287	5 904.9	766	542	27 888	339.7	20 190	200 392	533 399	5 565.2
1991 Jan	13 339	172 495	509 337	5 346.2	639	476	25 453	310.7	12 700	172 019	483 884	5 035.5
Feb	12 857	169 585	355 853	3 766.8	576	409	22 857	280.3	12 281	169 176	332 996	3 486.4
Mar	15 455	195 107	506 944	5 404.8	643	544	29 851	365.2	14 812	194 563	477 093	5 039.6
Apr	13 284	191 574	532 583	5 707.7	629	562	31 242	383.6	12 655	191 012	501 341	5 324.1
May	13 754	200 000	594 509	6 358.9	635	597	34 771	424.2	13 119	199 403	559 738	5 934.7
Jun	14 010	210 915	639 949	6 824.5	585	540	35 151	425.9	13 425	210 375	604 798	6 398.6
Jul	13 656	201 363	686 241	7 324.5	578	576	36 367	441.9	13 078	200 787	649 874	6 882.6
Aug	13 967	194 300	712 619	7 594.4	530	605	37 213	450.4	13 437	193 695	675 406	7 144.0
Sep	14 410	201 452	679 548	7 258.6	611	586	37 140	451.7	13 799	200 866	642 408	6 806.9
Oct	15 961	215 025	658 700	7 020.6	661	618	34 599	425.2	15 300	214 407	624 101	6 595.4
Nov	18 293	221 505	555 201	5 912.0	607	588	29 526	362.6	17 686	220 917	525 675	5 549.4
Dec	23 623	206 500	576 204	6 093.4	720	554	27 921	339.1	22 903	205 946	548 283	5 754.3
1992 Jan	14 827	188 679	584 778	6 173.9	606	501	27 495	334.4	14 221	188 178	557 283	5 839.5
Feb	14 237	205 584	524 484	5 609.9	619	511	26 425	324.6	13 618	205 073	498 059	5 285.3
Mar	15 280	221 696	616 266	6 606.3	672	566	30 111	372.9	14 608	221 130	586 155	6 233.3

1 Scheduled services only. All kilometre statistics are based on standard
  (Great Circle) distance.
2 Including weight of freight mail, excess baggage and diplomatic bags, but
  excluding passengers' and crews' permitted baggage.

Source: Civil Aviation Authority

13.10 Merchant vessels registered in the United Kingdom (500 gross tons and over)[1]

	Bulk, tanker and dry			Other			Total		
	Number	Grt million	Dwt million	Number	Grt million	Dwt million	Number	Grt million	Dwt million
	BMJG	BMJH	BMJI	BMJJ	BMJK	BMJL	BMJM	BMJN	BMJO
1985	315	9.0	15.8	378	3.2	3.1	693	12.2	18.9
1986	219	4.9	8.8	326	2.8	2.6	545	7.7	11.4
1987	220	4.3	7.8	286	2.7	2.4	506	7.1	10.2
1988	210	4.1	7.3	283	2.7	2.3	493	6.8	9.6
1989	178	3.5	6.3	272	2.5	2.1	450	6.0	8.4
1990	162	3.0	5.4	265	2.5	2.0	427	5.5	7.4
1991	156	2.7	4.7	253	2.3	1.8	409	5.0	6.5
End Quarter									
1988 Q1	214	4.3	7.8	287	2.7	2.4	501	7.0	10.1
Q2	210	4.0	7.1	285	2.8	2.4	495	6.8	9.5
Q3	212	4.0	7.2	281	2.7	2.3	493	6.7	9.5
Q4	205	4.0	7.1	277	2.6	2.2	482	6.6	9.3
1989 Q1	205	3.9	7.0	270	2.5	2.1	475	6.4	9.1
Q2	193	3.9	7.0	269	2.5	2.1	462	6.3	9.0
Q3	186	3.8	6.9	270	2.5	2.1	456	6.3	9.0
Q4	178	3.5	6.3	272	2.5	2.1	450	6.0	8.4
1990 Q1	176	3.6	6.5	265	2.5	2.1	441	6.1	8.5
Q2	166	3.1	5.5	262	2.4	2.0	428	5.5	7.5
Q3	163	2.7	5.4	262	2.8	2.0	425	5.5	7.4
Q4	162	3.0	5.4	265	2.5	2.0	427	5.5	7.4
1991 Q1	158	3.0	5.3	263	2.5	2.0	421	5.4	7.3
Q2	156	2.9	5.2	254	2.3	1.8	410	5.2	7.0
Q3	156	2.8	5.0	254	2.3	1.8	410	5.1	6.8
Q4	156	2.7	4.7	253	2.3	1.8	409	5.0	6.5
1992 Q1	151	2.7	4.9	251	2.3	1.7	402	5.0	6.6

1 Covers vessels registered within the United Kingdom, the Channel Isles and the Isle of Man.

Note: From Q1 1987 changes were made to the basis of these figures with consequent minor amendment to ship type definition.

Source: Department of Transport

Why...... waste time......searching...... for what we already have ???

When you need facts & figures fast get the

Guide to Official Statistics

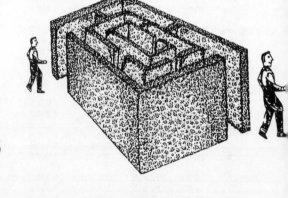

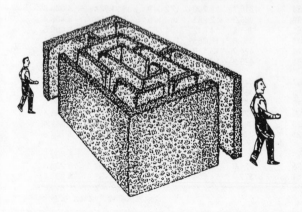

16 detailed chapters, with vital information about sources of government and important non-government statistics for the United Kingdom, make the 'Guide to Official Statistics' an invaluable fact-finder for libraries, businesses, industry, education and the media.

ISBN 0 11 620394 3

Central Statistical Office publications are published by HMSO
They are obtainable from HMSO bookshops and through booksellers.

HMSO £24.00 net

13.11 UK passenger movement by sea and air[1]

Thousands

Inward

	Sea						Air					Total sea and air
	Irish Republic	Other EC	Rest of Europe and Mediterranean Sea area	Rest of world	Pleasure cruises[2]	Total[3]	Irish Republic	Other EC	Rest of Europe and Mediterranean Sea area	Rest of world	Total[4]	
	BMKC	BMKD	BMKE	BMKF	BMKG	BMKB	BMKI	BMKJ	BMKK	BMKL	BMKH	BMKA
1985	1 440	11 380	257	25	66	13 167	904	8 438	8 668	7 948	25 958	39 125
1986	1 339	11 835	247	18	53	13 492	1 051	14 963	4 316	7 988	28 318	41 810
1987	1 299	11 447	233	20	61	13 061	1 364	17 158	5 119	9 240	32 881	45 942
1988	1 223	10 996	199	18	62	12 497	1 766	17 596	5 835	10 144	35 341	47 838
1989	1 353	12 782	209	15	62	14 421	2 052	18 003	6 281	10 987	37 322	51 722
1990	1 373	13 276	147	12	74	14 882	2 233	17 995	6 485	11 621	38 334	53 215
1991	1 511	13 862	126	12	83	15 598	..	..	..	..	..	..
1989 Q2	335	3 263	60	1	17	3 676	491	4 871	1 545	2 857	9 765	13 441
Q3	598	5 056	79	11	29	5 773	666	6 417	2 079	3 479	12 640	17 289
Q4	205	2 349	35	3	14	2 606	465	3 779	1 304	2 488	8 035	10 621
1990 Q1	187	1 947	19	-	4	2 157	475	3 093	1 372	2 339	7 279	9 436
Q2	342	3 713	50	2	15	4 122	579	4 851	1 683	3 065	10 179	14 301
Q3	618	5 220	51	6	36	5 931	717	6 252	2 155	3 659	12 783	18 714
Q4	226	2 395	27	4	18	2 671	462	3 799	1 275	2 558	8 093	10 764
1991 Q1	196	2 033	5	-	4	2 239	410	2 640	1 081	2 090	6 220	8 459
Q2	410	3 668	40	7	22	4 147	493	4 366	1 031	3 156	9 045	..
Q3	669	5 385	47	7	33	6 141	637	6 181	1 277	4 134	12 228	..
Q4	235	2 775	33	3	25	3 071	446	3 856	911	3 221	8 434	..
1992 Q1	194	2 274	18	-	6	2 492	432	3 122	1 051	3 062	7 668	..

Outward

	Sea						Air					Total sea and air
	Irish Republic	Other EC	Rest of Europe and Mediterranean Sea area	Rest of world	Pleasure cruises[2]	Total[3]	Irish Republic	Other EC	Rest of Europe and Mediterranean Sea area	Rest of world	Total[4]	
	BMKO	BMKP	BMKQ	BMKR	BMKS	BMKN	BMKU	BMKV	BMKW	BMKX	BMKT	BMKM
1985	1 426	11 384	220	18	71	13 119	903	8 472	8 615	7 996	25 986	39 105
1986	1 289	11 731	213	18	54	13 304	1 056	14 973	4 282	8 106	28 418	41 722
1987	1 281	11 470	207	21	63	13 043	1 357	17 225	5 094	9 340	33 016	46 059
1988	1 211	11 027	178	16	65	12 496	1 756	17 564	5 803	10 282	35 406	47 902
1989	1 389	12 864	215	15	67	14 545	2 041	17 888	6 240	11 132	37 301	51 827
1990	1 399	13 308	147	10	79	14 943	2 202	17 861	6 443	11 750	38 257	53 201
1991	1 527	13 770	127	17	89	15 530	..	..	..	..	..	..
1989 Q2	302	3 407	62	-	21	3 792	473	5 109	1 549	2 666	9 798	13 591
Q3	623	5 048	83	11	28	5 793	669	6 312	2 053	3 599	12 633	17 311
Q4	263	2 225	33	3	17	2 541	508	3 481	1 277	2 678	7 944	10 466
1990 Q1	145	1 901	19	1	3	2 069	426	3 069	1 349	2 317	7 161	9 230
Q2	343	3 893	45	-	20	4 301	568	5 046	1 737	2 886	10 237	14 538
Q3	641	5 162	58	6	38	5 905	716	6 218	2 131	3 786	12 852	18 757
Q4	271	2 353	25	2	18	2 669	492	3 528	1 226	2 761	8 007	10 676
1991 Q1	179	2 183	5	1	3	2 370	380	2 685	1 068	2 104	6 237	8 607
Q2	405	3 692	37	5	26	4 165	480	4 567	1 034	3 039	9 119	..
Q3	678	5 209	52	6	34	5 979	634	6 169	1 268	4 231	12 302	..
Q4	264	2 686	33	4	26	3 013	468	3 563	921	3 400	8 352	..
1992 Q1	158	2 329	20	1	4	2 512	402	3 149	1 037	2 981	7 569	..

EC=European Community. Spain and Portugal have now joined the EC.

1 Excluding movement by land across the frontier between the Irish Republic and Northern Ireland, passengers travelling between the Channel Islands and Great Britain, passengers carried in aircraft chartered by British government departments and as far as possible, passengers travelling by sea on day trips and HM and other Armed Forces travelling in the course of their duties.

2 To avoid disclosure the figure for the first quarter of each year is included with that for the second quarter.

3 Including passengers on pleasure cruises beginning and/or ending at UK seaports.

4 The figures do not include oil rigs.

Sources: Department of Transport; Civil Aviation Authority

13.12 UK passenger movement by sea and air
Analysis of countries of landing and of embarkation

Thousands

		1989	1990	1991	1990 Q2	1990 Q3	1990 Q4	1991 Q1	1991 Q2	1991 Q3	1991 Q4	1992 Q1
European continent and Mediterranean Sea area												
By sea[1]												
Belgium	BMLB	3 444	3 587	3 510	991	1 403	649	548	867	1 411	684	541
France[2]	BMLC	19 247	20 103	21 248	5 788	7 944	3 467	3 232	5 720	8 197	4 099	3 683
Netherlands	BMLD	2 364	2 507	2 459	709	880	563	382	664	821	592	351
Other European Community[3]	BMLE	471	230	416	62	86	46	55	109	166	86	28
Other countries	BMLF	545	449	252	150	177	76	11	76	98	67	38
Total	BMLA	26 071	26 876	27 849	7 700	10 490	4 801	4 227	7 436	10 658	5 528	4 641
By air												
Austria	BMLH	851	908	844	183	235	130	292	164	238	150	328
Belgium	BMLI	1 309	1 408	1 351	364	351	362	272	348	347	384	346
Denmark	BMLJ	781	885	909	235	247	228	176	243	259	231	204
Finland	BMLK	340	378	343	104	109	94	62	97	101	83	67
France	BMLL	5 711	6 236	5 918	1 639	1 738	1 397	1 267	1 540	1 705	1 406	1 537
Eastern Europe[4]	BMLM	863	997	1 083	234	341	208	230	262	370	221	252
Germany FR	BMLN	4 960	5 744	5 275	1 495	1 668	1 332	1 092	1 321	1 552	1 310	1 224
Greece	BMLO	3 528	3 577	3 459	1 145	1 859	448	87	960	1 953	459	112
Irish Republic	BMLP	4 093	4 437	3 948	1 147	1 434	954	790	972	1 271	915	834
Italy	BMLQ	3 314	3 451	3 079	916	1 243	651	493	780	1 145	661	659
Malta	BMLR	1 092	1 012	1 013	270	370	216	136	243	385	249	188
Netherlands	BMLS	3 073	3 292	3 162	890	883	813	616	839	867	840	754
Norway	BMLT	797	864	769	223	244	214	141	198	222	208	192
Portugal	BMLU	1 981	2 053	2 193	588	790	401	287	612	855	439	332
Spain	BMLV	11 110	8 916	8 406	2 587	3 608	1 605	930	2 243	3 595	1 638	1 062
Sweden	BMLW	841	940	835	248	259	236	146	223	233	233	190
Switzerland	BMLX	2 655	2 738	2 541	665	702	548	741	597	660	543	776
Turkey	BMLY	866	747	524	211	361	111	44	113	264	103	64
Yugoslavia	BMLZ	1 052	1 144	257	370	595	120	60	147	37	13	13
Other countries[5]	BMMA	576	537	460	142	156	118	86	113	146	115	92
Total	BMLG	49 791	50 265	46 373	13 655	17 194	10 186	7 949	12 016	16 207	10 201	9 225
Mediterranean Area												
Cyprus	BMMC	1 071	1 326	1 322	400	503	250	95	326	535	366	257
Near East[6]	BMMD	569	574	535	154	192	100	73	118	197	147	126
North Africa[7]	BMME	931	860	604	212	256	190	68	122	214	200	204
Total	BMMB	2 570	2 761	2 461	766	952	540	235	567	946	713	586
Rest of World												
By sea												
United States of America	BMMG	29.3	18.0	29.5	-	11.6	6.0	0.3	10.0	12.9	6.3	0.3
Canada	BMMH	-	-	-	-	-	-	-	-	-	-	-
Australia	BMMI	0.4	1.7	1.7	0.9	-	0.3	0.5	0.8	-	0.4	0.3
New Zealand	BMMJ	0.1	0.3	0.3	0.1	-	-	0.2	0.1	-	-	0.1
South Africa	BMMK	0.1	0.7	0.8	-	-	0.1	0.1	0.5	0.1	0.1	-
West Africa	BMML	0.1	0.3	0.5	0.1	0.1	-	0.1	0.2	0.1	0.1	-
British West Indies and Bermuda	BMMM	-	-	0.1	-	-	-	-	-	-	0.1	-
Other countries[8]	BMMN	1.0	0.5	0.8	0.4	0.1	-	-	0.7	0.1	-	-
Total	BMMF	31.1	21.7	34.0	1.6	11.8	6.4	1.3	12.4	13.2	7.1	1.5
By air												
Australia and New Zealand	BMMP	486	615	753	144	174	163	184	183	199	187	206
Canada	BMMQ	1 996	2 088	1 853	573	849	379	250	493	745	365	268
Canary Islands	BMMR	3 125	2 937	3 246	689	886	731	689	691	972	894	912
Caribbean[9]	BMMS	692	671	677	172	198	166	142	175	194	166	145
Central Africa[10]	BMMT	83	84	76	22	21	21	19	18	24	15	15
Central America[11]	BMMU	153	85	48	23	31	21	-	15	23	10	-
East Africa[12]	BMMV	300	352	417	73	116	91	79	89	139	110	97
Far East[13]	BMMW	1 785	1 963	1 997	481	564	487	417	475	578	527	500
Indian Continent[14]	BMMX	930	997	898	229	254	255	240	191	223	244	251
Japan	BMMY	699	822	820	190	230	209	130	178	268	244	265
Middle East[15]	BMMZ	1 175	1 136	1 088	278	337	219	178	257	364	289	292
Southern Africa[16]	BMNA	541	608	614	145	162	154	145	144	158	167	165
South America[17]	BMNB	192	249	285	53	78	64	64	64	86	71	72
United States of America	BMNC	9 447	10 244	9 697	2 768	3 409	2 214	1 546	2 478	3 260	2 413	2 057
West Africa[18]	BMND	395	402	431	82	104	115	108	96	106	121	123
Other countries[19]	BMNE	262	316	329	74	78	87	82	81	81	85	89
Oil rigs	BMNF	728	833	842	209	214	229	208	221	205	208	201
Total	BMMO	22 991	24 398	24 073	6 204	7 703	5 603	4 482	5 850	7 625	6 116	5 658

1 Passengers to and from North Africa and Middle East Mediterranean countries have been attributed to the European continent and Mediterranean Sea areas.

2 Including hovercraft passengers.

3 Consists of Denmark, Germany (Federal Republic) and Italy.

4 Including Albania, Bulgaria, Czechoslovakia, German Democratic Republic, Hungary, Poland, Rumania and Commonwealth of Independent States.

5 Including Faroes, Gibraltar, Iceland, Luxembourg, Croatia and Slovenia.

6 Including Jordan, Lebanon, Israel and Syria.

7 Including Algeria, Egypt, Libya, Morocco and Tunisia.

8 Figures for Other countries cover mainly passengers to or from the Canary Islands, Madeira and the Azores.

9 Including Bahamas, Barbados, Bermuda, Cayman Islands, French Antilles, Jamaica, Leeward Islands, Netherlands Antilles, Puerto Rico, Trinidad and Tobago, Turks and Caicos Islands, US Virgin Islands and Windward Islands.

10 Including Angola, Central African Republic, Chad, Congo, Malawi, Zaire and Zambia.

11 Including Belize, Costa Rica, Cuba, Dominican Republic, El Salvador, Guatemala, Haiti, Honduras, Mexico, Nicaragua and Panama.

12 Including Burundi, Djibouti, Ethiopia, Kenya, Rwanda, Somali Republic, Sudan, Tanzania and Uganda.

13 Including Bandar Seri Begawan, Burma, China, Hongkong, Indonesia, Kampuchea , Korea, Laos, Malaysia, Nepal, Philippines, Singapore, Taiwan, Thailand and Vietnam.

14 Including Afghanistan, Bangladesh, India, Pakistan and Sri Lanka.

15 Including Iran, Iraq, Kuwait, Persian Gulf States, Republic of North Yemen, Republic of South Yemen, Saudi Arabia and United Arab Emirates.

16 Including Botswana, Lesotho, Mozambique, Namibia, South African Republic, Swaziland and Zimbabwe.

17 Including Argentina, Bolivia, Brazil, Chile, Colombia, Ecuador, Guyana, Paraguay, Peru, Uruguay and Venezuela.

18 Including Benin, Cameroon, Equatorial Guinea, Gabon, Gambia, Ghana, Guinea, Guinea Bissau, Ivory Coast, Liberia, Mali, Mauritania, Niger, Nigeria, Senegal, Sierra Leone, Togo, Upper Volta and Western Sahara.

19 Atlantic Ocean Islands, Indian Ocean Islands and Pacific Ocean Islands and Madeira.

Sources: Department of Transport;
Civil Aviation Authority

14 Retailing

14.1 Index numbers of retail sales[1,2]

Sales: weekly average 1985=100, seasonally adjusted

	Volume							Value						
			Mixed retail busi-nesses	Non-food retailers						Mixed retail busi-nesses	Non-food retailers			
	All retail-ers	Food retail-ers		Total	Clothing and footwear	Household goods	Other non-food	All retail-ers	Food retail-ers		Total	Clothing and footwear	Household goods	Other non-food
Sales in 1985 (£m)	87 920	32 986	15 865	39 069	8 677	14 717	15 675	87 920	32 986	15 865	39 069	8 677	14 717	15 675
	FAAM	FAAN	FAAO	FSAL	FAAP	FAAQ	FAAR	FAAL	FSAA	FSAB	FSAK	FSAC	FSAD	FSAE
1987	110.7	106.7	109.6	114.6	115	122	107	117.4	113.5	116.0	121.3	121	126	117
1988	117.7	111.5	114.4	124.3	120	136	115	128.8	122.8	124.8	135.4	130	143	131
1989	119.9	115.0	113.3	126.6	119	138	120	137.4	133.8	129.6	143.5	135	150	142
1990	120.4	117.4	111.8	126.4	119	137	121	146.4	147.1	134.5	150.6	141	154	153
1991	119.5	119.1	109.7	123.7	117	136	116	153.5	157.6	138.0	156.3	142	162	159
1991 Q3	119.7	120.0	109.1	123.6	117	136	116	155.0	160.0	138.2	157.6	142	163	161
Q4	119.6	119.3	109.7	123.9	117	137	116	156.2	159.9	140.8	159.4	145	165	163
1992 Q1	120.0†	120.2	108.1	123.6	114	139	115	157.5	163.4	138.2	160.2	138	168	165
Q2	120.2	121.1	109.1	..	116	137	115	159.0	..	..	..	..	..	..
1991 Oct	119.2	119.6	110.7	122.3	115	134	115	155.1	159.6	141.3	157.1	142	161	162
Nov	120.4	119.6	113.2	124.0	119	135	116	157.1	160.4	144.8	159.3	146	163	163
Dec*	119.3	118.8	106.2	125.2	116	140	116	156.3	159.7	137.1	161.2	145	168	163
1992 Jan	119.7	121.5	107.4	123.2	115	136	116	156.9	164.5	136.7	158.8	139	163	166
Feb	120.1	120.0	110.6	124.1	115	140	115	158.1	162.9	141.4	160.8	139	169	165
Mar	118.9	119.4	106.6	123.4	112	141	113	157.4	163.0	136.9	160.9	137	171	165
Apr[3]	119.9	121.0	110.0	123.0	115	138	113	158.3	163.8	140.9	160.7	141	167	166
May	120.4	121.3	108.5	124.3	119	136	116	158.6	164.9	139.1	161.1	143	165	168
Jun	120.2	121.0†	108.9	124.2	115	137	117	159.0	164.0	140.0	162.0	140	166	168

1 Great Britain only. The motor trades are excluded. Information for periods earlier than those shown is available from CSO Newport (tel. 0633 812987).
2 A new statutory panel of contributors has been used to calculate the April 1992 retail sales index. Further details of the changes are available from CSO Newport (0633 812987).
3 Provisional.

Source: Central Statistical Office

14.2 Index numbers of retail sales: retail stocks[1,2]

Sales: weekly average 1985=100, not seasonally adjusted value series

	Food retailers								Clothing and footwear retailers			
	All retailers	Total value of sales	Grocers	Dairymen	Butchers	Fishmongers	Green-grocers, fruiterers	Bread and flour confec-tioners	Total value of sales	Men's and boys' wear retailers	Women's wear and general clothing retailers, leather and travel	Footwear
Sales in 1985 (£m)	87 920	32 986	25 895	1 843	2 749	210	1 285	1 004	8 677	1 267	5 323	2 087
	FHBJ	FSAF	FSAM	FSAN	FSAO	FSAP	FSAQ	FSAR	FSAG	FSAS	FSBK	FSAT
1987	117	114	115	116	98	114	107	117	121	130	122	113
1988	129	123	126	132	97	112	107	118	130	153	130	114
1989	137	134	139	140	101	118	114	123	135	156	137	118
1990	146	147	155	145	100	125	118	131	141	157	144	124
1991	154	158	168	147	98	123	118	134	142	148	147	126
1991 Q2	148	158	168	152	95	127	128	134	134	134	137	128
Q3	150	158	168	151	93	126	117	137	141	146	143	132
Q4	178	167	179	154	107	124	113	136	178	186	190	142
1992 Q1	146	158	169	131	94	112	119	134	113	117	117	100
1991 Aug	148	157	168	146	92	127	118	138	140	146	142	134
Sep*	149	156	166	153	94	123	104	137	136	135	141	127
Oct	154	157	168	147	98	119	106	140	141	136	146	130
Nov	169	163	175	148	98	120	106	136	162	153	178	125
Dec*	204	179	191	163	120	132	125	133	221	253	235	165
1992 Jan	145	154	165	127	96	114	113	129	118	137	118	105
Feb	145	158	169	134	94	113	119	135	107	110	112	96
Mar	148†	161	173	132	92	109	123	137	114	107	120	100
Apr	155	166	180	124	94	110	127	138	130	125	133	126
May	153	164	178	121	89	107	138	132	143	126	146	144

1 Index numbers of sales in Great Britain; value of stocks in the United Kingdom. Excludes the motor trades.
2 A new statutory panel of contributors has been used to calculate the April 1992 retail sales index. The not seasonally adjusted figures for January, February and March have been recalculated. Further details of the changes are available from CSO Newport (0633 812987).

Source: Central Statistical Office

14.2 Index numbers of retail sales: retail stocks[1,2]
continued

Sales: weekly average 1985=100, not seasonally adjusted value series

Household goods retailers

	Total value of sales	Furniture, carpet, and household textiles retailers	Electrical and music goods retailers, gas and electricity showrooms	Hardware, china and fancy goods	DIY retailers	TV and other hire and repair businesses
Sales in 1985 (£m)	14 717	4 902	5 011	1 194	2 357	1 253
	FSAH	FSAU	FSAV	FSAW	FSAX	FSAZ
1987	126	124	125	130	137	112
1988	143	144	143	150	161	107
1989	150	147	144	162	182	108
1990	154	146	146	176	198	113
1991	162	151	151	184	220	121
1991 Q2	152	142	127	181	230	113
Q3	156	144	139	181	228	114
Q4	184	160	195	210	225	132
1992 Q1	163	164	144	176	216	127
1991 Aug*	151	140	132	175	225	113
Sep*	159	146	144	178	227	119
Oct	165	150	153	179	234	129
Nov	178	161	174	199	240	125
Dec*	204	166	246	243	206	139
1992 Jan	171	175	155	172	211	139
Feb	162	163	141	170	216	129
Mar	159	157	136	183	221	117
Apr	165	155	132	183	264	130
May	156	138	121	188	269	125

	All other non-food retailers								Mixed retail businesses				Stocks at end of period £m
	Total value of sales	Confectioners, tobacconists and newsagents	Off-licences	Chemists[3]	Booksellers, stationers and newsagents	Jewellers	Toys, hobby and sports goods and cycle retailers	All other non-food	Total value of sales	Large mixed businesses	Other mixed businesses	General mail order	All kinds of businesses
Sales in 1985 (£m)	15 675	7 161	2 287	1 445	1 208	1 246	1 054	1 274	15 865	11 965	928	2 972	9 959
	FSAI	FSBA	FSBB	FSBC	FSBG	FSBD	FSBE	FSBF	FSAJ	FSBH	FSBI	FSBJ	FSBL
1987	117	113	115	123	119	120	126	123	116	118	100	114	12 006
1988	131	124	122	143	137	138	144	149	125	129	97	116	13 228
1989	142	131	128	159	153	162	157	164	130	135	106	116	14 180
1990	153	143	136	168	166	171	172	173	135	141	116	117	15 131
1991	159	153	143	178	170	162	170	175	138	144	122	120	15 030
1991 Q3	157	155	145	183	162	139	172	162	126	130	121	109	14 799
Q4	186	168	167	201	219	259	233	167	184	200	147	134	15 030
1992 Q1	149	154	131	166	164	122	128	170	121	121	113	121	15 053†
Q2	..	..	..	..	..	..	..	..	..	..	..	..	14 870
1991 Aug	156	153	153	184	149	136	180	158	121	126	122	104	..
Sep*	156	155	135	174	183	144	157	159	126	129	113	117	..
Oct	156	153	141	169	181	136	166	164	140	142	119	141	..
Nov	169	163	143	174	214	195	207	142	178	186	137	156	..
Dec*	225	183	207	247	254	408	308	190	225	257	177	112	..
1992 Jan	143	148	124	167	161	117	130	135	120	120	116	120	..
Feb	151	155	133	166	168	122	127	170	119	118	109	127	..
Mar	154	158	134	165	162	125	127	198	122	124	114	118	..
Apr	160	165	141	169	144	116	159	215	132†	135	117	121	..
May	163	161	145	175	135	121	166	252	124	128	119	110	..

1 Index numbers of sales in Great Britain; value of stocks in the United Kingdom. Excludes the motor trades.
2 A new statutory panel of contributors has been used to calculate the April 1992 retail sales index. The not seasonally adjusted figures for January, February and March have been recalculated. Further details of the changes are available from CSO Newport (0633 812987).
3 Excluding receipts under the National Health Service.

Source: Central Statistical Office

15 External trade

15.1 Value of exports (f.o.b.) and imports (c.i.f.): analysis by commodity classes

£ million, seasonally adjusted

		Food, beverages and tobacco	Basic materials	Fuels	Total manufactures	Manufactures excluding erratics[1]								Total
						Semi-manufactures[2]		Finished manufactures[3]					
	Total					Chemicals	Total	Total	Passenger motor cars[4]	Other consumer[4]	Intermediate[4]	Capital[4]	Total	
SITC (Rev. 3) Section, Division or Group		0 and 1	2 and 4	3	5 to 8	5	6 less PS	5 and 6 less PS	781			7 and 8	5 to 8 less SNA	less SNAPS
Exports	CGKI	BOCB	BOCC	BOCD	BOCE	BOCH	BOCI	BOCG	BOCK	BOCL	BOCM	BOCN	BOCJ	BOCF
1986	72 782	5 487	2 100	8 654	54 546	9 697	8 938	18 632	1 362	5 529	14 321	9 803	31 016	49 647
1987	79 760	5 598	2 243	8 746	61 005	10 541	9 817	20 359	1 981	6 788	15 250	11 036	35 053	55 409
1988	82 072	5 534	2 120	6 258	66 195	11 331	10 578	21 910	2 033	6 644	16 012	13 367	38 056	59 967
1989	93 798	6 555	2 349	6 175	76 407	12 351	12 211	24 561	2 639	8 029	18 237	15 651	44 555	69 117
1990	103 691	7 112	2 249	7 869	84 165	13 182	13 553	26 734	3 320	9 563	20 620	16 809	50 313	77 048
1991	104 816	7 749	2 013	7 144	86 058	13 784	13 519	27 300	4 090	9 425	21 272	16 547	51 334	78 633
1990 Nov	8 816	599	187	746	7 100	1 104	1 134	2 238	356	764	1 759	1 364	4 244	6 482
Dec	8 521	605	170	696	6 877	1 058	1 089	2 147	351	731	1 729	1 325	4 136	6 283
1991 Jan	8 360	637	167	501	6 880	1 087	1 090	2 177	341	762	1 679	1 305	4 087	6 264
Feb	8 377	622	170	580	6 847	1 073	1 089	2 161	334	751	1 706	1 293	4 084	6 245
Mar	8 530	605	162	624	6 978	1 100	1 114	2 213	314	793	1 768	1 365	4 240	6 453
Apr	8 555	597	171	505	7 139	1 161	1 147	2 309	333	787	1 855	1 359	4 333	6 642
May	8 624	625	171	556	7 132	1 109	1 120	2 229	344	775	1 806	1 392	4 317	6 546
Jun	9 045	629	175	607	7 449	1 197	1 147	2 344	430	793	1 805	1 421	4 449	6 793
Jul	8 927	616	175	550	7 439	1 158	1 144	2 302	413	772	1 776	1 390	4 351	6 653
Aug	9 149	653	172	671	7 509	1 190	1 194	2 384	305	770	1 853	1 441	4 369	6 753
Sep	8 635	663	163	650	7 011	1 126	1 081	2 207	355	812	1 682	1 394	4 243	6 449
Oct	8 749	664	158	575	7 199	1 199	1 139	2 337	340	800	1 704	1 367	4 211	6 548
Nov	8 803	687	166	657	7 135	1 206	1 121	2 327	299	795	1 827	1 415	4 336	6 663
Dec	9 062	751	163	668	7 340	1 178	1 133	2 310	282	815	1 811	1 405	4 314	6 624
1992 Jan	8 388	641	155	505	6 945	1 189	1 047	2 236	334	785	1 763	1 328	4 210	6 446
Feb	9 075	677	165	523	7 566	1 246	1 191	2 436	337	868	1 907	1 410	4 522	6 958
Mar	8 976	697	175	561	7 369	1 255	1 129	2 385	338	851	1 828	1 389	4 406	6 790
Apr	8 905	676†	165†	595	7 289†	1 224	1 105†	2 328†	329†	818†	1 902†	1 328	4 377†	6 705†
May	9 280†	737†	166†	615	7 581†	1 224†	1 157†	2 381†	322†	807†	1 975†	1 527†	4 631†	7 012†
Jun	8 959	784	168	553	7 281	1 206	1 129	2 335	343	799	1 862	1 352	4 355	6 690
Imports	CGHM	BODB	BODC	BODD	BODE	BODH	BODI	BODG	BODK	BODL	BODM	BODN	BODJ	BODF
1986	85 658	10 032	5 067	6 385	62 800	7 361	13 234	20 593	4 809	10 145	13 249	10 640	38 844	59 438
1987	94 043	10 130	5 688	6 099	70 966	8 347	14 970	23 316	5 024	11 488	15 365	12 181	44 060	67 374
1988	106 556	10 616	5 983	5 038	83 483	9 314	17 423	26 737	6 750	12 603	17 915	14 616	51 885	78 623
1989	122 000	11 429	6 491	6 429	95 975	10 439	19 530	29 969	7 619	14 827	21 199	16 818	60 462	90 429
1990	126 086	12 316	6 098	7 863	98 067	10 834	19 709	30 545	7 398	15 808	22 258	15 886	61 353	91 899
1991	118 867	12 326	5 065	7 582	92 103	10 973	18 439	29 414	5 509	14 917	21 739	15 058	57 224	86 637
1990 Nov	10 135	987	441	780	7 787	919	1 621	2 540	530	1 263	1 794	1 211	4 798	7 339
Dec	9 796	939	423	754	7 534	930	1 514	2 445	513	1 244	1 767	1 171	4 695	7 140
1991 Jan	9 992	974	407	761	7 710	933	1 578	2 511	485	1 243	1 740	1 163	4 631	7 142
Feb	9 466	985	414	573	7 348	897	1 530	2 428	489	1 174	1 774	1 155	4 592	7 020
Mar	9 729	1 019	412	581	7 597	875	1 555	2 431	458	1 250	1 810	1 205	4 722	7 153
Apr	9 733	1 014	408	605	7 541	824	1 527	2 351	467	1 265	1 776	1 209	4 717	7 068
May	9 884	1 011	425	621	7 675	883	1 523	2 406	471	1 275	1 842	1 255	4 843	7 249
Jun	9 862	1 047	423	627	7 645	893	1 513	2 407	495	1 194	1 829	1 264	4 782	7 189
Jul	9 862	1 058	450	664	7 557	905	1 547	2 451	502	1 263	1 778	1 273	4 816	7 268
Aug	10 294	1 017	447	753	7 894	977	1 552	2 529	414	1 261	1 881	1 310	4 867	7 395
Sep	9 860	1 009	417	576	7 711	935	1 508	2 443	441	1 275	1 773	1 271	4 760	7 203
Oct	9 960	1 010	421	612	7 756	931	1 537	2 468	447	1 235	1 786	1 289	4 757	7 225
Nov	10 112	1 074	416	625	7 823	1 015	1 514	2 529	416	1 261	1 877	1 380	4 935	7 463
Dec	10 113	1 108	425	584	7 846	905	1 555	2 460	424	1 221	1 873	1 284	4 802	7 262
1992 Jan	9 835	1 067	419	492	7 697	826	1 480	2 306	552	1 236	1 822	1 326	4 936	7 242
Feb	10 424	1 083	431	543	8 232	917	1 575	2 492	507	1 296	1 899	1 401	5 103	7 595
Mar	10 224	1 047	438	529	8 079	924	1 576	2 501	539	1 281	1 879	1 297	4 996	7 496
Apr	10 616	1 088	445	608	8 330	922	1 565	2 487	557	1 323	1 986	1 353	5 218	7 705
May	10 450†	1 112†	427†	588†	8 175†	947†	1 585†	2 533†	587†	1 334†	1 951†	1 357†	5 229†	7 762†
Jun	10 140	1 126	436	610	7 845	926	1 561	2 487	569	1 278	1 833	1 304	4 984	7 471

The statistics are on an overseas trade basis (see footnote 1 to Table 15.7)
1 These are defined as ships, North Sea installations (together comprising SITC(Rev 3)(793), aircraft (792), precious stones (667) and silver (681.1).
2 Excluding precious stones and silver (PS).
3 Excluding ships, North Sea installations and aircraft (SNA).
4 Based on the *Classification by Broad Economic categories* (BEC) published by the United Nations.

Source: Central Statistical Office

15.2 Value of United Kingdom exports (f.o.b.)[1,2]

£ million

		1990	1991	1992 Q1	1992 Q2	1992 Apr	1992 May	1992 Jun
0. Food and live animals chiefly for food	BQRA	4 341.9	4 716.6	1 280.3	1 205.1	407.2	393.6	404.4
00. Live animals other than animals of Division 03	BQRB	258.0	288.4	75.6	51.5	13.8	15.8	21.9
01. Meat and meat preparations	BQRC	610.3	672.6	187.5	177.9	60.4	58.1	59.3
02. Dairy products and birds' eggs	BQRD	458.2	451.9	120.1	142.9	47.3	37.8	57.8
03. Fish (not marine mammals), crustaceans, molluscs and aquatic invertebrates and preparations thereof	BQRE	505.3	574.4	121.7	129.9	43.1	42.8	43.9
04. Cereals and cereal preparations	BQRF	1 061.6	1 102.8	345.5	287.3	102.4	105.0	79.6
05. Vegetables and fruit	BQRG	263.7	299.1	76.7	75.6	28.2	25.1	22.2
06. Sugar, sugar preparations and honey	BQRH	240.4	247.5	63.6	73.1	22.5	23.4	27.2
07. Coffee, tea, cocoa, spices and manufactures thereof	BQRI	438.7	465.2	130.4	105.8	37.3	32.2	36.3
08. Feeding stuff for animals (not including unmilled cereals)	BQRJ	238.9	302.9	80.5	76.9	23.9	26.2	26.8
09. Miscellaneous edible products and preparations	BQRK	266.8	311.7	78.6	84.4	28.4	27.2	29.9
1. Beverages and tobacco	BQRL	2 770.2	3 032.3	708.3	814.7	248.8	259.2	306.7
11. Beverages	BQRM	2 112.8	2 251.6	488.7	604.5	188.1	190.7	225.8
12. Tobacco and tobacco manufactures	BQRN	657.5	780.7	219.7	210.0	60.7	68.5	80.9
2. Crude materials, inedible, except fuels	BQRO	2 162.5	1 919.8	473.7	474.4	156.7	155.1	162.6
21. Hides, skins and fur skins, raw	BQRP	188.8	135.1	33.7	32.9	10.9	10.8	11.2
22. Oil seeds and oleaginous fruit	BQRQ	67.3	52.6	10.5	3.6	2.2	1.1	0.3
23. Crude rubber (including synthetic and reclaimed)	BQRR	221.9	198.1	48.8	55.8	18.2	18.2	19.4
24. Cork and wood	BQRS	27.7	27.9	7.0	7.9	2.2	2.9	2.8
25. Pulp and waste paper	BQRT	53.1	38.8	13.6	8.8	3.5	2.6	2.8
26. Textile fibres (other than wool tops and other combed wool) and their wastes (not manufactured into yarn fabric)	BQRU	494.5	466.4	127.5	123.3	42.5	40.9	40.0
27. Crude fertilisers other than those of division 56, and crude minerals (excluding coal, petroleum and precious stones)	BQRV	369.9	365.5	90.3	94.2	27.4	31.0	35.8
28. Metalliferous ores and metal scrap	BQRW	633.5	526.8	109.1	119.0	39.0	38.6	41.4
29. Crude animal and vegetable materials	BQRX	105.9	108.6	33.2	28.7	10.8	9.1	8.9
3. Mineral fuels, lubricants and related materials	BQRY	7 868.7	7 145.3	1 587.8	1 601.4	561.0	529.6	510.8
33. Petroleum, petroleum products and related materials	BQRZ	7 544.6	6 792.6	1 482.2	1 545.3	542.0	510.4	492.8
32, 34 and 35. Coal, coke, gas and electric current	BQSA	324.1	352.8	105.6	56.2	19.0	19.1	18.0
4. Animal and vegetable oils, fats and waxes	BQSB	87.7	95.9	23.9	23.7	10.2	6.9	6.6
5. Chemicals and related products	BQSC	13 181.6	13 782.0	3 720.6	3 746.3	1 281.7	1 218.1	1 246.5
51. Organic chemicals	BQSD	3 351.6	3 469.1	936.9	950.9	354.4	287.8	308.5
52. Inorganic chemicals	BQSE	951.6	997.1	316.5	279.0	86.1	94.3	98.6
53. Dyeing, tanning and colouring materials	BQSF	1 193.5	1 216.5	312.9	341.2	112.2	114.2	114.7
54. Medicinal and pharmaceutical products	BQSG	2 257.5	2 555.6	698.3	718.3	251.2	214.8	252.3
55. Essential oils and perfume materials; toilet, polishing and cleansing materials	BQSH	1 161.9	1 298.2	345.2	358.3	114.4	123.9	120.0
56. Fertilisers (other than those of group 272)	BQSI	110.3	103.2	32.6	30.5	13.8	8.8	7.9
57. Plastic in primary forms	BQSJ	1 342.4	1 333.0	329.6	344.7	111.0	118.5	115.2
58. Plastics in non-primary forms esters and ethers	BQSK	781.7	786.6	194.8	206.0	64.9	71.6	69.5
59. Chemical materials and products, not elsewhere specified[2]	BQSL	2 031.1	2 022.7	553.7	517.6	173.7	184.3	159.7
6. Manufactured goods classified chiefly by material	BQSM	15 821.6	15 575.3	3 560.5	4 153.0	1 354.7	1 412.7	1 385.7
61. Leather, leather manufactures n.e.s., and dressed fur skins	BQSN	311.8	258.0	63.1	68.5	23.5	21.4	23.6
62. Rubber manufactures n.e.s.	BQSO	872.8	887.9	234.3	247.9	81.7	83.5	82.7
63. Cork and wood manufactures (excluding furniture)	BQSP	114.2	116.4	30.0	35.0	10.4	11.2	13.4
64. Paper, paperboard and articles of paper pulp, of paper or of paperboard	BQSQ	1 539.4	1 623.8	411.6	435.9	139.0	151.7	145.2
65. Textile yarn, fabrics, made-up articles n.e.s., and related products	BQSR	2 447.0	2 349.2	609.6	634.7	214.0	206.5	214.1
66. Non-metallic mineral manufactures n.e.s.	BQSS	3 191.3	3 172.1	557.0	927.0	311.8	311.0	304.1
67. Iron and steel	BQST	3 036.0	3 011.6	723.9	790.4	242.3	288.4	259.5
68. Non-ferrous metals	BQSU	2 193.6	1 974.2	404.6	450.2	144.7	157.1	148.4
69. Manufactures of metal n.e.s.	BQSV	2 115.6	2 182.2	526.3	563.5	187.2	181.8	194.5

1 The numbers on the left hand side of the table refer to the Section and Division code numbers of the *Standard International Trade Classification*, Revision 3, which was introduced in January 1988.

2 The broad structure of SITC(R3) follows that of SITC(R2) but two major changes should be noted:
1) Explosives and Pyrotechnic products, Division 57 in SITC(R2), forms part of Division 59 in SITC(R3) and

2) Military equipment, part of Section 9 in SITC(R2) forms part of Division 89 in SITC(R3). However, from June 1988, military equipment has been transferred back to Section 9 to remove the problem of discontinuity in trends for Trade in manufactures (Sections 5-8) over time.

Source: Department of Trade and Industry

15.2
continued

Value of United Kingdom exports (f.o.b.)[1,2]

£ million

		1990	1991	1992 Q1	1992 Q2	1992 Apr	1992 May	1992 Jun
7. Machinery and transport equipment	BQSW	41 850.6	43 600.0	10 588.9	11 144.7	3 737.2	3 766.5	3 641.1
71. Power generating machinery and equipment	BQSX	5 250.7	5 073.1	1 317.3	1 408.1	460.5	497.7	449.9
72. Machinery specialised for particular industries	BQSY	4 234.1	3 921.7	960.1	1 054.0	339.7	359.9	354.4
73. Metalworking machinery	BQSZ	912.5	812.7	178.3	181.1	60.5	62.4	58.2
74. General industrial machinery and equipment n.e.s., and machine parts n.e.s.	BQTA	4 545.7	4 520.2	1 077.6	1 186.5	394.8	393.6	398.1
75. Office machines and automatic data processing equipment	BQTB	6 341.7	6 581.2	1 537.1	1 641.5	540.0	557.2	544.3
76. Telecommunications and sound recording and reproducing apparatus and equipment	BQTC	2 685.5	2 943.3	668.1	660.9	224.1	240.9	195.9
77. Electrical machinery, apparatus and appliances n.e.s., and electrical parts thereof (including non-electrical counterpart n.e.s., of electrical household type equipment)	BQTD	5 648.2	5 723.6	1 448.8	1 550.2	517.4	540.1	492.8
78. Road vehicles (including air cushion vehicles)	BQTE	7 296.5	8 554.0	2 241.7	2 270.4	770.7	736.2	763.5
79. Other transport equipment	BQTF	4 935.7	5 470.3	1 159.8	1 192.3	429.7	378.6	384.0
8. Miscellaneous manufactured articles	BQTG	13 349.0	13 143.0	3 279.2	3 423.9	1 154.0	1 083.7	1 186.2
81. Prefabricated buildings, sanitary plumbing, heating and lighting fixtures and fittings n.e.s.	BQTH	260.3	267.3	61.5	68.0	24.3	20.2	23.5
82. Furniture and parts thereof, bedding, mattresses, mattress supports, cushions and similar stuffed furnishings	BQTI	533.2	564.2	145.6	163.3	55.7	56.0	51.6
83. Travel goods, handbags and similar containers	BQTJ	69.9	72.4	18.1	17.2	5.8	5.4	6.1
84. Articles of apparel and clothing accessories	BQTK	1 699.4	1 920.1	445.3	430.5	150.5	134.2	145.8
85. Footwear	BQTL	274.4	314.8	80.6	71.3	25.6	23.7	21.9
87. Professional, scientific and controlling instruments and apparatus n.e.s.	BQTM	2 945.2	2 995.5	722.7	846.0	258.9	245.4	341.7
88. Photographic apparatus, equipment and supplies and optical goods n.e.s., watches and clocks	BQTN	1 167.0	1 266.0	291.7	357.8	120.1	115.4	122.2
89. Miscellaneous manufactured articles n.e.s.[2]	BQTO	6 399.5	5 742.7	1 513.6	1 469.9	513.1	483.5	473.3
5-8. Manufactured goods	BQTP	84 202.8	86 100.3	21 149.1	22 468.1	7 527.6	7 481.0	7 459.5
9. Commodities and transactions not classified elsewhere	BQTQ	2 258.5	1 808.2	433.7	501.3	176.7	174.1	150.4
Total United Kingdom exports	BQTR	103 692.4	104 818.4	25 656.8	27 088.6	9 088.2	8 999.5	9 000.9

1 The numbers on the left hand side of the table refer to the Section and Division code numbers of the *Standard International Trade Classification*, Revision 3, which was introduced in January 1988.

2 The broad structure of SITC(R3) follows that of SITC(R2) but two major changes should be noted:
1) Explosives and Pyrotechnic products, Division 57 in SITC(R2), forms part of Division 59 in SITC(R3) and

2) Military equipment, part of Section 9 in SITC(R2) forms part of Division 89 in SITC(R3). However, from June 1988, military equipment has been transferred back to Section 9 to remove the problem of discontinuity in trends for Trade in manufactures (Sections 5-8) over time.

Source: Department of Trade and Industry

15.3 Value of United Kingdom imports (c.i.f)[1]

£ million

		1990	1991	1992 Q1	1992 Q2	1992 Apr	1992 May	1992 Jun
0. Food and live animals chiefly for food	BQUA	10 408.7	10 390.1	2 635.6	2 912.9	941.8	971.1	1 000.0
00. Live animals other than animals of Division 03	BQUB	290.7	203.2	45.2	35.7	11.6	9.6	14.5
01. Meat and meat preparations	BQUC	1 887.8	1 845.1	461.8	534.6	173.0	185.6	176.0
02. Dairy products and birds' eggs	BQUD	913.7	871.0	205.9	274.3	88.7	91.8	93.8
03. Fish (not marine animals), crustaceans, and aquatic invertebrates and preparations thereof	BQUE	968.9	979.0	230.0	254.5	79.1	84.8	90.6
04. Cereals and cereal preparations	BQUF	785.1	818.5	204.2	224.9	76.8	69.6	78.5
05. Vegetables and fruit	BQUG	2 964.5	3 003.2	788.3	875.7	284.3	295.4	295.9
06. Sugar, sugar preparations and honey	BQUH	639.2	681.2	169.2	188.3	48.0	71.3	69.0
07. Coffee, tea, cocoa, spices and manufactures thereof	BQUI	904.4	869.7	224.2	205.1	73.0	64.6	67.4
08. Feeding stuff for animals (not including unmilled cereals)	BQUJ	624.6	618.8	184.5	160.0	58.9	47.1	53.9
09. Miscellaneous edible products and preparations	BQUK	429.9	500.4	122.2	160.0	48.5	51.2	60.3
1. Beverages and tobacco	BQUL	1 907.1	1 936.1	339.9	498.5	145.2	155.9	197.5
11. Beverages	BQUM	1 529.7	1 464.9	243.7	394.3	114.3	123.0	157.0
12. Tobacco and tobacco manufactures	BQUN	377.4	471.2	96.2	104.2	30.8	32.8	40.5
2. Crude materials, inedible, except fuels	BQUO	5 721.1	4 679.3	1 177.0	1 230.1	412.8	394.3	422.9
21. Hides, skins and fur skins, raw	BQUP	100.5	68.8	23.8	19.5	7.8	6.6	5.1
22. Oil seeds and oleaginous fruit	BQUQ	273.0	224.0	54.2	66.7	23.4	21.5	21.9
23. Crude rubber (including synthetic and reclaimed)	BQUR	244.9	223.6	59.7	56.7	19.3	19.0	18.4
24. Cork and wood	BQUS	1 409.9	1 043.7	236.3	274.2	86.7	87.9	99.6
25. Pulp and waste paper	BQUT	777.2	608.0	150.9	160.5	58.9	51.6	50.0
26. Textile fibres (other than wool tops and other combed wool) and their wastes (not manufactured into yarn or fabric)	BQUU	548.9	452.6	128.5	129.0	44.5	39.4	45.0
27. Crude fertilisers other than those of Division 56, and crude minerals (excluding coal, petroleum and precious stones)	BQUV	344.7	285.8	67.8	68.1	23.0	21.7	23.3
28. Metalliferous ores and metal scrap	BQUW	1 479.2	1 232.7	291.0	330.3	102.5	105.5	122.4
29. Crude animal and vegetable materials	BQUX	542.7	540.1	164.8	125.0	46.7	41.2	37.1
3. Mineral fuels, lubricants and related materials	BQUY	7 864.5	7 581.0	1 648.0	1 701.5	571.9	578.8	550.7
33. Petroleum, petroleum products and related materials	BQUZ	6 285.1	5 843.8	1 167.2	1 288.3	440.3	430.3	417.8
32, 34 and 35. Coal, coke, gas and electric current	BQVA	1 579.4	1 737.1	480.8	413.1	131.6	148.6	132.9
4. Animal and vegetable oils, fats and waxes	BQVB	377.3	387.5	99.4	103.4	37.6	30.2	35.6
5. Chemicals and related products	BQVC	10 834.0	10 978.1	2 789.2	2 833.8	955.5	917.5	960.8
51. Organic chemicals	BQVD	2 593.4	2 618.9	672.3	671.6	223.6	222.0	225.9
52. Inorganic chemicals	BQVE	1 000.1	1 033.6	181.1	207.8	67.9	66.6	73.4
53. Dyeing, tanning and colouring materials	BQVF	651.3	620.9	164.6	175.4	60.1	55.7	59.6
54. Medicinal and pharmaceutical products	BQVG	1 157.8	1 371.1	389.3	400.1	134.9	134.0	131.3
55. Essential oils and perfume materials; toilet, polishing and cleansing materials	BQVH	756.1	798.1	205.9	227.3	72.3	72.5	82.6
56. Fertilisers (other than those of group 272)	BQVI	285.6	282.9	98.9	55.3	28.9	14.2	12.2
57. Plastic in primary forms	BQVJ	2 212.6	2 053.2	510.0	505.5	166.7	167.8	171.0
58. Plastics in non-primary forms	BQVK	1 015.0	975.8	249.2	258.8	84.9	84.9	89.0
59. Chemical materials and products, not elsewhere specified[2]	BQVL	1 162.1	1 223.5	317.9	331.9	116.2	99.8	116.0
6. Manufactured goods classified chiefly by material	BQVM	21 902.4	20 520.6	5 203.4	5 335.6	1 817.6	1 741.8	1 776.1
61. Leather, leather manufactures n.e.s., and dressed fur skins	BQVN	240.8	185.9	45.1	46.3	16.0	14.0	16.3
62. Rubber manufactures n.e.s.	BQVO	880.4	872.2	252.7	247.8	85.0	79.2	83.6
63. Cork and wood manufactures (excluding furniture)	BQVP	949.3	821.6	215.8	220.7	72.0	69.9	78.9
64. Paper, paperboard and articles of paper pulp, of paper or of paperboard	BQVQ	4 014.3	3 869.0	960.6	1 931.2	322.3	314.3	334.0
65. Textile yarn, fabrics, made-up articles n.e.s., and related products	BQVR	3 936.1	3 738.5	988.6	980.0	321.3	326.0	332.6
66. Non-metallic mineral manufactures n.e.s.	BQVS	3 601.9	3 332.9	753.3	897.8	342.3	299.8	255.7
67. Iron and steel	BQVT	2 683.4	2 620.3	678.2	660.6	227.0	208.3	225.4
68. Non-ferrous metals	BQVU	3 003.3	2 556.3	682.3	649.9	208.6	210.5	230.9
69. Manufactures of metal n.e.s.	BQVV	2 592.9	2 524.0	626.9	661.8	223.3	219.9	218.7

The statistics are on an overseas trade statistics basis (see footnote 1 to Table 15.7) to which a number of changes have been made to the coverage, with effect from 1 January 1981. The changes, which are described below, were previously taken into account by means of balance of payments adjustments.

a) Trade in precious stones now excludes consignments which cross national boundaries on a temporary basis only, ie for valuation or for exhibition, previously these were included in the *Overseas Trade Statistics* figures each time they arrived in or left the United Kingdom.

b) Trade in secondhand aircraft is excluded where the aircraft are being imported or exported solely for the purpose of repair or modification, but the value of the work done in undertaking the repair or modification is included.

c) Certain atomic energy materials previously excluded are now included.

1 The numbers on the left hand side of the table refer to the Section and Division code numbers of the *Standard International Trade Classification*, Revision 3, which was introduced in January 1988.

2 The broad structure of SITC(R3) follows that of SITC(R2) but two major changes should be noted:

1) Explosives and Pyrotechnic products, Division 57 in SITC(R2), forms part of Division 59 in SITC(R3) and

2) Military equipment, part of Section 9 in SITC(R2), forms part of Division 89 in SITC(R3). However, from June 1988, Military equipment has been transferred back to Section 9 to remove the problem of discontinuity in trends for Trade in manufactures (Sections 5-8) over time.

Source: Department of Trade and Industry

15.3 Value of United Kingdom imports (c.i.f)[1]

continued

£ million

		1990	1991	1992 Q1	1992 Q2	1992 Apr	1992 May	1992 Jun
7. Machinery and transport equipment	BQVW	47 160.9	43 124.7	11 479.8	12 204.1	4 289.6	3 916.7	4 002.1
71. Power generating machinery and equipment	BQVX	3 518.4	3 345.7	800.5	921.1	324.0	304.6	292.5
72. Machinery specialised for particular industries	BQVY	3 521.9	3 005.4	768.6	848.4	293.7	277.3	277.5
73. Metalworking machinery	BQVZ	993.4	861.3	230.0	228.8	95.3	68.9	64.6
74. General industrial machinery and equipment n.e.s. and machine parts n.e.s.	BQWA	4 359.8	4 202.7	1 117.7	1 128.2	376.9	376.8	374.5
75. Office machines and automatic data processing equipment	BQWB	7 715.0	7 586.3	2 011.4	2 034.6	730.4	641.6	662.6
76. Telecommunications and sound recording and reproducing apparatus and equipment	BQWC	3 486.8	3 351.9	722.2	787.1	258.7	264.9	263.5
77. Electrical machinery, apparatus and appliances n.e.s. and electrical parts thereof (including non-electrical counterpart n.e.s. of electrical household type equipment)	BQWD	6 921.9	7 079.4	1 775.6	1 922.6	643.9	631.1	647.6
78. Road vehicles (including air cushion vehicles)	BQWE	12 594.2	10 217.2	2 868.3	3 271.9	1 034.8	1 058.4	1 183.0
79. Other transport equipment	BQWF	4 049.5	3 474.9	1 185.6	1 061.4	532.0	293.2	236.3
8. Miscellaneous manufactured articles	BQWG	18 252.5	17 560.4	4 480.2	4 479.4	1 483.1	1 465.4	1 530.9
81. Prefabricated buildings, sanitary plumbing, heating and lighting fixtures and fittings n.e.s.	BQWH	394.5	368.3	96.9	92.6	30.9	30.9	30.9
82. Furniture and parts thereof, bedding, mattresses, mattress supports, cushions and similar stuffed furnishings	BQWI	1 112.0	1 005.3	262.4	285.6	95.0	92.9	97.7
83. Travel goods, handbags and similar containers	BQWJ	309.1	285.1	70.5	75.6	25.0	23.5	27.1
84. Articles of apparel and clothing accessories	BQWK	3 904.1	4 129.4	1 105.1	909.6	316.2	284.9	308.5
85. Footwear	BQWL	1 168.9	1 168.5	308.2	258.3	101.2	78.6	78.5
87. Professional, scientific and controlling instruments and apparatus n.e.s.	BQWM	2 482.1	2 525.3	651.3	651.7	217.6	214.0	220.1
88. Photographic apparatus, equipment and supplies and optical goods n.e.s., watches and clocks	BQWN	1 591.5	1 565.2	362.2	413.2	139.0	137.3	137.0
89. Miscellaneous manufactured articles n.e.s.[2]	BQWO	7 290.3	6 513.3	1 623.6	1 792.7	558.3	603.4	631.0
5-8. Manufactured goods	BQWP	98 149.8	92 183.8	23 952.6	24 852.9	8 545.8	8 041.4	8 269.9
9. Commodities and transactions not classified elsewhere	BQWQ	1 657.6	1 713.5	422.2	403.6	141.3	138.1	123.2
Total United Kingdom imports	BQWR	126 086.1	118 871.4	30 274.7	31 702.9	10 797.5	10 309.9	10 599.8

The statistics are on an overseas trade statistics basis (see footnote 1 to Table 15.7) to which a number of changes have been made to the coverage, with effect from 1 January 1981. The changes, which are described below, were previously taken into account by means of balance of payments adjustments.

a) Trade in precious stones now excludes consignments which cross national boundaries on a temporary basis only, ie for valuation or for exhibition, previously these were included in the *Overseas Trade Statistics* figures each time they arrived in or left the United Kingdom.

b) Trade in secondhand aircraft is excluded where the aircraft are being imported or exported solely for the purpose of repair or modification, but the value of the work done in undertaking the repair or modification is included.

c) Certain atomic energy materials previously excluded are now included.

1 The numbers on the left hand side of the table refer to the Section and Division code numbers of the *Standard International Trade Classification*, Revision 3, which was introduced in January 1988.

2 The broad structure of SITC(R3) follows that of SITC(R2) but two major changes should be noted:
1) Explosives and Pyrotechnic products, Division 57 in SITC(R2), forms part of Division 59 in SITC(R3) and
2) Military equipment, part of Section 9 in SITC(R2), forms part of Division 89 in SITC(R3). However, from June 1988, Military equipment has been transferred back to Section 9 to remove the problem of discontinuity in trends for Trade in manufactures (Sections 5-8) over time.

Source: Department of Trade and Industry

15.4 Value of exports (f.o.b.) and imports (c.i.f.): analysis by area

£ million, seasonally adjusted

	European Community	Rest of Western Europe	E Europe & former USSR	North America	Other OECD	Oil exporting countries	Other Countries	Total
Exports								
	BOGB	BOGC	OBWN	BOGD	BOGE	BOGF	OBWE	CGKI
1986	35 025	6 730	1 275	12 063	2 829	5 494	8 923	72 782
1987	39 497	7 415	1 241	12 992	3 195	5 220	9 786	79 760
1988	41 052	7 210	1 285	12 794	3 520	5 019	10 009	82 072
1989	47 540	7 987	1 473	14 437	4 519	5 831	11 084	93 798
1990	55 072	9 039	1 480	14 972	4 828	5 572	12 173	103 691
1991	59 412	8 608	1 253	13 134	3 986	5 717	12 063	104 816
1990 Nov	4 939	775	114	1 298	413	430	983	8 816
Dec	4 730	708	93	1 128	370	305	963	8 521
1991 Jan	4 812	701	88	915	333	468	967	8 360
Feb	4 828	674	103	1 022	304	399	943	8 377
Mar	4 840	680	106	1 039	339	452	948	8 530
Apr	4 879	734	109	1 120	321	472	948	8 555
May	4 908	722	104	1 116	341	472	949	8 624
Jun	5 019	700	115	1 173	351	495	961	9 045
							1 019	
Jul	4 937	706	100	1 166	371	497	1 019	8 927
Aug	5 063	754	112	1 296	334	448	1 030	9 149
Sep	4 777	703	104	1 107	303	506	1 036	8 635
Oct	4 957	774	107	1 044	334	425	1 061	8 749
Nov	5 088	714	106	1 074	324	525	1 035	8 803
Dec	5 304	746	99	1 062	331	558	1 095	9 062
1992 Jan	4 667	670	118	1 025	301	408	1 009	8 388
Feb	5 145	723	114	1 120	339	541	1 012	9 075
Mar	5 062	726	97	1 130	341	474	993	8 976
Apr	4 956	668	115	1 169	336	587	1 004	8 905
May	5 278[†]	723[†]	152[†]	1 208[†]	330[†]	498	1 087[†]	9 280[†]
Jun	4 891	706	159	1 106	330	606	1 032	8 959
Imports								
	BOGJ	BOGK	OBWQ	BOGL	BOGM	BOGN	OBWH	CGHM
1986	44 727	11 718	1 477	9 995	6 100	2 061	8 842	85 658
1987	49 736	12 710	1 696	10 781	6 722	1 699	10 243	94 043
1988	55 958	13 831	1 629	12 903	7 817	2 085	11 663	106 556
1989	63 807	15 155	1 781	15 929	8 514	2 313	11 663	106 556
1990	65 956	15 717	1 798	16 753	8 413	2 974	13 748	122 000
1991	61 308	14 306	1 691	15 740	8 104	2 786	14 165	126 086
								118 867
1990 Nov	5 232	1 294	162	1 295	706	309	1 099	10 135
Dec	5 054	1 223	145	1 358	625	205	1 136	9 796
1991 Jan	5 099	1 393	187	1 286	664	263	1 116	9 992
Feb	5 115	1 056	132	1 241	585	169	1 120	9 466
Mar	5 132	1 152	132	1 204	706	207	1 185	9 729
Apr	4 924	1 224	120	1 298	718	208	1 180	9 733
May	5 067	1 217	124	1 314	657	205	1 212	9 884
Jun	5 013	1 125	130	1 365	665	248	1 166	9 862
Jul	5 029	1 226	135	1 269	662	232	1 253	9 862
Aug	5 248	1 288	136	1 365	665	268	1 155	10 294
Sep	5 110	1 249	150	1 310	606	248	1 161	9 860
Oct	5 107	1 227	125	1 377	643	229	1 191	9 960
Nov	5 240	1 074	148	1 360	727	273	1 216	10 112
Dec	5 224	1 075	172	1 351	806	236	1 210	10 113
1992 Jan	5 084	1 044	109	1 325	712	190	1 216	9 835
Feb	5 445	1 082	119	1 410	822	216	1 279	10 424
Mar	5 324	1 232	100	1 379	763	210	1 174	10 224
Apr	5 484	1 251	135	1 386	852	229	1 304	10 616
May	5 580[†]	1 162[†]	155	1 293[†]	794[†]	213	1 258	10 450[†]
Jun	5 251	1 135	131	1 178	705	321	1 267	10 140

The statistics are on an overseas trade statistics basis (see footnote 1 to Table 15.7).

Source: Central Statistical Office

15.5 United Kingdom exports, by countries (f.o.b)

£ million

		1990	1991	1992 Q1	1992 Q2	1992 Apr	1992 May	1992 Jun
Total trade	BQXA	103 692.4	104 818.4	25 656.8	27 088.6	9 088.2	8 999.5	9 000.9
European Community:								
France	BQXC	10 894.5	11 591.1	2 773.2	2 818.6	981.4	886.8	950.5
Belgium and Luxembourg	BQXD	5 649.4	5 870.9	1 352.9	1 566.7	528.7	538.4	499.7
Netherlands	BQXE	7 561.3	8 258.5	2 157.6	2 052.1	718.1	688.0	646.1
Germany[1]	BRAE	13 141.8	14 654.0	3 646.4	3 666.9	1 194.7	1 269.2	1 202.9
Italy	BQXG	5 553.0	6 145.0	1 603.2	1 643.2	552.2	532.8	558.2
Irish Republic	BQXH	5 313.0	5 295.9	1 223.2	1 431.2	450.2	497.2	483.8
Denmark	BQXI	1 419.3	1 408.5	357.2	385.2	122.4	139.9	123.0
Greece	BQXJ	682.9	667.7	191.9	180.1	62.2	58.6	59.3
Portugal	BQXK	1 031.8	1 085.1	284.3	301.6	96.6	96.0	109.1
Spain	BQXL	3 620.9	4 278.8	1 072.80	1 200.60	398.6	393.1	409.0
Total	BRAF	54 868.0	59 255.6	14 662.7	15 246.2	5 105.1	5 100.0	5 041.6
Other Western Europe:								
Norway	BQXN	1 292.0	1 357.3	307.9	359.3	116.6	129.7	113.1
Sweden	BQXO	2 712.3	2 471.5	594.2	589.4	198.4	187.9	203.2
Finland	BQXP	1 041.7	847.7	262.5	251.2	98.7	88.7	63.8
Switzerland	BQXQ	2 358.9	2 105.7	479.9	463.5	139.1	151.1	173.2
Austria	BQXR	705.8	766.7	193.9	192.4	61.8	67.1	63.5
Turkey	BQXT	614.0	730.0	163.0	161.8	53.0	53.7	55.1
Other countries	BQXU	584.0	361.6	81.0	94.4	32.3	30.4	31.6
Total	BRAG	9 308.7	8 640.5	2 082.4	2 112.0	699.9	708.6	703.5
Eastern Europe and the former USSR:								
Former USSR	BQZX	606.6	354.7	79.4	125.4	26.4	47.6	51.3
Poland	BQZZ	221.7	347.1	103.7	123.0	36.7	38.3	48.0
Czechoslovakia	BRAA	133.1	129.4	44.1	47.2	15.8	16.2	15.3
Romania	BRAB	85.9	58.7	10.6	15.1	6.3	4.7	4.0
Yugoslavia[1]	BQXS	261.0	193.8	34.9	32.3	12.4[†]	12.7	7.3
Other countries	BRAH	171.4	171.3	47.0	61.6	18.6[†]	23.8	19.3
Total	BRAI	1 479.7	1 255.0	319.7	404.6	116.2	143.3	145.2
North America:								
Canada	BQXW	1 906.4	1 701.1	379.7	377.3	133.1	134.3	109.9
United States	BQXX	12 966.8	11 340.0	2 695.5	2 987.1	990.8	1 012.2	991.7
Other countries	BQXY	72.3	83.2	30.7	28.9	8.0	7.5	13.7
Total	BQXV	14 945.5	13 124.3	3 105.9	3 393.3	1 131.9	1 154.0	1 115.3
Other OECD countries:								
Japan	BQYB	2 631.3	2 257.6	560.2	548.4	197.2	172.7	178.4
Australia	BQYC	1 632.9	1 355.1	320.6	334.6	114.4	105.5	114.7
New Zealand	BQYD	439.6	260.1	55.6	63.1	21.4	18.4	23.2
Total	BRAJ	4 703.8	3 872.8	936.4	946.1	333.0	296.6	316.6
Oil exporting countries:								
Algeria	BQYF	73.8	55.7	7.8	7.9	3.2	1.5	3.1
Libya	BQYG	244.8	255.7	64.7	59.3	22.1	18.5	18.7
Nigeria	BQYH	499.8	544.6	134.1	162.1	53.6	42.1	66.4
Gabon	BQYI	17.6	30.6	4.3	4.4	1.3	1.6	1.5
Saudi Arabia	BQYJ	2 011.4	2 229.0	437.3	574.1	179.3	142.4	252.4
Kuwait	BQYK	181.5	178.3	62.6	54.4	18.3	18.5	17.5
Bahrain	BQYL	127.3	147.5	48.6	51.6	19.3	17.3	15.0
Qatar	BQYM	98.5	109.2	31.4	27.1	11.1	7.0	9.0
Abu Dhabi	BQYN	170.2	220.1	71.1	63.8	21.1	15.4	27.2
Dubai	BQYO	444.0	478.8	130.2	141.4	49.7	48.2	43.5
Sharjah etc	BQYP	50.5	60.8	13.7	16.1	6.0	4.5	5.7
Oman	BQYQ	272.1	237.9	60.8	53.7	17.0	20.6	16.2
Iraq	BQYR	293.4	4.4	6.9	15.9	4.9	4.2	6.8
Iran	BQYS	384.2	511.5	142.1	159.4	48.5	58.5	52.4
Brunei	BQYT	224.6	215.2	27.7	30.7	21.3	6.0	3.5
Indonesia	BQYU	198.0	198.0	83.1	88.1	31.9	28.7	27.4
Trinidad and Tobago	BQYV	49.9	62.5	12.6	12.2	3.9	4.5	3.8
Venezuela	BQYW	204.9	166.7	40.0	46.9	12.8	19.2	14.9
Ecuador	BQYX	30.2	45.2	10.7	7.5	1.7	2.9	2.8
Total	BQYE	5 576.6	5 751.7	1 389.7	1 576.5	527.2	461.6	587.8

The statistics are on an overseas trade statistics basis (see footnote 1 to Table 15.7).

1 From January 1991 back data has been recalculated to take into account changes in country grouping and country definitions.
The changes are as follows:
(a) FR GERMANY and GDR become GERMANY.

(b) REST OF WESTERN EUROPE becomes OTHER WESTERN EUROPE and YUGOSLAVIA is excluded.
(c) OTHER DEVELOPED COUNTRIES changed to OTHER OECD COUNTRIES and excludes SOUTH AFRICA.
(d) OTHER DEVELOPING COUNTRIES now becomes OTHER COUNTRIES and includes SOUTH AFRICA.
(e) CENTRALLY PLANNED ECONOMIES changed to EASTERN EUROPE AND THE (former) USSR and the GDR is replaced by YUGOSLAVIA.

Source: Department of Trade and Industry

15.5 United Kingdom exports, by countries (f.o.b)
continued

£ million

		1990	1991	1992 Q1	1992 Q2	1992 Apr	1992 May	1992 Jun
Other countries:								
Egypt	BQYZ	298.3	282.9	74.1	61.2	17.1	21.3	22.8
Ghana	BQZA	162.1	169.3	39.4	49.9	18.7	13.7	17.5
Kenya	BQZB	243.1	206.9	40.9	32.2	11.7	11.0	9.6
Tanzania	BQZC	84.7	72.8	19.3	19.4	6.2	6.6	6.6
Zambia	BQZD	92.8	62.7	12.6	14.9	4.9	4.3	5.7
South Africa[1]	BQYA	1 113.6	1 023.5	272.3	267.5	79.3	112.5	75.7
Cyprus	BQZE	204.9	209.9	49.7	58.3	20.0	19.6	18.8
Lebanon	BQZF	53.3	87.8	24.9	21.9	9.5	6.6	5.9
Israel	BQZG	567.7	529.5	127.0	160.2	52.0	51.7	56.4
Pakistan	BQZH	251.8	272.1	84.6	71.0	21.6	24.5	24.9
India	BQZI	1 264.2	1 017.4	230.0	287.3	112.7	76.8	97.7
Thailand	BQZJ	416.6	463.4	121.9	94.6	35.3	29.0	30.3
Malaysia	BQZK	550.7	582.2	141.5	148.4	56.1	45.0	47.3
Singapore	BQZL	1 040.7	1 018.4	257.0	290.1	122.1	85.6	82.4
Taiwan	BQZM	430.6	519.8	126.7	141.9	45.0	51.2	45.7
Hong Kong	BQZN	1 238.0	1 386.9	400.7	369.3	132.2	117.9	119.2
South Korea	BQZO	620.7	786.2	149.6	164.5	55.8	56.6	52.2
Philippines	BQZP	158.0	146.6	40.7	49.4	16.9	16.4	16.0
Jamaica	BQZQ	58.7	54.7	9.7	10.9	4.5	3.0	3.4
Mexico	BQZR	263.0	276.6	59.8	72.8	20.4	23.1	29.4
Chile	BQZS	130.4	106.6	26.6	28.2	10.7	8.6	8.9
Brazil	BQZT	320.5	339.4	63.6	69.1	22.4	26.8	20.0
Argentina	BQZU	36.0	69.7	23.1	24.1	7.1	7.4	9.6
Other countries	BRAK	2 360.4	2 455.7	578.9	635.3	205.4	212.9	208.3
Total	BRAL	11 960.8	12 141.0	2 974.6	3 142.4	1 087.6	1 032.1	1 014.3
Low value trade[2]	BRAD	850.1	777.5	185.4	267.5	87.3	103.3	76.9

The statistics are on an overseas trade statistics basis (see footnote 1 to Table 15.7).

1 See footnote 1 on the previous page.

2 Prior to January 1986 items valued at less than £200 have not been allocated to specific countries and areas. With effect from 1 January 1986 the threshold was raised to £475, increased to £600 as from 1 January 1988.

Source: Department of Trade and Industry

For the latest official macro-economic data from the Central Statistical Office simply phone or fax the following numbers
(you may have to select "polling" mode on your fax machine)

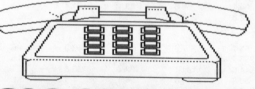

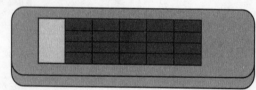

CSO STATCALL
0839 3383 PLUS ..

CSO STATFAX
0336 4160 PLUS ..

Retail prices index	
Monthly trade figures	37
Balance of payments	38
PSBR	39
Index of production	40
Producer prices	41
Retail sales index	42
Credit business	43
Gross domestic product	44
and for forthcoming economic release dates	45
	46

Calls are charged at 36p per minute cheap rate; 48p per minute at all other times

CSO   Great George Street London SWIP 3AQ

15.6 United Kingdom imports, by countries (c.i.f)

£ million

		1990	1991	1992 Q1	1992 Q2	1992 Apr	1992 May	1992 Jun
Total trade	BGAA	126 086.1	118 871.4	30 274.7	31 702.9	10 797.5	10 309.9	10 599.8
European Community:								
France	BGAC	11 872.3	11 066.1	2 787.7	3 110.1	1 094.8	949.8	1 065.6
Belgium and Luxembourg	BGAD	5 732.0	5 472.7	1 498.1	1 401.4	460.7	457.0	483.6
Netherlands	BGAE	10 483.2	9 970.0	2 505.4	2 444.1	832.0	797.3	814.8
Germany[1]	BRAM	19 912.5	17 741.1	4 535.2	4 817.2	1 602.6	1 618.3	1 596.3
Italy	BGAG	6 732.8	6 378.9	1 619.8	1 748.9	551.7	546.2	651.1
Irish Republic	BGAH	4 497.4	4 416.2	1 144.5	1 224.6	398.3	414.2	412.2
Denmark	BGAI	2 278.5	2 226.7	581.3	603.4	187.2	200.8	215.4
Greece	BGAJ	400.5	378.1	93.9	97.6	33.7	32.4	31.5
Portugal	BGAK	1 176.2	1 043.5	279.6	278.2	94.9	95.9	87.5
Spain	BGAL	2 870.7	2 627.9	739.0	750.8	242.4	241.0	267.3
Total	BRAN	65 956.0	61 321.1	15 784.5	16 476.3	5 498.3	5 352.9	5 625.3
Other Western Europe:								
Norway	BGAN	4 132.8	4 232.8	947.7	892.9	344.0	302.4	246.5
Sweden	BGAO	3 594.5	3 142.4	807.1	838.0	275.7	268.8	293.5
Finland	BGAP	1 775.7	1 522.3	380.8	412.0	136.3	135.3	140.3
Switzerland	BGAQ	4 247.9	3 754.6	870.2	1 018.2	375.7	308.0	334.5
Austria	BGAR	957.8	916.3	233.6	230.1	80.3	75.3	74.6
Turkey	BGAT	550.8	402.8	110.7	104.5	34.3	36.2	34.0
Other countries	BGAU	538.9	316.1	79.6	86.7	25.2	28.6	33.0
Total	BRAO	15 798.4	14 287.3	3 429.7	3 582.4	1 271.5	1 154.6	1 156.4
Eastern Europe and the former USSR:								
Former USSR	BGCX	917.7	901.8	100.4	197.4	65.6	68.4	63.4
Poland	BGCZ	367.6	313.8	84.6	87.2	27.8	32.9	26.6
Czechoslovakia	BGDA	136.1	131.4	37.9	44.3	13.6	13.5	17.2
Romania	BGDB	61.2	58.5	12.5	14.5	4.7	3.9	5.9
Yugoslavia[1]	BGAS	189.4	147.9	31.6	32.8	11.5	11.6	9.7
Other countries	BRAP	135.9	141.0	40.6	50.1	14.8	15.7	19.6
Total	BRAQ	1 807.9	1 694.4	307.6	426.3	138.0	146.0	142.4
North America:								
Canada	BGAW	2 207.7	1 922.5	441.9	578.8	221.5	179.9	177.5
United States	BGAX	14 352.7	13 711.5	3 695.0	3 562.0	1 288.5	1 201.4	1 075.8
Other countries	BGAY	134.3	114.9	29.5	31.2	9.7	8.7	9.0
Total	BGAV	16 694.7	15 748.9	4 166.4	4 172.0	1 519.7	1 390.0	1 262.3
Other OECD countries:								
Japan	BGBB	6 761.3	6 753.6	1 806.4	1 901.9	694.8	617.3	594.1
Australia	BGBC	1 020.7	870.8	312.6	279.1	70.6	113.7	94.7
New Zealand	BGBD	483.6	391.6	106.7	132.2	44.3	50.9	37.0
Total	BRAR	8 265.6	8 016.0	2 225.7	2 313.2	809.7	781.9	725.8
Oil exporting countries:								
Algeria	BGBF	260.0	194.9	20.1	52.0	12.2	15.7	24.2
Libya	BGBG	151.6	121.2	27.7	49.9	15.0	16.9	17.9
Nigeria	BGBH	297.4	249.3	78.7	29.9	6.3	7.1	16.5
Gabon	BGBI	1.8	3.2	0.6	0.7	0.1	0.5	0.2
Saudi Arabia	BGBJ	794.6	963.9	175.5	251.2	80.2	66.1	105.0
Kuwait	BGBK	109.0	29.9	13.2	4.6	2.8	0.7	1.2
Bahrain	BGBL	48.5	39.1	15.0	12.3	3.9	5.3	3.1
Qatar	BGBM	7.0	5.5	5.2	1.7	0.4	0.8	0.5
Abu Dhabi	BGBN	76.4	109.0	16.6	36.9	3.4	10.6	22.9
Dubai	BGBO	95.5	97.1	40.0	53.3	14.2	11.1	28.0
Sharjah etc	BGBP	9.6	25.8	4.8	7.3	1.7	2.5	3.1
Oman	BGBQ	89.4	73.6	22.9	23.2	13.4	7.0	2.8
Iraq	BGBR	101.6	2.5	0.2	0.1	-	-	-
Iran	BGBS	279.1	158.4	26.9	40.7	9.1	17.2	14.4
Brunei	BGBT	158.5	147.7	13.3	23.3	5.1	2.9	15.3
Indonesia	BGBU	327.9	415.3	120.4	117.1	40.6	34.2	42.4
Trinidad and Tobago	BGBV	45.1	41.7	3.3	20.3	7.7	1.1	11.4
Venezuela	BGBW	101.7	100.2	28.2	32.7	11.3	12.3	9.1
Ecuador	BGBX	19.6	16.3	2.7	3.0	1.2	0.5	1.3
Total	BGBE	2 974.2	2 794.5	615.2	760.3	228.6	212.5	319.2

The statistics are on an overseas trade statistics basis (see footnote 1 to Table 15.7).

1 See footnote 1 to Table 15.5 on page 91.

Source: Department of Trade and Industry

15.6 United Kingdom imports, by countries (c.i.f)
continued

£ million

		1990	1991	1992 Q1	1992 Q2	1992 Apr	1992 May	1992 Jun
Other countries:								
Egypt	BGBZ	145.3	136.4	47.2	43.0	19.2	17.9	5.9
Ghana	BGCA	105.1	77.3	14.7	24.6	8.0	6.7	9.9
Kenya	BGCB	149.5	142.0	34.4	33.2	11.0	9.6	12.5
Tanzania	BGCC	25.6	20.9	8.0	5.4	1.7	2.1	1.6
Zambia	BGCD	19.3	22.5	1.7	1.8	0.5	0.7	0.6
South Africa[1]	BGBA	1 079.5	954.7	214.6	247.6	71.5	75.8	100.4
Cyprus	BGCE	152.9	141.1	32.6	53.1	13.6	12.4	27.1
Lebanon	BGCF	6.2	8.5	1.7	3.2	1.7	3.0	0.4
Israel	BGCG	506.1	455.8	127.5	122.6	45.0	40.8	36.7
Pakistan	BGCH	236.4	261.3	63.9	67.9	21.6	24.2	22.1
India	BGCI	799.4	777.0	202.1	212.0	73.5	71.0	67.4
Thailand	BGCJ	484.3	625.4	145.7	132.0	45.7	39.9	46.4
Malaysia	BGCK	775.5	930.0	215.7	277.5	89.8	85.7	102.0
Singapore	BGCL	1 021.1	1 134.4	232.0	282.9	100.4	97.7	84.9
Taiwan	BGCM	1 211.8	1 272.6	310.0	334.3	120.9	104.6	108.9
Hong Kong	BGCN	1 972.1	2 147.6	519.7	508.3	166.5	159.1	182.8
South Korea	BGCO	963.8	924.6	214.2	222.2	75.3	70.2	76.7
Philippines	BGCP	220.7	230.0	56.6	55.1	20.4	15.9	18.8
Jamaica	BGCQ	136.5	123.8	31.4	47.9	11.7	17.9	18.3
Mexico	BGCR	172.1	147.2	44.4	37.3	10.5	9.2	17.6
Chile	BGCS	222.5	177.9	54.9	57.5	20.1	17.8	19.6
Brazil	BGCT ·	719.8	766.1	191.7	210.7	77.5	61.3	71.9
Argentina	BGCU	144.2	135.5	28.2	29.1	6.5	8.9	13.7
Other countries	BRAS	2 568.5	2 653.9	757.2	764.0	252.1	255.5	256.4
Total	BRAT	13 838.2	14 265.9	3 550.1	3 775.2	1 264.7	1 207.9	1 302.6
Low value trade[2]	BGDD	778.1	743.3	195.5	196.9	67.0	64.1	65.8

The statistics are on an overseas trade statistics basis (see footnote 1 to Table 15.7).

1 See footnote 1 to Table 15.5 on page 91.
2 Prior to January 1986 items valued at less than £200 have not been allocated to specific countries and areas. With effect from 1 January 1986 the threshold was raised to £475, increased to £600 as from 1 January 1988.

Source: Department of Trade and Industry

15.7 Volume and unit value index numbers on a balance of payments basis[1]

1985=100

	Volume index numbers		Unit value index numbers		
	Seasonally adjusted		Not seasonally adjusted		
	Exports	Imports	Exports (f.o.b.)	Imports (f.o.b.)	Terms of trade[2]
	CGTR	CGTS	CGTO	CGTP	CGTQ
1988	111.6	130.1[†]	93.4	96.9[†]	96.4[†]
1989	116.6[†]	140.5	100.8	104.1	96.8
1990	124.2	142.1	106.2	108.0	98.3
1991	126.3	138.1	106.4	108.4	98.2
1991 Feb	123.7[†]	131.2[†]	104.5	106.2[†]	98.4[†]
Mar	125.4	137.4	104.8	106.5	98.4
Apr	123.6	138.3	105.5	107.2	98.4
May	123.1	136.5	106.1	108.1	98.1
Jun	131.4	138.1	106.0	108.1	98.1
Jul	127.1	138.8	106.5	108.9	97.8
Aug	130.9	144.7	107.9	109.9	98.2
Sep	125.4	135.8	107.7	109.9	98.0
Oct	125.9	137.4	107.4	109.9	97.7
Nov	128.3	139.3	107.8	110.2	97.8
Dec	132.1	141.0	106.2[†]	109.6	96.9
1992 Jan	121.7	137.0	106.6	108.0	98.7
Feb	130.8	147.4	107.3	107.7	99.6
Mar	130.7	145.2	107.0	107.9	99.2
Apr	129.4	150.8	108.3	108.0	100.3
May	134.4	147.0	108.5	107.2	101.2
Jun	128.1	146.3	108.2	106.5	101.6

1 Statistics of visible trade on a balance of payments basis (shown in Table 16.1) are obtained by making certain adjustments in respect of valuation and coverage to the statistics recorded in the *Overseas Trade Statistics*.

These adjustments are described in detail in *United Kingdom Balance of Payments 1983 Edition*.
2 Export unit value as a percentage of the import unit value index.

Source: Central Statistical Office

15.8 Export and import volume indices

1985=100, seasonally adjusted

	Total	Food, beverages and tobacco	Basic materials	Fuels	Total manufactures	Manufactures excluding erratics[1]								
						Total	Semi-manufactures excluding precious stones (P) and silver			Finished manufactures exc ships, North Sea installations and aircraft SNA				
							Total	Chemicals	Total	Total	Passenger motor cars[2]	Other consumer[2]	Intermediate[2]	Capital[2]
SITC (Rev 3) Section or division	0 to 9	0 and 1	2 and 4	3	5 to 8	5 to 8 less SNAPS	5 and 6 less PS	5	6 less PS	7 and 8 less SNA	781			
Weights	1 000	64	28	214	670	619	234	121	114	385	17	65	180	122
Exports														
	BOKO	BOKP	BOKQ	BOKR	BOKS	BOKT	BOKU	BOKV	BOKW	BOKX	BOKY	BOKZ	BOKA	BOKB
1987	109.8	112.1	114.4	100.8	112.3	110.6	110.4	112.1	108.6	110.6	117.3	125.7	103.5	112.3
1988	112.5	112.3	99.9	93.8	119.6	117.7	116.9	118.0	115.7	118.2	122.8	122.5	104.5	135.4
1989	117.3	123.5	104.3	75.1	131.1	129.1	121.9	119.7	124.1	133.6	153.1	144.4	114.5	153.1
1990	125.1	124.1	102.0	80.7	141.1	140.5	129.4	123.8	135.3	147.3	183.4	169.1	126.8	160.9
1991	126.9	130.2	98.3	78.4	144.7	144.6	135.2	129.4	141.3†	150.4	219.2	169.3	128.9	162.5
1991 Mar	126.1	122	96	84	143	144	133	126	141	150	206	173	131	159
Apr	124.4	120	100	68	145	148	139	132	146	153	222	171	137	157
May	123.9	125	99	72	143	143	133	126	141	150	224	166	128	161
Jun	130.7	129	102	80	149	149	140	137	144	155	276	169	129	169
Jul	127.8	125	100	72	149	145	136	130	143	150	265	162	126	163
Aug	131.4	132	98	86	149	148	139	133	146	153	191	163	134	170
Sep	125.6	132	96	86	140	141	130	126	134	148	225	177	119	166
Oct	126.8	135	94	77	145	145	138	134	142	149	216	173	123	164
Nov	128.8	138	99	87	144	147	137	134	140	154	186	172	133	169
Dec	132.8	149	97	91	148	147	138	132	144	153	170	174	132	170
1992 Jan	121.7	127	88	75	139	141	134	131	136	146	200	170	126	156
Feb	130.6	130	96	77	151	152	146	139	153	156	205	183	136	165
Mar	130.1	136	100	84	147	149	144	141	146	152	199	177	129	165
Apr	129.1	130	96	84	146	147	141	140	142	152	191	175	135	158
May	134.5†	145	98†	86†	152	154	145†	139†	150†	160	194†	168†	139	180
Jun	128.2	155	97	74	146	147	141	136	146	150	206	174	129	160
Weights	1 000	109	65	125	686	647	230	81	148	417	49	106	143	119
Imports														
	BONO	BONP	BONQ	BONR	BONS	BONT	BONU	BONV	BONW	BONX	BONY	BONZ	BONA	BONB
1987	114.8	109.4	116.9	105.1	117.7	118.6	116.8	119.5	115.3	119.5	99.1	127.4	123.7	115.8
1988	130.5	115.0	118.1	108.3	138.5	139.1	131.4	128.4	133.1	143.3	130.1	141.6	148.1	144.4
1989	140.8	118.3	116.7	117.7	151.1	152.0	139.3	140.0	138.8	159.0	135.1	159.0	164.9	161.6
1990	142.7	121.5	114.3	125.6	152.1	152.9	144.1	145.8	143.1	157.8	121.4	169.1	166.6	152.1
1991	138.6	122.5	114.7	128.0	145.6	146.9	144.3	147.9	142.4	148.3	85.8	159.7	163.1	146.2
1991 Mar	138.0	124	114	121	146	148	143	141	145	151	87	166	169	141
Apr	138.7	127	109	132	145	146	141	133	145	149	86	165	164	141
May	137.1	120	108	128	144	146	138	144	135	151	87	164	167	146
Jun	138.5	124	114	137	144	146	142	147	140	148	94	151	165	146
Jul	139.0	125	115	139	144	147	144	145	143	149	93	159	160	149
Aug	144.9	119	123	157	149	150	150	161	144	149	76	158	167	151
Sep	136.1	118	111	117	145	145	145	152	141	145	80	160	156	147
Oct	138.1	119	115	123	146	146	146	149	144	146	85	157	157	150
Nov	140.1	127	127	117	148	151	149	164	140	152	77	160	163	161
Dec	142.1	131	128	124	149	149	149	147	150	148	76	155	166	151
1992 Jan	137.2	128	112	109	146	147	140	138	141	151	98	156	163	154
Feb	147.6	129	123	127	157	157	155	152	157	158	92	163	170	164
Mar	145.4	124	130	122	155	155	158	157	159	153	101	158	168	153
Apr	150.9	129	126	141	159	159	154	157	152	161	102	167	180	159
May	147.3†	131	117	130	156†	159†	153†	159	150†	162†	109†	171†	178†	158†
Jun	145.8	133	122	133	153	156	156	156	156	156	106	169	167	151

The statistics are on an overseas trade statistics basis (see footnote 1 to Table 15.7).
1 These are defined as ships, North Sea installations (together comprising SITC (Rev 3) (793), aircraft (792), precious stones (667) and silver (6811).

2 Based on the *Classification by Broad Economic Categories*, (BEC) published by the United Nations.

Source: Central Statistical Office

15.9 Export and import unit value index numbers

1985=100

	Total	Food, beverages and tobacco	Basic materials	Fuels	Total manufactures	Manufactures excluding erratics[1]								
						Total	Semi-manufactures excluding precious stones (P) and silver			Finished manufactures exc ships, North Sea installations and aircraft SNA				
							Total	Chemicals	Total	Total	Pass-enger motor cars[2]	Other con-sumer[2]	Inter-mediate[2]	Capital[2]
SITC (Rev 3) Section or Division	0 to 9	0 and 1	2 and 4	3	5 to 8	5 to 8 less SNAPS	5 and 6 less PS	5	6 less PS	7 and 8 less SNA	781			
Weights	1 000	64	28	214	670	619	234	121	114	385	17	65	180	122
Exports														
	BOLC	BOLD	BOLE	BOLF	BOLG	BOLH	BOLI	BOLJ	BOLK	BOLL	BOLM	BOLN	BOLO	BOLP
1987	93.8	105	94	52	106	106	103	102	104	107	123	108	107	104
1988	94.1	107	99	40	109	110	107	106	107	111	122	110	113	108
1989	101.6	114	107	49	116	116	114	113	115	117	132	115	118	115
1990	107.0	123	103	59	121	120	118	118	119	121	137	120	122	119
1991	107.3	127	95	55	122	122	117	119	115	124	144	122	127	119
1991 Mar	105.6	123	92	52	121	121	117	119	114	123	141	122	126	118
Apr	106.4	126	93	52	122	121	117	119	114	124	143	120	127	118
May	107.0	128	96	53	122	121	117	119	115	124	142	120	128	118
Jun	106.8	128	97	52	122	121	117	120	114	124	140	122	128	117
Jul	107.4	129	97	54	122	123	118	121	115	126	142	123	129	119
Aug	108.7	129	96	54	124	123	118	120	116	126	148	123	130	121
Sep	108.5	129	96	55	124	123	118	120	115	126	146	122	128	121
Oct	108.3	128	94	57	123	122	117	120	114	125	144	121	128	120
Nov	108.7	127	95	58	123	122	117	120	114	125	149	123	127	121
Dec	107.1[†]	128	95	52	123	122	116[†]	119	113[†]	125	154	123	127	119
1992 Jan	106.7	127	95	49	123	122	116	120	112	126	156	124	128	120
Feb	107.4	128	96	49	124	123	116	120	112	127	157	125	129	121
Mar	107.1	129	96	48	124	123	116	120	112	127	155	124	129	121
Apr	108.3	129	93	51	125	124	116	119	113	129	159	126	132	121
May	108.6	130	92[†]	51	125	124	116	120	112	129	161	125	132	122
Jun	108.3	130	93	52	124	123	116	121	112	127	159	121	132	120
Weights	1 000	109	65	125	686	647	230	81	148	417	49	106	143	119
Imports														
	BOLQ	BOLR	BOLS	BOLT	BOLU	BOLV	BOLW	BOLX	BOLY	BOLZ	BOKC	BOKD	BOKE	BOKF
1987	97.7	101	90	56	105	105	104	102	106	106	122	102	103	107
1988	97.0	101	93	45	106	106	108	106	109	105	124	102	103	102
1989	104.0	107	103	53	113	112	114	110	117	111	135	108	109	106
1990	107.9	112	101	60	117	116	117	113	119	116	141	110	116	110
1991	108.4	111	90	57	119	118	114	113	115	121	154	111	123	113
1991 Mar	106.6	109	91	55	117	116	114	115	114	117	153	108	116	111
Apr	107.3	110	90	54	118	117	114	114	115	119	158	108	119	112
May	108.2	112	91	56	119	118	115	113	115	119	159	107	121	112
Jun	108.1	112	90	54	119	118	115	113	116	120	153	109	122	113
Jul	108.8	113	90	56	119	120	115	113	117	122	154	111	125	114
Aug	109.8	112	90	55	121	120	114	112	115	124	156	113	128	114
Sep	109.8	112	89	56	121	120	114	112	115	124	155	115	128	114
Oct	109.7	112	89	57	121	120	114	112	115	123	151	115	129	113
Nov	109.9	112	90	60	120	120	113	110	115	123	154	114	127	114
Dec	109.4	112	88	54	121	120	113	110	114	124	162	114	128	114
1992 Jan	107.7	111	88	52	119	118	111	109	112	122	160	112	125	113
Feb	107.5	112	87	50	119	118	110	109	111	122	158	114	124	114
Mar	107.6	112	88	51	119	118	110	108	112	122	154	115	124	114
Apr	107.8	114	88	51	119	118	110	107	112	122	159	113	124	113
May	107.0[†]	113	89	52	118[†]	117[†]	109	107	111	121[†]	158	111[†]	122[†]	114[†]
Jun	106.3	112	89	53	117	116	108	106	109	120	156	109	121	113

The statistics are on an overseas trade statistics basis (see footnote 1 to Table 15.7).

1 These are defined as ships, North Sea installations (together comprising SITC (Rev 3) (793), aircraft (792), precious stones (667) and silver (6811).

2 Based on the *Classification by Broad Economic Categories*, (BEC) published by the United Nations.

Source: Central Statistical Office

15.10 Import penetration and export sales ratios for products of manufacturing industry[1,2,3]
Standard Industrial Classification 1980

Twelve months ending, per cent

Ratio 1 Imports/Home demand Division/Class		SIC	1984 Dec	1985 Dec	1986 Dec	1987 Dec	1988 Mar	1988 Jun	1988 Sep	1988 Dec	1989 Mar	1989 Jun
Total Manufacturing	BYAA	2-4	33.4	34.3	34.3	35.2	35.3	35.5	35.6	35.6	36.2	36.7
Extraction of minerals and ores other than fuels; manufacture of metals, mineral products and chemicals	BYAB	2	32	33	32	32	32	33	33	33	33	33
Extraction and preparation of metalliferous ores	BYAC	21	98.0	100.0	-	-	-	-	-	-	-	-
Metal manufacturing	BYAD	22	29	29	25	24	25	26	27	29	30	31
Extraction of minerals not elsewhere specified	BYAE	23	42	43	37	36	32	30	27	21	21	21
Manufacture of non-metallic mineral products	BYAF	24	12	13	16	16	16	17	17	17	17	17
Chemical industry	BYAG	25	38	40	40	41	41	41	41	41	41	42
Production of man-made fibres	BYAH	26	68	71	68	66	66	67	67	67	68	69
Metal goods, engineering and vehicle industries	BYAI	3	43	44	45	45	45	46	46	46	47	48
Manufacture of metal goods not elsewhere specified	BYAJ	31	14	16	16	18	17	18	17	17	18	18
Mechanical engineering	BYAK	32	34	36	37	38	38	39	39	39	40	40
Manufacture of office machinery and data processing equipment	BYAL	33	105	100	100	93	90	89	88	91	94	95
Electrical and electronic engineering	BYAM	34	44	47	47	49	49	50	50	50	51	52
Manufacture of motor vehicles and parts thereof	BYAN	35	51	50	51	48	49	49	50	50	50	51
Manufacture of other transport equipment	BYAO	36	51	45	45	42	42	46	44	45	49	49
Instrument engineering	BYAP	37	58	57	55	58	58	59	58	58	60	60
Other manufacturing industries	BYAQ	4	25	25	25	26	26	26	26	26	26	26
Food, drink and tobacco manufacturing industries	BYAR	41/42	18	18	18	18	18	18	18	18	18	18
Textile industry	BYAS	43	44	44	45	47	47	48	48	48	48	48
Manufacture of leather and leather goods	BYAT	44	44	49	46	49	49	50	49	49	51	52
Footwear and clothing industries	BYAU	45	36	35	36	39	39	39	39	39	40	40
Timber and wooden furniture industries	BYAV	46	32	30	31	31	30	30	30	30	30	30
Manufacture of paper and paper products; printing and publishing	BYAW	47	21	21	21	22	22	22	22	21	22	22
Processing of rubber and plastics	BYAX	48	25	26	27	28	27	27	27	26	26	26
Other manufacturing industries	BYAY	49	39	38	39	46	45	44	44	44	44	45

1 The ratios were first introduced in an article in the August 1977 edition of *Economic Trends* 'The Home and Export Performance of United Kingdom Industries' which described the conceptual and methodological problems involved in measuring such variables as 'import penetration'. The latest ratios for the full detail within manufacturing (over 200 Activity Headings) are shown in Business Monitor *MQ12 Import Penetration and Export Sales for Manufacturing Industry.*

2 The calculation of the ratios is inappropriate for certain industries. In such cases, and where suitable data are not available, the industry has been omitted from the analysis. The Activity Headings (AHs) concerned are:

AH2247.2 Precious metals, AH2396(pt) Unworked precious stones, AH2436 Ready-mixed concrete, AH3138 Heat and surface treatment of metals, AH3246 Process engineering contractors, AH3480 Electrical equipment installation, AH4121 Slaughterhouses, AH4370 Textile finishing, AH4560 Fur goods, AH4672 Shop and office fittings, AH4820 Retreading and specialist repairing of rubber tyres, AH4910 Jewellery and coins and AH4930 Photographic and cinematographic processing laboratories.

3 As a result of recommendations made in the 1989 review of Department of Trade and Industry statistics, quarterly sales data for most manufacturing idustries, which are used in the calculation of this ratio, are no longer collected. Data for the third quarter of 1989 and onwards are therefore not available.

Source: Department of Trade and Industry

15.10
continued

Import penetration and export sales ratios for products of manufacturing industry[1,2,3]
Standard Industrial Classification 1980

Twelve months ending, per cent

Ratio 2 Imports/Home demand plus Exports Division/Class	SIC	1984 Dec	1985 Dec	1986 Dec	1987 Dec	1988 Mar	1988 Jun	1988 Sep	1988 Dec	1989 Mar	1989 Jun
Total Manufacturing	BYBA	2-4	26.4	26.7	26.9	27.5	27.6	27.9	28.0	28.1	28.5	28.8
Extraction of minerals and ores other than fuels; manufacture of metals, mineral products and chemicals	BYBB	2	24	24	23	24	24	24	24	24	25	25
Extraction and preparation of metalliferous ores	BYBC	21	94	96	-	-	-	-	-	-	-	-
Metal manufacturing	BYBD	22	23	23	20	19	20	21	22	23	24	25
Extraction of minerals not elsewhere specified	BYBE	23	38	40	35	33	30	28	25	19	20	19
Manufacture of non-metallic mineral products	BYBF	24	11	11	13	14	14	14	14	14	15	15
Chemical industry	BYBG	25	26	26	26	27	27	27	27	27	28	28
Production of man-made fibres	BYBH	26	37	39	41	42	41	41	41	40	40	40
Metal goods, engineering and vehicle industries	BYBI	3	31	31	32	32	33	33	33	34	34	35
Manufacture of metal goods not elsewhere specified	BYBJ	31	13	14	15	16	15	16	16	15	16	16
Mechanical engineering	BYBK	32	24	24	25	26	27	27	27	28	28	28
Manufacture of office machinery and data processing equipment	BYBL	33	60	54	56	52	52	51	50	51	52	53
Electrical and electronic engineering	BYBM	34	32	33	33	35	35	36	36	36	36	37
Manufacture of motor vehicles and parts thereof	BYBN	35	38	39	41	38	39	39	40	41	41	41
Manufacture of other transport equipment	BYBO	36	28	27	26	24	24	26	27	27	28	28
Instrument engineering	BYBP	37	39	40	39	40	40	40	40	40	40	41
Other manufacturing industries	BYBQ	4	22	22	22	23	23	23	23	23	23	23
Food, drink and tobacco manufacturing industries	BYBR	41/42	17	17	17	17	16	16	16	16	16	16
Textile industry	BYBS	43	35	35	36	38	38	38	38	38	38	39
Manufacture of leather and leather goods	BYBT	44	34	37	36	37	37	37	37	37	38	39
Footwear and clothing industries	BYBU	45	32	31	31	33	33	34	34	34	35	35
Timber and wooden furniture industries	BYBV	46	31	29	30	30	29	29	29	29	29	29
Manufacture of paper and paper products; printing and publishing	BYBW	47	20	19	19	20	20	20	20	20	20	20
Processing of rubber and plastics	BYBX	48	21	22	22	23	23	23	22	22	22	22
Other manufacturing industries	BYBY	49	32	31	31	36	36	35	35	35	35	36

1 The ratios were first introduced in an article in the August 1977 edition of *Economic Trends* 'The Home and Export Performance of United Kingdom Industries' which described the conceptual and methodological problems involved in measuring such variables as 'import penetration'. The latest ratios for the full detail within manufacturing (over 200 Activity Headings) are shown in Business Monitor *MQ12 Import Penetration and Export Sales for Manufacturing Industry*.

2 The calculation of the ratios is inappropriate for certain industries. In such cases, and where suitable data are not available, the industry has been omitted from the analysis. The Activity Headings (AHs) concerned are:

AH2247.2 Precious metals, AH2396(pt) Unworked precious stones, AH2436 Ready-mixed concrete, AH3138 Heat and surface treatment of metals, AH3246 Process engineering contractors, AH3480 Electrical equipment installation, AH4121 Slaughterhouses, AH4370 Textile finishing, AH4560 Fur goods, AH4672 Shop and office fitting, AH4820 Retreading and specialist repairing of rubber tyres, AH4910 Jewellery and coins and AH4930 Photographic and cinematographic processing laboratories.

3 As a result of recommendations made in the 1989 review of Department of Trade and Industry statistics, quarterly sales data for most manufacturing industries, which are used in the calculation of this ratio, are no longer collected. Data for the third quarter of 1989 and onwards are therefore not available.

Source: Department of Trade and Industry

15.10
continued

Import penetration and export sales ratios for products of manufacturing industry[1,2,3]

Standard Industrial Classification 1980

Twelve months ending, per cent

Ratio 3 Exports/Sales

Division/Class	SIC	1984 Dec	1985 Dec	1986 Dec	1987 Dec	1988 Mar	1988 Jun	1988 Sep	1988 Dec	1989 Mar	1989 Jun
Total Manufacturing	BYCA	2-4	28.4	30.2	29.6	30.3	29.9	29.9	29.6	29.2	29.7	30.0
Extraction of minerals and ores other than fuels; manufacture of metals, mineral products and chemicals	BYCB	2	33	35	35	35	35	35	35	35	35	35
Extraction and preparation of metalliferous ores	BYCC	21	70	95	-	-	-	-	-	-	-	-
Metal manufacturing	BYCD	22	24	25	23	23	22	23	24	25	25	26
Extraction of minerals not elsewhere specified	BYCE	23	13	13	9	12	11	10	19	18	18	9
Manufacture of non-metallic mineral products	BYCF	24	14	15	17	17	17	17	17	16	17	16
Chemical industry	BYCG	25	44	47	47	46	46	46	47	46	46	46
Production of man-made fibres	BYCH	26	72	73	68	64	64	65	66	67	69	70
Metal goods, engineering and vehicle industries	BYCI	3	41	43	42	42	42	42	41	41	42	42
Manufacture of metal goods not elsewhere specified	BYCJ	31	13	14	13	13	13	14	13	13	13	13
Mechanical engineering	BYCK	32	42	43	42	43	41	41	40	39	40	39
Manufacture of office machinery and data processing equipment	BYCL	33	107	100	100	91	89	87	87	90	93	93
Electrical and electronic engineering	BYCM	34	39	43	43	43	44	44	45	44	45	46
Manufacture of motor vehicles and parts thereof	BYCN	35	37	37	34	34	33	33	32	32	32	33
Manufacture of other transport equipment	BYCO	36	63	55	58	58	55	58	54	55	59	60
Instrument engineering	BYCP	37	53	50	48	52	52	53	53	53	54	54
Other manufacturing industries	BYCQ	4	14	14	14	15	15	15	14	14	14	14
Food, drink and tobacco manufacturing industries	BYCR	41/42	10	11	11	12	11	11	11	11	11	12
Textile industry	BYCS	43	30	31	30	32	32	32	32	32	32	32
Manufacture of leather and leather goods	BYCT	44	35	38	36	40	39	40	40	38	40	41
Footwear and clothing industries	BYCU	45	18	19	18	21	20	20	20	19	19	19
Timber and wooden furniture industries	BYCV	46	6	6	5	5	5	5	4	4	4	4
Manufacture of paper and paper products; printing and publishing	BYCW	47	10	11	10	11	11	11	10	10	10	10
Processing of rubber and plastics	BYCX	48	22	22	21	22	21	21	21	20	20	20
Other manufacturing industries	BYCY	49	28	28	28	34	33	33	32	31	30	30

1 The ratios were first introduced in an article in the August 1977 edition of *Economic Trends* 'The Home and Export Performance of United Kingdom Industries' which described the conceptual and methodological problems involved in measuring such variables as 'import penetration'. The latest ratios for the full detail within manufacturing (over 200 Activity Headings) are shown in Business Monitor *MQ12 Import Penetration and Export Sales for Manufacturing Industry*.

2 The calculation of the ratios is inappropriate for certain industries. In such cases, and where suitable data are not available, the industry has been omitted from the analysis. The Activity Headings (AHs) concerned are:

AH2247.2 Precious metals, AH2396(pt) Unworked precious stones, AH2436 Ready-mixed concrete, AH3138 Heat and surface treatment of metals, AH3246 Process engineering contractors, AH3480 Electrical equipment installation, AH4121 Slaughterhouses, AH4370 Textile finishing, AH4560 Fur goods, AH4672 Shop and office fitting, AH4820 Retreading and specialist repairing of rubber tyres, AH4910 Jewellery and coins and AH4930 Photographic and cinematographic processing laboratories.

3 As a result of recommendations made in the 1989 review of Department of Trade and Industry statistics, quarterly sales data for most manufacturing industries, which are used in the calculation of this ratio, are no longer collected. Data for the third quarter of 1989 and onwards are therefore not available.

Source: Department of Trade and Industry

15.10
continued

Import penetration and export sales ratios for products of manufacturing Industry[1,2,3]

Standard Industrial Classification 1980

Twelve months ending, per cent

Ratio 4 Export/Sales plus Imports Division/Class		SIC	1984 Dec	1985 Dec	1986 Dec	1987 Dec	1988 Mar	1988 Jun	1988 Sep	1988 Dec	1989 Mar	1989 Jun
Total Manufacturing	BYDA	2-4	20.9	22.1	21.6	22.0	21.6	21.5	21.3	21.0	21.2	21.3
Extraction of minerals and ores other than fuels; manufacture of metals, mineral products and chemicals	BYDB	2	25	27	27	27	27	27	27	27	27	27
Extraction and preparation of metalliferous ores	BYDC	21	4	4	-	-	-	-	-	-	-	-
Metal manufacturing	BYDD	22	18	19	18	18	18	18	18	19	20	20
Extraction of minerals not elsewhere specified	BYDE	23	8	8	6	8	8	7	7	7	6	7
Manufacture of non-metallic mineral products	BYDF	24	13	14	15	15	15	15	14	14	14	14
Chemical industry	BYDG	25	33	35	35	34	34	34	34	33	33	33
Production of man-made fibres	BYDH	26	45	44	40	37	38	38	39	40	41	42
Metal goods, engineering and vehicle industries	BYDI	3	28	29	28	28	28	28	27	27	27	28
Manufacture of metal goods not elsewhere specified	BYDJ	31	11	12	11	11	11	11	11	11	11	11
Mechanical engineering	BYDK	32	32	33	32	31	30	30	29	28	28	28
Manufacture of office machinery and data processing equipment	BYDL	33	43	46	44	43	43	42	43	44	44	44
Electrical and electronic engineering	BYDM	34	26	29	28	28	28	28	29	28	29	29
Manufacture of motor vehicles and parts thereof	BYDN	35	23	22	20	21	20	20	19	19	19	20
Manufacture of other transport equipment	BYDO	36	45	40	44	43	42	43	40	40	43	43
Instrument engineering	BYDP	37	32	30	29	32	31	32	32	32	32	32
Other manufacturing industries	BYDQ	4	11	11	11	11	11	11	11	11	11	11
Food, drink and tobacco manufacturing industries	BYDR	41/42	9	9	9	10	9	9	9	9	9	10
Textile industry	BYDS	43	19	20	19	20	20	20	20	19	20	20
Manufacture of leather and leather goods	BYDT	44	23	24	23	25	25	25	25	24	25	25
Footwear and clothing industries	BYDU	45	13	13	13	14	14	13	13	13	13	12
Timber and wooden furniture industries	BYDV	46	4	4	4	3	3	3	3	3	3	3
Manufacture of paper and paper products; printing and publishing	BYDW	47	8	9	9	9	8	8	8	8	8	8
Processing of rubber and plastics	BYDX	48	17	17	17	17	17	17	16	15	15	15
Other manufacturing industries	BYDY	49	19	20	19	21	21	21	21	20	20	19

1 The ratios were first introduced in an article in the August 1977 edition of *Economic Trends* 'The Home and Export Performance of United Kingdom Industries' which described the conceptual and methodological problems involved in measuring such variables as 'import penetration'. The latest ratios for the full detail within manufacturing (over 200 Activity Headings) are shown in Business Monitor *MQ12 Import Penetration and Export Sales for Manufacturing Industry*.

2 The calculation of the ratios is inappropriate for certain industries. In such cases, and where suitable data are not available, the industry has been omitted from the analysis. The Activity Headings (AHs) concerned are:

AH2247.2 Precious metals, AH2396(pt) Unworked precious stones, AH2436 Ready-mixed concrete, AH3138 Heat and surface treatment of metals, AH3246 Process engineering contractors, AH3480 Electrical equipment installation, AH4121 Slaughterhouses, AH4370 Textile finishing, AH4560 Fur goods, AH4672 Shop and office fitting, AH4820 Retreading and specialist repairing of rubber tyres, AH4910 Jewellery and coins and AH4930 Photographic and cinematographic processing laboratories.

3 As a result of recommendations made in the 1989 review of Department of Trade and Industry Statistics, quarterly sales data for most manufacturing industries, which are used in the calculation of this ratio, are no longer collected. Data for the third quarter of 1989 and onwards are therefore not available.

Source: Department of Trade and Industry

16 Overseas finance

16.1 Balance of payments
Summary

£ million

	Seasonally adjusted						Not seasonally adjusted					
		Invisible (balance)						UK external assets and liabilities			Allocation of SDRS and gold subscription to IMF	Balancing item
	Visible trade (balance)	Services	Interest, profits and dividends	Transfers	Total	Current balance	Current balance	Transactions in assets[1]	Transactions in liabilities[1]	Net transactions		
	AIMA	AIMC	AIMD	AIME	AIMB	AIMF	AIMG	HEPZ	HEQW	HEQU	AIMI	AASA
1979	-3 343	3 895	1 205	-2 210	2 890	-454[†]	-453	-40 189	39 447	-742	195	1 000
1980	1 357	3 653	-182	-1 984	1 487	2 841	2 843	-43 439	39 499	-3 940	180	917
1981	3 252	3 792	1 251	-1 547	3 496	6 748	6 748	-50 769	43 334	-7 436	158	530
1982	1 910	3 022	1 460	-1 741	2 741	4 648	4 649	-31 433	28 916	-2 519	-	-2 130
1983	-1 537	4 064	2 831	-1 593	5 302	3 793	3 765	-30 378	25 818	-4 562	-	797
1984	-5 336	4 519	4 345[†]	-1 730	7 134[†]	1 965	1 798[†]	-31 915[†]	23 502[†]	-8 414[†]	-	6 616[†]
1985	-3 345	6 687	2 560	-3 111	6 136	3 003	2 790	-50 493	46 761	-3 733	-	943
1986	-9 559	6 808	4 974	-2 157	9 625	66	66	-92 551	89 417	-3 134	-	3 068
1987	-11 582	6 745	3 754	-3 400	7 099	-4 482	-4 482	-82 205	86 539	4 334	-	148
1988	-21 480[†]	4 397[†]	4 423	-3 518	5 302	-16 179	-16 179	-58 475	67 870	9 396	-	6 783
1989	-24 683	4 039	3 495	-4 578	2 956	-21 726	-21 726	-88 912	108 172	19 259	-	2 467
1990	-18 809	4 581	2 094	-4 897	1 778	-17 029	-17 029	-79 498	90 591	11 091	-	5 938
1991	-10 290	4 990	328	-1 349	3 969	-6 321	-6 321	-20 780	26 030	5 249	-	1 072
1982 Q2	138	776	433	-743	466	605	154	-20	1 218	1 197	-	-1 351
Q3	549	591	402	-647	346	896	921[†]	-18 422	16 438	-1 985	-	1 064[†]
Q4	961	716	532	-476	772	1 728[†]	2 417	-1 375	-92	-1 467	-	-950
1983 Q1	-217	1 080	797	53	1 930	1 709	1 453	-10 796	8 578	-2 219	-	766
Q2	-575	973	374	-675	672	100	-394	-241	419	178	-	216
Q3	-142	938	1 002	-417	1 523	1 388	1 367	-11 530	11 897	366	-	-1 733
Q4	-603	1 073	658	-554	1 177	596	1 339	-7 811	4 924	-2 887	-	1 548
1984 Q1	-448	1 189	866[†]	-309	1 746[†]	1 316	850	-14 083	12 673[†]	-1 410[†]	-	560
Q2	-1 387	1 009	877	-649	1 237	-105	-711	-8 836[†]	6 622	-2 215	-	2 926
Q3	-1 534	1 124	949	-636	1 437	-40	95	-557	-709	-1 266	-	1 171
Q4	-1 967	1 197	1 653	-136	2 714	794	1 564	-8 439	4 916	-3 523	-	1 959
1985 Q1	-1 962	1 456	886	-835	1 507	-392	-778	-16 479	13 842	-2 637	-	3 415
Q2	-214	1 747	605	-651	1 701	1 539	866	-6 452	6 423	-29	-	-837
Q3	-538	1 797	735	-881	1 651	1 163	1 250	-15 168	9 754	-5 414	-	4 164
Q4	-631	1 687	334	-744	1 277	693	1 452	-12 394	16 742	4 347	-	-5 799
1986 Q1	-1 585	1 771	1 045	66	2 882	1 296	669	-15 545	14 436	-1 109	-	440
Q2	-2 162	1 567	1 180	-544	2 203	41	-179	-14 987	13 278	-1 709	-	1 888
Q3	-2 895	1 702	1 377	-803	2 276	-619	-790	-43 641	45 473	1 832	-	-1 042
Q4	-2 917	1 768	1 372	-876	2 264	-652	366	-18 378	16 230	-2 148	-	1 782
1987 Q1	-1 848	1 763	1 109	-767	2 105	257	-31	-14 044	18 119	4 075	-	-4 044
Q2	-2 791	1 733	893	-759	1 867	-924	-1 241	-26 713	28 208	1 495	-	-254
Q3	-3 071	1 825	1 012	-981	1 856	-1 215	-1 658	-27 343	24 444	-2 899	-	4 557
Q4	-3 872	1 424	740	-893	1 271	-2 600	-1 552	-14 105	15 768	1 663	-	-111
1988 Q1	-4 329[†]	1 173[†]	932	-1 045	1 060	-3 269	-3 631	-4 516	11 434	6 918	-	-3 287
Q2	-4 800	1 233	1 192	-888	1 537	-3 263	-3 616	-20 805	21 501	696	-	2 920
Q3	-5 648	1 100	1 252	-202	2 150	-3 498	-3 957	-23 807	25 716	1 909	-	2 048
Q4	-6 703	891	1 047	-1 383	555	-6 149	-4 975	-9 347	9 219	-127	-	5 102
1989 Q1	-6 371	892	1 207	-706	1 393	-4 978	-5 115	-27 973	36 417	8 443	-	-3 328
Q2	-6 692	1 301	911	-844	1 368	-5 325	-5 874	-16 795	19 167	2 372	-	3 502
Q3	-6 753	1 056	744	-1 396	404	-6 349	-7 065	-23 658	34 529	10 871	-	-3 806
Q4	-4 867	790	633	-1 632	-209	-5 074	-3 672	-20 486	18 059	-2 427	-	6 099
1990 Q1	-6 082	1 442	-29	-925	488	-5 594	-6 197	-16 969	23 747	6 777	-	-580
Q2	-5 407	1 193	13	-1 303	-97	-5 504	-5 991	-7 168	6 815	-354	-	6 345
Q3	-4 059	1 072	1 154	-1 111	1 115	-2 944	-3 781	-35 524	37 340	1 816	-	1 965
Q4	-3 261	874	956	-1 558	272	-2 987	-1 060	-19 837	22 689	2 852	-	-1 792
1991 Q1	-3 040	1 039	-559	-144	336	-2 704	-3 602	-9 383	10 255	872	-	2 730
Q2	-2 234	1 401	84	198[†]	1 683	-551	-839	-3 764	-6 907	-10 672	-	11 511
Q3	-2 385	1 482	491	-965	1 008	-1 378	-2 220	-9 096	10 354	1 258	-	962
Q4	-2 631	1 068	312	-438	942	-1 688	340	1 463	12 328	13 791	-	-14 131
1992 Q1	-3 066	1 040	452	-1 062	430	-2 636	-3 034	-11 773	1 834	-9 939	-	12 973
Q2	-3 107	..	..	..	..	..	..	..	..	..	..	..

1 Prior to 1979 foreign currency lending and borrowing abroad by UK banks (other than certain export credit extended) is recorded on a net basis under liabilities.

Source: Central Statistical Office

16.2 Balance of payments
Current account

£ million

| | Seasonally adjusted | | | | | | | | | Not seasonally adjusted: current balance |
| | Visible trade | | | Invisibles | | | | Net seasonal influences on current account | |
	Exports	Imports	Visible balance	Credits	Debits	Invisible balance[1]	Current balance		
	CGKG	CGHK	AIMA	CGKR	CGHT	AIMB	AIMF	HHHI	AIMG
1986	72 627	82 186	-9 559	77 255†	67 630†	9 625†	66†	-	66†
1987	79 153	90 735	-11 582	79 826	72 726	7 099	-4 482	-	-4 482
1988	80 346	101 826†	-21 480†	87 739	82 438	5 302	-16 179	-	-16 179
1989	92 154†	116 837	-24 683	107 778	104 821	2 956	-21 726	-†	-21 726
1990	101 718	120 527	-18 809	115 150	113 370	1 778	-17 029	-	-17 029
1991	103 413	113 703	-10 290	116 164	112 195	3 969	-6 321	-	-6 321
1990 Q4	25 614†	28 875†	-3 261†	29 608†	29 334†	272†	-2 987†	1 927†	-1 060†
1991 Q1	24 883	27 923	-3 040	29 086	28 750	336	-2 704	-898	-3 602
Q2	25 926	28 160	-2 234	30 822	29 139	1 683	-551	-288	-839
Q3	26 377	28 762	-2 385	28 678	27 671	1 008	-1 378	-842	-2 220
Q4	26 227	28 858	-2 631	27 578	26 635	942	-1 688	2 028	340
1992 Q1	26 190	29 256	-3 066	28 594	28 164	430	-2 636	-398	-3 034
Q2	26 834	29 941	-3 107	..	..	..	..	..	..
1991 Jun	9 020†	9 422†	-402†	..	..	561†	159†	..	-601†
Jul	8 798	9 441	-643	..	..	336	-307	..	-592
Aug	9 034	9 872	-838	..	..	336	-502	..	-1 038
Sep	8 545	9 449	-904	..	..	336	-568	..	-589
Oct	8 614	9 533	-919	..	..	314	-605	..	-447
Nov	8 689	9 674	-985	..	..	314	-671	..	-358
Dec	8 924	9 651	-727	..	..	314	-413	..	1 145
1992 Jan	8 287	9 448	-1 161	..	..	143	-1 018	..	-1 226
Feb	8 985	9 999	-1 014	..	..	144	-870	..	-907
Mar	8 918	9 809	-891	..	..	143	-748	..	-901
Apr	8 828	10 183	-1 355	..	..	200	-1 155	..	..
May	9 165	9 995	-830	..	..	200	-630	..	..
Jun	8 841	9 763	-922	..	..	200	-722	..	..

1 Monthly data is one third of the appropriate calendar quarters estimate or projection.

Source: Central Statistical Office

16.3 Balance of payments
Summary of transactions in UK external assets and liabilities[1]

£ million

| | Transactions in assets | | | | | | | Transactions in liabilities | | | | | | |
| | UK investment overseas | | Lending etc to overseas residents by UK banks | Deposits and lending overseas by UK residents other than banks and general government[2] | Official reserves | Other external assets of central government | Total transactions in assets | Overseas investment in the United Kingdom | | Borrowing etc from overseas residents by UK banks | Borrowing from overseas by UK residents other than banks and general government[2] | Other external liabilities of general government | Total transactions in liabilities | Net transactions |
	Direct	Portfolio						Direct	Portfolio					
	HHBV	CGOS	HEYN	HETJ	AIPA	HEUJ	HEPZ	HHBU	HEYR	HEYS	HTEV	HEUR	HEQW	HEQU
1986	-11 678†	-22 277†	-53 747†	-1 450†	-2 891	-509	-92 551†	5 837†	12 181†	66 868†	4 354†	177†	89 417†	-3 134†
1987	-19 239	5 163	-50 500	-4 821	-12 012	-796	-82 205	9 449	19 535	52 433	3 292	1 829	86 539	4 334
1988	-20 944	-11 239	-19 690	-2 955	-2 761	-887†	-58 475	12 006	15 564	34 088	5 382	832	67 870	9 396
1989	-21 515	-35 486	-28 612	-7 866	5 440	-873	-88 912	18 567	14 603	44 739	27 482	2 781	108 172	19 259
1990	-9 553	-15 844	-41 240	-11 759	-79	-1 025	-79 498	18 634	5 276	47 612	18 151	918	90 591	11 091
1991	-10 261	-30 908	32 231	-8 287	-2 662	-894	-20 780	12 045	16 627	-24 024	23 694	-2 311	26 030	5 249
1991 Q1	-3 378†	-7 524†	4 052†	-156†	-2 147	-230	-9 383†	4 908†	5 120†	-2 179†	3 724†	-1 318	10 255†	872†
Q2	-3 900	-7 395	16 112	-7 533	-847	-201	-3 764	2 856	5 664	-20 382	4 654	301	-6 907	-10 672
Q3	-2 831	-8 720	4 053	-1 513	152	-237†	-9 096	2 044	2 477	109	6 240	-515	10 354	1 258
Q4	-152	-7 269	8 014	915	180	-226	1 463	2 237	3 366	-1 572	9 076	-779†	12 328	13 791
1992 Q1	-2 512	-6 057	3 642	-6 394	-315	-137	-11 773	4 376	5 136	-12 310	4 725	-93	1 834	-9 939

1 UK assets: increase-/decrease+. UK liabilities: increase+/decrease-.
2 Only partial coverage for the most recent quarter.

Source: Central Statistical Office

17 Home finance

17.1 Central government borrowing on own account (CGBR(O))

£ million

	Cash receipts						Cash outlays				Own account borrowing (CGBR(O))
	Inland Revenue	Customs and Excise	Social security contributions[1]	Interest and dividends	Other receipts[2]	Total	Interest payments	Privatisation proceeds	Net departmental outlays[3]	Total	
	1	2	3	4	5	6	7	8	9	10	11
	ACAB	ACAC	ABIA	ABIB	ABIC	ABID	ABIE	ABIF	ABIG	ABIH	ABEB
1988	67 102	48 768	30 090	9 181	4 283	159 423	17 043	-6 087	137 898	148 854	-10 569
1989	75 639	52 005	30 566	9 890	3 991	172 090	16 680	-4 561	150 314	162 433	-9 656
1990	81 851	54 786	32 500	9 470	13 181	191 787	16 395	-4 285	178 565	190 675	-1 113
1991	80 824	59 166	34 311	9 480	15 267†	199 048†	15 073	-8 627	199 189	205 635	6 587†
1988/89	68 813	49 565	30 702	9 438	4 031	162 549	16 886	-7 069	139 688	149 505	-13 044
1989/90	76 674	52 190	31 020	9 879	3 783	173 545	16 598	-4 219	155 797	168 176	-5 369
1990/91	82 322	55 337	33 013	9 464	14 790	194 925	15 880	-5 345	181 468	192 003	-2 922
1991/92	79 353	61 827	34 391	9 815	16 077	201 463	15 364	-7 923	205 763	213 204	11 741
1990 Q4	21 632	14 923	7 393	2 256	4 719	50 923	3 541	-1 944	45 555	47 152	-3 771
1991 Q1	25 002	13 162	9 304	2 632	2 040	52 140	4 278	-1 681	46 131	48 728	-3 412
Q2	16 755	14 029	8 727	2 216	4 467	46 194	3 413	-2 255	51 510	52 668	6 474
Q3	18 605	15 155	8 354	2 565	4 490	49 169	4 077	-1 427	50 190	52 840	3 671
Q4	20 462	16 820	7 926	2 067	4 270†	51 545†	3 305	-3 264	51 358	51 399	-146†
1992 Q1	23 531	15 823	9 384	2 967	2 850	54 555	4 569	-977	52 705†	56 297†	1 742
Q2	16 146	14 737	9 430	1 876†	3 772	45 961	3 215†	-1 836†	55 022	56 401	10 440
1991 Aug	4 297	6 325	2 653	469	1 689	15 433	1 138	-145	16 529	17 522	2 089
Sep	5 157	4 107	2 568	1 490	1 434	14 756	1 330	22	16 592	17 944	3 188
Oct	9 812	4 785	2 964	822	1 340†	19 723†	1 147	-1 486	17 964	17 625	-2 098†
Nov	4 759	7 375	2 391	570	1 419	16 514	1 527	15	16 036	17 578	1 064
Dec	5 891	4 660	2 571	675	1 511	15 308	631	-1 793	17 358	16 196	888
1992 Jan	13 267	4 525	3 428	682	1 423	23 325	1 641	-68	17 892	19 465	-3 860
Feb	4 917	6 400	2 869	661	741	15 588	1 316	-817	16 864	17 363	1 775
Mar	5 347	4 898	3 087	1 624	686	15 642	1 612	-92	17 949†	19 469†	3 827
Apr	7 074	4 813	3 179	742†	989	16 797	1 132	-595†	19 093	19 630	2 833
May	4 373	5 965	3 025	529	1 354	15 246	1 499	-799	17 793	18 493	3 247
Jun	4 699	3 959	3 226	605	1 429	13 918	584†	-442	18 136	18 278	4 360
Jul	8 507	4 803	3 059	565	1 364	18 298	1 760	-1 662	18 971	19 069	771

Relationships between columns 1+2+3+4+5=6; 7+8+9=10; 10-6=11
Note: For further details see *Financial Statistics* table 3.12.
1 Excluding Northern Ireland contributions
2 Including some elements of expenditure that are not separately identified.
3 Net of certain receipts, on-lending to local authorities and public corporations.

17.2 Public sector borrowing requirement[1]

£ million

	Total		Contributions by:			Financed by:				
						Banks and building societies/Overseas sector			Other private sector	
						External finance				
	Not seasonally adjusted	Seasonally adjusted[2]	Central government (own account)[3]	Local authorities[4]	Public corporations[4]	Borrowing in sterling from banks	Foreign currency borrowing from banks	Other external finance	Notes and coin	Other
	ABEN	ABFP	ABEB	ABEG	ABEM	AQXV	AQXW	ABGH	AQUP	AQGG
1988	-11 868	-11 976	-10 569	607	-1 906	-686	-572	-823	1 040	-7 080
1989	-9 276	-9 605	-9 656	585	-205	-3 577	-46	4 272	897	-10 186
1990	-2 120	-2 467	-1 113	3 904	-4 911	169	-29	-4 454	-101	940
1991	7 681†	7 327†	6 587†	1 875†	-781†	-972	37	2 868	461	4 484
Financial years										
1989/90	-7 932	-7 932	-5 369	1 321	-3 884	-620	-89	1 674	841	-9 822
1990/91	-457	-457	-2 922	3 443	-978	-543	105	-2 618	711	1 147
1991/92	13 733	13 733	11 741	1 689	303	1 087	36	5 070	-732	7 531
1991 Q1	-2 583†	-57†	-3 412	1 349	-520†	-2 324	-95	-224	466	-831
Q2	6 989	1 908	6 474	270	245	3 393	-7	1 960	-37	1 129
Q3	3 774	2 886	3 671†	264†	-161	-1 097	19	785	-396	4 358
Q4	-499	2 590	-146†	-8†	-345	-944	120	347	428	-172
1992 Q1	3 469	6 349	1 742	1 163	564	-265	-96	1 978	-727	2 216
Q2	10 688	5 607	10 440	125	123	..	..	..	..	..

1 For further details see *Financial Statistics* Tables 2.3, 2.5 and 2.6.
2 Financial year constrained.
3 An increase in debt is shown positive.
4 Includes direct borrowing from central government.

Source: Central Statistical Office

17.3 Selected financial statistics[1]

£ million

	National savings[2]	Building societies Deposits Not seasonally adjusted	Building societies Deposits Seasonally adjusted	Building societies Advances Not seasonally adjusted	Building societies Advances Seasonally adjusted	Unit trusts	Total capital issues (net)	Net inflow into life assurance & super-annuation funds
Amount outstanding 31 Dec	ACUV	AHIX		AHIF		AGXB		
1991	39 534	..		204 297		55 145		
Net transactions	ACVX	AHKB	AHHR	AAMN	AHHU	AGXE	AJAD	AALV
1988	1 492	20 685	..	24 926	..	1 796	7 062	23 978
1989	-1 489	17 517	..	26 460	..	3 864	7 863	33 781
1990	932	18 052	..	26 338	..	393	2 901	37 225
1991	2 254	17 890	..	21 843	..	2 770	11 054	41 594
1991 Q2	585	4 833	5 153	5 543	5 493	426	4 032	11 931
Q3	771	4 013	3 999	5 911	5 566	785	2 451	11 181
Q4	601	2 909	3 317	5 402	5 173	283	4 044	9 855
1992 Q1	1 248†	4 727	3 922	3 764	4 394	256	1 823†	7 869
Q2	1 516	1 988	2 400	4 309	4 256	464	1 585	..
1991 Aug	244	418	1 284	1 955	1 829	221	751	..
Sep	249	1 472	1 378	1 821	1 746	358	574	..
Oct	263	860	1 274	1 845	1 712	123	2 696	..
Nov	191	196	1 425	2 222	1 829	59	906	..
Dec	147	1 853	618	1 335	1 632	101	442	..
1992 Jan	345†	3 270	1 428	1 485	1 699	54	931†	..
Feb	372†	455	1 212	1 022	1 537	-33	299	..
Mar	531	1 002	1 282	1 257	1 158	235	593	..
Apr	510	772	480	1 550	1 683	253	490	..
May	573	643	1 136	1 310	1 327	235	347	..
Jun	433	573	784	1 449	1 246	-24	748	..
Jul	..	..	..	..	..	..	811	..

	Banks[3] UK private sector deposits Sterling Not seasonally adjusted	Banks[3] UK private sector deposits Sterling Seasonally adjusted	Banks[3] UK private sector deposits Other currencies	Banks[3] Lending to the private sector Sterling Not seasonally adjusted	Banks[3] Lending to the private sector Sterling Seasonally adjusted	Banks[3] Lending to the private sector Other currencies	Credit business: Total agreements Not seasonally adjusted	Credit business: Total agreements Seasonally adjusted	Consumer credit Not seasonally adjusted	Consumer credit Seasonally adjusted
Amount outstanding 31 Dec	AEAS		AGAK	AECE		AECK	RKZE		AILA	
1991	321 617†		37 393†	405 705†		62 055	63 862†		53 449	
Net transactions	AEAT	AEAW	AEAZ	AECF	AECI	AECL	RKZF	RKZJ	-AIKL	-AIKM
1988	36 020		3 453	56 930		9 705	8 321		6 745†	
1989	45 258†		9 364†	64 171		16 301	7 523		6 551	
1990	31 788		10 610	46 768		2 554	4 514†		4 399	
1991	13 038		4 611	13 753†		9 108	29		2 208	
1991 Q2	5 585†	3 222†	1 673†	521	3 777	889	743†	544†	980†	850
Q3	2 675	2 658	3 290	7 060	4 253	888	150	-118	822	555
Q4	3 774	4 475	-1 863	155†	847†	5 584	-18	-340	528	423
1992 Q1	541	2 196	2 738	2 483	1 277	-2 354	-759	-39	-692	-582
Q2	5 630	3 427	344	2 838	6 102	-116	113	-112	199	..
1991 Aug	580†	..	213	902	..	-688	..	..	..	..
Sep	4 514	..	1 764†	6 941†	..	2 582	..	..	..	..
Oct	-2 049	..	-60†	-3 093†	..	2 127	..	..	..	..
Nov	1 231	..	-187	714	..	3 028†	..	..	..	..
Dec	4 592	..	-1 616	2 534	..	429	..	..	..	..
1992 Jan	-3 357	..	2 322	-1 032	..	-181	..	..	..	..
Feb	143	..	-885	-936	..	-1 687	..	..	..	..
Mar	3 755	..	1 301	4 450	..	-486	..	..	..	..
Apr	208	..	994	-1 086	..	381	..	..	..	..
May	2 147	..	-719	-1 140	..	691	..	..	..	..
Jun	3 275	..	69	5 063	..	-1 188	..	..	..	..

1 For further details see *Financial Statistics*, Tables 3.9, 6.1, 6.8, 6.9, 7.1, 7.5, 7.7, 9.3, 12.1.
2 Total administered by the Department for National Savings.
3 Monthly figures relate to calendar months.

Sources: Central Statistical Office;
Department for National Savings;
Building Societies Association;
Unit Trust Association;
Bank of England;
Department of Trade and Industry

17.4 Monetary aggregates

£ million

	Amount outstanding					
	'Narrow' money		'Broad' money			
	M0-the wide monetary base		M2		M4	
	Not seasonally adjusted	Seasonally adjusted	Not seasonally adjusted	Seasonally adjusted	Not seasonally adjusted	Seasonally adjusted
	AVAD	AVAE	AUYC	AUYG	AUYM	AUYN
1985	15 161	14 278	145 701	144 699	224 899	225 094
1986	15 945	15 027	167 120	166 040	261 400	261 219
1987	16 633	15 663	185 468	184 291	303 662	302 999
1988	18 040	16 868	214 968	213 442	356 420	355 407
1989	19 006	17 828	236 257	234 521	423 405[†]	422 369[†]
1990	19 493	18 295	255 202	253 607	474 293	473 366
1991	20 073	18 848	278 286	276 628	502 005	501 121
1989 Q4	19 006	17 828	236 257	234 521	423 405[†]	422 369[†]
1990 Q1	17 600	18 017	239 062	238 528	439 207	438 209
Q2	18 194	18 238	245 486	244 122	456 665	453 609
Q3	18 325	18 288	250 041	249 594	466 892	464 101
Q4	19 493	18 295	255 202	253 607	474 293	473 366
1991 Q1	18 161	18 465	263 587	262 776	483 079	481 876
Q2	18 581	18 594	271 047	269 446	493 165	489 579
Q3	18 757	18 713	273 265	273 148	497 691	495 495
Q4	20 073	18 848	278 286	276 628	502 005	501 121
1992 Q1	18 383	18 879	280 529	279 742	507 142	505 697
Q2	18 847	18 825	281 616	280 109	514 934	511 364
1991 May	18 566	18 527	267 930	267 833	489 058[†]	489 041[†]
Jun	18 581	18 594	271 047	269 446	493 165	489 579
Jul	18 771	18 605	270 294	270 331	491 658	491 438
Aug	18 915	18 594	270 293	272 121	492 416	493 328
Sep	18 757	18 713	273 265	273 148	497 691	495 495
Oct	18 700	18 767	273 806	274 341	495 911	497 293
Nov	18 749	18 809	275 476	275 578	498 446	499 410
Dec	20 073	18 848	278 286	276 628	502 005	501 121
1992 Jan	18 598	18 839	276 355	277 014	501 584	503 275
Feb	18 330	18 867	275 892[†]	278 052[†]	502 309	505 429
Mar	18 383	18 879	280 529	279 742	507 142	505 697
Apr	18 913	18 960	279 343	278 563	508 974	509 576
May	19 095	18 984	280 400	280 316	510 756	510 839
Jun	18 847	18 825	281 616	280 109	514 934	511 364

Source: Bank of England

17.5 Selected interest rates, exchange rates and security prices

	Selected retail banks' base rate	Average discount rate on Treasury bills	Inter-bank 3 month rate	British government securities 20 years yield[1]	Sterling exchange rate index 1985=100	Exchange rate US spot	Ordinary share price index[2]
		AJNB		AJLX	AJHV	AJGA	AJMA
1991 Jul	11.00	10.45	11.13-11.13	10.10	90.3	1.6840	1 208.52
Aug	11.00	10.07	10.78-10.81	9.89	90.7	1.6760	1 244.49
Sep	10.50	9.69	10.19-10.25	9.54	91.1	1.7505	1 265.42
Oct	10.50	9.98	10.50-10.56	9.62	90.5	1.7380	1 245.25
Nov	10.50	10.08	10.59-10.63	9.68	91.0	1.7630	1 210.28
Dec	10.50	10.19	10.94-11.00	9.56	91.2	1.8678	1 156.90
1992 Jan	10.50	9.88	10.63-10.66	9.34	90.8	1.7925	1 203.07
Feb	10.50	9.74	10.31-10.34	9.21	90.8	1.7580	1 218.70
Mar	10.50	10.21	10.78-10.81	9.54	90.1	1.7350	1 199.04
Apr	10.50	9.81	10.50-10.56	9.33	91.3	1.7727	1 225.16
May	10.50	9.43	10.00-10.00	8.99	92.8	1.8312	1 310.73
Jun	10.00	9.46	10.06-10.13	9.02	92.8	1.9030	1 205.01
Jul	10.00	9.61	10.31-10.25	8.88	..	..	1 171.62

Source: Bank of England

1 Average of working days.
2 *Financial Times* Actuaries share indices 10 April 1962 = 100. All classes
(750 shares) index.

18 Prices and wages

18.1 General index of retail prices[1]

	All items	All items except seasonal food[2]	Food	Alcoholic drink	Tobacco	Housing	Fuel and light	Durable household goods	Clothing and footwear	Transport and vehicles	Miscellaneous goods	Services	Meals bought and consumed outside the home
15 January 1974=100													
Annual averages													
	CBAB	CBAP	CBAN	CBAA	CBAC	CBAH	CBAG	CBAE	CBAD	CBAO	CBAJ	CBAM	CBAI
1982	320.4	322.0	299.3	341.0	413.3	358.3	433.3	243.8	210.5	343.5	325.8	331.6	341.7
1983	335.1	337.1	308.8	366.4	440.9	367.1	465.4	250.4	214.8	366.3	345.6	342.9	364.0
1984	351.8	353.1	326.1	387.7	489.0	400.7	478.8	256.7	214.6	374.7	364.7	357.3	390.8
1985	373.2	375.4	336.3	412.1	532.4	452.3	499.3	263.9	222.9	392.5	392.2	381.3	413.3
1986	385.9	387.9	347.3	430.6	584.9	478.1	506.0	266.7	229.2	390.1	409.2	400.5	439.5
1987 Jan 1	394.5	396.4	354.0	100.0	602.9	502.4	506.1	265.6	230.8	399.7	413.0	408.8	454.8

		All items	Food and catering	Alcohol and tobacco	Housing and household expenditure	Personal expenditure	Travel and leisure	All items except seasonal food[2]	All items except food	Seasonal food[2,3]	Non-seasonal food[3]	All items except housing	Nationalised industries[4]	Consumer durables
13 January 1987=100														
Weights 1991		*1000*	*198*	*109*	*353*	*101*	*239*	*976*	*849*	*24*	*127*	*808*		*128*
Weights 1992		*1000*	*199*	*116*	*344*	*99*	*242*	*978*	*848*	*22*	*130*	*828*		*127*
Annual averages														
		CHAW	CHBS	CHBT	CHBU	CHBV	CHBW	CHAX	CHAY	CHBP	CHBB	CHAZ	CHBX	CHBY
1987		101.9	101.4	101.2	102.1	101.4	102.6	101.9	102.0	101.6	101.0	101.6	100.9	101.2
1988		106.9	105.7	105.7	108.4	105.2	107.2	107.0	107.3	102.4	105.0	105.8	106.7	103.7
1989		115.2	111.9	110.8	121.9	111.2	112.8	115.5	116.1	105.0	111.6	111.5	..	107.2
1990		126.1	120.8	120.5	139.0	117.6	119.8	126.4	127.4	116.4	119.9	119.2	..	111.3
1991		133.5	128.6	136.2	142.2	123.6	128.9	133.8	135.1	121.6	126.3	128.3	..	114.8
1990 Jan	16	119.5	117.2	113.7	128.4	113.4	114.8	119.6	120.2	116.3	116.0	114.6	..	108.0
Feb	13	120.2	118.1	114.3	129.0	114.7	115.4	120.3	120.9	118.7	116.7	115.3	..	109.1
Mar	13	121.4	118.7	114.8	131.3	115.6	115.9	121.4	122.1	119.6	117.3	115.9	..	109.9
Apr	10	125.1	119.9	118.6	138.5	117.0	118.0	125.1	126.3	123.4	118.0	117.6	..	111.0
May	15	126.2	121.2	120.9	139.8	117.6	118.6	126.3	127.4	123.6	119.4	118.8	..	111.6
Jun	12	126.7	121.3	121.3	140.7	117.5	119.1	126.9	128.0	118.3	120.3	119.1	..	111.5
Jul	17	126.8	120.6	122.4	141.4	116.0	119.6	127.3	128.4	108.1	120.7	119.1	..	109.7
Aug	14	128.1	121.7	123.0	142.5	117.2	121.4	128.5	129.6	112.2	121.4	120.3	..	110.7
Sep	11	129.3	120.3	123.5	143.6	119.3	123.5	129.8	131.1	111.5	121.8	121.6	..	112.5
Oct	16	130.3	122.5	124.4	144.8	120.3	124.6	130.7	132.2	111.8	121.9	122.6	..	113.2
Nov	13	130.0	123.4	124.6	143.8	121.1	123.7	130.4	131.7	114.5	122.4	122.7	..	113.8
Dec	11	129.9	124.1	125.1	143.8	121.1	122.4	130.2	131.4	119.2	122.6	122.6	..	114.1
1991 Jan	15	130.2	124.9	126.0	144.2	118.6	122.8	130.4	131.6	121.2	123.1	122.7	..	110.7
Feb	12	130.9	126.2	126.8	145.0	119.7	123.1	131.1	132.2	125.9	124.0	123.5	..	111.8
Mar	12	131.4	126.4	127.3	145.5	120.9	123.6	131.6	132.8	124.4	124.4	123.9	..	113.0
Apr	16	133.1	128.5	136.9	141.7	123.6	127.5	133.3	134.5	125.6	125.8	127.6	..	115.2
May	14	133.5	128.6	137.9	141.5	124.2	128.9	133.8	135.1	122.5	126.2	128.5	..	116.0
Jun	11	134.1	129.8	138.4	141.7	124.6	129.4	134.3	135.5	126.0	127.1	129.3	..	116.1
Jul	16	133.8	128.8	139.1	141.0	122.3	130.6	134.2	135.4	117.3	126.8	129.2	..	113.2
Aug	13	134.1	129.7	139.6	140.9	122.7	130.9	134.4	135.6	121.6	127.3	129.8	..	113.9
Sep	10	134.6	129.1	140.0	141.3	125.6	131.6	135.2	136.4	114.9	127.4	130.4	..	116.2
Oct	15	135.1	129.4	140.3	141.0	126.7	132.8	135.6	136.9	116.1	127.4	131.1	..	116.9
Nov	12	135.6	130.4	140.8	141.3	127.0	133.1	135.9	137.3	121.3	127.8	131.7	..	117.3
Dec	10	135.7	130.9	141.0	141.6	127.0	132.9	136.0	137.4	122.7	128.0	131.8	..	117.6
1992 Jan	14	135.6	131.9	141.8	141.7	123.5	132.9	135.9	137.1	125.2	129.0	131.6	..	113.2
Feb	11	136.3	132.6	142.3	142.2	124.7	133.7	136.6	137.8	126.0	129.7	132.3	..	114.4
Mar	10	136.7	133.0	142.7	141.9	126.1	134.6	137.0	138.2	124.8	130.2	133.0	..	115.7
Apr	14	138.8	132.8	146.6	144.8	127.3	136.9	139.2	140.7	122.4	130.1	134.4	..	116.2
May	12	139.3	133.4	147.3	145.1	127.5	137.5	139.7	141.2	120.9	131.0	134.9	..	116.4
Jun	9	139.3	133.1	147.6	145.0	127.7	137.8	139.9	141.3	117.4	131.0	135.0	..	116.4
Jul	14	138.8	131.9	148.1	145.0	125.0	137.8	139.6	141.1	105.8	130.9	134.3	..	113.1

1 Following the recommendation of the Retail Price Index Advisory Committee, the index has been re-referenced to make 13 January, 1987=100. Further details can be found in the April 1987 edition of *Employment Gazette*.

2 Seasonal food is defined as; items of food the prices of which show significant seasonal variations. These are fresh fruit and vegetables, fresh fish, eggs and home-killed lamb.

3 For the February, March and April 1988 indices, the weights for seasonal and non-seasonal food were 24 and 139 respectively. Thereafter the weight for home-killed lamb (a seasonal item) was increased by 1 and that for imported lamb (a non-seasonal item) correspondingly reduced by 1 in the light of new information about their relative shares of household expenditure.

4 From December 1989 the Nationalised Industries Index is no longer published. Industries remaining nationalised in December 1989 were coal, electricity, post and rail.

Source: Central Statistical Office

18.2 General index of retail prices[1]
Detailed figures for various groups, sub-groups and sections

13 January 1987=100

		Group and sub-group weights in 1992	1992 Jan	1992 Feb	1992 Mar	1992 Apr	1992 May	1992 Jun	1992 Jul
Day of month			14	11	10	14	12	9	14
All items	CHAW	1000	135.6	136.3	136.7	138.8	139.3	139.3	138.8
All items excluding mortgage interest	CHMK	924	133.1	133.8	134.5	136.7	137.1	137.2	136.7
Food	CHBA	152	128.4	129.1	129.4	128.9	129.5	129.0	127.2
Bread	DOAA	7	133.3	135.0	134.9	134.8	135.4	135.2	134.1
Cereals	DOAB	4	135.5	136.5	136.6	136.6	136.0	135.4	136.1
Biscuits and cakes	DOAC	9	132.4	132.8	134.4	133.8	135.1	134.8	136.5
Beef	DOAD	7	125.8	125.1	125.7	124.5	125.5	125.2	123.6
Lamb	DOAE	3	113.3	115.9	116.1	123.6	122.2	115.2	109.7
of which home-killed lamb	DOAF	2	114.1	122.6	123.0	129.9	127.9	116.6	109.1
Pork	DOAG	3	125.4	124.9	127.5	128.3	133.6	130.5	126.4
Bacon	DOAH	4	135.6	136.8	137.8	137.5	137.8	138.8	137.9
Poultry	DOAI	6	111.0	111.7	114.2	109.6	112.7	109.7	112.5
Other meat	DOAJ	9	121.8	123.4	123.5	123.2	124.1	123.9	123.0
Fish	DOAK	5	127.7	126.6	125.6	124.5	125.8	124.6	126.4
of which fresh fish	DOAL	1	147.7	143.0	144.7	144.0	145.8	136.4	140.4
Butter	DOAM	1	126.3	125.3	125.1	127.2	127.0	127.0	126.8
Oils and fats	DOAN	2	127.2	127.8	127.0	128.3	129.0	128.7	126.7
Cheese	DOAO	4	126.7	128.7	130.1	130.1	133.1	134.2	132.7
Eggs	DOAP	2	119.4	119.2	116.8	115.3	116.0	113.9	111.8
Milk, fresh	DOAQ	11	135.9	136.1	136.5	136.1	136.4	137.6	138.7
Milk products	DOAR	3	135.8	135.9	136.4	137.6	137.7	138.8	136.1
Tea	DOAS	2	152.3	152.3	152.9	152.3	151.9	150.9	150.6
Coffee and other hot drinks	DOAT	2	91.4	91.4	90.9	90.8	91.2	91.4	90.8
Soft drinks	DOAU	12	151.6	154.7	156.0	156.1	156.2	156.1	155.8
Sugar and preserves	DOAV	2	138.8	139.2	138.8	137.7	137.6	137.3	136.8
Sweets and chocolate	DOAW	13	118.5	119.3	119.8	120.1	121.4	121.8	122.7
Potatoes	DOAX	7	126.8	126.9	126.7	128.6	132.4	122.6	121.2
of which unprocessed potatoes	DOAY	3	119.3	119.6	118.0	121.9	126.8	103.6	99.8
Vegetables	DOAZ	10	122.9	121.7	122.0	114.1	111.6	113.0	99.7
of which other fresh vegetables	DOBA	7	119.4	117.1	117.8	106.2	102.6	105.7	88.0
Fruit	DOBB	9	132.6	134.9	132.6	133.4	131.1	132.4	121.0
of which fresh fruit	DOBC	7	134.8	137.6	134.1	135.3	132.0	133.7	119.1
Other foods	DOBD	15	133.0	133.5	133.6	134.3	134.0	135.0	135.0
Catering	CHBC	47	144.3	144.8	145.3	146.3	147.2	147.9	148.3
Restaurant meals	DOBE	25	144.2	144.7	145.1	146.0	146.8	147.3	147.8
Canteen meals	DOBF	7	146.2	146.5	147.2	148.1	148.7	150.1	150.4
Take-aways and snacks	DOBG	15	143.5	144.0	144.9	146.1	147.0	147.7	148.2
Alcoholic drink	CHBD	80	143.9	144.6	145.2	147.1	147.9	148.4	149.2
Beer	DOBH	46	148.0	148.7	149.1	150.7	151.5	151.9	153.0
Beer on sales	DOBI	40	150.0	150.5	150.8	152.5	153.2	153.8	155.0
Beer off sales	DOBJ	6	134.0	136.2	137.1	138.1	139.2	138.7	138.5
Wines and spirits	DOBK	34	137.9	138.8	139.6	141.8	142.6	143.2	143.7
Wines and spirits on sales	DOBL	13	143.8	144.4	145.2	147.8	148.7	149.1	149.6
Wines and spirits off sales	DOBM	21	133.6	134.6	135.4	137.4	138.2	138.8	139.3
Tobacco	CHBE	36	137.4	137.5	137.5	145.7	146.1	146.1	146.0
Cigarettes	DOBN	32	138.0	138.1	138.1	146.6	147.1	147.0	146.9
Other tobacco	DOBO	4	133.4	133.8	133.9	139.5	139.9	139.9	139.9
Housing	CHBF	172	156.0	156.5	155.1	161.1	161.4	161.1	161.5
Rent	DOBP	35	158.3	158.5	158.7	168.5	168.7	168.7	168.9
Mortgage interest payments	DOBQ	64	188.1	189.3	184.3	182.8	183.6	183.5	181.4
Community Charge	DOBR	31	120.9	120.9	120.9	137.0	136.6	136.6	136.6
Water and other charges	DOBS	9	174.1	174.1	174.1	191.7	191.8	191.8	191.8
Repairs and maintenance charges	DOBT	9	141.5	141.8	142.0	143.2	143.5	143.8	144.1
Do-it-yourself materials	DOBU	16	139.5	140.2	141.5	140.3	141.0	137.5	143.2
Dwelling insurance and ground rent	CHMJ	8	190.6	190.5	190.0	189.7	189.9	190.2	200.6

Indices are given to one decimal place to provide as much information as is available but precision is greater at higher levels of aggregation, ie at sub-group and group levels.

1 *Retail Prices Index 1914-1990* (HMSO Price £10.95 net) contains group and sub-group indices and weights back to 1956, group indices back to 1947, together with cost of living indices as far back as 1914.

Source: Central Statistical Office

18.2 General index of retail prices[1]
Detailed figures for various groups, sub-groups and sections
continued

13 January 1987 = 100

		Group and sub-group weights in 1992	1992 Jan	1992 Feb	1992 Mar	1992 Apr	1992 May	1992 Jun	1992 Jul
	Day of month		14	11	10	14	12	9	14
Fuel and light	CHBG	47	127.7	127.8	127.6	127.8	128.2	128.3	128.4
Coal and solid fuels	DOBW	3	117.5	117.6	117.6	117.6	116.5	112.0	112.1
Electricity	DOBX	24	139.6	139.6	139.6	140.0	141.0	142.0	142.7
Gas	DOBY	18	119.5	119.5	119.5	119.5	119.5	119.5	118.9
Oil and other fuel	DOBZ	2	104.5	106.7	103.5	103.0	103.8	103.2	103.4
Household goods	CHBH	77	123.9	125.0	126.3	126.4	126.9	126.8	125.1
Furniture	DOCA	19	123.6	125.6	127.5	127.1	128.1	126.7	124.9
Furnishings	DOCB	13	120.2	121.6	123.3	123.1	123.3	124.1	120.9
Electrical appliances	DOCC	11	109.5	110.4	112.1	112.8	112.0	112.3	108.9
Other household equipment	DOCD	9	129.9	131.0	130.9	131.7	131.9	132.3	130.1
Household consumables	DOCE	16	140.6	141.7	141.8	142.3	144.0	143.9	144.5
Pet care	DOCF	9	119.2	118.4	120.1	120.0	119.6	120.2	120.3
Household services	CHBI	48	135.3	135.3	135.5	136.6	136.6	136.6	138.1
Postage	DOCG	2	138.1	138.1	138.1	138.1	138.1	138.1	138.1
Telephones, telemessages etc	DOCH	16	120.9	120.8	120.8	120.7	120.7	120.6	120.6
Domestic services	DOCI	8	146.8	147.3	148.0	148.9	149.6	150.0	150.8
Fees and subscriptions	DOCJ	22	143.1	143.0	143.2	145.4	145.1	145.2	148.3
Clothing and footwear	CHBJ	59	115.7	117.2	118.9	120.0	120.0	120.3	115.5
Men's outerwear	DOCK	11	115.0	117.7	120.6	119.6	121.8	121.9	114.3
Women's outerwear	DOCL	18	104.9	106.1	107.5	110.8	109.5	109.9	104.6
Children's outerwear	DOCM	7	115.5	117.1	119.6	120.6	120.8	120.8	115.8
Other clothing	DOCN	11	131.4	133.0	135.2	135.1	135.3	135.7	132.7
Footwear	DOCO	12	121.8	122.2	122.8	123.0	123.0	123.2	120.5
Personal goods and services	CHBQ	40	138.4	139.2	139.9	141.3	141.8	142.0	143.1
Personal articles	DOCP	11	111.5	112.6	113.5	113.7	114.0	114.1	113.2
Chemists goods	DOCQ	17	142.5	143.1	143.9	146.1	146.6	146.7	148.1
Personal services	DOCR	12	164.5	164.9	165.4	166.9	167.8	168.4	171.6
Motoring expenditure	CHBK	143	134.0	135.0	136.4	139.1	140.0	140.3	140.3
Purchase of motor vehicles	DOCS	67	127.4	128.4	129.9	130.3	131.0	131.6	131.4
Maintenance of motor vehicles	DOCT	21	149.6	150.8	151.2	152.0	152.6	153.2	153.6
Petrol and oil	DOCU	33	124.6	126.0	128.0	132.4	134.1	133.8	133.6
Vehicle tax and insurance	DOCV	22	157.5	157.5	157.5	168.0	168.0	168.0	168.9
Fares and other travel costs	CHBR	20	140.9	141.4	141.8	142.6	142.9	145.0	144.9
Rail fares	DOCW	5	150.7	150.7	150.7	150.8	151.3	151.2	151.2
Bus and coach fares	DOCX	6	150.1	150.1	150.8	153.4	153.9	154.4	154.5
Other travel costs	DOCY	9	128.2	129.2	129.6	129.6	129.8	133.8	133.5
Leisure goods	CHBL	47	119.3	119.9	120.4	120.8	121.1	120.9	120.7
Audio-visual equipment	DOCZ	11	84.3	84.5	84.6	84.5	84.1	83.9	81.9
Records, tapes and CDs	DODA	6	110.4	110.7	110.9	111.4	111.7	111.8	111.9
Toys, photographic and sports goods	DODB	10	119.3	120.1	120.9	120.8	121.4	121.5	120.8
Books and newspapers	DODC	15	147.4	148.3	149.4	150.9	151.4	152.1	153.0
Gardening products	DODD	5	136.3	137.2	138.3	138.2	138.6	135.7	139.4
Leisure services	CHBM	32	145.5	145.6	145.8	149.6	150.0	150.2	150.2
Television licences and rentals	DODE	9	118.1	118.1	118.1	121.0	121.0	121.0	119.8
Entertainment and other recreation	DODF	23	162.1	162.3	162.5	166.9	167.5	167.8	168.4

Indices are given to one decimal place to provide as much information as is available but precision is greater at higher levels of aggregation, ie at sub-group and group levels.

1 *Retail Prices Index 1914-1990* (HMSO Price £10.95 net) contains group and sub-group indices and weights back to 1956, group indices back to 1947, together with cost of living indices as far back as 1914.

Source: Central Statistical Office

18.3 General index of retail prices (all items)[1]

	Annual average	Jan	Feb	Mar	Apr	May	Jun	Jul	Aug	Sep	Oct	Nov	Dec
January 1974 =100													
	CBAB												
1963	54.0	53.5	54.0	54.1	54.2	54.2	54.2	53.9	53.7	53.9	54.1	54.2	54.3
1964	55.8	54.6	54.6	54.8	55.3	55.8	56.0	56.0	56.2	56.2	56.3	56.7	56.9
1965	58.4	57.1	57.1	57.3	58.4	58.6	58.8	58.8	58.9	58.9	59.0	59.2	59.5
1966	60.7	59.6	59.6	59.7	60.5	60.9	61.1	60.8	61.2	61.1	61.2	61.6	61.7
1967	62.3	61.8	61.8	61.8	62.3	62.3	62.5	62.1	62.0	61.9	62.4	62.8	63.2
1968	65.2	63.4	63.7	63.9	65.1	65.1	65.4	65.4	65.5	65.6	65.9	66.1	66.9
1969	68.7	67.3	67.7	67.9	68.7	68.6	68.9	68.9	68.7	68.9	69.4	69.6	70.1
1970	73.1	70.6	71.0	71.4	72.5	72.7	72.9	73.5	73.4	73.8	74.6	75.1	75.6
1971	80.0	76.6	77.1	77.7	79.4	79.9	80.4	80.9	81.0	81.1	81.5	82.0	82.4
1972	85.7	82.9	83.3	83.6	84.4	84.8	85.3	85.6	86.3	86.8	88.0	88.3	88.7
1973	93.5	89.3	89.9	90.4	92.1	92.8	93.3	93.7	94.0	94.8	96.7	97.4	98.1
1974	108.5	100.0	101.7	102.6	106.1	107.6	108.7	109.7	109.8	111.0	113.2	115.2	116.9
1975	134.8	119.9	121.9	124.3	129.1	134.5	137.1	138.5	139.3	140.5	142.5	144.2	146.0
1976	157.1	147.9	149.8	150.6	153.5	155.2	156.0	156.3	158.5	160.6	163.5	165.8	168.0
1977	182.0	172.4	174.1	175.8	180.3	181.7	183.6	183.8	184.7	185.7	186.5	187.4	188.4
1978	197.1	189.5	190.6	191.8	194.6	195.7	197.2	198.1	199.4	200.2	201.1	202.5	204.2
1979	223.5	207.2	208.9	210.6	214.2	215.9	219.6	229.1	230.9	233.2	235.6	237.7	239.4
1980	263.7	245.3	248.8	252.2	260.8	263.2	265.7	267.9	268.5	270.2	271.9	274.1	275.6
1981	295.0	277.3	279.8	284.0	292.2	294.1	295.8	297.1	299.3	301.0	303.7	306.9	308.8
1982	320.4	310.6	310.7	313.4	319.7	322.0	322.9	323.0	323.1	322.9	324.5	326.1	325.5
1983	335.1	325.9	327.3	327.9	332.5	333.9	334.7	336.5	338.0	339.5	340.7	341.9	342.8
1984	351.8	342.6	344.0	345.1	349.7	351.0	351.9	351.5	354.8	355.5	357.7	358.8	358.5
1985	373.2	359.8	362.7	366.1	373.9	375.6	376.4	375.7	376.7	376.5	377.1	378.4	378.9
1986	385.9	379.7	381.1	381.6	385.3	386.0	385.8	384.7	385.9	387.8	388.4	391.7	393.0
1987	..	394.5	..	..	..	..	..	..	..	..	..	..	..
January 1987=100													
	CHAW												
1987	101.9	100.0	100.4	100.6	101.8	101.9	101.9	101.8	102.1	102.4	102.9	103.4	103.3
1988	106.9	103.3	103.7	104.1	105.8	106.2	106.6	106.7	107.9	108.4	109.5	110.0	110.3
1989	115.2	111.0	111.8	112.3	114.3	115.0	115.4	115.5	115.8	116.6	117.5	118.5	118.8
1990	126.1	119.5	120.2	121.4	125.1	126.2	126.7	126.8	128.1	129.3	130.3	130.0	129.9
1991	133.5	130.2	130.9	131.4	133.1	133.5	134.1	133.8	134.1	134.6	135.1	135.6	135.7
1992	..	135.6	136.3	136.7	138.8	139.3	139.3	138.8	..	..	..	..	..

1 *Retail Prices Index 1914-1990* (HMSO Price £10.95 net) contains group and sub-group indices and weights back to 1956, group indices back to 1947, together with cost of living indices as far back as 1914.

Source: Central Statistical Office

18.4 Internal purchasing power of the pound (based on RPI)[1,2]

Pence

	Year in which purchasing power was 100p															
	1976	1977	1978	1979	1980	1981	1982	1983	1984	1985	1986	1987	1988	1989	1990	1991
	BAMI	BAMJ	BAMK	BAML	BAMM	BAMN	BAMO	BAMP	BAMQ	BAMR	BAMS	BAMT	BAMU	BAMV	BAMW	BASX
1976	100	116	125	142	168	188	204	213	224	238	246	256	268	289	317	335
1977	86	100	108	123	145	162	176	184	193	205	212	221	232	250	273	289
1978	80	92	100	113	134	150	163	170	178	189	196	204	214	231	252	267
1979	70	81	88	100	118	132	143	150	157	167	173	180	189	203	223	236
1980	60	69	75	85	100	112	122	127	133	142	146	152	160	172	189	200
1981	53	62	67	76	89	100	109	114	119	127	131	136	143	154	169	179
1982	49	57	62	70	82	92	100	105	110	116	120	125	132	142	155	164
1983	47	54	59	67	79	88	96	100	105	111	115	120	126	136	148	157
1984	45	52	56	64	75	84	91	95	100	106	110	114	120	129	141	150
1985	42	49	53	60	71	79	86	90	94	100	103	108	113	122	133	141
1986	41	47	51	58	68	76	83	87	91	97	100	104	109	118	129	136
1987	39	45	49	56	66	73	80	83	87	93	96	100	105	113	124	131
1988	37	43	47	53	63	70	76	79	83	89	92	95	100	108	118	125
1989	35	40	43	49	58	65	71	74	77	82	85	88	93	100	109	116
1990	32	37	40	45	53	59	64	67	71	75	78	81	85	91	100	106
1991	30	35	37	42	50	56	61	64	67	71	73	76	80	86	94	100

1 To find the purchasing power of the pound in 1980, given that it was 100 pence in 1976, select the column headed 1976 and look at the 1980 row. The result is 60 pence.

2 These figures are calculated by taking the inverse ratio of the respective annual averages of the General Index of Retail Prices. See table above.

Source: Central Statistical Office

18.5 Tax and price index

	January 1978=100 BSAA									January 1987=100 DQAB					
	1979	1980	1981	1982	1983	1984	1985	1986	1987	1987	1988	1989	1990	1991	1992
January	106.1	123.2	140.4	162.3	170.7	177.9	184.7	192.9	198.0	100.0	101.4	107.1	113.9	123.6	128.1
February	107.2	125.3	141.9	162.4	171.6	178.8	186.4	193.7	..	100.5	101.8	108.0	114.7	124.3	128.8
March	108.2	127.2	144.3	164.0	171.9	179.4	188.4	194.0	..	100.7	102.3	108.5	115.9	124.9	128.8
April	110.5	130.8	151.3	166.0	171.8	178.8	190.2	192.5	..	99.7	101.4	109.8	118.2	125.4	129.6
May	111.6	132.2	152.4	167.4	172.6	179.6	191.2	192.9	..	99.8	101.9	110.5	119.4	125.8	130.2
June	113.8	133.6	153.5	168.0	173.1	180.1	191.7	192.8	..	99.8	102.3	110.9	119.9	126.5	130.2
July	113.8	134.9	154.2	169.0	174.2	179.9	191.3	192.1	..	99.7	102.4	111.1	120.0	126.2	129.6
August	114.9	135.3	155.5	169.0	175.1	181.8	191.8	192.9	..	100.0	103.7	111.4	121.4	126.5	..
September	116.2	136.3	156.6	168.9	176.0	182.2	191.7	194.0	..	100.4	104.3	112.2	122.7	127.0	..
October	117.6	137.3	158.2	169.9	176.7	183.5	191.4	194.3	..	100.9	105.4	111.7	123.8	127.5	..
November	118.8	138.5	160.1	170.9	177.5	184.1	192.1	196.3	..	101.5	106.0	112.8	123.4	128.1	..
December	119.8	139.4	161.2	170.5	178.0	183.9	192.4	197.1	..	101.4	106.3	113.1	123.3	128.2	..

Percentage changes on one year earlier

Tax and price index

	1979	1980	1981	1982	1983	1984	1985	1986	1987	1987	1988	1989	1990	1991	1992
January	6.1	16.1	14.0	15.6	5.2	4.2	3.8	4.4	2.6		1.4	5.6	6.3	8.5	3.6
February	6.5	16.9	13.2	14.4	5.7	4.2	4.3	3.9	..	2.7	1.3	6.1	6.2	8.4	3.6
March	6.6	17.6	13.4	13.7	4.8	4.4	5.0	3.0	..	2.8	1.6	6.1	6.8	7.8	3.1
April	12.3	18.4	15.7	9.7	3.5	4.1	6.4	1.2	..	2.5	1.7	8.3	7.7	6.1	3.3
May	12.6	18.5	15.3	9.8	3.1	4.1	6.5	0.9	..	2.4	2.1	8.4	8.1	5.4	3.5
June	13.8	17.4	14.9	9.4	3.0	4.0	6.4	0.6	..	2.5	2.5	8.4	8.1	5.5	2.9
July	13.2	18.5	14.3	9.6	3.1	3.3	6.3	0.4	..	2.8	2.7	8.5	8.0	5.2	2.7
August	13.4	17.8	14.9	8.7	3.6	3.8	5.5	0.6	..	2.6	3.7	7.4	9.0	4.2	..
September	14.1	17.3	14.9	7.9	4.2	3.5	5.2	1.2	..	2.4	3.9	7.6	9.4	3.5	..
October	14.8	16.8	15.2	7.4	4.0	3.8	4.3	1.5	..	2.9	4.5	6.0	10.8	3.0	..
November	15.1	16.6	15.6	6.7	3.9	3.7	4.3	2.2	..	2.4	4.4	6.4	9.4	3.8	..
December	14.9	16.4	15.6	5.8	4.4	3.3	4.6	2.4	..	1.9	4.8	6.4	9.0	4.0	..

Retail prices index

	1979	1980	1981	1982	1983	1984	1985	1986	1987	1987	1988	1989	1990	1991	1992
January	9.3	18.4	13.0	12.0	4.9	5.1	5.0	5.5	3.9		3.3	7.5	7.7	9.0	4.1
February	9.6	19.1	12.5	11.0	5.3	5.1	5.4	5.1	..	3.9	3.3	7.8	7.5	8.9	4.1
March	9.8	19.8	12.6	10.4	4.6	5.2	6.1	4.2	..	4.0	3.5	7.9	8.1	8.2	4.0
April	10.1	21.8	12.0	9.4	4.0	5.2	6.9	3.0	..	4.2	3.9	8.0	9.4	6.4	4.3
May	10.3	21.9	11.7	9.5	3.7	5.1	7.0	2.8	..	4.1	4.2	8.3	9.7	5.8	4.3
June	11.4	21.0	11.3	9.2	3.7	5.1	7.0	2.5	..	4.2	4.6	8.3	9.8	5.8	3.9
July	15.6	16.9	10.9	8.7	4.2	4.5	6.9	2.4	..	4.4	4.8	8.2	9.8	5.5	3.7
August	15.8	16.3	11.5	8.0	4.6	5.0	6.2	2.4	..	4.4	5.7	7.3	10.6	4.7	..
September	16.5	15.9	11.4	7.3	5.1	4.7	5.9	3.0	..	4.2	5.9	7.6	10.9	4.1	..
October	17.2	15.4	11.7	6.8	5.0	5.0	5.4	3.0	..	4.5	6.4	7.3	10.9	3.7	..
November	17.4	15.3	12.0	6.3	4.8	4.9	5.5	3.5	..	4.1	6.4	7.7	9.7	4.3	..
December	17.2	15.1	12.0	5.4	5.3	4.6	5.7	3.7	..	3.7	6.8	7.7	9.3	4.5	..

Note: The purpose and methodology of the Tax and price index were described in an article in the August 1979 issue of *Economic Trends* and in the September *Economic Progress Report* published by the Treasury. The purpose is to produce a single index which measures changes in both direct taxes (including national insurance contributions) and in retail prices for a representative cross-section of taxpayers. Thus, while the Retail prices index may be used to measure changes in the purchasing power of after-tax income (and of the income of non-taxpayers) the Tax and price index takes account of the fact that taxpayers will have more or less to spend according to changes in direct taxation. The index measures the change in gross taxable income which would maintain after tax income in real terms.

The months April, May and June for the years 1979 and 1980 are affected by the late timing of the 1979 Budget.

Source: Central Statistical Office

18.6 Index numbers of producer prices

1985=100, monthly averages

	Materials and fuel purchased[1,2]													
	Manufacturing industry	Materials	Fuel	Manufacturing industry (seasonally adjusted)	Manufacturing other than food, drink and tobacco	Food, drink and tobacco manufacturing industries	Metal manufacturing	Extraction of minerals not elsewhere specified	Non-metallic mineral products	Chemical industry	Man-made fibres	Metal goods, engineering and vehicle industries	Metal goods not elsewhere specified	Mechanical engineering
SIC 1980 Division Class or Group	2 to 4		2 to 4		2 to 4 excl. 41/42	41/42	22	23	24	25	26	3	31	32
	DZBR	DZBS	DZBT	DZDQ	DZBU	DZBX	DZBY	DZBZ	DZCA	DZCB	DZCC	DZCD	DZCE	DZCF
1987	95.3	97.4	85.5	95.3	94.0	99.5	99.2	91.4	98.0	86.8	97.8	101.6	101.0	104.4
1988	98.4	101.5	84.3	98.4	98.4	100.9	110.3	91.7	101.2	85.7	100.6	110.0	111.4	111.6
1989	104.0	107.5	88.9	104.0	103.7	107.1	116.3	97.4	105.8	90.2	103.6	116.3	117.5	118.9
1990	103.8	106.6	91.3	103.8	102.8	109.2	111.8	103.0	110.6	95.2	105.4	114.9	114.2	122.5
1991	102.6	104.9	92.7	102.6	100.5	110.9	110.9	106.8	113.4	96.4	104.1	114.2	112.3	126.3
1988 Nov	99.8	102.8	86.3	99.8	100.0	102.1	114.1	92.8	103.3	85.8	103.4	113.3	115.1	114.5
Dec	102.6	103.6	97.7	100.4	103.3	103.4	117.4	97.7	105.8	87.6	104.6	115.8	117.4	115.8
1989 Jan	104.0	105.2	98.7	101.3	105.2	103.9	119.9	99.2	106.8	89.8	105.4	117.0	118.6	117.4
Feb	101.9	105.2	87.6	101.6	102.6	103.5	115.9	95.0	104.4	88.6	103.7	115.4	116.7	117.2
Mar	102.4	106.9	82.4	102.8	102.6	104.7	116.6	93.5	105.5	89.3	103.1	115.7	117.5	117.4
Apr	103.9	108.1	84.9	103.9	103.5	107.0	116.8	95.2	106.5	90.5	104.2	116.2	117.8	118.3
May	104.7	109.1	85.2	104.7	104.3	107.8	117.8	96.5	107.3	91.2	104.4	116.7	118.4	119.1
Jun	104.7	109.1	84.8	105.0	103.9	108.2	116.6	96.4	105.9	91.3	104.6	116.7	118.3	119.4
Jul	102.8	106.9	84.8	104.1	101.6	107.7	112.4	95.8	103.4	89.3	103.9	115.2	116.2	118.9
Aug	102.7	106.8	84.6	104.1	102.2	106.5	115.0	95.5	103.2	88.7	102.2	116.0	117.3	119.3
Sep	103.8	108.0	85.2	104.9	103.0	107.8	116.2	96.4	103.9	89.4	102.4	116.5	117.9	119.7
Oct	104.1	108.1	86.5	105.0	102.8	108.8	116.1	97.4	104.4	89.3	101.7	116.1	117.4	119.7
Nov	105.7	108.3	94.4	105.6	104.8	109.6	116.2	101.0	107.3	91.4	103.1	116.4	116.9	120.0
Dec	107.7	107.9	107.2	105.4	107.6	110.1	116.2	106.5	110.6	93.9	105.0	117.3	117.0	120.7
1990 Jan	107.4	107.5	107.8	104.8	107.5	110.1	113.9	108.1	111.8	95.9	106.8	116.7	116.0	121.8
Feb	104.6	106.9	94.9	104.4	103.5	109.8	109.6	102.4	108.8	93.4	104.8	114.2	113.4	120.9
Mar	105.1	108.8	88.8	105.5	103.7	110.8	113.9	100.1	109.4	91.8	104.1	115.6	114.9	121.4
Apr	104.7	108.8	86.2	104.4	102.4	112.0	113.0	99.4	109.4	91.1	104.4	115.4	115.0	122.2
May	103.6	107.8	84.5	103.4	101.3	111.0	113.0	98.8	108.7	89.8	104.0	115.0	114.9	122.2
Jun	102.1	106.3	83.2	102.3	99.8	110.1	111.7	98.0	108.4	88.4	103.6	114.1	113.9	122.1
Jul	101.1	104.9	83.5	102.2	98.8	109.2	110.5	98.0	108.5	88.6	103.0	114.0	113.3	122.3
Aug	101.9	105.3	87.1	103.1	101.6	106.6	111.4	101.7	110.1	96.1	103.4	114.4	113.8	122.5
Sep	104.1	107.6	88.4	105.3	104.7	106.8	114.8	104.0	111.3	101.4	103.9	115.6	115.3	123.4
Oct	103.4	106.3	91.3	104.1	104.1	106.6	111.8	106.6	112.4	103.6	107.5	114.6	113.6	123.4
Nov	103.0	104.7	95.4	102.8	102.7	107.7	108.4	107.8	112.9	101.3	108.9	114.2	112.4	123.4
Dec	104.7	104.7	104.9	102.9	104.1	109.5	110.1	111.3	115.2	100.6	110.2	115.5	113.3	124.2
1991 Jan	104.4	104.6	104.0	102.7	103.4	110.2	110.0	112.2	115.8	100.9	108.4	115.4	112.9	125.5
Feb	102.3	103.5	97.1	102.5	99.9	110.9	107.5	108.8	114.3	95.9	106.2	114.4	112.4	125.3
Mar	102.4	105.3	89.2	102.6	99.4	111.9	109.6	104.5	112.7	95.3	105.0	114.3	112.8	125.6
Apr	103.6	106.5	91.4	103.4	100.8	113.0	112.0	105.3	113.1	95.6	104.1	115.2	113.7	126.5
May	103.5	106.4	90.0	103.2	100.2	113.0	111.2	105.1	113.1	96.2	103.5	114.5	113.0	126.5
Jun	103.2	106.6	87.7	103.5	100.5	112.3	112.4	104.8	112.5	95.4	103.3	114.4	112.8	126.8
Jul	102.5	105.6	88.5	103.6	100.6	110.5	112.6	104.9	112.9	95.4	102.5	114.4	112.7	126.8
Aug	101.1	104.1	87.6	102.3	100.0	108.2	111.8	104.7	112.6	96.1	102.0	113.8	112.0	126.3
Sep	101.0	103.9	88.2	102.0	99.6	108.6	111.2	105.6	112.5	95.8	102.2	113.4	111.5	126.3
Oct	101.5	104.2	89.3	101.9	99.9	109.3	111.1	106.1	112.5	97.0	102.8	113.2	111.2	126.4
Nov	102.6	104.2	95.6	102.4	100.6	110.9	111.1	108.7	113.7	97.2	103.9	113.5	111.1	126.6
Dec	103.4	103.4	103.6	101.6	101.0	112.1	110.6	111.0	115.2	95.9	105.2	114.1	111.3	127.1
1992 Jan	103.2	103.2	103.4	101.5	100.6	112.4	110.0	110.3	115.3	96.0	105.1	114.0	110.7	127.7
Feb	103.2	104.4	97.8	103.2	99.8	113.7	110.2	108.1	114.4	95.4	104.2	113.8	111.2	127.7
Mar	102.2	105.1	89.3	102.4	98.3	113.9	110.2	105.5	113.2	93.8	103.1	113.7	111.3	127.9
Apr	102.7	105.1	92.2	102.3	98.9	114.2	110.0	107.3	113.6	94.7	103.9	114.0	111.6	128.4
May	102.2†	104.6†	91.3†	101.9†	98.3†	113.8	109.3†	107.5†	113.3†	94.7	103.8†	113.6†	110.9†	128.4†
Jun[3]	101.7	104.0†	91.3	102.1	97.9	113.1†	108.5	108.1	112.9	95.2†	103.8	113.6	110.9	128.4
Jul[3]	101.0	103.4	90.7	102.1	97.1	112.9	108.1	108.1	112.7	94.1	103.9	113.5	110.8	128.3

Note: The dagger symbol beside a figure indicates the earliest revised value for each series. Figures for the last two months and where indicated are provisional.

1 Index numbers are constructed on a net sector basis ie transactions within sector are excluded.

2 Index numbers are compiled exclusive of VAT. Revenue duties (on cigarettes, tobacco and alcoholic liquor) are included, as is duty on hydrocarbon oils.

3 Provisional.

Source: Central Statistical Office

18.6 Index numbers of producer prices

continued

1985=100, monthly averages

Price index numbers of materials and fuel purchased[1,2]

	Electrical and electronic engineering	Motor vehicles and parts	Other transport equipment	Instrument engineering	Food manufacturing industries	Materials	Fuel	Textile industry	Footwear and clothing industries	Timber and wooden furniture industries	Paper and paper products	Processing of rubber and plastics	Other manufacturing industries	Construction materials	House-building materials
SIC 1980 Division Class or Group	34	35	36	37	411 to 423			43	45	46	47	48	49	5	part of 5
	DZCG	DZCH	DZCI	DZCJ	DZCK	DZCL	DZCM	DZCN	DZCO	DZCP	DZCQ	DZCR	DZCS	DZCT	DZCU
1987	104.1	106.8	105.1	105.8	99.5	100.4	83.3	103.2	104.5	105.5	108.1	104.8	104.9	109.3	110.1
1988	113.0	113.0	112.1	112.6	101.0	102.0	81.2	107.9	106.9	109.4	113.5	111.1	109.4	115.4	116.2
1989	119.4	119.5	118.3	119.0	107.5	108.6	85.9	115.0	109.8	116.9	120.1	111.7	114.7	123.4	124.1
1990	120.3	124.2	123.2	123.9	109.2	110.3	89.1	112.8	113.6	126.6	123.2	113.9	115.7	129.6	130.2
1991	120.8	128.6	128.2	128.2	110.8	111.8	90.2	109.1	115.6	128.3	121.8	112.3	115.7	133.6	134.0
1988 Nov	116.5	115.4	114.1	115.1	102.3	103.3	82.5	110.4	107.2	111.2	115.3	112.3	112.3	118.5	119.2
Dec	118.5	116.6	115.8	116.2	103.5	104.0	92.8	111.4	107.3	112.3	116.8	113.4	113.2	118.8	119.6
1989 Jan	119.9	118.2	117.2	117.3	104.2	104.9	94.0	113.8	108.2	113.5	117.9	114.2	114.0	120.1	120.9
Feb	118.5	118.0	117.0	117.2	103.7	104.7	84.1	112.0	108.1	113.2	117.2	112.7	112.7	120.6	121.5
Mar	119.0	118.0	117.1	117.4	105.1	106.4	79.4	112.2	107.7	113.5	117.3	112.0	113.8	122.3	123.0
Apr	119.3	118.6	117.6	118.2	107.6	109.0	82.0	112.4	108.3	114.2	119.2	112.6	114.4	122.9	123.5
May	119.6	119.1	118.1	118.9	108.4	109.8	82.9	113.8	108.8	115.2	119.5	112.3	114.3	123.1	123.8
Jun	119.3	119.2	118.2	119.1	108.7	110.1	82.5	116.0	109.7	116.2	119.9	111.6	114.8	123.1	123.6
Jul	118.0	119.1	118.2	118.9	107.8	109.1	82.5	113.7	110.0	117.0	120.6	110.5	113.4	123.4	124.0
Aug	119.3	119.6	118.6	119.2	106.4	107.7	82.0	114.3	110.2	117.9	120.6	109.9	114.5	124.1	124.8
Sep	119.9	120.4	118.8	119.7	108.0	109.3	82.7	116.8	110.7	118.7	121.0	109.9	115.5	125.1	125.8
Oct	120.0	120.6	119.0	120.1	109.3	110.6	84.2	116.8	111.3	119.4	121.1	110.0	115.5	125.3	126.1
Nov	119.9	121.1	119.8	120.5	110.0	111.0	91.3	118.1	112.0	120.9	122.4	111.4	116.5	125.4	126.1
Dec	120.1	122.0	120.5	121.0	110.4	110.8	102.8	119.6	112.4	122.6	124.3	113.1	116.8	125.3	126.2
1990 Jan	120.0	123.3	121.7	122.5	110.3	110.6	103.6	120.3	113.9	124.4	125.6	114.4	116.5	126.5	127.4
Feb	118.6	122.6	121.1	122.0	110.0	111.0	91.8	118.1	113.6	124.1	123.8	112.9	115.4	126.6	127.6
Mar	120.6	122.9	121.5	122.7	111.3	112.6	86.3	115.7	113.6	124.8	123.5	112.3	116.8	128.2	128.7
Apr	120.8	123.5	122.4	123.3	112.5	114.0	84.2	115.8	114.3	125.7	122.8	112.3	116.9	129.5	130.0
May	120.6	123.5	122.5	123.4	111.5	113.1	82.4	113.8	113.5	126.2	123.0	112.3	116.5	129.8	130.2
Jun	119.9	123.4	122.6	123.4	110.4	111.9	81.1	112.8	113.4	126.6	122.6	111.9	115.3	129.7	130.1
Jul	119.8	123.8	122.9	123.6	109.0	110.6	81.1	110.4	113.2	126.8	122.8	111.9	115.2	130.4	130.9
Aug	120.5	124.3	123.6	124.1	106.1	107.2	85.3	109.3	113.0	127.3	122.7	112.2	115.6	130.7	131.1
Sep	121.7	125.1	124.2	124.8	106.5	107.5	87.4	110.1	113.3	127.7	123.1	113.5	116.3	130.7	131.1
Oct	120.4	125.4	124.9	125.2	106.2	107.1	90.4	109.6	113.3	128.0	122.3	115.5	114.6	131.0	131.5
Nov	119.8	125.6	125.2	125.4	107.3	108.1	93.6	108.2	113.7	128.3	123.1	118.0	114.0	131.1	131.6
Dec	120.5	126.4	126.3	126.2	109.3	109.7	101.9	110.0	114.3	129.0	123.6	119.6	114.8	131.0	131.6
1991 Jan	121.5	127.8	127.8	127.5	109.9	110.4	101.0	110.3	115.1	129.4	123.1	119.6	115.3	132.6	133.0
Feb	120.6	127.5	127.8	127.5	110.6	111.5	94.3	108.1	114.9	129.0	122.6	117.7	114.3	132.6	133.2
Mar	120.8	127.8	127.4	127.5	112.0	113.3	86.9	107.7	114.9	128.4	120.9	115.4	115.4	133.8	134.0
Apr	121.5	128.6	128.1	128.1	113.2	114.5	89.2	109.0	115.2	128.3	121.8	112.8	116.6	134.0	134.2
May	120.9	128.5	128.1	128.0	113.2	114.6	87.8	109.4	115.5	128.3	121.6	111.1	116.0	134.1	134.4
Jun	120.9	128.5	128.2	128.2	112.2	113.6	85.6	109.7	116.3	128.5	121.5	110.7	117.1	133.4	133.7
Jul	121.0	128.5	128.3	128.4	110.2	111.4	86.2	109.9	116.5	128.7	121.7	110.3	117.2	133.7	134.1
Aug	120.3	128.6	128.0	128.2	107.6	108.8	85.4	109.4	116.1	128.0	121.2	109.9	115.8	133.8	134.3
Sep	120.4	128.9	128.1	128.3	108.1	109.3	86.1	108.4	115.5	127.8	121.1	110.1	115.5	133.6	134.1
Oct	120.3	128.9	128.3	128.5	109.0	110.2	87.1	108.0	115.3	127.6	121.2	109.6	115.8	133.8	134.4
Nov	120.4	129.3	128.5	128.6	110.9	111.8	92.9	108.9	115.7	127.6	121.9	109.5	115.2	133.6	134.3
Dec	120.6	129.9	129.3	129.1	112.1	112.8	99.8	110.1	116.0	127.9	123.6	110.6	114.4	133.6	134.2
1992 Jan	120.8	130.7	130.1	130.0	112.6	113.3	99.1	108.6	116.7	128.0	122.4	111.4	114.6	134.0	134.7
Feb	121.0	130.6	130.2	130.1	114.0	115.0	94.3	108.8	117.0	127.7	121.8	110.9	115.3	133.9	134.5
Mar	120.9	130.5	129.8	130.1	114.2	115.6	86.9	108.5	117.2	127.7	120.9	109.9	115.8	134.8	135.3
Apr	121.2	131.1	130.4	130.5	114.6	115.9	89.7	108.0	116.9	128.1	121.7	109.8	115.4	134.8	135.3
May	120.9	131.2	130.5	130.6	114.0	115.3	89.0[†]	107.7	116.8	128.0[3]	121.2	109.5[†]	114.7	134.6	135.1
Jun[3]	121.1[†]	131.3[†]	130.7[†]	130.7[†]	113.3[†]	114.6[†]	89.1	105.9[†]	116.5[†]	128.0	121.2[†]	109.6	114.5[†]	134.6[†]	135.1[†]
Jul[3]	121.3	131.3	130.6	130.9	113.1	114.4	88.5	105.0	116.1	127.9	121.0	109.6	114.6	134.9	135.4

Note: The dagger symbol beside a figure indicates the earliest revised value for each series. Figures for the last 2 months and where indicated are provisional.

1 Index numbers are constructed on a net sector basis ie transactions within sector are excluded.

2 Index numbers are compiled exclusive of VAT. Revenue duties (on cigarettes, tobacco and alcoholic liquor) are included, as is duty on hydrocarbon oils.

3 Provisional.

Source: Central Statistical Office

18.6 Index numbers of producer prices
continued

1985=100, monthly averages

Output:[1,2] home sales

	Output of manufactured products	Products of manufacturing industries other than food, drink and tobacco	Products of manufacturing industries other than food, drink and tobacco seasonally adjusted	Products of the food, drink and tobacco manufacturing industries	Metal manufacturing	Extraction of minerals not elsewhere specified	Non-metallic mineral products	Chemical industry	Man-made fibres	Metal goods engineering and vehicles	Metal goods not elsewhere specified	Mechanical engineering
SIC1980 Division Class or Group	2 to 4	2 to 4 excl. 41/42	2 to 4 excl. 41/42	41/42	22	23	24	25	26	3	31	32
	DZCV	DZCW	DZDU	DZCX	DZCY	DZCZ	DZDA	DZDB	DZDC	DZDD	DZDE	DZDF
1987	108.3	108.6	108.7	107.5	101.3	109.8	108.9	105.8	105.7	108.6	107.9	109.0
1988	113.2	113.8	113.9	111.5	109.8	115.2	114.4	111.5	106.9	113.7	114.0	114.8
1989	119.0	120.0	120.0	116.6	118.2	123.0	121.8	116.4	107.9	120.0	121.6	122.7
1990	126.0	127.3	127.3	123.0	117.5	130.4	129.8	121.7	112.1	127.5	128.2	132.7
1991	133.0	133.6	133.6	131.3	114.8	131.7	136.0	126.5	115.2	134.3	135.4	140.3
1988 Nov	115.2	115.7	116.1	113.6	114.6	116.9	116.7	113.6	105.6	115.8	116.6	116.9
Dec	115.4	115.9	116.5	114.1	115.9	116.2	116.6	113.7	105.8	116.0	116.9	117.2
1989 Jan	116.4	117.4	117.2	114.2	117.1	117.4	118.0	114.8	108.1	117.5	118.6	118.8
Feb	116.8	117.9	117.6	114.4	116.9	116.6	119.0	115.3	107.5	117.9	119.8	119.4
Mar	117.2	118.4	118.1	114.7	118.5	121.8	120.8	115.7	107.2	118.1	120.4	120.1
Apr	117.8	118.9	118.5	115.5	118.8	122.6	121.1	116.1	107.7	118.7	120.8	121.0
May	118.3	119.5	119.1	115.9	118.2	122.8	121.6	116.7	108.1	119.5	121.2	122.5
Jun	118.6	119.8	119.7	115.9	118.5	124.6	121.6	116.7	108.0	119.7	121.6	122.8
Jul	119.2	120.2	120.2	116.8	117.8	124.8	122.5	116.4	108.4	120.0	121.9	123.2
Aug	119.7	120.6	120.8	117.5	118.6	124.0	122.8	116.1	108.6	120.6	122.3	123.6
Sep	120.2	121.2	121.4	117.9	119.7	125.0	123.2	117.0	108.4	121.3	122.7	124.0
Oct	120.8	121.7	122.0	118.5	119.0	125.0	123.5	116.7	108.7	122.0	123.0	125.2
Nov	121.2	122.2	122.6	118.7	117.9	126.0	123.9	117.2	107.3	122.4	123.6	125.6
Dec	121.5	122.5	123.2	119.2	116.8	125.2	123.8	117.5	107.2	122.6	123.6	125.8
1990 Jan	122.5	123.9	123.6	119.4	116.4	126.0	125.5	118.6	110.0	124.2	125.7	128.2
Feb	123.0	124.5	124.2	119.8	115.3	125.7	126.4	119.2	110.2	124.8	126.5	129.1
Mar	123.8	125.3	125.0	120.5	117.4	130.1	128.0	120.0	109.7	125.0	126.5	129.5
Apr	125.1	126.2	125.8	122.6	118.7	131.4	129.1	120.3	110.5	126.1	127.3	131.3
May	125.8	126.9	126.4	123.3	118.9	130.4	129.9	120.5	111.3	126.9	127.4	132.0
Jun	126.1	127.1	127.0	123.7	118.1	131.2	129.8	120.8	111.8	127.3	127.9	132.6
Jul	126.4	127.4	127.5	123.7	118.0	132.3	130.4	121.1	111.5	127.5	128.3	133.0
Aug	126.9	128.0	128.2	124.1	118.2	132.0	130.6	121.8	111.7	128.2	128.9	133.3
Sep	127.2	128.6	128.8	124.0	118.3	132.0	131.6	122.4	113.4	128.7	129.2	133.4
Oct	127.9	129.3	129.5	124.6	117.5	132.6	132.2	123.8	113.5	129.5	129.8	134.0
Nov	128.2	129.7	130.0	125.0	116.4	131.2	132.3	125.7	115.1	129.7	130.1	134.2
Dec	128.6	130.0	130.5	125.4	116.3	130.4	132.4	126.2	116.6	130.0	130.3	134.6
1991 Jan	130.0	131.7	131.5	126.3	115.9	131.5	134.2	128.0	116.8	131.9	133.2	137.4
Feb	130.5	132.5	132.3	126.6	115.7	130.6	134.1	128.3	116.9	133.0	134.2	138.3
Mar	131.4	132.8	132.5	128.3	116.0	134.4	136.6	128.2	115.5	133.3	134.1	138.9
Apr	132.8	133.3	132.9	131.1	116.3	134.1	136.7	126.6	116.4	134.0	135.1	139.9
May	133.2	133.7	133.2	131.7	115.9	133.8	137.0	125.9	115.8	134.3	135.4	140.2
Jun	133.3	133.4	133.4	132.3	114.9	132.4	136.4	125.3	115.1	134.3	135.5	140.4
Jul	133.6	133.8	133.9	132.6	114.7	132.9	136.4	125.6	115.4	134.5	135.8	140.7
Aug	133.9	134.1	134.3	132.7	114.7	133.0	136.0	125.8	115.6	134.8	135.9	141.0
Sep	134.1	134.3	134.6	132.9	114.0	131.1	135.9	126.0	114.1	135.2	136.3	141.3
Oct	134.3	134.5	134.8	133.1	113.5	129.9	135.9	126.0	113.2	135.2	136.4	141.2
Nov	134.7	134.7	135.1	133.9	113.0	128.4	136.4	125.9	112.8	135.5	136.4	142.1
Dec	134.8	134.8	135.3	134.2	112.7	129.0	136.2	126.0	114.5	135.7	136.6	142.5
1992 Jan	135.8	135.7	135.4	135.0	111.7	129.5	137.1	127.2	114.5	136.6	137.9	143.7
Feb	136.3	136.2	135.9	135.6	112.5	130.8	136.6	127.8	113.6	137.3	138.3	144.0
Mar	137.3	136.7	136.4	137.4†	114.2	131.6	137.1	128.2	113.0	137.7	138.2	144.5
Apr	137.8†	137.0	136.6	138.0†	114.6	131.6	137.4	128.3	115.8	138.1	138.9	145.1
May	137.9†	137.2	136.7	138.2	114.2†	131.5†	137.3	128.5	115.6†	138.3	139.0	145.2
Jun[3]	138.0	137.3†	137.3†	138.3	114.4†	130.2	137.5†	128.7†	115.9†	138.3	138.9†	145.4
Jul[3]	138.2	137.5	137.6	138.5	114.5	130.2	137.5	129.3	115.9	138.3	139.0	145.1

Note: The dagger symbol beside a figure indicates the earliest revised value for each series. Figures for the last 2 months and where incicated are provisional.

1 Index numbers are constructed on a net sector basis ie transactions within sector are excluded.

2 Index numbers are compiled exclusive of VAT. Revenue duties (on cigarettes, tobacco and alcoholic liquor) are included, as is duty on hydrocarbon oils.

3 Provisional.

Source: Central Statistical Office

18.6 Index numbers of producer prices
continued

	Office machinery and data processing equipment	Electrical and electronic engineering	Motor vehicles and parts	Instrument engineering	Food manufacturing industries	Drink and tobacco manufacturing industries	Textile industries	Footwear and clothing industries	Timber and wooden furniture industries	Paper and paper products, printing and publishing	Processing of rubber and plastics	Other manufacturing industries	Construction output price index[3]	Index of average price of new dwellings: mortgages approved[4,5]
SIC1980 Division Class or Group	33	34	35	411 to 37	424 to 423	429	43	45	46	47	48	49		
	DZDS	DZDG	DZDH	DZDI	DZDJ	DZDT	DZDK	DZDL	DZDM	DZDN	DZDO	DZDP	BAEL	FCAZ
1987	..	108.2	114.3	109.3	105.5	..	109.4	108.3	110.6	109.3	108.8	111.5	112	136.6
1988	..	111.9	122.7	114.3	109.5	..	115.2	113.5	115.8	113.6	114.4	115.6	125	173.2
1989	89.6	116.0	131.6	121.4	114.9	..	120.5	118.3	121.5	119.8	119.6	120.8	141	201.0
1990	92.0	121.9	140.8	129.3	119.8	129.1	126.2	123.6	130.8	127.2	125.7	130.9	147	211.6
1991	85.2	128.2	149.7	138.4	125.2	142.8	131.2	129.8	135.2	133.3	133.1	139.4	140	204.9
1988 Nov	..	113.5	125.9	116.1	111.4	..	116.6	115.2	117.7	115.1	116.1	116.5	132	187.5
Dec	..	113.7	126.2	116.6	112.1	..	116.7	115.3	117.6	115.3	116.4	116.1	-	190.7
1989 Jan	90.8	114.4	129.3	119.1	112.3	..	118.4	117.2	118.5	116.7	117.8	118.0	-	184.5
Feb	90.8	114.8	129.4	119.6	112.2	..	118.7	117.2	118.9	117.2	118.0	118.2	136	190.6
Mar	90.9	114.4	129.5	119.8	112.8	..	118.9	117.5	119.8	117.5	118.5	117.9	-	199.2
Apr	91.5	115.0	129.6	120.1	113.9	..	119.5	117.6	120.1	117.9	119.1	118.5	-	200.4
May	91.7	115.5	130.0	120.3	114.3	..	120.0	117.8	120.5	119.1	119.4	118.6	140	200.2
Jun	92.1	115.4	130.5	121.0	114.4	..	120.5	118.0	121.4	119.6	119.9	119.3	-	204.3
Jul	91.6	115.8	130.5	121.9	115.2	119.9	121.3	118.3	121.6	120.1	120.0	122.3	-	205.7
Aug	91.6	116.2	132.2	121.9	115.8	120.8	121.4	118.9	122.3	120.5	120.0	122.3	-	203.0
Sep	93.3	117.1	133.9	122.5	116.0	121.3	121.4	119.1	122.7	120.9	120.3	122.7	144	202.8
Oct	93.3	117.5	134.6	123.2	116.8	121.6	121.6	119.1	123.6	122.2	120.5	123.6	-	201.1
Nov	93.3	117.8	134.8	123.4	117.2	121.6	121.8	119.4	123.9	122.8	120.5	123.8	-	203.2
Dec	93.3	117.9	134.8	124.0	118.0	121.6	122.2	119.6	124.7	123.0	121.0	124.8	145	211.4
1990 Jan	90.8	119.0	137.6	126.0	118.0	122.2	124.0	120.7	126.0	124.2	122.4	127.3	-	210.8
Feb	90.8	119.4	137.6	126.3	118.2	122.7	124.7	121.6	127.0	124.6	123.1	128.1	147	211.3
Mar	90.9	119.7	137.9	126.7	118.4	124.8	125.1	122.2	129.4	125.2	123.4	128.6	-	209.7
Apr	91.5	121.0	138.2	127.7	119.3	129.2	125.8	122.9	130.1	125.9	124.2	129.9	-	213.8
May	91.7	121.6	140.0	128.2	120.0	129.5	126.1	123.2	130.3	126.8	124.6	131.0	147	213.8
Jun	92.1	121.6	140.3	128.7	120.4	129.9	126.2	123.5	130.7	127.0	124.9	130.6	-	212.2
Jul	91.6	121.7	140.4	129.1	120.3	130.2	126.5	123.9	131.4	127.4	125.7	132.0	-	215.5
Aug	91.6	122.6	141.2	130.5	120.2	131.3	126.5	124.6	132.2	127.6	126.1	132.0	147	214.8
Sep	93.3	123.1	142.9	131.1	120.0	131.6	126.7	124.8	132.7	128.3	126.5	132.6	-	210.8
Oct	93.3	124.0	144.3	132.2	120.6	132.4	127.2	124.9	133.2	129.5	128.0	132.6	-	204.7
Nov	93.3	124.0	144.4	132.5	121.1	132.3	127.4	125.2	133.3	130.0	129.4	132.5	145	206.7
Dec	93.3	124.6	144.4	132.8	121.4	132.8	127.7	125.5	132.8	130.4	129.9	133.2	-	217.3
1991 Jan	95.1	125.4	146.1	135.9	122.8	133.0	129.9	128.0	133.7	131.6	132.0	136.0	-	201.1
Feb	94.4	125.7	148.6	136.1	122.9	133.2	130.1	128.5	134.4	132.1	132.3	135.9	143	200.3
Mar	92.2	126.4	149.4	136.2	123.5	137.0	130.2	129.0	134.7	131.4	132.9	136.8	-	206.2
Apr	84.9	127.9	149.7	136.6	124.5	143.5	130.6	129.2	133.9	132.6	133.2	138.4	-	203.2
May	84.8	128.5	149.8	136.6	125.2	143.9	130.9	129.7	134.8	133.6	132.9	139.1	141	209.3
Jun	83.1	128.2	150.0	137.7	125.7	144.6	131.1	129.9	134.6	133.1	132.8	139.1	-	208.1
Jul	82.5	128.5	149.9	139.0	126.0	145.2	131.7	130.0	135.0	133.4	133.2	141.0	-	206.9
Aug	82.1	128.8	150.1	139.5	125.9	145.7	131.8	130.1	135.6	134.1	133.2	140.9	138	209.6
Sep	82.2	129.3	150.8	140.0	126.0	145.9	131.7	130.5	136.1	134.0	133.6	141.2	-	201.2
Oct	81.6	129.6	150.4	140.6	126.1	146.5	132.1	130.8	136.6	134.5	133.7	141.3	-	204.7
Nov	79.8	129.9	150.6	141.2	126.6	147.7	132.1	131.0	136.5	134.6	133.8	141.6	136	202.7
Dec	79.3	129.9	150.7	141.4	127.0	147.7	132.4	131.1	136.2	134.4	134.1	142.0	-	202.8
1992 Jan	79.3	130.8	151.2	142.9	128.3	147.7	133.6	133.4	137.0	135.0	135.0	143.4	-	199.6
Feb	79.1	131.5	152.7	143.0	128.7	148.7	133.7	133.2	137.2	135.7	135.1	144.6	133	192.7
Mar	78.9	132.0	153.5	143.2	129.2	152.7	134.4	133.5	137.6	136.1	135.5	145.3	..	195.6
Apr	79.3†	132.4	153.8	143.5	129.3†	154.5	134.3	133.8†	137.7	136.4	135.8	145.3	..	193.4
May	79.3	132.7	153.7	143.8	129.5	154.6†	134.5	133.9	137.7	137.0†	136.2	145.4[6]	..	194.3
Jun[6]	79.3	132.7†	153.5	144.2	129.6	154.9	134.8	134.1	137.8	137.0	136.4	145.3	..	197.0
Jul[6]	79.3	132.9	153.5	145.3	129.7	155.2	135.1	134.4	137.9	137.5	136.6	145.6	..	196.0

Note: The dagger symbol beside a figure indicates the earliest revised value for each series. Figures for the last 2 months and where indicated are provisional.

1 Index numbers are constructed on a net sector basis ie transactions within sector are excluded.

2 Index numbers are compiled exclusive of VAT. Revenue duties (on cigarettes, tobacco and alcoholic liquor) are included, as is duty on hydrocarbon oils.

3 A base weighted (1985=100) combination of the separate price indices for contractor's output in the five new work sectors.

4 The index covers only dwellings on which building societies have approved mortgages during the period. The cost of land is included.

5 The Abbey National ceased to operate as a building society in July 1989 but to ensure continuity in the data its results are included in the building society sector wherever possible.

6 Provisional.

Sources: Central Statistical Office;
Department of the Environment

18.7 Average weekly and hourly earnings and hours of full-time employees on adult rates: Great Britain
At April

	Manufacturing industries[1]					All industries and services				
	Weekly earnings(£)			Hourly earnings(£)[2]		Weekly earnings(£)			Hourly earnings(£)[2]	
	Including those whose pay was affected by absence	Excluding those whose pay was affected by absence	Hours[2]	Including overtime pay and overtime hours	Excluding overtime pay and overtime hours	Including those whose pay was affected by absence	Excluding those whose pay was affected by absence	Hours[2]	Including overtime pay and overtime hours	Excluding overtime pay and overtime hours
Total										
	BAPL	BAPM	BAQJ	BAPN	BAPO	BAPX	BAPY	BAQM	BAPZ	BAQA
1983	142.2	147.0	41.4	3.52	3.47	144.5	147.4	40.1	3.63	3.60
1984	155.2	160.8	41.9	3.81	3.75	155.8	159.3	40.3	3.90	3.87
1985	169.2	174.7	41.9	4.12	4.05	167.4	171.0	40.4	4.17	4.13
1986	183.1	188.6	41.9	4.44	4.38	181.2	184.7	40.4	4.51	4.47
1987	196.0	202.0	42.0	4.74	4.68	194.9	198.9	40.4	4.85	4.81
1988	212.7	219.4	42.3	5.09	5.02	213.6	218.4	40.6	5.29	5.26
1989	231.7	239.5	42.5	5.55	5.48	234.3	239.7	40.7	5.81	5.79
1990	255.1	262.8	42.4	6.09	6.01	258.0	263.1	40.5	6.37	6.34
1991	271.3	280.7	41.3	6.69	6.62	278.9	284.7	40.0	7.00	6.98
Men										
	BAPP	BAPQ	BAQK	BAPR	BAPS	BAQB	BAQC	BAQN	BAQD	BAQE
1983	156.4	161.2	42.2	3.78	3.75	161.1	164.7	41.4	3.93	3.91
1984	171.2	176.8	42.8	4.10	4.06	174.3	178.8	41.7	4.23	4.21
1985	187.2	192.6	42.9	4.44	4.39	187.9	192.4	41.9	4.53	4.50
1986	202.3	207.8	42.9	4.79	4.74	203.4	207.5	41.8	4.89	4.87
1987	217.0	222.3	43.0	5.11	5.07	219.4	224.0	41.9	5.27	5.26
1988	236.3	242.3	43.3	5.50	5.44	240.6	245.8	42.1	5.74	5.73
1989	257.3	264.6	43.6	5.98	5.94	263.5	269.5	42.3	6.28	6.29
1990	282.2	289.2	43.4	6.55	6.50	290.2	295.6	42.2	6.88	6.89
1991	299.5	308.1	42.1	7.20	7.15	312.9	318.9	41.5	7.55	7.57
Women										
	BAPT	BAPU	BAQL	BAPV	BAPW	BAQF	BAQG	BAQO	BAQH	BAQI
1983	94.7	97.9	38.6	2.53	2.51	107.6	109.5	37.2	2.91	2.90
1984	101.7	105.5	38.8	2.71	2.69	114.9	117.2	37.2	3.10	3.09
1985	110.6	114.7	38.8	2.94	2.92	123.9	126.4	37.3	3.34	3.32
1986	119.2	123.2	38.8	3.16	3.13	134.7	137.2	37.3	3.63	3.61
1987	128.2	133.4	39.0	3.39	3.36	144.9	148.1	37.5	3.88	3.86
1988	138.4	144.3	39.2	3.66	3.62	160.1	164.2	37.6	4.31	4.29
1989	152.7	159.1	39.1	4.04	4.00	178.1	182.3	37.6	4.80	4.78
1990	170.3	177.1	39.1	4.48	4.44	197.0	201.5	37.5	5.30	5.28
1991	184.2	192.9	38.8	4.94	4.91	217.2	222.4	37.4	5.91	5.89

1 Results for manufacturing industries relate to divisions 2,3 and 4 of the *Standard Industrial Classification 1980.*
2 Excluding those whose pay was affected by absence.

Source: New Earnings Survey: Department of Employment

115

18.8 Average weekly and hourly earnings of full-time employees on adult rates by industry division: Great Britain
At April

£

	Agriculture, forestry, fishing	Energy & water supply	Mineral/ore extraction (exc. fuels) Mineral, metal & chemical manufacture	Metal goods engineering & vehicle manuf-acture	Other manuf-acturing industries	Construction	Distribution, Hotels, Catering, repairs	Transport & commun-ication	Banking, finance, insurance, business services & leasing	Other services
SIC 1980 Division	0	1	2	3	4	5	6	7	8	9

Full time employees on adult rates whose pay was unaffected by absence

Average gross weekly earnings

Total

	0	1	2	3	4	5	6	7	8	9
	BAQP	BAQQ	BAQR	BAQS	BAQT	BAQU	BAQV	BAQW	BAQX	BAQY
1985	130.5	208.8	187.1	179.1	163.3	165.8	139.4	188.8	193.2	165.9
1986	135.7	229.1	200.4	193.3	177.0	179.5	150.4	200.7	209.5	179.4
1987	142.7	248.1	216.6	207.0	188.7	194.1	162.2	214.9	230.7	191.5
1988	161.6	271.1	233.1	226.2	205.2	212.6	178.8	229.6	260.1	211.0
1989	169.7	295.0	254.8	249.7	220.8	236.3	197.1	248.3	284.6	232.3
1990	190.5	326.8	275.2	272.6	245.1	268.5	214.0	266.3	317.7	253.8
1991	207.9	363.2	295.3	291.1	261.6	285.7	230.3	288.4	336.9	281.8

Men

	0	1	2	3	4	5	6	7	8	9
	BAQZ	BARA	BARB	BARC	BARD	BARE	BARF	BARG	BARH	BARI
1985	132.7	218.4	201.7	192.3	188.1	169.6	161.2	198.8	237.6	195.3
1986	138.8	240.3	216.8	207.5	203.3	168.8	174.0	211.2	257.0	210.1
1987	145.1	251.5	233.6	222.0	216.5	198.6	188.1	226.8	284.5	224.1
1988	167.0	286.0	251.6	243.1	236.3	218.1	206.1	241.4	320.1	247.0
1989	174.5	312.1	273.5	268.3	254.4	242.9	227.8	262.0	350.9	269.2
1990	195.7	345.8	295.4	292.9	280.3	277.3	247.8	281.2	390.5	293.4
1991	214.2	385.4	316.3	311.6	298.7	294.9	264.3	302.7	412.8	327.3

Women

	0	1	2	3	4	5	6	7	8	9
	BARJ	BARK	BARL	BARM	BARN	BARO	BARP	BARQ	BARR	BARS
1985	109.2	148.3	122.9	117.4	110.6	110.8	101.0	139.7	134.6	136.9
1986	106.7	158.5	130.4	126.5	118.8	121.7	109.2	148.6	147.9	149.6
1987	122.3	169.6	142.3	137.0	128.3	134.8	118.3	158.2	160.8	160.1
1988	124.9	186.2	155.0	148.7	138.4	151.0	131.0	175.0	183.6	177.6
1989	135.5	203.5	174.2	164.9	151.5	166.7	144.9	191.2	202.5	198.5
1990	150.5	226.0	193.3	180.3	170.5	178.5	157.2	207.7	227.7	218.4
1991	164.3	255.4	211.7	197.8	184.6	195.5	174.1	229.8	244.7	242.9

Average gross hourly earnings (excluding overtime)

Total

	0	1	2	3	4	5	6	7	8	9
	BART	BARU	BARV	BARW	BARX	BARY	BARZ	BASA	BASB	BASC
1985	2.60	5.14	4.37	4.13	3.79	3.78	3.32	4.17	5.00	4.29
1986	2.87	5.53	4.70	4.48	4.09	4.06	3.60	4.45	5.49	4.64
1987	3.05	6.04	5.07	4.79	4.33	4.44	3.87	4.76	6.06	4.91
1988	3.30	6.55	5.41	5.16	4.66	4.80	4.25	5.07	6.82	5.43
1989	3.50	7.09	5.95	5.66	5.05	5.31	4.69	5.50	7.41	6.04
1990	3.91	7.76	6.43	6.20	5.58	6.02	5.07	5.92	8.25	6.60
1991	4.21	8.64	7.04	6.89	6.08	6.47	5.48	6.49	8.85	7.37

Men

	0	1	2	3	4	5	6	7	8	9
	BASD	BASE	BASF	BASG	BASH	BASI	BASJ	BASK	BASL	BASM
1985	2.60	5.34	4.64	4.38	4.26	3.83	3.74	4.28	6.08	4.89
1986	2.89	5.76	5.01	4.75	4.58	4.13	4.06	4.58	6.66	5.25
1987	3.06	6.31	5.40	5.08	4.85	4.51	4.36	4.91	7.41	5.57
1988	3.33	6.85	5.75	5.48	5.22	4.88	4.76	5.20	8.31	6.15
1989	3.52	7.43	6.29	6.00	5.66	5.39	5.27	5.65	9.05	6.76
1990	3.94	8.12	6.80	6.57	6.22	6.14	5.70	6.07	10.06	7.38
1991	4.25	9.05	7.44	7.30	6.77	6.59	6.11	6.64	10.75	8.25

Women

	0	1	2	3	4	5	6	7	8	9
	BASN	BASO	BASP	BASQ	BASR	BASS	BAST	BASU	BASV	BASW
1985	2.54	3.92	3.18	2.96	2.81	2.95	2.60	3.58	3.66	3.69
1986	2.62	4.16	3.36	3.20	3.02	3.15	2.82	3.79	4.03	4.02
1987	3.00	4.48	3.66	3.43	3.22	3.45	3.05	4.02	4.35	4.25
1988	3.09	4.90	3.98	3.70	3.47	3.93	3.37	4.42	4.99	4.74
1989	3.34	5.35	4.50	4.11	3.80	4.40	3.71	4.83	5.45	5.36
1990	3.69	5.89	4.89	4.51	4.26	4.68	4.02	5.31	6.13	5.89
1991	3.93	6.68	5.46	5.04	4.66	5.15	4.46	5.86	6.65	6.60

Source: New Earnings Survey: Department of Employment

18.9 Average weekly and hourly earnings of full-time employees by age group: Great Britain
At April

£

| | Full time employees whose pay was unaffected by absence | | | | | | | | |
	Under 18	18-20	21-24	25-29	30-39	40-49	50-59	60-64	All ages
Average gross weekly earnings									
Total									
	BANJ	BANK	BANL	BANM	BANN	BANO	BANP	BANQ	BANR
1984	61.2	91.6	120.0	150.1	177.6	178.4	167.8	158.2	155.9
1985	67.3	96.4	128.4	160.1	190.3	192.8	180.7	167.9	167.4
1986	72.4	103.3	137.6	172.4	206.2	208.6	195.3	181.7	181.1
1987	79.0	110.1	147.5	186.2	221.0	226.2	211.4	194.4	195.3
1988	88.4	120.9	162.5	205.8	242.8	248.9	230.6	211.1	214.7
1989	95.2	132.2	180.5	226.1	265.0	272.1	252.9	226.4	235.3
1990	103.0	144.1	196.2	248.8	291.4	297.6	274.9	240.9	258.6
1991	108.7	155.0	209.6	266.5	313.0	323.3	297.6	261.9	280.8
Men									
	BANS	BANT	BANU	BANV	BANW	BANX	BANY	BANZ	BAOA
1984	63.3	101.1	133.9	163.1	193.6	200.5	185.4	163.7	175.2
1985	69.5	106.4	144.0	174.0	207.5	217.3	200.0	173.6	188.6
1986	72.7	113.5	153.6	186.8	225.0	234.8	216.2	186.7	203.6
1987	79.4	119.7	164.2	202.1	241.9	256.5	233.9	200.3	220.1
1988	89.3	131.6	179.6	222.5	265.5	283.0	255.5	217.1	241.6
1989	94.7	142.4	199.5	244.2	289.7	309.1	279.5	234.5	264.5
1990	101.5	154.2	215.6	269.7	318.2	339.1	305.6	249.9	290.3
1991	109.9	163.4	228.7	286.1	340.8	368.2	329.5	273.6	314.2
Women									
	BAOB	BAOC	BAOD	BAOE	BAOF	BAOG	BAOH	BAOI	BAOJ
1984	58.6	82.3	103.5	126.2	130.8	124.7	121.1	115.7	114.8
1985	64.7	86.9	110.8	135.7	142.1	135.1	130.1	123.1	123.9
1986	72.1	93.3	119.5	146.6	154.7	147.1	140.8	138.1	134.7
1987	78.5	100.6	128.6	159.1	167.0	156.9	152.5	143.5	145.5
1988	87.4	110.3	143.2	177.3	186.3	173.3	166.5	160.3	161.6
1989	95.7	122.3	159.3	196.5	206.6	191.2	184.6	170.6	179.3
1990	105.0	133.8	174.6	215.9	229.5	211.0	198.6	184.8	198.6
1991	107.4	146.3	189.3	237.0	252.3	233.4	220.9	198.8	220.0
Average gross hourly earnings (excluding overtime)									
Total									
	BAOK	BAOL	BAOM	BAON	BAOO	BAOP	BAOQ	BAOR	BAOS
1984	1.54	2.29	2.97	3.69	4.33	4.31	4.06	3.75	3.78
1985	1.67	2.39	3.16	3.92	4.60	4.64	4.35	3.95	4.04
1986	1.81	2.56	3.39	4.22	5.01	5.04	4.72	4.28	4.38
1987	1.97	2.73	3.62	4.55	5.38	5.47	5.09	4.57	4.72
1988	2.20	2.98	3.96	5.00	5.89	6.00	5.52	4.91	5.16
1989	2.39	3.26	4.41	5.50	6.45	6.57	6.05	5.30	5.68
1990	2.61	3.58	4.81	6.04	7.08	7.16	6.59	5.62	6.23
1991	2.75	3.89	5.20	6.58	7.73	7.94	7.24	6.23	6.89
Men									
	BAOT	BAOU	BAOV	BAOW	BAOX	BAOY	BAOZ	BAPA	BAPB
1984	1.53	2.42	3.17	3.86	4.60	4.72	4.38	3.83	4.13
1985	1.66	2.52	3.37	4.10	4.88	5.08	4.69	4.04	4.41
1986	1.75	2.67	3.60	4.41	5.31	5.52	5.08	4.35	4.77
1987	1.91	2.82	3.85	4.77	5.73	6.04	5.50	4.66	5.17
1988	2.13	3.08	4.18	5.20	6.25	6.63	5.96	4.99	5.63
1989	2.29	3.34	4.64	5.70	6.84	7.24	6.50	5.40	6.17
1990	2.49	3.66	5.03	6.27	7.50	7.92	7.12	5.71	6.76
1991	2.68	3.93	5.41	6.80	8.17	8.77	7.80	6.39	7.45
Women									
	BAPC	BAPD	BAPE	BAPF	BAPG	BAPH	BAPI	BAPJ	BAPK
1984	1.54	2.17	2.73	3.37	3.50	3.29	3.18	3.05	3.02
1985	1.68	2.27	2.91	3.60	3.78	3.57	3.43	3.24	3.25
1986	1.89	2.45	3.14	3.88	4.13	3.88	3.71	3.54	3.54
1987	2.04	2.63	3.36	4.18	4.42	4.09	3.98	3.70	3.79
1988	2.29	2.87	3.72	4.65	4.94	4.54	4.36	4.23	4.22
1989	2.50	3.19	4.15	5.16	5.49	5.04	4.83	4.56	4.70
1990	2.77	3.50	4.57	5.68	6.07	5.53	5.19	5.00	5.20
1991	2.85	3.84	4.97	6.24	6.75	6.24	5.86	5.33	5.82

Source: New Earnings Survey: Department of Employment

18.10 Average earnings index: all employees: by industry
Great Britain Classified according to the Standard Industrial Classification 1980

	Agriculture and forestry[1]	Coal and coke[2]	Mineral oil and natural gas	Electricity, gas, other energy and water supply	Metal processing and manufacturing	Mineral extraction and manufacturing	Chemicals and man-made fibres	Mechanical engineering	1985=100 Electrical and electronic engineering. 1988=100 and Instrument engineering	Motor vehicles and parts	Other transport equipment	1985=100 Metal goods and instruments. 1988=100 Metal goods n.e.s.	Food, drink and tobacco
SIC 1980 Class	(01-02)	(11-12)	(14)	(15-17)	(21-22)	(23-24)	(25-26)	(32)	(33-34)	(35)	(36)	(31,37)	(41-42)
1985=100													
	DNET	DNEU	DNEV	DNEW	DNEX	DNEY	DNEZ	DNFA	DNFB	DNFC	DNFD	DNFE	DNFF
1983	85.4	99.6	82.8	87.2	83.0	86.1	84.9	82.6	83.9	82.1	83.8	85.5	85.5
1984	92.0	50.0	91.0	93.3	92.0	92.5	92.1	90.6	91.7	88.2	92.1	92.6	92.0
1985	100.0	100.0	100.0	100.0	100.0	100.0	100.0	100.0	100.0	100.0	100.0	100.0	100.0
1986	105.5	113.3	109.5	106.9	106.5	107.8	107.9	106.9	108.0	108.7	107.9	107.4	108.7
1987	112.2	121.6	120.0	115.0	116.5	116.9	116.9	114.7	117.6	118.0	115.7	116.0	116.9
1988	117.7	135.8	133.0	122.0	128.0	126.2	126.9	125.3	128.5	129.0	120.0	126.3	126.3
SIC 1980 Class	(01,02)	(11)	(13,14)	(15-17)	(21,22)	(23,24)	(25,26)	(32)	(33,34,37)	(35)	(36)	(31)	(41,42)
1988=100													
	DNAI	DNAJ	DNAK	DNAL	DNAM	DNAN	DNAO	DNAP	DNAQ	DNAR	DNAS	DNAT	DNAU
1988	100.0	100.0	100.0	100.0	100.0	100.0	100.0	100.0	100.0	100.0	100.0	100.0	100.0
1989	108.0	113.3	110.3	109.8	107.2	109.4	109.0	109.8	109.5	109.9	112.7	107.9	109.3
1990	120.0	125.0	126.7	121.6	115.5	119.1	122.6	119.3	119.3	119.5	125.6	117.5	121.7
1991	132.1	141.9	140.4	134.2	122.8	125.9	134.0	130.2	129.5	129.1	136.2	124.7	134.6
1989 Jul	110.5	112.5	114.7	114.7	121.7	109.9	107.3	110.6	110.5	111.8	114.4	110.1	110.6
Aug	119.5	115.6	111.0	118.3	101.2	108.7	109.6	109.1	109.6	107.8	111.3	110.7	108.9
Sep	126.3	115.1	110.0	110.9	103.0	111.1	108.5	110.2	110.7	108.7	112.9	109.2	110.2
Oct	120.4	117.2	110.1	113.0	118.6	110.8	109.6	111.6	112.0	110.1	114.3	109.5	110.9
Nov	111.6	122.2	120.5	114.9	104.2	112.6	117.5	113.2	113.5	112.2	115.5	111.3	113.4
Dec	108.3	119.6	118.9	114.4	109.6	114.2	120.8	115.6	113.6	119.4	115.7	110.8	115.9
1990 Jan	104.3	124.7	123.1	112.6	111.5	112.6	115.7	114.4	113.5	109.3	115.3	112.7	112.7
Feb	103.8	124.5	118.2	113.3	104.9	114.4	117.2	116.2	115.4	109.4	118.1	113.3	114.1
Mar	108.1	124.5	120.4	114.8	107.9	115.7	117.7	118.9	118.4	122.8	123.8	115.5	114.5
Apr	110.8	124.2	121.6	116.3	121.2	117.9	120.2	116.9	116.2	122.0	121.7	116.1	120.5
May	110.6	121.7	123.3	118.7	109.4	119.3	120.9	118.4	117.9	118.4	125.3	117.0	122.3
Jun	122.6	123.1	125.3	126.5	119.8	121.4	123.4	119.9	119.2	122.3	127.7	118.8	123.9
Jul	124.9	122.5	130.7	124.3	131.8	121.8	121.9	121.5	119.9	121.3	127.3	119.0	124.3
Aug	133.3	125.9	129.2	127.2	112.6	118.3	122.7	118.2	119.0	119.4	127.3	118.0	122.2
Sep	139.3	125.9	130.8	125.8	114.7	119.6	122.0	120.0	121.2	119.1	127.3	118.9	123.7
Oct	136.0	128.3	130.4	126.9	122.0	120.5	122.3	120.7	122.1	121.5	127.9	118.9	122.9
Nov	126.5	131.1	131.4	126.8	113.0	122.6	130.2	122.3	123.5	124.0	132.1	121.4	127.3
Dec	120.1	123.7	135.8	125.4	117.7	124.8	136.9	124.7	124.7	125.0	132.8	120.6	130.9
1991 Jan	118.7	137.8	139.6	125.7	123.2	122.3	126.3	124.2	123.6	124.5	135.0	119.9	127.0
Feb	122.0	141.0	131.5	127.8	114.9	121.9	129.7	126.6	125.3	124.8	132.4	121.8	128.4
Mar	120.9	142.7	136.0	126.4	116.9	122.2	135.4	127.8	127.3	124.9	135.7	122.0	131.3
Apr	129.9	139.3	140.0	127.8	127.2	123.7	129.9	129.1	127.1	139.4	139.2	122.6	135.5
May	126.4	140.6	140.8	140.9	119.5	125.8	130.7	129.2	129.4	126.7	133.2	123.9	135.9
Jun	127.1	142.2	141.7	129.0	119.8	128.0	131.6	131.6	132.1	131.2	135.5	124.4	135.5
Jul	134.4	139.7	145.1	133.4	128.6	127.5	132.4	131.0	131.0	131.3	136.0	127.4	134.5
Aug	160.4	141.5	140.8	140.8	125.9	126.5	134.6	130.5	129.3	124.9	136.2	124.3	134.3
Sep	147.6	140.7	140.4	146.1	120.8	127.2	135.5	130.6	129.6	127.0	135.3	126.7	134.7
Oct	137.6	141.8	141.1	136.2	130.1	127.3	136.8	132.6	131.7	129.1	139.8	125.9	135.0
Nov	130.4	152.7	141.1	139.1	121.8	128.5	140.6	134.5	133.0	131.5	139.0	128.0	141.3
Dec	129.7	142.8	146.5	137.6	125.2	130.2	144.4	135.1	134.6	134.3	137.6	129.4	141.5
1992 Jan	126.6	156.2	142.1	136.5	130.1	128.0	138.7	134.7	134.6	133.8	139.4	129.2	137.8
Feb	121.4	155.7	143.4	137.1	124.2	129.3	138.9	136.0	134.9	137.8	140.3	130.6	139.6
Mar	128.1	158.9	155.8	137.7	126.2	130.4	150.4	140.5	140.1	141.5	144.0	134.5	149.7
Apr	137.1	161.3	142.8	142.4	134.5	130.0	138.9	135.8	135.9	137.6	140.3	132.3	140.6
May	139.6†	153.4	144.2	144.3†	126.3†	131.7	139.4	136.4†	138.2†	152.0†	140.5†	133.3†	143.3†
Jun[3]	134.0	149.5	147.7	143.6	126.9	133.7	140.1	139.0	138.9	144.5	142.4	135.0	144.0

Note: For a detailed account of the revised Average Earnings Index based on 1988=100 please see the article in *Employment Gazette* November 1989 p.606-612.

1 England and Wales only.

2 The index series for this group has been based on average 1985 figures, excluding January and February, which were seriously affected by a dispute in the coal mining industry, (1985=100 series only).

3 Provisional.

Source: Department of Employment

18.10 continued

Average earnings index: all employees: by industry
Great Britain   Classified according to the Standard Industrial Classification 1980

	Textiles	Leather, footwear and clothing	Timber and wooden furniture[3]	Rubber, plastics and other manufacturing[3]	Paper products, printing and publishing	Construction	Distribution and repairs	Hotels and catering	Transport and communication[1]	Banking, finance, insurance and business services	Public administration	Education and health services	Other services[2]
SIC 1980 Class	(43)	(44-45)	(46)	(48-49)	(47)	(50)	(61-65, 67)	(66)	(71-72, 75-77,79)	(81-82 83pt-84pt)	(91-92pt)	(93,95)	(97pt-98pt)
1985=100	DNFG	DNFH	DNFI	DNFK	DNFJ	DNFL	DNFM	DNFN	DNFO	DNFP	DNFQ	DNFR	DNFS
1983	84.6	86.2	86.9	84.8	84.7	87.3	86.9	87.7	86.8	85.3	88.4	91.7	85.6
1984	91.0	92.4	93.3	92.6	92.0	92.5	93.2	94.1	92.7	92.2	94.3	95.5	92.9
1985	100.0	100.0	100.0	100.0	100.0	100.0	100.0	100.0	100.0	100.0	100.0	100.0	100.0
1986	107.2	107.4	107.1	107.9	107.5	107.9	107.0	107.3	106.5	110.1	105.6	110.1	107.9
1987	116.1	114.5	116.5	116.9	116.2	116.5	114.9	115.7	114.9	121.8	112.8	117.9	115.3
1988	123.7	123.9	131.9	126.5	124.0	129.1	125.1	126.0	122.0	131.8	124.2	130.2	123.1

	Textiles	Leather, footwear and clothing	Rubber, plastics and other manufacturing[3]	Paper products, printing and publishing	Construction	Distribution and repairs	Hotels and catering	Transport and communication[1]	Banking, finance, insurance and business services	Public administration	Education and health services	Other services[2]
SIC 1980 Class	(43)	(44,45)	(46,48,49)	(47)	(50)	(61,62,64,65,67)	(66)	(71-72,75-77,79)	(81-82 83pt-84pt)	(91-92pt)	(93,95)	(92pt-94,96pt,97,98pt)
1988=100	DNAV	DNAW	DNFT	DNAY	DNBA	DNBB	DNBC	DNBD	DNBE	DNBF	DNBG	DNBH
1988	100.0	100.0	100.0	100.0	100.0	100.0	100.0	100.0	100.0	100.0	100.0	100.0
1989	107.4	107.1	107.7	106.1	111.8	108.6	107.6	107.6	109.9	108.8	108.6	111.3
1990	117.6	115.8	117.5	113.5	124.6	117.3	118.4	118.8	121.2	120.7	118.0	122.9
1991	128.1	123.7	126.0	121.6	134.6	124.7	128.8	128.6	129.4	130.0	129.1	132.7
1989 Jul	109.6	108.8	109.1	107.2	112.3	108.1	106.6	109.1	111.5	106.8	111.7	114.2
Aug	107.8	106.2	107.6	106.8	109.3	107.5	107.5	107.2	108.0	106.3	113.8	110.5
Sep	108.7	107.8	109.4	108.8	114.0	110.1	108.0	107.6	107.5	110.7	114.6	114.1
Oct	109.3	108.5	108.2	107.7	113.9	108.4	108.9	111.1	109.5	115.6	110.6	116.7
Nov	112.7	109.0	110.4	108.3	119.0	109.1	111.1	111.9	115.6	115.1	110.2	118.6
Dec	110.6	109.2	111.2	109.3	121.5	114.3	117.6	110.6	118.1	115.2	111.7	117.7
1990 Jan	111.7	112.3	111.9	108.6	118.0	111.7	112.2	114.7	116.2	114.7	111.7	117.7
Feb	112.1	112.5	115.7	108.7	117.7	112.8	111.6	112.1	115.4	116.5	110.3	118.6
Mar	115.0	113.8	116.3	111.4	123.2	117.6	114.1	114.2	124.3	116.6	111.7	118.5
Apr	114.1	113.3	115.0	111.5	122.5	117.1	115.4	115.6	119.4	115.7	113.8	124.0
May	117.5	116.1	115.7	112.1	121.6	117.0	119.3	116.3	120.3	118.2	120.2	119.3
Jun	119.9	116.4	118.0	114.3	126.1	117.7	118.9	120.7	121.7	121.0	118.0	122.0
Jul	118.9	116.9	118.3	114.5	126.8	117.7	118.2	120.9	122.8	120.8	119.9	125.4
Aug	118.4	115.1	116.4	114.7	123.2	117.5	120.1	117.8	119.5	124.4	125.4	124.9
Sep	120.0	116.8	119.3	116.5	125.1	118.4	120.0	118.6	119.5	123.4	122.0	124.2
Oct	119.7	117.1	118.8	115.8	127.0	117.7	120.0	119.6	120.6	126.3	120.6	122.9
Nov	122.1	118.6	121.1	116.7	131.3	118.7	121.9	122.1	126.6	125.7	121.3	127.3
Dec	121.4	120.6	123.4	117.1	132.6	123.8	129.6	133.1	128.3	125.2	121.3	129.7
1991 Jan	120.8	119.1	120.3	117.0	129.7	120.1	123.6	125.1	126.5	125.7	122.3	125.8
Feb	121.9	120.1	122.8	116.1	130.8	120.8	124.3	124.8	123.7	126.5	122.6	128.5
Mar	123.1	121.9	122.9	118.0	131.9	125.5	124.3	125.9	134.9	126.9	123.5	130.7
Apr	124.5	122.6	123.7	119.1	133.4	124.3	125.0	126.5	126.8	125.7	126.4	129.7
May	126.7	123.6	125.6	120.1	132.1	124.8	127.6	126.8	127.6	127.5	127.9	130.6
Jun	129.7	125.8	127.9	122.5	137.4	125.7	129.8	125.7	129.4	126.9	129.1	132.3
Jul	132.9	124.8	127.2	123.4	137.0	125.5	128.7	127.8	129.0	131.7	133.9	130.8
Aug	130.6	123.3	125.4	122.9	132.5	124.8	132.1	130.6	128.3	131.1	136.3	134.9
Sep	129.7	123.9	126.8	124.0	134.8	125.1	129.6	133.7	127.5	133.7	131.8	133.4
Oct	131.6	125.5	128.1	123.5	135.5	123.6	129.6	131.7	128.3	134.5	131.4	138.2
Nov	132.0	126.7	129.3	125.5	137.8	128.4	131.8	133.2	135.2	134.2	134.1	142.1
Dec	133.9	126.6	132.1	127.2	142.4	128.1	138.6	131.9	135.7	134.2	134.1	142.1
1992 Jan	133.2	126.3	128.7	124.6	136.9	126.5	132.7	132.4	134.2	134.1	133.2	137.6
Feb	135.1	127.9	133.3	124.8	138.5	128.5	132.6	133.1	135.9	134.9	133.1	139.0
Mar	138.7	129.9	138.0	128.5	143.3	133.8	134.7	134.5	147.4	136.7	134.7	139.0
Apr	133.0	125.2†	130.1	127.1	137.9	130.0	137.2†	133.4	135.8†	136.0†	134.6	139.3†
May	138.0†	129.0†	132.2	128.4†	137.7†	129.1†	137.9†	135.8†	136.0†	134.4	140.9†	139.3†
Jun[4]	140.4	130.6	133.6	129.1	142.2	127.9	134.1	137.3	134.7	137.5	141.5	137.9

Note: For a detailed account of the revised Average Earnings Index based on 1988=100 please see the article in *Employment Gazette* November 1989 p.606-612.

1 Excluding sea transport.
2 Excluding private domestic and personal services.
3 For 1988=100 these series have been merged.
4 Provisional.

Source: Department of Employment

18.11 Average earnings Index: all employees: main Industrial sectors
Great Britain Classified according to the Standard Industrial Classification 1980

	Whole economy (Divisions 0-9)			Manufacturing industries (Divisions 2-4)			Production industries (Divisions 1-4)			Service industries (Divisions 6-9)		
	Actual	Seasonally adjusted	Underlying rate	Actual	Seasonally adjusted	Underlying rate	Actual	Seasonally adjusted	Underlying rate	Actual	Seasonally adjusted	Underlying rate
1985=100												
	DNFV			DNFW			DNFX			DNFY		
1985	100.0			100.0			100.0			100.0		
1986	107.9			107.7			108.0			107.7		
1987	116.3			116.3			116.7			116.0		
1988	126.4			126.2			126.5			126.2		
1988=100												
	DNAA			DNAC			DNAE			DNDU		
1988	100.0			100.0			100.0			100.0		
1989	109.1			108.7			109.1			108.9		
1990	119.7			118.9			119.4			119.4		
1991	129.3			128.7			129.7			128.5		
		DNAB	DNEM		DNAD	DNEO		DNAF	DNEN		DNDV	DNDX
1989 Jul	110.3	109.1	8.75	110.3	109.1	8.50	110.8	109.5	9.00	109.7	108.8	8.25
Aug	109.1	109.6	8.75	108.3	109.8	8.75	109.2	110.3	9.25	108.7	109.0	8.50
Sep	110.7	111.3	9.00	109.5	110.7	8.75	109.8	110.9	9.00	110.4	111.2	8.75
Oct	111.7	112.6	9.25	110.6	111.5	9.00	111.0	111.8	9.25	111.6	112.9	9.00
Nov	113.2	112.9	9.25	112.2	112.1	8.75	112.9	112.5	9.00	112.7	112.5	9.25
Dec	114.7	112.9	9.25	113.8	112.7	8.50	114.3	113.3	9.00	114.3	111.9	9.00
1990 Jan	113.8	114.7	9.50	112.7	113.6	8.75	113.2	114.1	9.25	113.9	115.0	9.25
Feb	114.0	115.4	9.50	113.9	114.7	9.25	114.3	115.1	9.50	113.7	115.0	9.25
Mar	117.4	116.5	9.50	116.8	116.5	9.50	117.0	117.0	9.75	117.2	115.8	9.25
Apr	117.3	117.5	9.75	117.2	116.2	9.50	117.4	116.6	9.75	116.9	117.2	9.50
May	118.5	118.8	9.75	117.9	117.5	9.25	118.2	117.8	9.75	118.6	118.8	9.75
Jun	120.5	119.9	10.00	120.1	118.8	9.50	120.7	119.7	9.75	119.8	119.4	10.00
Jul	121.2	120.0	10.25	120.8	119.5	9.50	121.3	119.9	10.00	120.5	119.5	10.00
Aug	120.9	121.6	10.00	118.8	120.5	9.50	119.7	120.9	9.75	121.1	121.5	10.00
Sep	121.3	122.0	10.00	120.2	121.6	9.50	121.0	122.1	9.75	120.6	121.5	10.00
Oct	121.7	122.7	9.75	120.8	121.7	9.25	121.6	122.4	9.75	120.9	122.2	9.75
Nov	123.8	123.5	9.75	123.0	122.9	9.50	123.7	123.3	9.75	123.0	122.8	9.75
Dec	126.3	124.2	9.75	125.1	123.8	9.50	125.2	124.1	9.75	126.3	123.7	9.50
1991 Jan	124.3	125.2	9.50	123.4	124.4	9.25	124.3	125.2	9.50	123.8	125.0	9.50
Feb	124.7	126.2	9.25	124.3	125.1	8.75	125.2	126.1	9.00	123.8	125.3	9.00
Mar	127.5	126.5	9.00	126.1	125.8	8.50	126.8	126.9	9.00	127.6	126.1	8.75
Apr	127.4	127.5	8.75	128.0	126.9	8.50	128.6	127.7	9.00	126.1	126.4	8.25
May	128.1	128.4	8.50	127.7	127.3	8.75	129.2	128.9	9.00	127.1	127.3	8.00
Jun	129.2	128.5	8.00	129.7	128.3	8.25	130.3	129.2	8.75	127.9	127.4	7.50
Jul	130.5	129.1	7.75	130.0	128.5	8.25	130.8	129.3	8.50	129.5	128.5	7.50
Aug	130.8	131.5	7.75	128.7	130.6	8.00	130.2	131.4	8.25	130.4	130.8	7.50
Sep	130.8	131.7	7.75	129.2	130.6	8.00	130.9	132.1	8.00	130.1	131.1	7.50
Oct	130.9	132.0	7.50	130.8	131.8	8.00	131.7	132.6	8.50	129.8	131.3	7.25
Nov	133.3	133.0	7.50	132.6	132.4	8.00	133.8	133.4	8.25	132.7	132.5	7.25
Dec	134.5	132.3	7.25	134.1	132.7	7.75	134.8	133.7	8.00	133.6	130.8	7.00
1992 Jan	133.0	134.0	7.25	132.7	133.8	7.75	133.9	134.9	7.75	132.3	133.5	7.00
Feb	134.0	135.7	7.50	134.0	134.9	8.25	135.0	136.1	8.25	133.3	134.9	7.25
Mar	138.6	137.6	7.25	139.1	138.8	7.75	140.0	140.0	7.75	137.6	136.0	7.25
Apr	135.3	135.5	7.00	134.4	133.3	7.50	135.9	135.1	7.50	134.7	135.0	7.00
May	136.3†	136.6†	6.25†	136.6	136.1	6.25†	137.7†	137.4	6.50†	135.4†	135.6†	6.50
Jun[1]	136.8	136.0	6.00	137.4	135.9	6.00	138.4	137.2	6.25	135.4	134.9	6.25

Note: The seasonal adjustment factors currently used for the SIC 1980 series are based on data up to April 1991.

Note: For a detailed account of the revised Average Earnings Index based on 1988=100 please see the article in *Employment Gazette* November 1989 p.606-612.

1 Provisional.

Source: Department of Employment

18.12 Index of purchase prices of the means of agricultural production and of producer prices of agricultural products[1]

1985=100

		Weights	1991[2]	1991 Jun	1991 Jul	1991 Aug	1991 Sep	1991 Oct	1991 Nov	1991 Dec	1992 Jan	1992 Feb	1992 Mar	1992 Apr	1992 May	1992 Jun
Purchase prices																
Goods and services currently consumed	BYEA	100.0	117.6	118.1	118.7	117.8	116.8	117.1	118.2	118.1	119.8	119.7	120.2	120.0	120.4†	120.5
Seeds	BYEB	3.9	109.0	114.5	114.1	107.1	105.0	104.6	108.0	104.5	114.8	115.5	117.7	119.5	119.4	119.4
Animals for production	BYEC	1.1	109.5	108.8	114.4	110.4	106.7	94.1	103.5	110.6	122.0	119.0	107.8	110.2	113.1†	113.1
Energy, lubricants	BYED	9.6	95.8	94.3	96.0	95.6	95.9	97.0	97.7	94.0	91.0	89.6	91.2	92.2	93.2†	94.1
Fertilizer and soil improvers	BYEE	13.8	91.0	88.1	88.0	87.5	86.5	86.2	86.3	86.4	89.3	90.4	91.0	90.7†	91.1†	91.0
Plant protection products	BYEF	4.8	141.5	140.9	141.9	141.9	142.2	144.4	145.0	144.1	146.3	146.6	146.5	148.2	148.0†	148.0
Animal feedingstuffs	BYEG	41.0	115.7	117.7	118.6	116.9	114.6	115.0	116.7	117.6	118.6	118.6	118.6	117.4	117.8	117.8
Material and small tools	BYEH	3.6	139.7	139.0	139.1	141.0	142.3	142.3	142.4	142.6	143.3	143.5	143.9	143.9	144.0	144.3
Maintenance of plant	BYEI	7.2	150.6	150.1	149.7	151.3	153.7	154.5	156.2	156.4	158.1	159.2	159.6	160.4	161.4†	161.5
Maintenance and repair of buildings	BYEJ	4.2	133.6	133.4	133.7	133.8	133.6	133.8	133.6	133.6	134.0	133.9	134.8	134.8	134.6†	134.9
Veterinary services	BYEK	2.1	127.9	128.0	128.1	128.2	128.3	128.3	127.1	127.1	140.0	128.7	128.8	127.8	128.2	128.5
General expenses	BYEL	8.7	138.0	139.3	139.0	139.4	139.0	139.3	139.4	138.7	139.7	140.4	142.1	142.0	142.2	142.2
Goods and services contributing to investment in agriculture	BYEM	100.0	139.3	138.9	139.0	139.1	140.4	141.6	141.8	142.3	142.8	143.4	144.4	144.1†	144.2†	144.3
Machinery and other equipment	BYEN	57.8	136.9	135.8	136.1	136.3	138.5	139.8	139.8	140.6	141.4	141.7	142.0	142.4†	142.6†	142.6
Buildings	BYEO	42.2	142.6	143.2	142.9	143.0	143.1	144.0	144.4	144.6	144.8	145.6	147.6†	146.5†	146.5†	146.6
Producer prices																
All products	BYEP	100.0	112.0	113.2	111.9	110.8	108.6	110.5	109.1	112.5	114.3†	116.4†	116.2†	115.4†	113.8†	108.0
All crop products	BYEQ	37.4	115.6	129.7	113.4	107.5	103.5	106.0	110.0	114.8	115.9†	118.8	118.3	119.2	123.2	108.0
Cereals	BYER	19.9	104.1	112.8	105.0	94.9	95.6	99.0	101.5	103.4	106.1†	107.3	107.7	106.8	105.8	104.0
Root crops	BYES	4.9	169.5	216.9	131.6	156.2	151.4	155.1	163.1	168.9	172.4	174.0	180.0	189.6	199.4	131.6
Fresh vegetables	BYET	6.4	112.8	136.1	125.9	105.7	87.3	90.5	99.7	112.9	104.6	116.9	104.6	106.1	115.0	109.5
Fresh fruit	BYEU	1.9	136.0	140.0	138.0	130.6	127.9	125.6	118.9	138.3	145.1	150.0	162.2	170.2	175.0	113.7
Seeds	BYEV	1.0	125.9	129.4	129.7	117.3	120.3	126.5	126.6	134.3	132.2	140.2	136.5	129.7	129.9	115.0
Flowers and plants	BYEW	1.1	107.2	105.0	106.0	101.7	102.5	104.4	108.0	104.8	106.0	105.0	107.2	108.6	107.2	102.7
Other crop products	BYEX	2.2	90.5	102.4	76.2	75.9	77.2	79.4	83.0	84.3	85.6	86.7	87.5	89.2	90.9	90.9
Animals and animal products	BYEY	62.6	109.8	103.7	111.0	113.0	111.8	113.3	108.6	111.1	113.4	115.0†	114.9†	113.1†	108.3†	108.0
Animals for slaughter	BYEZ	36.9	102.9	106.0	98.8	96.4	95.2	96.7	100.6	104.8	109.7	113.2	114.2	115.3	114.0	112.5
Milk	BYFA	21.0	125.9	105.3	139.9	149.5	147.0	146.4	124.4	123.2	121.9†	121.8†	120.4†	113.5†	102.4†	105.1
Eggs	BYFB	4.3	93.0	78.7	77.4	81.3	86.4	97.9	102.6	109.1	106.6	99.9	96.6	95.4	89.7	85.4
Other animal products	BYFC	0.4	85.7	82.6	82.6	82.6	82.6	82.6	82.6	82.6	82.6	82.6	82.6	82.6	83.9†	83.9

1 Index numbers for the years 1983 to 1989 on 1985=100 base and also at a more detailed level are available from the Ministry of Agriculture, Fisheries and Food, Room A509, Statistics Division (CP)A, Government Buildings, Epsom Road, Guildford, Surrey GU1 2LD.
2 Annual average.

Source: Ministry of Agriculture, Fisheries and Food

19 Leisure

19.1 Television licences

| | Television licences current | | | Television licences current | |
| | End of period | | | End of period | |
	Monochrome	Colour		Monochrome	Colour
	BTAA	BTAB	1990 Jan	1 728	17 840
1984	3 014	15 667	Feb	1 788	17 882
1985	2 733	15 887	Mar	1 681	17 964
1986	2 497	16 408	Apr	1 660	17 969
1987	2 283	16 902	May	1 638	17 866
1988	2 012	17 310	Jun	1 628	17 941
1989	1 762	17 846	Jul	1 615	17 994
1990	1 518	18 086	Aug	1 601	17 976
1991	1 259	18 149	Sep	1 589	17 988
			Oct	1 563	18 037
1988 Mar	2 220	17 134	Nov	1 537	18 024
Apr	2 203	17 158	Dec	1 518	18 086
May	2 183	17 186			
Jun	2 165	17 204	1991 Jan	1 487	18 062
			Feb	1 462	18 105
Jul	2 150	17 224	Mar	1 435	18 111
Aug	2 127	17 187	Apr	1 413	18 052
Sep	2 114	17 266	May	1 399	18 080
Oct	2 075	17 320	Jun	1 381	18 073
Nov	2 036	17 284			
Dec	2 012	17 310	Jul	1 376	18 165
			Aug	1 378	18 170
1989 Jan	1 986	17 420	Sep	1 333	18 202
Feb	1 965	17 473	Oct	1 297	18 129
Mar	1 927	17 469	Nov	1 274	18 135
Apr	1 911	17 492	Dec	1 259	18 149
May	1 893	17 547			
Jun	1 873	17 550	1992 Jan	1 230	18 185
			Feb	1 224	18 343
Jul	1 862	17 630	Mar	1 205	18 426
Aug	1 851	17 653	Apr	1 186	18 459
Sep	1 838	17 718	May	1 171	18 459
Oct	1 805	17 762	Jun	1 159	18 486
Nov	1 780	17 772			
Dec	1 762	17 846	Jul	1 150	18 551

Source: Post Office

19.2 Overseas travel and tourism: earnings and expenditure

£ million, current prices, seasonally adjusted

	Expenditure by overseas visitors to UK	Expenditure by UK residents abroad	Net earnings in UK		Expenditure by overseas visitors to UK	Expenditure by UK residents abroad	Net earnings in UK
	BWAA	BWAB	BWAC	1990 Nov	689	843	-154
1982	3 188	3 640	-452	Dec	596	828	-231
1983	4 003	4 090	-87				
1984	4 614	4 663	-49	1991 Jan	559	792	-233
1985	5 442	4 871	571	Feb	525	757	-232
1986	5 553	6 083	-530	Mar	573	778	-205
				Apr	584	942	-359
1987	6 260	7 280	-1 020	May	636	803	-167
1988	6 184	8 216	-2 032	Jun	575	722	-147
1989	6 945	9 357	-2 412				
1990	7 785	9 916	-2 131	Jul	577	835	-258
1991	7 166	9 824	-2 658	Aug	594	805	-211
				Sep	601	824	-223
1990 Q4	1 898	2 498	-600	Oct	613	867	-254
				Nov	708	858	-150
1991 Q1	1 656	2 327	-670	Dec	622	843	-221
Q2	1 795	2 467	-673				
Q3	1 772	2 463	-692	1992 Jan[1]	629	962†	-333†
Q4	1 943	2 567	-624	Feb[1]	615	870	-255
				Mar[1]	633	894	-262
1992 Q1	1 877	2 727†	-850†	Apr[1]	696	981	-285

1 Rounded to the nearest £5 million.

Source: Department of Employment (Employment Gazette)

Index

Figures indicate table numbers

ISBN 0 11 620540 7

ISSN 0308-6666

Annual Abstract of Statistics 1992

Price £21.00
ISBN 0 11 620498 2

338 tables in 18 separate chapters cover just about every aspect of economic, social and industrial life. Most of the data in the Abstract are annual and cover periods of about 10 years.

For about 140 years the Annual Abstract of Statistics has probably been the most quoted source of statistics about the United Kingdom.

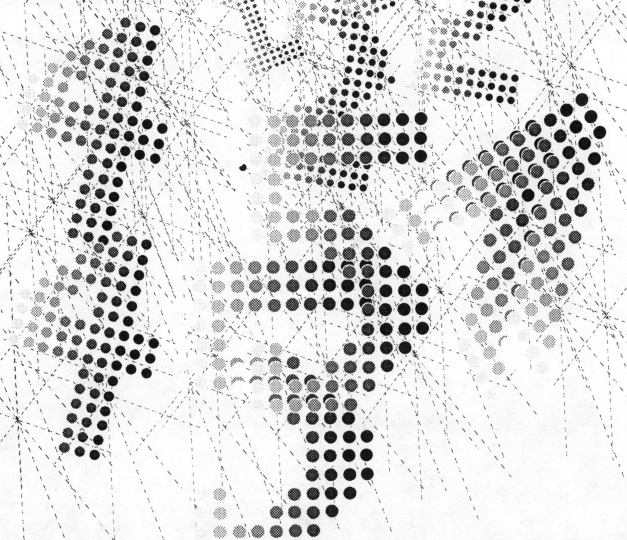

CENTRAL STATISTICAL OFFICE

Financial Statistics

Financial Statistics provides data on a wide variety of financial topics including financial accounts for sectors of the economy, government income and expenditure, public sector borrowing, banking statistics, monetary aggregates, institutional investment, company finance and liquidity, security prices and exchange and interest rates.

Many figures in this publication are included in the **CSO** Databank.

Price £8.95

Central Statistical Office publications are published by HMSO.
They are obtainable from HMSO bookshops and through booksellers.

Family Spending

A report on the 1990
Family Expenditure Survey

The Family Expenditure Survey is based on responses given by some 7,000 households in the UK and has been in continuous operation since 1957. It represents a unique and reliable source of household data on expenditure, income and other aspects of household finances, and provides a perspective of the changes and developments in spending on items as diverse as food, clothes, fuel and alcohol over more than a quarter of a century.

HMSO £19.50 net
ISBN 0 11 620502 4

Units of measurement

Length

1 millimetre (mm)		= 0.039 370 1 inch
1 centimetre (cm)	= 10 millimetres	= 0.393 701 inch
1 metre (m)	= 1 000 millimetres	= 1.093 61 yards
1 kilometre (km)	= 1 000 metres	= 0.621 371 mile
1 inch (in.)		= 25.4 millimetres or 2.54 centimetres
1 foot (ft.)	= 12 inches	= 0.304 8 metre
1 yard (yd.)	= 3 feet	= 0.914 4 metre
1 mile	= 1 760 yards	= 1.609 34 kilometres

Area

1 square millimetre (mm^2)		= 0.001 55 square inch
1 square metre (m^2)	= one million square millimetres	= 1.195 99 square yards
1 hectare (ha)	= 10 000 square metres	= 2.471 05 acres
1 square kilometre (km^2)	= one million square metres	= 247.105 acres
1 square inch (sq. in.)		= 645.16 square millimetres or 6.451 6 square centimetres
1 square foot (sq. ft.)	= 144 square inches	= 0.092 903 square metre or 929.03 square centimetres
1 square yard (sq. yd.)	= 9 square feet	= 0.836 127 square metre
1 acre	= 4 840 square yards	= 4 046.86 square metres or 0.404 686 hectare
1 square mile (sq. mile)	= 640 acres	= 2.589 99 square kilometres or 258.999 hectares

Volume

1 cubic centimetre (cm^3)		= 0.061 023 7 cubic inch
1 cubic decimetre (dm^3)	= 1 000 cubic centimetres	= 0.035 314 7 cubic foot
1 cubic metre (m^3)	= one million cubic centimetres	= 1.307 95 cubic yards
1 cubic foot (cu. ft.)		= 0.028 316 8 cubic metre or 28.316 8 cubic decimetres
1 cubic yard (cu. yd.)	= 27 cubic feet	= 0.764 555 cubic metre

Capacity

1 litre (l)	= 1 cubic decimetre	= 0.220 gallon
1 hectolitre (hl)	= 100 litres	= 22.0 gallons
1 pint		= 0.568 litre
2 pints	= 1 quart	= 1.137 litres
8 pints	= 1 gallon	= 4.546 09 cubic decimetres or 4.546 litres
36 gallons (gal.)	= 1 bulk barrel	= 1.636 56 hectolitres

Weight

1 gram (g)		= 0.035 274 0 ounce
1 hectogram (hg)	= 100 grams	= 3.527 4 ounces or 0.220 462 pound
1 kilogram (kg)	= 1 000 grams or 10 hectograms	= 2.204 62 pounds
1 tonne (t)	= 1 000 kilograms	= 1.102 31 short tons or 0.984 2 long ton
1 ounce avoirdupois (oz.)		= 28.349 5 grams
1 pound avoirdupois (lb.)	= 16 ounces	= 0.453 592 37 kilogram
1 hundredweight (cwt.)	= 112 pounds	= 50.802 3 kilograms
1 short ton	= 2 000 pounds	= 907.184 74 kilograms or 0.907 184 74 tonne
1 long ton (referred to as ton)	= 2 240 pounds	= 1 016.05 kilograms or 1.016 05 tonnes
1 ounce troy	= 480 grains	= 31.103 5 grams

Energy

British thermal unit (Btu)	= 0.252 kilocalorie (kcal) = 1.05 506 kilojoule (kj)
Therm	= 100 000 British thermal units = 25 200 kcal = 105 506 kj
Megawatt (Mw)	= 10^6 watts
Gigawatt hour (GWh)	= 10^6 kilowatt hours = 34 121 therms

Food and drink

Butter	23 310 litres milk	= 1 tonne butter (average)
Cheese	10 070 litres milk	= 1 tonne cheese
Condensed milk	2 550 litres milk	= 1 tonne full cream condensed milk
	2 953 litres skimmed milk	= 1 tonne skimmed condensed milk
Milk	1 million litres	= 1 030 tonnes
Milk powder	8 054 litres milk	= 1 tonne full cream milk powder
	10 740 litres skimmed milk	= 1 tonne skimmed milk powder
Eggs	17 126 eggs	= 1 tonne (approximate)
Sugar	100 tonnes raw sugar	= 95 tonnes refined sugar
Beer	1 bulk barrel	= 36 gallons irrespective of gravity

Shipping

Gross tonnage	= The total volume of all the enclosed spaces of a vessel, the unit of measurement being a ton of 100 cubic feet.
Deadweight tonnage	= Deadweight tonnage is the total weight in tons of 2 240 lb. that a ship can legally carry, that is the total weight of cargo, bunkers, stores and crew.

Printed in the United Kingdom for HMSO   Dd. 295372   C38   9/92   4073